MW01708588

D

May you have many great explorations of your own.

love

Aunt Anne

& Uncle Paul

Journeys of THE GREAT EXPLORERS

Rosemary Burton, Richard Cavendish, Bernard Stonehouse

Writers: Rosemary Burton, Richard Cavendish and Bernard Stonehouse

Copy editor: Helen Douglas-Cooper

Published by AA Publishing, which is a trading name of Automobile Association Developments Limited, whose registered office is at Norfolk House, Priestley Road, Basingstoke, Hampshire RG24 9NY, registered number 1878835.

Published by AA Publishing, a trading name of Automobile Association Developments Limited, whose registered office is Norfolk House, Priestley Road, Basingstoke, Hampshire RG24 9NY.
Registered number 1878835.

A catalogue record for this book is available from the British Library.

Hardback ISBN 0 7495 3189 4
Paperback ISBN 0 7495 1010 2

Typeset in Caslon and Gill by Servis Filmsetting Ltd, Manchester
Colour Reproduction by L. C. Repro and Sons Ltd., Aldermaston
Printed in Dubai by Oriental Press

Endpapers *An engraving showing the start of the successful yet fatal expedition of Burke and Wills to cross Australia from south to north.*

Title page *A Viking picture stone from the 8th century AD.*

This page *Cortés and his army approaching the city of Mexico.*

Contents

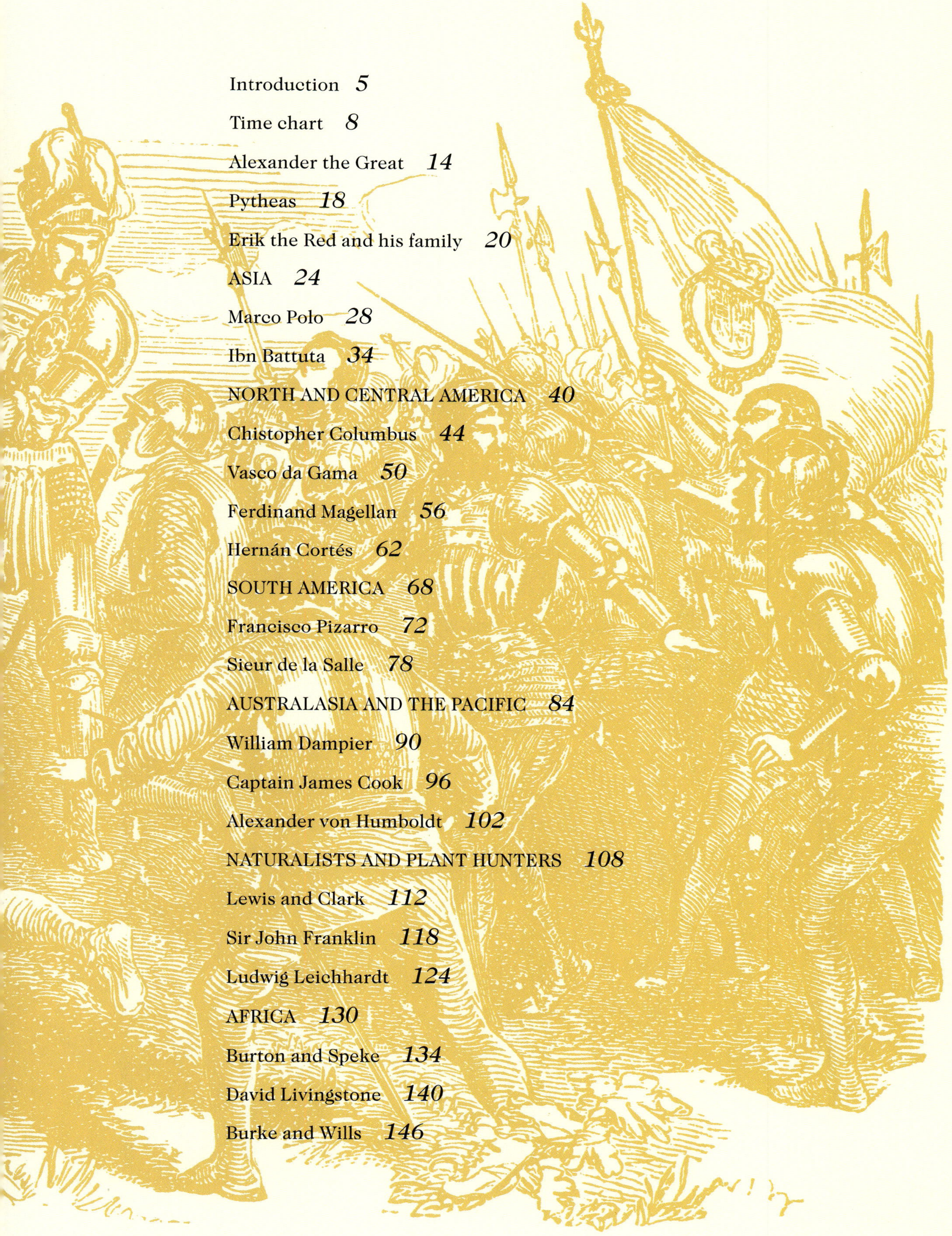

Right and below
Compasses and other navigational instruments from the 18th century.

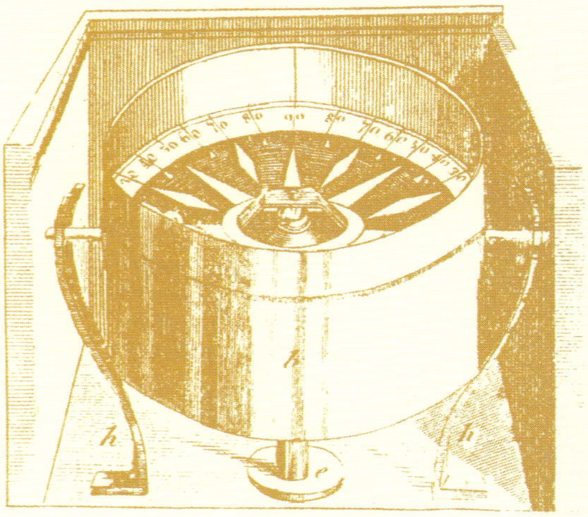

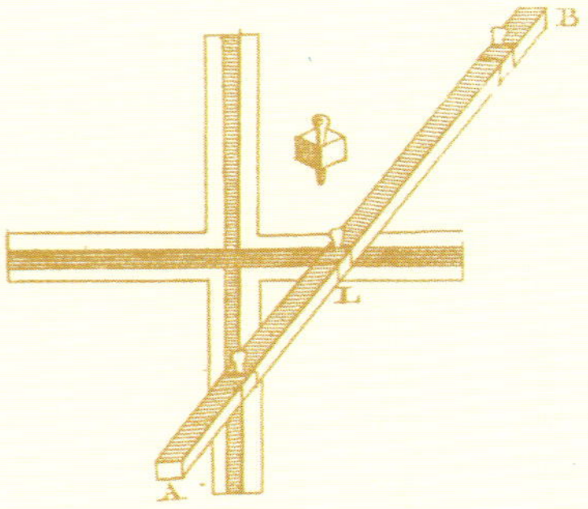

Some explorers made their principal discoveries on land; others spent most of their time at sea, sailing between countries and continents; while others concentrated on opening up the Arctic and Antarctic. This is reflected in the background tint colour used for the short features on each explorer.

land-based explorer

seafaring explorer

explorer of the polar regions

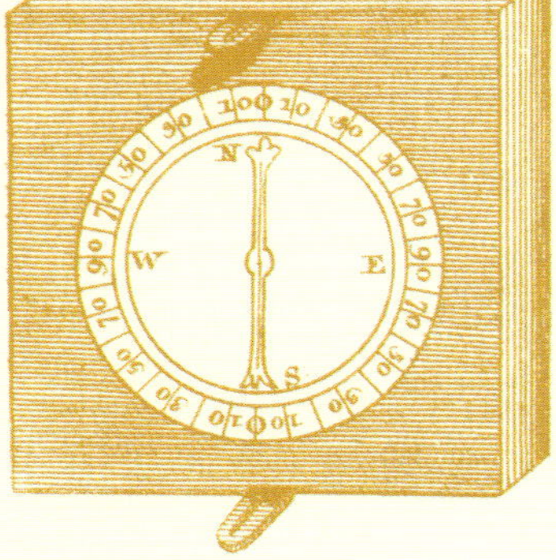

INTRODUCTION

Tom, he was a piper's son,
He learnt to play when he was young,
And all the tune that he could play
Was 'Over the hills and far away'.

Nursery rhyme

It was in Africa millions of years ago, according to the currently accepted theory, that the first human beings evolved, and from Africa that they spread out to colonise the globe, in the process developing different physical characteristics, different languages, different religious, political and social systems. Most of the world was first explored, settled and tamed long ago by people who had no system of writing and could leave behind them no record of their journeys and their feats of courage, determination and skill. Their adventures, tribulations and achievements are lost in the darkness of the unrecorded past.

This book describes epic journeys of a later time, in general, and of individual explorers rather than migrating peoples. We begin with Alexander of Macedon, who is remembered mainly for his conquests throughout Asia. However, apart from his huge army, scientists and surveyors accompanied him to collect data on climate, geography and natural history and to record distances and draw maps. Continuing with the exploits of such famous figures as Marco Polo and Christopher Columbus, Ferdinand Magellan and Captain Cook, David Livingstone and Roald Amundsen, we end in our own time with the first voyage to the moon – perhaps the most remarkable feat of exploration in all human history.

The explorers are arranged in chronological order and interspersed with their adventures are general features on continents and other topics to supply the historical background to the individual exploits. Because human societies have traditionally been male-dominated, most explorers have been men, but there have been intrepid, determined and successful women in the field too, and the book reflects that. It also reflects the fact that since the Renaissance the exploration of the world has been led and dominated by Europeans.

One world

From Columbus on, the great explorers have played a vital role in the process by which, during the last 500 years, the West has extended its influence over the entire globe. Reversing, in a way, the evolutionary spread of the human race across the world, European explorers have travelled to countries far distant geographically, culturally and psychologically from their own, and so have made people all over the world more aware of each other and less separate from each other. Exploration has made one world where there were formerly many.

Below The Landing at Mallicolo *by William Hodges. Cook steps into the water to accept a palm branch, a symbol of peace, from a Pacific Islander.*

European explorers often received much help from the local inhabitants. After Columbus had made his successful landfall in the West Indies he was guided to other islands by helpful natives in their dugout canoes, while he contemplated with satisfaction how readily they could be turned into dutiful Christian converts and obedient slave labourers. The astonishing achievement of Hernán Cortés in overthrowing the Aztec Empire was greatly aided by his shrewd mistress Doña Marina, and thousands of Indian warriors. The brutal Francisco Pizarro and his handful of Spanish soldiers seized control of the empire of the Incas with assistance from disaffected members of the ruling regime. When Lewis and Clark found their way through the Rocky Mountains they had a Shoshoni woman as a guide and were welcomed by her people.

The explorers themselves, however were almost always rootedly Eurocentric in their outlook. When they treated native people considerately, it was still with a fundamentally superior attitude that has tarnished the innocent word 'native' itself. Certainty of their own superiority caused many explorers to fail to take sensible advantage of local helpfulness and local knowledge of how to survive in harsh and unfamiliar environments. On the other hand, it was certainty of their own superiority that gave explorers the confidence to venture into the unknown.

Motives for venturing into the unknown include longing for fame, greed for wealth and the urge to convert other people to one's own beliefs. The lure of the fabled riches of the Far East drew the first European expeditions round Africa and across the Indian Ocean, over the Atlantic – where the Americas were found inconveniently in the way – and across the trackless wastes of the Pacific. Hunger for gold inspired both the heroism and the vicious brutality of the conquerors of Mexico and Peru. Meanwhile far into the 19th century much exploration was also impelled by the earnest zeal to carry Christianity to the ends of the earth; this in time blended with the impulse to convert the rest of the world to European parliamentary democracy and Western ways.

Beyond the horizon

Powerful as these motives have been, there is also present in human nature a fundamental, compelling curiosity about what lies round the next bend or beyond the hills on the horizon. Many a traveller sets out lured by the fascination and romance of the unknown, and 'Over the hills and far away' is a tune that has drawn many explorers on. Ultima Thule and Terra Australis Incognita in their time had the intense attraction more recently exercised by the North Pole, the South Pole and the summit of Mount Everest, not because they held gold or slaves or converts for the taking, but because they were there.

The urge to satisfy scientific curiosity has been the driving force of explorers from Captain Cook and Alexander von Humboldt to Sven Hedin and Thor Heyerdahl. In the footsteps of the first pioneers followed the naturalists and plant-hunters, the geologists, zoologists and anthropologists, as greedy to find species unknown to science as any conquistador for the gold of El Dorado.

To satisfy ambition and scratch the itch of curiosity, explorers have driven their way into the furthest and most inhospitable regions of the earth – and in this century deep into the ocean and far out into the sky. They have sailed down the Amazon and the Mississippi, crossed the Gobi Desert and the Empty Quarter of Arabia, penetrated forbidden cities in peril of death, negotiated the North-West Passage and floated across the Pacific on a raft. With tiny armies they have outfaced powerful potentates, defeated hostile hordes and brought down empires. They have braved the most acute dangers of impossible terrain, blizzards and tempests, hunger and thirst, icebergs

Below *Apollo astronaut Schweickart, on a space walk. First practised by Leonov in 1965, the technique was later used to repair external spacecraft damage.*

and frostbite, destroying heat, murderous diseases, wild animals and mutinous subordinates.

Many died on the way: Captain Cook killed in the Hawaiian Islands and Magellan in the Philippines; La Salle murdered by his own men; Verrazzano eaten by cannibals; Franklin and his crews frozen in the Arctic ice; Burke and Wills succumbing to starvation in the Australian outback; Captain Scott and his gallant party dying of exhaustion and disappointment huddled in a tiny hut in the vast empty space of Antarctica.

Others, like Columbus, returned home safely and in triumph to find their glory turning to dust and ashes, and to die forgotten and embittered. There is a story about Hernán Cortés, who brought Mexico and all its glittering plunder to Spain, belittled and ignored in his last years in his own country. One day he pushed his way through a crowd to stand on the step of Emperor Charles V's carriage. The emperor, puzzled, asked who he was. 'I am a man who has given you more provinces than your ancestors left you cities,' said Cortés and turned away.

Explorers have driven themselves and their companions on through the most desperate hardships. Magellan and his men, sailing on across the endless Pacific, were reduced to eating sawdust soup and toasted strips of leather from the rigging. Rats were a great treat. Charles Sturt and his party, trapped by drought for months in the Australian bush, had to dig an underground bunker to live in, so ferocious was the sun. When Robert Peary took off his boots after a long trek in the Arctic, bits of his frostbitten toes came off with them, and the story of polar exploration amply proves the determination of human beings to conquer even the most desolate places of the earth.

Who dares, wins
The history of exploration reflects every facet of humble nature, good and bad. Courage, determination and problem-solving intelligence are on one side of the coin, brutality, greed, treachery and arrogance on the other.

The great explorers, on the whole, have not been the most attractive of characters or the easiest to get on with. Like high achievement in other spheres, successful exploration tends to demand ruthless drive and ambition, dedicated selfishness and a fierce competitiveness, whose most recent large-scale manifestation was the race between the United States and the Soviet Union to be the first to put a man on the moon. Many of the great explorers have been driven personalities, convinced they had a special mission and a special destiny in life, restlessly unhappy and dissatisfied with the known world, and consequently impelled to seek out an unknown one.

The records of exploring expeditions brim over with personality clashes, jealousies, resentments, wounded feelings, violent and sometimes murderous quarrels. The Lewis and Clark expedition across North America is a rare exception, but Burton and Speke cordially loathed each other and Peary and Cook were savagely hostile rivals. On completing his pioneer trek across Northern Australia, Ludwig Leichhardt recorded that he was sick of the sight of his companions, and there is little doubt that they were equally sick of the sight of him.

When all is said and done, however, it is impossible not to thrill to the courage, determination, eager curiosity, resourcefulness and adamant refusal to admit defeat of men and women pressing on into unknown territory against overwhelming odds and often at the risk of life itself. The story of the great explorers is a celebration of something indomitable in the human spirit. As Bernal Diaz wrote, looking back in old age to his memories of Cortés and the conquest of Mexico, 'What men in all the world have shown such daring?'

TIME CHART

	ASIA	NORTH AND CENTRAL AMERICA	SOUTH AMERICA
500 BC	**c. 445** Herodotus travelled through Egypt and central Asia. **334–325** Alexander led his army across Persia into India and back. **138** Chang Ch'ien travelled across central Asia to Samarkand and Tibet.		
AD 1	**399** Fa Hsien travelled to India, Sri Lanka and Java.		
500	**600–700** Hsuan Tsang crossed the Gobi Desert to India.		
1000	**1271–95** Marco Polo travelled through Asia Minor, Persia, central Asia, Mongolia and China. **1325–7** Ibn Battuta travelled to Mecca via the Middle East. **1328–30** Ibn Battuta travelled through Arabia and down the east coast of Africa to Zanzibar. **1330–3** Ibn Battuta travelled through Anatolia and central Asia to Afghanistan. **1333–46** Ibn Battuta travelled through India and China and back to North Africa. **1405–33** Admiral Zheng Ho made several voyages exploring the Far East, Indian Ocean and east coast of Africa for the Chinese. **1488** Pedro de Covilhã was sent on a secret mission to find the sea route from Africa to India. **1497–8** Vasco da Gama sailed around the Cape of Good Hope and established the sea route from Europe to India.	**c. 1000** Leif Eriksson, sailing from Greenland, discovered Newfoundland. **1492–3** Christopher Columbus's first expedition to the New World. Discovered the Bahamas, Cuba and Hispaniola. **1493–6** Columbus's second expedition. Discovered Dominica, Guadeloupe, Puerto Rico and Jamaica. **1497** John Cabot explored the coastline of Canada, landing at Cape Breton. **1498–1500** Columbus's third expedition. Discovered Trinidad and mainland Venezuela.	**1499** Alonso de Ojeda explored the coasts of Guiana and Venezuela. **1499–1500** Amerigo Vespucci discovered the mouth of the Amazon. **1499** Vicente Yañez Pinzón led an expedition up the Colombian coast.
1500	**1503** Lodovico Vathema was probably the first Christian to visit Mecca. **1540s** Botanist Pierre Belon journeyed through Greece and the Middle East.	**1502–4** Columbus's fourth expedition. Explored the Central American coast. **1513** Vasco Nuñez de Balboa crossed Panama to reach the Pacific Ocean. **1513** Juan Ponce de Leon sailed north from Puerto Rico and discovered Florida and the Gulf Stream. **1517** Hernandez de Cordoba explored the Yucatan coast, and discovered the ruins of Mayan cities. **1524** Giovanni da Verrazzano crossed the Atlantic and sailed up the American coast from North Carolina to Newfoundland. **1530s** Jacques Cartier explored the Gulf of St Lawrence and the St Lawrence River. **1539** Francisco de Ulloa explored the Gulf of California. **1540** Francisco Vasquez de Coronado led an expedition into modern Arizona and New Mexico. **1542** Juan Rodriguez Cabrilho explored the Californian coast.	**1500** Alvarez Cabral claimed Brazil for Portugal, and sailed to India via the Cape of Good Hope. **1501–2** Amerigo Vespucci explored the Brazilian and Patagonian coasts. **1519–21** Hernán Cortés invaded Mexico and conquered the Aztec Empire. **1520** Ferdinand Magellan sailed down the east coast of South America and found a way through to the Pacific Ocean north of Tierra del Fuego. One ship from the expedition eventually returned to Portugal, completing the first circumnavigation of the world. **1524** Hernán Cortés led an expedition to Honduras. **1524–7** Francisco Pizarro led expeditions down the Pacific coast of South America. **1531** Francisco de Orellana journeyed from Ecuador down the Amazon River to the Atlantic coast. **1532–3** Pizarro led an expedition into Peru that conquered and destroyed the Inca Empire. **1535** Pedro de Mendoza crossed Peru and founded a settlement at the site of modern Buenos Aires.
1550	**1581** Yermak Timofeyevich led the Cossack Invasion of Siberia.		**1595** Sir Walter Raleigh travelled up the Orinoco River by canoe.
1600	**1620s** Antonio de Andrade explored the Himalayas. **1620–30s** Thomas Herbert provided a description of the dodo, seen on Mauritius, and published the first account of the ruins of Persepolis.	**1608** Samuel de Champlain founded a French colony at Quebec and explored the Great Lakes area. **1609** Henry Hudson sailed up the Hudson River and claimed the area for the Dutch. **1610** Hudson died in Hudson Bay while searching for the Northeast Passage.	**1616** Willem Schouten discovered a open–sea route round Cape Horn.

AUSTRALASIA AND THE PACIFIC	AFRICA	THE POLAR REGIONS	WORLD EVENTS
			c. 310 Pytheas of Marseilles explored the northern seas. **c. 215** Building of the Great Wall of China. **44** Assassination of Julius Caesar. **19** Virgil's *Aeneid* almost completed at the poet's death.
			14 Death of the Emperor Augustus. **33** Traditional date of the crucifixion of Jesus of Nazareth. **c. 150** Ptolemy's *Geography* completed.
			618–907 Tang dynasty in China. **632** Death of Muhammad. **800** Charlemagne crowned emperor.
	1349–54 Ibn Babbuta travelled through Somalia and Mali to Timbuktu. **1413** Anselme d'Isalguier reached Mali. **1470** Benedetto Dei claimed he had reached Timbuktu. **1482** Diego Cão discovered the Congo River (now the Zaïre). **1487** Bartolomeu Dias passed the Cape of Good Hope without seeing it. **1497** Vasco da Gama rounded the Cape of Good Hope and continued up the east coast.	**1497** John Cabot discovered Newfoundland.	**1096** The First Crusade. **1294** Death of Kublai Khan. **1321** Death of Dante. **1325** Aztec capital of Tenochtitlán founded. **1337** Beginning of the Hundred Years War. **1445** First European printed book produced by Johannes Gutenberg. **1453** Constantinople fell to the Turks.
1520 Ferdinand Magellan discovered islands in the Pacific during the first circumnavigation of the world. **1527** Hernán Cortés sent an expedition across the northern Pacific from Mexico to establish communication between New Spain and the Philippines.			**1512** Michelangelo completed the Sistine Chapel ceiling. **1517** Martin Luther attacked indulgences; beginning of the Reformation in Europe. **1519** Death of Leonardo da Vinci. **1526** The Mogul dynasty founded in India. **1543** Publication of the Copernican theory.
1567 Alvaro de Mendaña discovered the Solomon Islands. **1578–80** Sir Francis Drake sailed up and down the Pacific coast of South America and then made the second circumnavigation of the world. **1595** Alvaro de Mendaña found the Marquesas Islands.		**1570s** Humphrey Gilbert searched for the Northwest Passage. **1590s** Willem Barents led expeditions that discovered Bear Island and Svalbard, and rounded the northern tip of Novaya Zemlya.	**1556** Accession of Akbar, greatest of the Mogul emperors. **1559** Tobacco first imported into Europe. **1564** Birth of Galileo. **1566** Death of Suleiman the Magnificent, most powerful of the Ottoman Sultans. **1584** Death of Ivan the Terrible of Russia. **1588** Defeat of the Spanish Armada.
1605 While searching for the great southern continent, Pedro Fernandez de Quiros discovered the New Hebrides. **1605** Captain Willem Janszoon made the first European landing on Australia, in the Gulf of Carpentaria. **1642** Abel Tasman discovered Tasmania, and sailed on to New Zealand, Tonga and Fiji. **1644** Abel Tasman sailed along the north coast of Australia.			**1600–1** First performance of Shakespeare's *Hamlet*. **1605** Cervantes completed *Don Quixote*. **1606** Birth of Rembrandt. **1616** The Blue Mosque completed in Istanbul. **1620** The Pilgrim Fathers landed in New England on the *Mayflower*. **1628** Circulation of the blood announced by William Harvey. **1643** Accession of Louis XIV of France. **1644** The Ming dynasty of China replaced by the Manchu dynasty.

	ASIA	NORTH AND CENTRAL AMERICA	SOUTH AMERICA
1650	**1658** Quaker missionaries Katherine Evans and Sarah Cheevers tried to reach Alexandra but were imprisoned on Malta. **1660s** Johann Gruebner and Albert D'Orville travelled in China and India, and were probably the first Europeans to visit Tibet.	**1679–81** Sieur de La Salle explored the Great Lakes area of Canada. **1681–2** Sieur de La Salle sailed down the Illinois and Mississippi rivers to the Gulf of Mexico. **1684–7** Sieur de La Salle led an expedition from France to the Gulf of Mexico to find the mouth of the Mississippi but failed to do so.	**1680s–1720s** Father Samuel Fritz worked as a missionary in the upper Amazon region.
1700	**1716** Lady Mary Montagu made a year-long journey to Constantinople with her husband. **1716–21** Ippolito Desideri visited Tibet.		**1730s** Charles-Marie de la Condamine travelled down the Amazon by canoe and raft.
1750		**1763** Captain James Cook surveyed the Newfoundland and Labrador coasts. **1766** Naturalist Sir Joseph Banks studied plants and insects in Newfoundland. **1775** Juan de Ayala discovered the harbour at San Francisco. **1778** Cook sailed up the Pacific coast of North America to Alaska and the Bering Strait in search of the Northwest Passage. **1789–93** Alexander Mackenzie made expeditions up the Mackenzie River to the Arctic Ocean and across to the Pacific Ocean. **1790s** George Vancouver surveyed the northwest coast of Canada.	**1799–1804** Baron Alexander von Humboldt explored northern South America and the Andes Mountains.
1800	**1812–25** William Moorcroft explored the Himalayas, Tibet and Kashmir.	**1804** Meriwether Lewis and William Clark pioneered the overland route to the Pacific across the Rocky Mountains. **1819–22** Sir John Franklin surveyed the area from Hudson Bay to the Coppermine River. **1820** John James Audubon travelled the Ohio and Mississippi rivers, studying and drawing birds in their natural habitats. **1822–34** David Douglas made expeditions through North and South America collecting plant specimens. **1825–7** Sir John Franklin explored the region between the Mackenzie River and northern Alaska.	**1831** Charles Darwin sailed with HMS Beagle, exploring the Atlantic and Pacific coasts. **1848** Alfred Russell Wallace and Henry Walker Bates travelled up the Amazon studying insects.
1850	**1850** Sir Richard Burton visited Mecca in disguise. **1857** Harriet Tytler was caught up in the Indian Mutiny. **1860s** W.G. Palgrave trekked across Jordan to the Persian Gulf. **1865** Père Armand David discovered a species of deer in China, which was later named after him. **1868** Alexandra David-Neel was the first western woman to enter Lhasa. **1870s** C.M. Doughty travelled across the Arabian desert with Bedouins.	**1873** Isabella Bird travelled in the Rocky Mountains.	**1850** Edward Whymper explored the Andes Mountains and was the first to climb Chimborazo in Ecuador, 20,702ft (6310m). **1897** Mattias Zurbriggen was the first to climb Aconcagua, the highest mountain in the Andes, 22,839ft (6959m).

AUSTRALASIA AND THE PACIFIC	AFRICA	THE POLAR REGIONS	WORLD EVENTS
679–91 William Dampier's first oyage, which included the Philippines, ustralia, India and Indo-China. **699–1701** Dampier's second voyage, n official expedition to Australia.			**1654** The Taj Mahal completed. **1663** John Milton finished *Paradise Lost*. **1682** Peter the Great became Tsar of Russia. **1685** Birth of Johann Sebastian Bach. **1687** Publication of Isaac Newton's *Principia*.
703–7 Dampier's third voyage, to he southern Pacific. **708–11** Dampier's fourth voyage, to he southern Pacific. **721** Jacob Roggeveen discovered aster Island and Samoa.		**1725** Vitus Bering's first trip to Siberia and the Arctic Ocean. **1732** Carl Linnaeus investigated the wildlife of Lapland. **1741** Bering's second voyage to the Arctic Ocean. Naturalist Georg Wilhelm Steller sailed with him.	**1719** *Robinson Crusoe* published. **1740** Frederick the Great became King of Prussia. **1742** First performance of Handel's *Messiah*, in Dublin. **1748** The ruins of Pompeii rediscovered.
760s Captain Wallis discovered Tahiti nd Captain Carteret discovered itcairn Island. **768** Louis Antoine de Bougainville isited Tahiti and made the first French ircumnavigation of the world. hilibert de Commerson sailed with im to search for exotic plants. **768–71** Captain Cook's first xpedition, to Tahiti, New Zealand nd Botany Bay. Naturalists Sir Joseph anks and Daniel Solander sailed with im. **772–5** Cook's second expedition, to lew Zealand and the Antarctic ircle (which he crossed twice), aster Island and the Marquesas. **776–9** Cook discovered Hawaii where he was killed in 1779), and hen crossed the Pacific to explore he northwest coast of America.	**1769–72** James Bruce searched for the source of the Nile, and found the source of the Blue Nile. **1770s** Francis Masson was sent by Kew Gardens to the Cape of Good Hope to collect plants and bulbs. **1795–7** Mungo Park led expeditions in search of the source of the River Niger.	**1770's** Captain Cook circumnavigated the world in Antarctic waters.	**1756** Birth of Wolfgang Amadeus Mozart. **1757** The battle of Plassey established British rule in India. **1759** Voltaire wrote *Candide*. **1762** Accession of Catherine the Great of Russia. **1769** James Watt patented his first steam engine. **1776** The American Declaration of Independence. **1783** The Montgolfier Brothers made the first manned balloon flight. **1788** Penal colony established at Botany Bay, Australia. **1789** Beginning of the French Revolution. **1796** Edward Jenner discovered vaccination.
801 Thomas-Nicholas Baudin was ent by Napoleon to explore the oast of Australia. **803** Matthew Flinders made the first ircumnavigation of Australia, urveying the coast. **814** Samuel Marsden was the first nissionary to arrive in New Zealand. **828** Charles Sturt travelled into the nterior of Australia and discovered he Darling River. **829** Sturt led an expedition along he Murrumbidgee and Murray rivers. **841** Edward Eyre led an overland xpedition from Adelaide to Perth. **844** Charles Sturt tried to reach the entre of Australia from the south and iscovered Cooper Creek. **844–5** Ludwig Leichhardt crossed ortheast Australia from Brisbane to he Gulf of Carpentaria, and on to the ast at Port Essington. **845–6** Sir Thomas Mitchell crossed he Great Dividing Range in Australia nd discovered the Barcoo River. **848** Ludwig Leichhardt attempted to ross Australia from east to west and isappeared.	**1830** Richard and John Lander discovered the source of the Niger. **1846–54** David Livingstone crossed Africa from coast to coast, west to east. **1848** Johann Rebmann discovered Mount Kilimanjaro.	**1818** Sir John Franklin sailed with an expedition to the Arctic Sea in search of the Northwest Passage. **1820** Captain Fabian Bellingshausen made the first sighting of Antarctica (the Princess Martha coast). **1827** William Parry attempted to reach the North Pole, but turned back at 82° 45'N, 500 miles (800km) short. **1839–45** James Clark Ross discovered the Ross Ice Shelf and Victoria Land in Antarctica. **1845–7** Sir John Franklin led an expedition to look for the Northwest Passage; it ended in the death of all members.	**1804** Napoleon Bonaparte crowned Emperor of the French by the Pope. **1808** Publication of the first part of Goethe's *Faust*. **1813** Birth of Richard Wagner. **1815** Napoleon defeated at the Battle of Waterloo. **1819** Simon Bolivar became President of Colombia. **1822** Independence of Brazil declared. **1827** Death of Ludwig van Beethoven. **1829** Building of George Stephenson's locomotive 'Rocket'. **1833** Slavery abolished in the British Empire. **1837** Morse code and Pitman's shorthand invented. **1848** Karl Marx and Friedrich Engels issued *The Communist Manifesto*.
858 Augustus Gregory travelled long the Barcoo River to Cooper reek. **860–1** Robert Burke and William Vills made the first crossing of ustralia from south to north but ied on the return journey. **860–2** John McDouall Stuart, on his hird attempt, reached the north coast f Australia from the south.	**1850–55** Heinrich Barth crossed the Sahara to Lake Chad and followed the Niger to Timbuktu. **1858** Sir Richard Burton and John Hanning Speke discovered Lake Tanganyika, and Speke discovered Lake Victoria – the source of the Nile. **1858–64** Livingstone led the Great Zambezi Expedition. **1859** Paul du Chaillu was the first white man to encounter the gorilla. **1860–3** John Hanning Speke led an expedition back to the source of the Nile.	**1850–54** Robert McClure led the first European expedition to traverse the Northwest Passage – but sledging overland and in the 'wrong' direction (west to east). **1878** Adolf Nordenskiöld sailed the Northeast Passage. **1879** George Washington de Long led an expedition to cross the Arctic Ocean, but the ship was crushed in ice and the crew died. **1886–95** Robert Peary made three expeditions to the northern part of the Greenland ice-cap.	**1851** Herman Melville completed *Moby Dick*; first performance of Verdi's *Rigoletto*. **1856** Birth of Sigmund Freud. **1859** Publication of Darwin's *Origin of Species*. **1861–5** The American Civil War. **1864** Founding of the Red Cross. **1868** Restoration of the Meiji dynasty in Japan opened the country to the West. **1869** Opening of the Suez Canal; Tolstoy completed *War and Peace*.

	ASIA	NORTH AND CENTRAL AMERICA	SOUTH AMERICA
1850 continued	**1870s** Ney Elias crossed the Gobi Desert and explored Chinese Turkestan. **1870s–80s** Nikolai Przhevalsky explored Mongolia, Chinese Turkestan and Tibet. **1875–80** Isabella Bird travelled in Japan and Malaysia. **1880s** Kishen Singh surveyed Tibet on behalf of the British. **1886** Svebn Hedin explored Persia, Iraq and Turkey. **1889–98** Isabella Bird travelled alone through Tibet, Persia, Korea and China. **1890** Sven Hedin travelled to Bukhara, Samarkand and Chinese Turkestan. **1893–7** Sven Hedin explored Central Asia. **1898–1914** Gertrude Bell explored the Arabian and Syrian deserts.		
1900	**1900–1** Sven Hedin explored Tibet and attempted to reach Lhasa. **1901** Isabella Bird visited Berber Arabs in the Atlas Mountains. **1904** Francis Younghusband led an expedition into Tibet. **1906–7** Sven Hedin travelled in Tibet. **1917–18** H. St John Philby explored the interior of Arabia. **1922** First Everest expedition. **1924** Second Everest expedition. **1927** Freya Stark travelled through the Middle East. **1930** Freya Stark explored the Valley of the Assassins. **1931** Bertram Thomas was the first to cross the Arabian desert. **1931** Frank Smythe reached the peak of Kamet in the Himalayas, the first mountain over 25,000ft (7620m) to be conquered. **1930s** Elia Maillart made a journey from Peking to Kashmir and travelled in India and Afghanistan. British-American party climbed Nanda Devi, over 25,000ft (7620m), in the Himalayas. **1940s** Wilfred Thesiger explored the Arabian desert.	**1913** Hudson Stuck climbed Mount McKinley, the highest mountain in North America.	**1911** Hiram Bingham discovered the ruins of the Inca city of Machu Picchu. **1925** Colonel Percy Fawcett disappeared in the forest of the Motto Grosso.
1950	**1950** Maurice Herzog climbed Annapurna, over 26,247ft (8,000m). **1953** Sir Edmund Hillary and Tenzing Norgay reached the summit of Mount Everest.		**1957** Richard Mason and Robin Hanbury-Tenison drove across South America at its widest point, from Recife to Lima. **1964** Robin Hanbury-Tenison travelled by dinghy from the Caribbean, down the Orinoco, Amazon and Paraguay rivers to the Atlantic at Buenos Aires.

AUSTRALASIA AND THE PACIFIC

900 Donald Mackay made a 240-day ip round Australia on a bicycle.
930s Donald Mackay organised the st aerial survey of the continent.
947 Thor Heyerdahl sailed on the ft Kon–Tiki from South America to e Philippines.

970 Thor Heyerdahl sailed from orocco to the West Indies in a reed oat, *Ra II*.
977–8 Thor Heyerdahl sailed across e Indian Ocean in a reed boat, *Tigris*.

AFRICA

1861 Samuel and Florence Baker travelled south through Egypt and Sudan and discovered Lake Albert Nyanza, a feeder of the White Nile.
1860s Gerhard Rohlfs explored the Sahara from Tripoli on the Mediterranean to Lagos on the Gulf of Guinea.
1866–73 Livingstone explored the cental African river system. He met H.M. Stanley at Lake Tanganyika in 1871.
1969–70 Georg Augustus Schweinfurth was the first European to encounter pygmies in the Congo.
1873–5 Verne Lovett Cameron surveyed Lake Tanganyika and made the first European east–west crossing of the African continent.
1874 Henry Morton Stanley explored Lake Victoria and confirmed it as the source of the Nile, and travelled down the Congo River to the west coast.
1870s–80s Count Pierre Savorgnan de Brazza explored Ogowé and the Congo.
1889 Hans Meyer and Ludwig Purtscheller were the first to climb Mount Kilimanjaro.
1893 Mary Kingsley explored parts of the French Congo (Zaïre, Congo and Gabon) in search of 'fish and fetish'.
1894–5 Kingsley travelled among the Fang tribes in present-day Gabon.

THE POLAR REGIONS

1888–9 Fridtjof Nansen made the first crossing of the Greenland ice-cap.
1893–6 Nansen's ship *Fram* drifted in pack–ice across the Arctic from Siberia to Svalbard. In 1895 Nansen reached 86° 15'N in a bid for the North Pole.
1895 Umberto Cagni reached 86° 34'N.
1897–9 Adrien de Gerlache's expedition was the first to winter in Antarctica, on board ship.
1899–1900 Karsten Borchgrevink's expedition was the first to winter on land in Antarctica.

1901–3 Captain Scott led the National Antarctic Expedition. Scott and Ernest Shackleton reached 86° 17'S in the journey towards the South Pole.
1903–6 Roald Amundsen sailed the Northwest Passage.
1905–6 Peary's first polar expedition. He claimed furthest north, 87°N.
1907–9 Shackleton led the British Antarctic Expedition and sledged to within 97 miles (156km) of the South Pole (1909).
1908 Frederick Cook claimed to have reached the North Pole.
1909 Peary claimed to have reached the North Pole.
1910–12 Amundsen's expedition to the South Pole – reached on 14 December 1911.
1910–12 Scott's second Antarctic expedition. They reached the South Pole on 17 January 1912, but all died on the return journey.
1914–17 Shackleton led the Imperial Trans–Antarctic Expedition but lost his ship in pack-ice.
1918–22 Amundsen's *Maud* expedition drifted across the Arctic Ocean.
1925 Richard Byrd made the first Arctic flights over Greenland and Ellesmere Island.
1926 Byrd made the first flight to the North Pole.
1926 Amundsen and Umberto Nobile flew over the North Pole in a balloon.
1929 Byrd made the first flight to the South Pole.
1935 Lincoln Ellsworth made the first flight across Antarctica.

1955–8 The British Commonwealth Trans–Antarctic Expedition led by Vivian Fuchs and Sir Edmund Hillary, made the first overland crossing of the continent.
1958 The American submarine Nautilus made the first voyage under the North Pole.
1969 Wally Herbert led the British Trans–Arctic Expedition, which made the first surface crossing of the Arctic.
1978 Naomi Uemura reached the North Pole solo.
1979–82 Sir Ranulph Fiennes and Charles Burton made the first circumnavigation of the globe via both poles.
1990 An international expedition crossed Antarctica at its widest point, 4,000 miles (6,435km).

WORLD EVENTS

1876 Alexander Graham Bell patented the telephone.
1885 First Benz and Daimler automobiles.
1895 Wilhelm Röntgen discovered X-rays.

1901 First transatlantic radio signal transmitted by Guglielmo Marconi.
1903 First powered aircraft flight, by the Wright Brothers.
1905 Einstein published his special theory of relativity.
1911 The Manchu dynasty overthrown in China.
1912 The sinking of the *Titanic*.
1914–18 World War I.
1917 The Bolshevik Revolution in Russia.
1919 The atom split for the first time, by Ernest Rutherford.
1922 Publication of James Joyce's *Ulysses*.
1924 Death of Lenin.
1928 Mickey Mouse made his debut.
1930 Amy Johnson flew solo from England to Australia.
1932 Amelia Earhart was the first woman to fly the Atlantic; record balloon ascent by August Piccard.
1933 Hitler came to power in Germany.
1934 William Beebe reached record ocean depth in a bathysphere.
1936 Outbreak of the Spanish Civil War.
1939–45 World War II.
1945 Atom bombs dropped on Japan.

1953 Death of Stalin.
1957 USSR launched first space satellite, Sputnik 1; Treaty of Rome and foundation of the European Economic Community.
1961 Yuri Gagarin was the first person in space.
1963 President Kennedy assassinated in Dallas, Texas.
1967 The first human heart transplant performed.
1969 The successful American moon landing.
1976 Death of Mao Tse-Tung.
1977 Naomi James was the first woman to sail round the world.
1989 The Berlin Wall taken down.
1991 Break-up of the USSR into independent states.

ALEXANDER THE GREAT

Alexander the Great led a life of relentless conquest and exploration, building an empire that stretched from Greece to India

In the space of 11 years during the 4th century BC, Alexander III of Macedon travelled 20,000 miles, leading a huge army on an unprecedented expedition all the way from central Europe to India. He opened up routes along which Greek culture spread through much of western Asia, and his name can be found in the literature of dozens of different countries stretching half-way across the world from the Malay Peninsula to the British Isles. He founded over 70 cities, and, as well as the one near the Nile delta still known today as Alexandria, he left another 20 or so Alexandrias scattered in his wake.

First named Alexander the Great by the Romans, he became a hero for the writers of medieval European romances, a revered man in the Judaic tradition, and a saint in the Coptic Church of Egypt. At the end of the 19th century tribal leaders in the Badakshan Mountains were still claiming to be his direct descendents, and the idea of Alexander as a superhuman figure remains a familiar one today. By the time of his death at the age of 33 he had defeated the huge power of the Persian Empire and could claim to rule an area of over 2 million square miles (5 million sq. km).

Early signs of greatness

Of Alexander's early life we know little. As a boy he is said to have impressed his elders when he won the trust of a difficult horse that no one else could approach. The animal was called Bucephalus and the two were to form a lasting partnership. Seeing this demonstration of his son's ability to assess a situation and act appropriately, King Philip is said to have remarked that Macedon would not be a large enough realm to contain such a man. In fact, Philip left Alexander heir to an empire that reached from the Danube and the coast of Dalmatia as far as islands in the Aegean. The historian, Plutarch, whose biography of Alexander was written around the end of the 1st century AD, says that the young man watched Philip's successes reluctantly, fearful that every triumph was depriving him of an opportunity for victory. Alexander, we are told, was not interested in inheriting a luxurious kingdom; he actually wanted a life of struggle, wars and relentless ambition. At the age of only 16 he was already proving himself a distinguished fighter and Philip was sufficiently impressed to appoint him regent of Macedon.

Philip died in mysterious circumstances when Alexander was 20, and his young heir was immediately faced with the need to impress his authority on the Greek city-states that his father had subjugated. He moved first into Thessaly to the north of

Below *Part of the ruins of Persepolis, the vast palace of the Persian kings, which Alexander looted and destroyed. It was said that 10,000 mules and 5,000 camels were needed to carry away the treasures of the palace.*

Alexander and the Gordian Knot

Perhaps the most celebrated of the stories about Alexander the Great is the one about the problem of the Gordian Knot. After his victory at the River Granikos, Alexander dealt with resistance at Miletus and Halicarnassus and campaigned south along the coast of Asia Minor before marching inland and north through Pisidia and Phrygia. At Gordium he visited the temple of Zeus, where an apparently inextricable knot held together parts of a chariot that had once belonged to Midas, King of Phrygia. A legend said that the man who was able to undo the knot would become King of Asia. When it proved impossible to untie he refused to accept defeat, drew his sword and sliced through it – an act that was symbolic of his ability always to find the unexpected solution to a problem. Alexander had been faced with deciding whether to continue campaigning in Asia or to return to Macedonia to deal with a possible threat from Persian forces there. The episode of the knot suggested to him, and his men, that he was right to continue and so it proved. The threat to Macedonia evaporated, Alexander went on to defeat Darius, and the image of cutting the Gordian Knot is one still used today.

***Right** Alexander is shown about to slice decisively through the Gordian knot in this imaginative painting.*

***Below** Alexander the Great conquered half the known world and was only 33 when he died. His career of conquest took him deep into the Egyptian desert, to far Samarkand and into northwestern India.*

Greece, and rather than risk an approach through a very narrow pass he contrived to lead his forces over the mountains, employing the element of surprise that was to become one of his tactical hallmarks. Accepted as ruler of Thessaly, he hurried on through the pass of Thermopylae and won the reluctant support of the Greeks. Within a short time he also subjugated the Triballian tribe, who had given his father trouble in the region of the Danube.

Into Asia

After ruthlessly destroying the rebellious Greek city of Thebes (an act which he was later to regret, believing that it earned him the curse of the god Dionysus) he divided his forces, leaving enough manpower behind to ensure control over Europe while he turned his attention to Asia. Now ostensibly acting as the leader of the Greeks in a campaign against their old enemy Persia (although his own army contained few Greeks while the Persian forces included large numbers of Greek mercenaries), he assembled perhaps 43,000 infantry and 6,000 cavalry. With him were teams of scientists who would collect data about climate, geography and natural history, and a number of specially trained runners and surveyors capable of assessing and recording the distances the army covered, presumably with a view to making accurate maps. He had recruited a fleet of Greek fighting ships and it was in command of one of these that he began his Asian expedition with a symbolic personal pilgrimage to the site of the ancient city of Troy. Alexander was a devotee of the *Iliad*, Homer's epic poem about the Trojan War, and he is said to have kept a copy of the book under his pillow and to have identified with the Greek hero Achilles.

Alexander becomes Pharaoh

A preliminary victory against the Persians at the River Granikos (Kocabas) in 334 BC was followed by another tough battle at Issus in 333, where Alexander's position was very vulnerable, but again, after a tough fight, he was victorious. Over 100,000 Persians were said to have been killed, but their king, Darius, remained free and Alexander continued in pursuit south along the Lebanese and Syrian coasts towards Egypt. The cities of Byblos (Jbail) and Sidon (Saïda) surrendered to him at once; Tyre (Soûr) fell only after an eight-month siege in 332, and Gaza gave way after a difficult battle. The same year saw Alexander proclaimed Pharaoh at Memphis in Egypt, where he remained from October 332 to April 331. During this period he established the city of Alexandria at a good strategic site near the mouth of the Nile, and staged another dramatic personal journey, this time a long trek to the oracle of Ammon (at modern-day Siwa) in the Libyan desert, which he was determined to reach regardless of dangerous dust storms and a serious shortage of water. His ability to survive such a journey was seen as evidence of god-like invincibility.

In 331 he faced Darius again at the Battle of Gaugamela in Mesopotamia; again, despite having far fewer men, his tactical skill triumphed. Darius escaped, defeated and dejected and Alexander was now well placed to assume his title as King of Asia. He pressed on through Babylonia to the Persian cities of Susa and Persepolis, where he stayed for six months before destroying the royal palace. He then marched 400 miles in 11 days towards Ecbatana (Hamadān), and learned that Darius had been killed by one of his own men, Bessus, who was now claiming the throne.

***Below** This Italian mosaic, from near Naples, depicts the Battle of the Issus, with King Darius in his chariot, while Alexander attacks from the left. Darius was defeated.*

Ambition takes hold and thousands die

At this point, as he led his troops eastwards through Hyrcania and Parthia in pursuit of Bessus, who was eventually caught and killed, there began to be talk of Alexander's desire to rule the whole of the known world. He posed as the heir and avenger of Darius, sometimes adopting an oriental style of dress, and some have argued that he had a vision of a political union between east and west. He fought a long, bitter campaign for the territories of Bactria and Sogdiana east of the Caspian Sea, and led his long-suffering troops through Afghanistan to Kābul and over the Hindu Kush. He succeeded in crossing the River Oxus (Amudar'ya), and establishing a number of permanent garrisons, but not before a part of his army had mutinied at the prospect of the continued journey north to Samarkand. The River Jaxartes (Syrdar'ya) marked the northeastern limit of his campaigns and he then tackled the Hindu Kush again and, in the spring of 327, began his assault on India. He met little serious opposition at first, but faced a fierce enemy in the Indian King Porus, whose elephants nearly terrorised Alexander's troops in battle at the River Hydaspes (Jhelum). Porus was defeated, but the battle did little for the morale of Alexander's men. Towards the end of 326 they rebelled, refusing his command to cross the River Hyphasis (River Sutlej) and venture further south into the unknown.

Alexander survived the crisis and made his return from India a mission of exploration. An entire fleet was assembled on the River Hydaspes, many ships being specially built on the spot, and, now supported by large numbers of reinforcements, Alexander sailed downriver from the Hydaspes into the Chenab and finally into the Indus, reaching the delta in the summer of 325. Here he instructed his admiral Nearchus to follow the coast all the way back to the Persian Gulf, while he and the greater part of the army took the overland route along the coast through the region known as Gedrosia (the Makran). Nearchus wrote an account of the journey, some of which survives in the work of the historian, Arrian. As the ships sighted Cape Maceta on the Arabian coast, the helmsman Onesicritus called for them to sail straight towards the Cape to avoid the trouble of coasting round the bay. Nearchus replied that this was to misunderstand the point of the voyage. 'Alexander desired to reconnoitre the coasts that lay along the line of the voyage, the roadsteads, the islets, and to explore thoroughly any bay which appeared and to learn of any cities on the coast, and to discover which land was fertile and which was desert.'

Ambition curtailed

The naval and the overland expeditions met up again at the end of 325. The fleet was safe at Hormuz, but Alexander had lost nearly 60,000 men through hunger, disease and natural disaster. He now began talking of ambitious schemes to send another expedition down the River Euphrates, round Arabia and Africa and into the Mediterranean from the west. It is hardly surprising that these ideas received no support. His unpopularity was increasing, aggravated by his announcement that he expected to be recognised as a god. After returning to Susa for several months and retreating further and further into isolation, which was compounded by grief at the death of his beloved companion and fellow commander, Hephaestion, he approached Babylon once more, in the knowledge that astrologers had predicted that he was facing disaster. In June 323, depressed and drinking heavily, he fell ill and died.

Alexander was, above all, a supreme tactician with a scientific approach to problems of strategy and an enquiring mind well trained by his tutor, the philosopher, Aristotle. That much is clear from the sheer scale of his adventures and successes, but it is rarely possible to separate the truth from the myths that he cultivated during his own short lifetime and which later ages have embroidered.

The historian Arrian, who wrote an account of Alexander's expedition in the second century AD, commented that there was no other figure about whom historical accounts had been more numerous or less in agreement with one another. Arrian could draw on a number of contemporary descriptions of Alexander, many of which indulged in shameless flattery (claiming, for example, that Alexander was a god, before whom the sea itself would bow in submission) and all of which, apart from a few fragments, have subsequently been lost. Arrian came to the conclusion that this was a man who would never voluntarily have retired from the life of conquest and exploration – even if he had extended his empire as far as the British Isles, 'he would have searched beyond for something unknown and in the absence of any other competition he would have competed against himself'.

Above *Fort Kait Bey at Alexandria in Egypt. The city is only one of many named after the great Macedonian, whose exploits caused contemporaries to hail him as a god.*

Biographical Notes

356 BC
Alexander born at Pella.

336
Succeeded to the throne of Macedonia.

334
Left Pella, leading huge army into Asia.

331
Defeated Persian forces at battle of Gaugamela.

329
Marched through Afghanistan and crossed the Hindu Kush.

327-5
Indian campaign extended his realm as far as the lower Indus. Fleet explored the sea-route from the Indus delta to the Persian Gulf.

323
Died in Babylon.

PYTHEAS

In the 4th century BC the Greek geographer and navigator, Pytheas, set off to find the western edge of the world.

The Greek historian Herodotus, who lived during the 5th century BC, wrote a book in which, among other things, he tried to give his readers all the information he could gather about the different countries of the world. After describing Arabia (where strange sheep were thoughtfully provided with wooden trailers to prevent their long tails from dragging on the ground), he turned his attention to the far west of Europe and admitted that he had no clear information about this area. He said there was a story about a river called the Eridanus, which was supposed to flow into a northern sea where there were lavish supplies of amber, but he could not believe this any more than he could confirm the existence of the Tin Islands, also supposedly in the west. Herodotus had never met anyone who had seen a sea to the northwest of Europe. Still, he had to admit that there was a well-established trade in tin and amber, which came to Greece from the far ends of the earth, but the exact place of origin remained a mystery.

Voyage into the unknown

A hundred years later in the Greek colony of Massalia, modern Marseilles, a geographer and astronomer called Pytheas appears to have set off in search of the answers to the questions that had defeated Herodotus. Pytheas's accounts of his discoveries, including a book with the title *Concerning the Ocean*, have not survived, but there are references to him in the work of later writers, which give a reasonable amount of information about his voyages.

Pytheas came from a city of seafarers. Massalia had been founded around 600 BC by Greeks from Phocaea (the most northerly of the Ionian cities in Asia Minor) who were eager to exploit the magnificent natural harbour there, and the city's great prosperity and powerful influence to east and west along the coast depended on outstanding competence at sea by its inhabitants.

An interest in astronomy and mathematics led Pytheas to conduct a number of experiments, and his observations of the sun and of the Pole Star contributed to a better understanding of relative latitude and to improved navigation techniques. He had enough faith in his own powers of navigation to risk a voyage into uncharted waters in an attempt to find the western edge of the world.

Britain and the island of Thule

In spite of a Carthaginian blockade of the Strait of Gibraltar, Pytheas appears to have sailed through and reached Cadiz without difficulty. He then followed the Spanish and French coast before heading north and crossing to the land of Belerion – in other words western Cornwall, or Land's End. Here he found the people friendly and he saw how tin was extracted from the earth, smelted and beaten into ingots before being taken across a causeway to an island called Ictis (the description fits St Michael's Mount), where foreign merchants bought it and transported it to mainland Europe.

Pytheas then sailed north, presumably up the west coast of Britain. He reckoned that the whole land mass was roughly triangular in shape and estimated that the northern tip was just over 1,000 miles (1,600km) from Marseilles – a very reasonable calculation. Continuing north, presumably at midsummer, he came to a place six days' journey from mainland Scotland (or perhaps from Orkney) where the sun set for only two or three hours in every 24. He named this land Thule. It may have been Shetland or, more probably, Iceland. For later authors and poets the word Thule came to stand for a strange place symbolising the ends of the earth.

Pioneer of Arctic exploration?

The Greek geographer Strabo, writing at the end of the 1st century BC, attacked Pytheas for wrongly calculating the length of the British coastline, and said that many people had been

Below The perils of unknown waters. A Greek ship of the century before Pytheas, driven by both oars and a sail, is shown on a vase in the British Museum, depicting Odysseus and the sirens.

Above *St Michael's Mount, reached by a causeway off the south Cornwall shore, fits Phytheas's description of an island where Cornish tin was traded to merchants from the Continent.*

misled by him. In the course of his attack, Strabo records Pytheas's description of a weird northern region, a further day's journey from Thule, which was neither sea nor land, but something between the two, on which one could neither walk nor sail. Whether this was an encounter with a semi-frozen sea in the vicinity of the Arctic Circle is far from clear.

After his discovery of Thule, Pytheas seems to have sailed along a northern coast and discovered a source of amber on an island near a large gulf. He may have been describing the Elbe estuary and Heligoland, but it is also possible that he sailed round the Jutland (Jylland) peninsula and towards the Baltic Sea. The Baltic area was an important source of amber for the ancient world and traders appear to have used Heligoland as a base, from which they sent consignments south through Germany and Italy. Much about his journey must remain in doubt, but he may well have returned from this northern coast to investigate the southeastern shores of England before setting sail for home.

Many later writers did their best to discredit Pytheas, dismissing his work as misleading and naive, but his influence was considerable and today he is still celebrated as a true pioneer explorer, one who was not content with the horizons of the known world and who was determined to go and find out what lay beyond.

Above *The details are necessarily a matter of conjecture, but the map indicates the main possibilities. Iceland may have been the place Pytheas called Thule.*

Primitive Navigation

Knowledge of navigation was very limited at the time of Pytheas's voyage and his journey into the unknown is the more remarkable for this reason. Although sailing was second nature to the Greeks, living as they did in an area where communication between numerous islands was essential, they depended largely on coastal navigation – keeping land in sight and steering according to their experience of particular waters – and on their knowledge of prevailing winds.

Pytheas, as a rational scientist, may not have feared that he would actually fall off the edge of the world if he ventured too far west, but he cannot have been certain that he would find his way home again. He, too, followed coasts as far as possible, but they were unknown coasts and he presumably had to make careful use of the device known as the lead line, to determine the depth of water in shallow areas. The position of his ship in relation to the sun would have given him some clues about his progress, but he knew nothing of the magnetic compass, which did not appear in the Mediterranean until the 11th century.

ERIK THE RED and his family

Five centuries before Columbus, Viking adventurers crossed the gale-swept North Atlantic to land in North America.

From their fjords and farms in Norway, Denmark and Sweden, the Vikings roamed the world, not only as pirates and plunderers, but as settlers and traders. Fierce and predatory in their serpent-prowed longships, they harried Britain, Ireland and France, looting and burning. Many of them settled down as farmers in these lands, too, and they pioneered the great trade route from the Baltic down the Russian rivers to Constantinople (Istanbul). The achievement that has specially caught the modern imagination, however, was the crossing of the wild North Atlantic and the discovery, long before Columbus, of the New World.

The age of Viking expansion began in the 8th century. Driven presumably by over-population and hungry for land, Norse settlers established themselves in Orkney and Shetland, the Hebrides and Ireland, and then further west in the Faeroes (Føroyar), or Islands of Sheep, in the Atlantic: where Irish hermits had already found refuges remote from the world of men. The Faeroes were a stepping stone to Iceland, still further west, which Irish priests reached in the 790s. The first boatloads of Viking settlers arrived there 70 years or so later, and their early terrible winters there inspired them to give the island the name it has borne ever since.

Below *The first Viking settlers reached Iceland in the 9th century and Iceland was the springboard from which Erik the Red discovered Greenland. Pushing further west, his family were the first Europeans, so far as is known, to land on the shore of North America.*

The discovery of Greenland

It was from Iceland that the next westward steps were taken. In the year 962 or thereabouts a seasoned adventurer named Erik the Red, who had earlier been expelled from his homeland in Norway for manslaughter, was banished from Iceland for three years after being involved in further quarrels and killings there. Needing somewhere to go and something to do, he raised a crew and sailed away to the west in search of an unexplored land that had been sighted 50 years or so earlier by a Norwegian named Gunnbjorn, whose ship had been driven off course in a storm.

It was a risky journey, with no chart and no pilot and with all the dangers of gales and fog, but after covering some 450 miles from Iceland, Erik and his men came to the east coast of what we now know to be the second-largest island in the world (after Australia): probably where the towering Ingolfsfjeld glacier looms up in the region of Angmagssalik.

Sailing south round Cape Farewell (Kap Farvel), they explored the south-western coast, where they found an uninhabited country rich in grassland, birds, fish and caribou. Erik named the country Greenland, for promotional purposes, and called various features of it after himself – Erik's Fjord, Erik's Island, and so on.

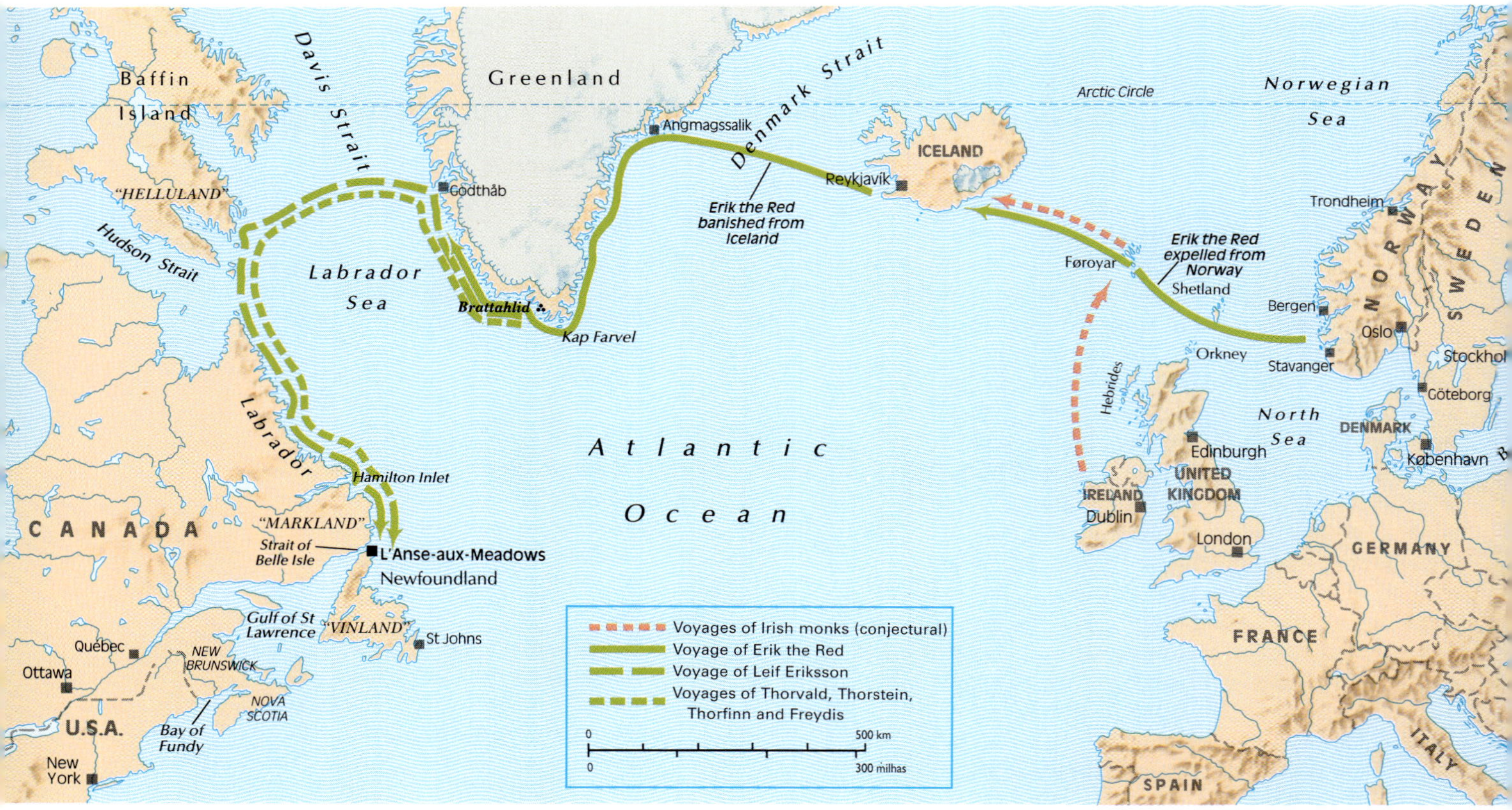

Land of Wine

"One evening news came that someone was missing: it was Tyrkir the Southerner. Leif was very displeased at this, for Tyrkir had been with the family for a long time, and when Leif was a child had been devoted to him. Leif rebuked his men severely, and got ready to make a search with twelve men.

They had gone only a short distance from the houses when Tyrkir came walking towards them, and they gave him a warm welcome. Leif quickly realized that Tyrkir was in excellent humour.

Leif said to him, 'Why are you so late, foster-father? How did you get separated from your companions?'

At first Tyrkir spoke for a long time in German, rolling his eyes in all directions and pulling faces, and no one could understand what he was saying. After a while he spoke in Icelandic.

'I did not go much farther than you,' he said. 'I have some news. I found vines and grapes.'

'Is that true, foster-father?' asked Leif.

'Of course it is true,' he replied. 'Where I was born there were plenty of vines and grapes.'

They slept for the rest of the night, and next morning Leif said to his men, 'Now we have two tasks on our hands. On alternate days we must gather grapes and cut vines, and then fell trees, to make a cargo for my ship.'

This was done. It is said that the tow-boat was filled with grapes. They took on a full cargo of timber; and in the spring they made ready to leave and sailed away. Leif named the country after its natural qualities and called it *Vinland*."

from *The Vinland Sagas* (translated by M. Magnusson and H. Pálsson)

When the three years were up, Erik returned to Iceland to recruit settlers. He was evidently an effective salesman and 25 ships sailed for Greenland with him, though it is an indication of the difficulties and dangers of the voyage that only 14 vessels arrived. The others either gave up and went back to Iceland or were lost at sea. Erik and his family settled down in the new land, of which he was the leading citizen. He had a comfortable farm that he called Brattahlid (which has been diligently excavated by modern archaeologists) and he had satisfied the three impulses that powered most Viking exploration: the longing for undying fame, curiosity and the drive to make money.

Erik had three sons by his wife, Thjodhild: Leif, Thorvald and Thorstein. He also had a natural daughter, Freydis. All of them played parts in what followed. According to one story, Erik resisted Christianity when the new faith came to Greenland, but Thjodhild was converted and promptly refused to let Erik into her bed, which he resented. She built a little turf-walled chapel, tactfully sited so that he did not have to see it every time he came out of his front door. The archaeologists have found the remains of it.

Above *The remains of Brattahlid, Erik the Red's farm in Greenland. Norse settlers were drawn to this newly discovered country by good grassland for their cattle and seaweed on which to pasture their sheep.*

Below *Erik the Red discovers Greenland, greeted by whales and seals, in this picture by a 19th-century Danish artist, Carl Rasmussen.*

Vinland the Good

A trader named Bjarni Herjolfsson, trying to reach Greenland from Iceland, went off course and drifted in a fog for many days. He came out of it to see land that did not fit the description of Greenland he had been given. He turned away and reached Greenland safely, but he was much criticised for his shameful lack of curiosity.

Some 15 years later, about AD 1000, Erik the Red's son Leif bought Bjarni's boat to set off for the unknown country. Erik was supposed to go, but he hurt his leg falling off his horse. This was a bad omen and he did not make the voyage.

Leif put out to sea with a crew of 35, headed west and duly came to land, which he called Helluland ('land of stone slabs'). This was probably the south part of Baffin Island, 200 miles (320km) west of Greenland across the Davis Strait, where flat slabs of stone do indeed project into the sea. Going south from there, he came to Markland ('land of woods'). Heavily forested, with white sandy beaches, it is now identified as the southern region of Labrador.

Sailing on, Leif and his crew came to a paradisal country with a mild climate, plentiful lush grass for pasture and streams abounding in fat salmon. One of the men, exploring from the camp, came back tipsy and explained, somewhat incoherently, that he had found wild grapes. So they called the place Vinland ('land of wine'). They spent the winter there and sailed back to Greenland in the summer with a cargo of grapes and timber, to find that in their absence Erik had died. As far as is yet known, they were the first Europeans to set foot on the soil of North America.

The killing of the Skraelings

Leif Eriksson, known as Leif the Lucky, made no more expeditions, but presently his brother Thorvald bought Bjarni's much-travelled boat and sailed westward again. He found the place where Leif had wintered and later sailed on from there to encounter for the first time the native people of the New World – aboriginal American Indians or Eskimos.

The meeting was all too grimly prophetic of the future. The Vikings saw three skin boats – canoes or kayaks – drawn up on a beach and killed the eight men in them, apparently entirely unprovoked. More skin boats appeared, buzzing with angry natives armed with bows and arrows. Thorvald was killed, shot in the armpit by an arrow. This may have happened at Hamilton Inlet in Labrador, or perhaps in the Bay of Fundy between New Brunswick and Nova Scotia. The other Vikings got away and went back to Greenland with stories of the aboriginals they called *skraelings* ('uglies').

Thorstein Eriksson, the third brother, tried to find Vinland again in Bjarni's same boat, but died of sickness. His widow married a rich Icelander, a merchant named Thorfinn Karlsefni, who made a fourth voyage. This time the intention was to found a settlement, and 60 men and 5 women went on the expedition, with all their livestock, including a bull. They reached their destination at Leif's original campsite and settled down there. Thorfinn's wife gave birth to a baby boy, called Snorri, the first European recorded to have been born in North America. The Vikings traded with the *skraelings* for furs, but one of the *skraelings* tried to steal some weapons and was promptly killed by one of the Vikings. This provoked a battle, which the Vikings won, but Thorfinn called off the whole enterprise and they all returned to Greenland.

Finally, Freydis, Erik the Red's natural daughter, led yet another expedition, but this was a disaster. Quarrels broke out, she had her two partners killed and she herself slaughtered their womenfolk with an axe. She went back to Greenland in disgrace.

Most of this comes from the *Greenlander's Saga*, which was written down in the 12th century and is considered the most reliable early account. The rival *Erik's Saga* was written later to boost the reputation of Leif Eriksson, who is credited with introducing Christianity to Greenland.

After the early 11th century, it seems, no more attempts were made to settle in Vinland. The westward wave of Viking expansion had reached its furthest and weakest extent; it had lapped at the North American shore and fallen back. Voyages were still being made to Vinland from Greenland 300 years later, presumably to bring away furs and timber. After that, silence fell. Norse civilisation in Greenland eventually died out during the 15th century, killed off by cold, malnutrition, disease and marauding Eskimos – at just the time when other Europeans were rediscovering America.

***Left** This Viking sword with its splendidly decorated silver hilt is now in the Statens Historiska Museum in Stockholm. Vikings lived in a hard world and needed to be handy with their swords.*

***Above** A scene in eastern Greenland. Although the land looks so barren, the Norse who colonised it supported themselves by farming and hunting until the 15th century. Walrus ivory was prized in Europe and the tusks were a valuable Greenland export.*

The Vinland Map, showing Greenland and Vinland.

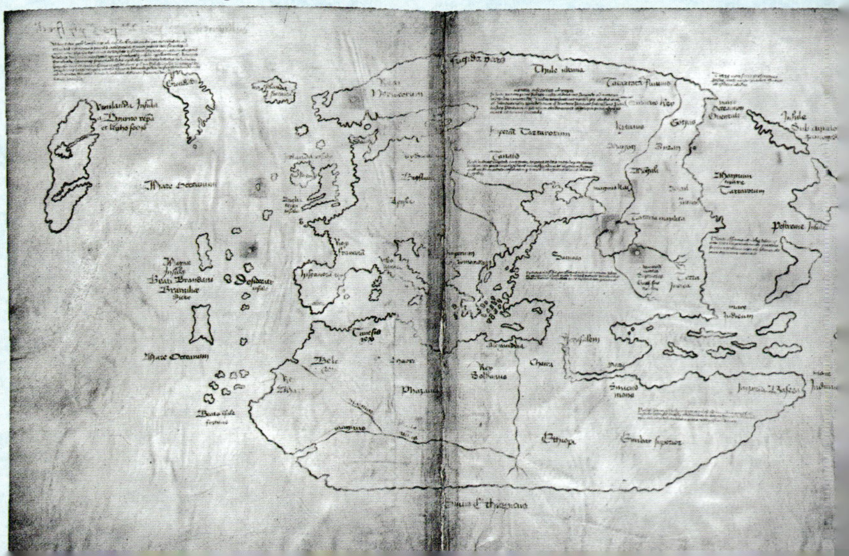

The difficulty is the grapes. Vinland was named for wine, but it is highly unlikely that wild grapes grew in Newfoundland 1,000 years ago. Perhaps the stories of wild vines and gentle winters, which the explorers brought back to Greenland, came from voyages that had probed further south from Newfoundland. Or perhaps the name Vinland was originally intended to mean 'grassland' and was misunderstood. Or possibly the Vikings mistook berries of some sort, such as currants, for grapes. Currants are still used for making wine in Scandinavia.

There is no longer room for any doubt that the Vikings landed in America. The precise location of Vinland, however, remains enticingly unsettled.

Where was Vinland?

Where exactly was the mysterious paradise of Vinland the Good, which Leif Eriksson discovered? The vagueness of the geography in the sagas has fuelled speculation, which has sited it along the American coast from Labrador to Florida. The weight of opinion at the moment favours the northern tip of Newfoundland, which in most respects fits the description in the sagas. What is more, archaeological investigation in the 1960s revealed the existence there of a Viking settlement of the right period. This was close to the village of L'Anse-aux-Meadows, where digging uncovered the remains of turf houses, a smithy, a sauna and boatsheds. No human skeletons were found, no weapons and only a few artefacts, but it is widely accepted that this was Leif Eriksson's base.

The Vinland Map

Excitement welled up in the media and in scholarly circles in 1965, when Yale University Press publishec what was claimed to be a map of the world dating from before Columbus's time and showing Vinland. Drawn on parchment and annotated in Latin, the map showed three islands in the North Atlantic: Iceland, Greenland further west and in remarkable agreement with modern maps, and further west still, 'Vinland Island discovered by the companions Bjarni and Leif'. Sadly, a scientific analysis commissioned by Yale University subsequently demonstrated that the ink used in the map could not have been manufactured before the 1920s. It was a forgery.

Did the Irish Discover America?

The Vikings were not the first explorers of the North Atlantic. Seafaring Irish monks, travelling in cockleshell boats called curraghs – made of leather stretched over a wooden frame, of a type still used in Ireland – were certainly in the Faeroes and Iceland before the Vikings. It is even possible that Irish voyagers reached America long before Leif Eriksson, though there is as yet no hard evidence of it.

The Celtic people of Britain and Ireland had old traditions of mysterious lands out to sea in the west, inhabited by gods or an unearthly race. A popular story grew up that St Brendan, a famous figure of 6th-century Ireland who founded the monastery at Clonfert, had set sail in a curragh to find the earthly paradise, the Land of Promise of the Saints, in the western ocean. In the course of the voyage he and his companions saw many marvels and came to numerous islands, including one of sheep, one of grapes, one of a fiery mountain. At one point they landed on the back of a sleeping whale, thinking it was an islet, and discovered their mistake when they lit a fire on it. Eventually they reached the Land of Promise, which was an open country rich in apple orchards.

Memories of real voyages could lie behind this legend. The island of sheep might be the Faeroes and the fiery mountain a volcano in Iceland, the island of grapes or the earthly paradise itself might be what the Norse later called Vinland. Tim Severin proved in the 1970s that the Irish could have reached America, by sailing a leather curragh, looking like a floating banana, from Ireland by way of the Hebrides, the Faeroes, Iceland and Greenland to Labrador, braving gales, ice and fog on the way. Whether the legend of St Brendan was based on real Irish voyages to America is still uncertain, but the story was one of the factors that influenced Christopher Columbus.

Biographical Notes

c.AD 982
Erik the Red, banished from Iceland for three years, sails westwards to explore a previously sighted but unknown land, and calls it Greenland.

c.935–6
Erik returns to Iceland and sails again for Greenland with 25 ships of settlers and livestock.

c.1000
Leif, one of Erik's sons, lands on what was probably the north coast of Newfoundland and calls it Vinland.

c.1001–10
Thorvald, Leifs brother, explores Vinland but is killed by native Indians. Thorstein, another brother, tries to find Vinland but dies of sickness.

c.1020
Thorstein's widow and her new husband settle in Vinland for about three years.

after 1020
Freydis, Erik's natural daughter, leads a disastrous expedition to Vinland.

Asia

'Or where the gorgeous East with richest hand,
Showers on her kings barbaric pearls and gold'

MILTON
Paradise Lost

Above *Looking towards Mount Annapurna, one of the highest peaks of the Himalayas, in the mountain kingdom of Nepal. Jesuit missionaries explored Tibet and Nepal in the 17th century, hoping to find a lost Christian community cut off among the eternal snows.*

The continent of Asia, which included Asia Minor, Mesopotamia, India and China, was the home of all the earliest advanced civilisations with the exception of that of Ancient Egypt. Early European travellers in Asia were not products of a superior culture exploring less developed territory. On the contrary, they were barbarians venturing into realms of glittering wealth, achievement and sophistication. The 'gorgeous East' has always held a special place and fascination in the European imagination – romantic, mysterious, inscrutable, profoundly alluring and profoundly sinister.

Long before Westerners arrived, of course, Asia had been explored by Asiatics. The Chinese were vigorous discoverers of the world about them. In 138 BC, for example, a man named Chang Ch'ien was sent on an imperial mission to central Asia that took him to the Samarkand area and Tibet. In AD 399 a monk named Fa Hsien went to India with three companions and spent years there in the study of Buddhism. He took his knowledge back to China by way of Sri Lanka and Java, and wrote an influential book about the peoples and places he had seen.

Another Chinese missionary was Hsuan Tsang, who rode across the Gobi Desert and over the mountains of the Hindu Kush to India in the 7th century. He spent years there and returned with a vast haul of Buddhist manuscripts, statues and relics. Between 1405 and 1433 the redoubtable Admiral Zheng Ho, a eunuch and a Muslim, commanded fleets of 60 and more ships on voyages all round the Indian Ocean, in which he visited Indo-China, the Malay Peninsula, Indonesia, Sri Lanka and southern India, the Persian Gulf, Arabia and the eastern coast of Africa.

Seeing the world

Simple greed lay behind some early Western adventuring in Asia. The saga of Jason and the Argonauts in pursuit of the Golden Fleece reflects avid Greek interest in the gold of the Caucasus. Curiosity impelled the Greek writer Herodotus to travel in Egypt and western Asia in the 5th century BC. The longing for fame and victory inspired Alexander the Great, who led his invincible Macedonian army across the whole breadth of Persia (modern Iran) and into north-west India in the following century.

The legend that St Thomas the Apostle – 'doubting Thomas' – travelled to southern India and founded churches there may be based on genuine Christian missionary work in India in the early centuries AD. By this time Greek ships were plying between the Red Sea ports, and Arab dhows sailed along the Persian Gulf and the Indian coast. By land, caravans carried luxury goods from China along the Silk Road across central Asia to Persia and on to the Mediterranean.

The Crusades brought Western fighting men to Syria and Palestine to wrestle with the Muslims for the Holy Places. Guidebooks were written for Christian pilgrims to Jerusalem, but few Europeans penetrated far into Asia in the Middle Ages. Much the most famous of those who did was Marco Polo, the 13th-century Venetian adventurer whose travels took him to Asia Minor, Persia, central Asia, Mongolia and China. A favourite of the Mongol emperor, Kublai Khan, he eventually returned to Europe by way of the South China Sea, the Malay Peninsula and the Indian Ocean.

Marco Polo's Arab counterpart was Ibn Battuta in the following century. Inspired by a passionate longing to see the world, he notched up an astonishing total of 75,000 miles in expeditions in Africa and Asia. He took the Silk Road to central Asia, he hobnobbed with such powerful potentates as the Khan of the Golden Horde and the Sultan of Delhi, and eventually saw China and Sumatra before returning to his native Tangier in Morocco to write a vivid account of his travels.

Paths to Cathay

A new era began at the end of the 15th century, when the royal courts of Spain and Portugal backed drives to open up new trade routes to the Far East to tap the fabled riches of Cathay (China). Columbus was trying to reach China and Japan when he accidentally discovered America. The Portuguese had been probing down the west coast of Africa.

Meanwhile, a secret agent named Pedro de Covilhã was employed by King John of Portugal to spy out a route from Africa to India. It was an undercover operation because the Muslim rulers who controlled trade in the Indian Ocean did not welcome Christian competition. Disguised as a Muslim honey merchant, Covilhã took passage down the Red Sea to Aden and from there to Calicut on the southwest coast of India, where he arrived in 1488. He went north up the coast to Goa, returned to Aden and visited the African east coast. Sending his information back to Portugal, where it was kept strictly secret, he vanished into the mountain strongholds of Ethiopia, where he was discovered living in comfortable retirement 30 years later.

The future, however, lay with the route to India round the Cape of Good Hope, which Vasco da Gama took to reach Calicut in 1498. He sent ships back to Lisbon loaded with a fortune in spices – pepper, ginger, cinnamon and cloves – and the King of Portugal now rejoiced to call himself 'Lord of the conquest, navigation and commerce of Ethiopia, Arabia, Persia and India'.

Soon after this, the engaging Italian adventurer Lodovico Varthema was the first Christian known to have visited the holy city of Mecca, which he did in 1503, disguised as a Muslim and in danger of his life if discovered. He went on to Aden, where he was unmasked and arrested as a Christian spy, but one of the Sultan's wives fell in love with him and obtained his release. Later journeys took him to southern Persia, India, Sri Lanka, Burma and Malaya, and he finally returned to Europe to write a popular book, the *Itinerario*.

Above *Cathay and the empire of the Great Khan, depicted on a map of the world drawn in 1459 by an Italian, Fra Mauro, for the ruling council of Venice. The Silk Road from China across central Asia to the Mediterranean had been travelled by merchant caravans since at least the 1st century* AD.

Left *The Chinese scholar Hsuan Tsang travelled to India in the 7th century* AD *in search of Buddhist texts, crossing the Gobi Desert and Kashmir on the way. After studying in Buddhist monasteries he returned to China and wrote an account of his travels.*

***Above** Musicians at the Pamionchi Monastery in Tibet. This remote country in central Asia, with its own idiosyncratic variety of Buddhism, was almost unknown to Europeans until well into the 19th century, when both Britain and Russia tried to bring it under their influence.*

An unknown quantity

The Portuguese built up a commercial empire in India. They were followed by the French and then by the British, who eventually took control of the whole subcontinent. China and Japan remained largely closed to foreign penetration until the 19th century. Vast regions of Central Asia, Siberia and Arabia meanwhile remained almost unknown to the outside world. They were explored by European merchants, missionaries, botanists, soldiers and intelligence agents.

Rumours of monasteries, black-robed monks and temple bells in a mysterious land north of the Himalayas drew Christian explorers, who hoped to discover a lost Christian community beyond the high peaks. The land was Tibet and the monasteries were real, but Buddhist.

An Italian Jesuit, Antonio de Antrade, struggled through the Himalayan snows into the western part of the country in the 1620s and founded a short-lived mission. Two more Jesuits, an Austrian named Johann Gruebner and a Belgian, Albert D'Orville, were probably the first Europeans to see Lhasa and the palace of the Dalai Lamas. They arrived there from China in 1661 and went on to India by way of the mountain kingdom of Nepal.

There was a Capuchin mission in Lhasa for a time in the 18th century, but the first European to make a thorough investigation of Tibet was an Italian Jesuit named Ippolito Desideri, who arrived in 1716 and spent five years in Lhasa. His description of the country was not published until long afterwards, in 1904, so Tibet remained largely an unknown quantity.

Siberia and the north

Russian armies began the conquest of Siberia in the 16th century, building forts and opening up trade in furs. The spearhead was the brutal Cossack leader Timofeyevich Yermak, who forced his way into Siberia in 1581. By 1639 the Russians had reached the Pacific at the Sea of Okhotsk. Tsar Peter the Great sent a Danish officer in the Russian navy, Vitus Bering, to explore the unknown area between Asia and America. Leaving St Petersburg in 1725, Bering and his men crossed the whole of Siberia, built a ship on the Kamchatka Peninsula and sailed it north into the Arctic Ocean. They established that the two continents were separated by sea and this was confirmed by Bering's second, tragic voyage in 1741, when he died of scurvy.

The roof of the world

In the 19th century the towering mountain ranges of central Asia on the borders of three great empires – the British, the Russian and the Chinese – were the stage for 'the great game', the rival spying and manoeuvring for position of the three powers. British and Indian soldiers and intelligence agents risked their lives in John Buchan-style adventures on 'the roof of the world'.

***Right** The Cossacks under Timofeyevich Yermak force their way into the Khanate of Siberia in a dramatic painting of 1895 by the Cossack painter Vasili Ivanovich Surikov. Like their opposite numbers in North America, the Cossacks had the advantage of guns.*

William Moorcroft, the veterinary surgeon who ran the East Indies Company's stud farm, was already engaged in anti-Russian intrigue when he explored the Himalayas, Tibet and Kashmir between 1812 and 1825. He apparently died in Bukhara, of either fever or poison, but rumour had it that he vanished into Lhasa, where he lived for 12 years in disguise and was then murdered on his way back to India.

With Tibet closed to Europeans, Lhasa achieved its enticing reputation as 'the forbidden city'. From 1865 on, however, the central Asian region was secretly explored and mapped by Indian surveyors in British pay. They carried Buddhist prayer wheels, but inside were rolls of blank paper for their notes, and they counted every 100 paces by the beads on their Tibetan rosaries. Their achievements were extraordinary. In 1882, for example, Kishen Singh returned after four years away in which he had been robbed, arrested more than once and imprisoned. Through his adventures he had meticulously surveyed 3,000 miles (4,750km) of terrain.

In 1872 an oddly named Englishman, Ney Elias, crossed the daunting Gobi Desert. He later penetrated Chinese Turkestan (now Xinjiang) and crossed the Pamir Mountains. A Russian army officer, Nikolai Przhevalsky, explored Mongolia, the Gobi, Chinese Turkestan and Tibet in the 1870s and 1880s.

The Tibetan nut was finally cracked and forced open when a British military expedition under Francis Younghusband entered Lhasa in 1904. Meantime, the distinguished Swedish explorer Sven Hedin, who had begun life as an interpreter in Iran, made extensive journeys in central Asia and was the first to make a detailed map of Tibet.

By World War I only the highest peaks of the Himalayas remained unconquered. They too yielded in time, including Everest itself in 1953, when Edmund Hillary and Tenzing Norgay stood on the highest summit in the world.

The Empty Quarter

As late as 1853, when the Englishman Richard Burton made the pilgrimage to Mecca in disguise, the blistering desert sands and the unpredictable wandering Bedouin had kept the interior of Arabia an unknown territory. The burning heat, the featureless dunes, the silence and solitude called to something deep in English temperaments and the exploration of the Arabian desert was an English achievement.

W.G. Palgrave, who made a hellish trek across the desert from what is now Jordan to the Persian Gulf in the 1860s, was a brilliant linguist, a botanist, a Roman Catholic missionary commissioned by the Pope and also an agent in the pay of the French government. C.M. Doughty joined groups of Bedouin to travel perilously in the desert in the 1870s. He was robbed and beaten, but he returned to write a famous book, *Travels in Arabia Deserta*.

Before World War I the redoubtable Gertrude Bell, archaeologist and mountaineer, travelled in the Syrian and Arabian deserts to the awed astonishment of people who had never seen a European before. In the 1930s Freya Stark travelled in remote regions of Iran and across the Yemen by donkey.

H. St John Philby explored the interior of Arabia in 1917–18 and became a convert to Islam and adviser to Ibn Saud, the ruler of Saudi Arabia. To his intense irritation, the feat of crossing the forbidding Empty Quarter in the south was pulled off in 1931 by someone else – Bertram Thomas, an obscure English financial adviser to the Sultan of Muscat. Philby hastened to make a more thorough exploration of the Empty Quarter himself in 1932, and the last of the great English Arabian explorers – Wilfred Thesiger, author of the marvellous *Arabian Sands* – was there in the 1940s. Even desert Arabia had at last yielded up her mysteries.

Above *Rising tier upon tier above its lake in Lhasa is the Potala Palace of the Dalai Lamas, from which Tibet was ruled for many centuries. Closed to Europeans in the 19th century, Lhasa gained a magnetic reputation as 'the forbidden city'.*

MARCO POLO

A merchant from Venice, Marco Polo travelled throughout China and the Far East in the service of the Great Khan.

Marco Polo was born in Venice (Venezia) in 1254, at a time of remarkable ambition and expansion. The fourth crusade, 50 years earlier, had left the city-state with vastly increased power and a considerable empire. At the same time, thousands of Mongol tribesmen under the leadership of Genghis Khan had brought terror and, eventually, a form of unity, to central Asia. They extended their power as far east as China where, by the middle of the 13th century, a descendant of the ruthless Genghis Khan was ruling over a remarkably advanced civilisation. With control over a network of ports stretching to Constantinople (Istanbul) and beyond, Venetian merchants now had an unprecedented opportunity to take their interests further east if they were prepared to risk the dangers of central Asia, and to investigate the remote corners of the Mongol empire. Two merchants who seized on this opportunity were Niccolò and Maffeo Polo, Marco Polo's father and uncle.

The Polos make their way to China

Niccolò and Maffeo Polo were involved in trade at Constantinople and they also had interests in the Crimea (Krym). In 1260 they saw that the time was right to take their goods further afield. A few missionary monks had already travelled to the Far East, eager to take the Christian message to the ends of the earth, and doubtless hoping to find the kingdom of Prester John – a fictitious Christian potentate rumoured to live somewhere beyond the Islamic world. The Polos, although they did not leave Constantinople with such an ambitious journey in mind, seem to have been the first Europeans to succeed in crossing the entire continent of Asia. They were pioneers and their achievement should be remembered alongside that of Marco Polo himself.

After profitable trading at Bolgara (Bulgar) and a long stay at Bukhara, they encountered an envoy who was on his way back to the court of Kublai Khan, the Mongol emperor of China. The envoy told them that the Khan had never met people of the Latin race before and would be eager to do so. He also talked of the profits to be made in the east and persuaded the Polos to go and see for themselves, although it is unlikely that they had hopes of gaining any part in the lucrative silk trade, whose routes were very closely guarded and controlled.

From Bukhara they had to travel for another whole year before they reached Kublai Khan's court at Cambaluc (Beijing), where they were treated with honour and respect. The Khan even gave the appearance of an interest in Christianity (his own mother had been a convert) and, providing them with a golden safe-conduct pass that required all his subject peoples to help them on their way, he instructed them to take letters to the Pope in which he asked to be supplied with 100 Christian theologians and oil from the lamp of the Holy Sepulchre in Jerusalem.

After three more years of travelling Niccolò and Maffeo arrived at Acre ('Akko), north of Jerusalem, in April 1269, only to learn that the Pope was dead. As no successor had been chosen they could not deliver the Khan's letters and they returned to Venice, their mission unfulfilled.

Marco Polo leaves Venice to visit the Great Khan

During their long absence Niccolò's wife had died and his son, Marco, had grown up. Niccolò and Maffeo waited in vain at Venice for news of the

Right *Marco Polo on his travels, from a French manuscript of the Venetian's* Book of Marvels, *which gave European readers their first full account of the mysterious Orient.*

appointment of a new Pope. Atter two years they decided, at the end of 1271, to return to the court of Kublai Khan, this time taking the 17-year-old Marco with them. They had not travelled far when they heard that a Pope, a man whom they had already met and who had chosen the name Gregory X, had finally been elected. He called them back and assigned two Dominican friars to accompany them to China. This small group was supposed to travel to the court of the Khan bearing letters and gifts from the Pope to the eastern ruler, but warfare in Armenia soon persuaded the friars that the enterprise was far too dangerous. They abandoned their mission and the three members of the Polo family were left to travel on alone.

Below *Marco Polo was the most travelled European of his day. Crossing the whole breadth of Asia to China, he spent 17 years there in the service of the Great Khan.*

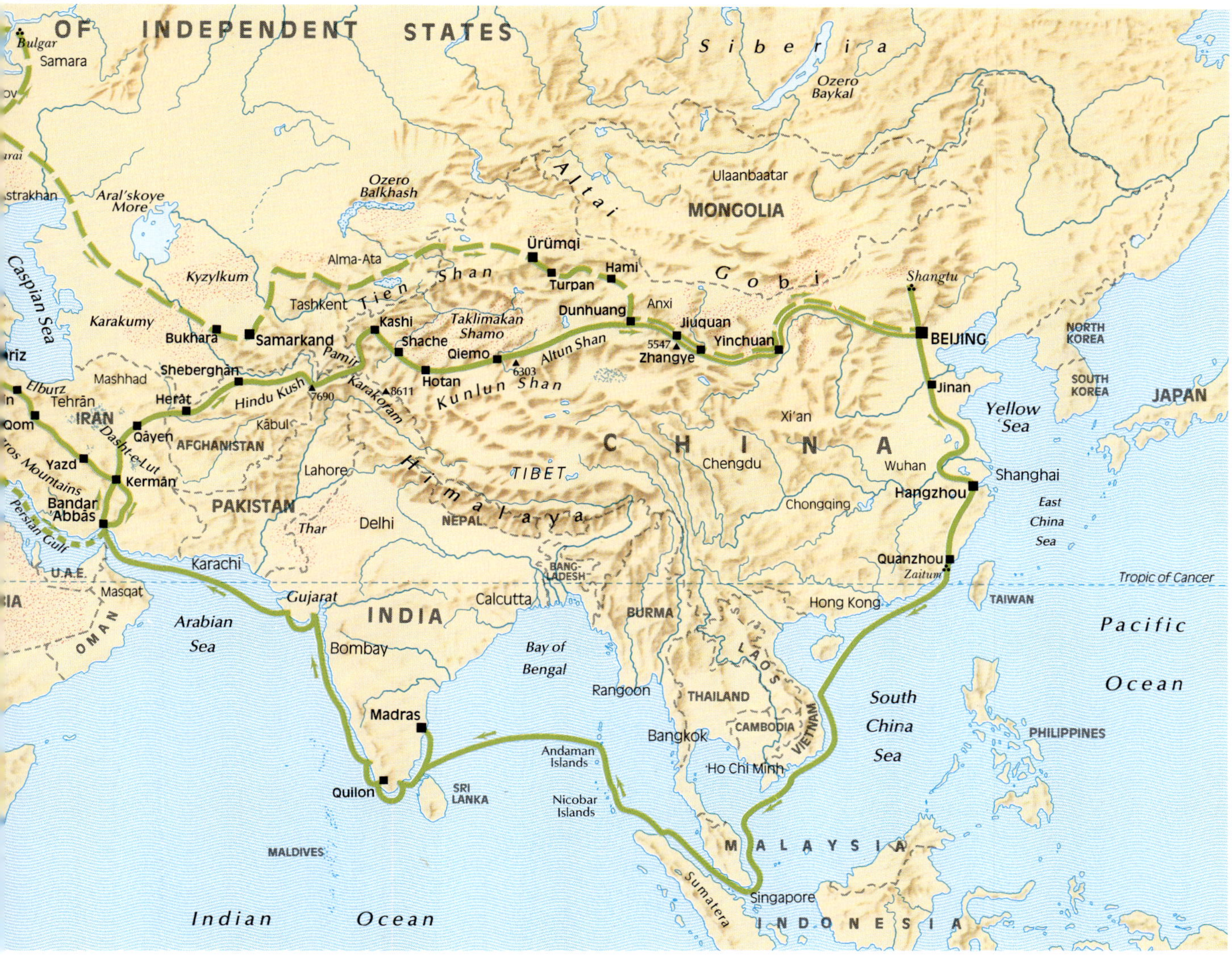

Above *Marco Polo and his father and uncle set out from Venice on their expedition to the Far East: from a French 14th-century manuscript,* Les Livres du Graunt Caam. *The ships are typical Mediterranean trading vessels of the period and Venice can be seen in the background.*

From Armenia they went to Tabrīz, and then to Hormuz (Bander Abbās) on the Persian Gulf, where they toyed with the idea of sailing to India. However, they chose not to risk a journey in the ships of the region which, to men accustomed to European construction techniques, looked flimsy and dangerous. The alternative was the overland route. The Polos crossed the khanate of the Persian Mongols. They reached the foot of the Pamir Mountains, where they stayed for the winter of 1271–2. They then spent 40 days traversing the mountain range, and came to the Takla Makan desert (Taklimakan Shamo) in western China. After crossing the desert they came to Kashgar (Kashi), and then entered the territory of the Great Khan at Khotan (Hotan), rich in minerals and vineyards. Finally they reached Kanchau (Zhangye). Storms and tempests caused countless delays and the whole journey took three and a half years. According to Marco Polo's account of his travels, this included a whole year spent in the city of Kanchau, where they must presumably have been engaged in business of some description – the delay suggests that the delivery of letters from the Pope, not to mention oil from the lamp of the Holy Sepulchre, was seen as a matter of no great urgency.

From Kanchau, their route took them on to Cambaluc, but the journey was still not over as the Khan was not in residence. They finally traced him to his summer headquarters at Shangtu, also known as Xanadu, where the young Marco immediately made a favourable impression and where Niccolò's polite suggestion that his son was at the Khan's service appears to have been interpreted literally.

Servant of the Great Khan

Nothing is known of Marco Polo's education during his early years in Venice, but at the court of the Great Khan he seems to have behaved studiously, learning about the customs of the country and apparently mastering four languages. A competent individual, and an asset to any ruler, he soon became a personal emissary of the Khan, a valued and high-ranking civil servant loyal to his foreign master for 17 years. He seems to have acted as an official reporter, travelling within the Mongol Empire with special instructions from the Khan to gather information about any unusual customs or phenomena that he observed. His book attempts to be a comprehensive gazetteer rather than a detailed account of one individual's itinerary, with the result that the actual route of Marco Polo's travels cannot be stated with certainty. It is reasonably clear that vast stretches of Asia were known to him, and he talks of lands from Armenia to Korea, and from Mongolia and Siberia to southern India; he also gives information about Japan, and about parts of tropical Africa, although it is doubtful that he went to these places himself.

As a servant of the Khan he seems to have visited Burma, and he describes a four-month journey to the province of 'Bengal', supposedly subjugated by the Mongols. It is doubtful that this was the real Bengal, however, because there is no record of any such victory. One of his most remarkable descriptions concerns the port of Hangchow (Hangzhou), or 'the city of heaven', on the eastern coast of China, an overwhelming place with canals and fine buildings that invited comparison with those of Venice. For Marco Polo, Hangchow was the finest city in the world. He explains that it was about 100 miles in circumference, that a huge river carried away all the city's waste, and that the air was remarkably pure. Town planning was obviously far advanced and there were 'ten principal market-places, not to speak of innumerable local ones'. Merchants from India and elsewhere stored their goods in large stone buildings accessible by land and water. Hangchow even had public baths. The locals, we are told, liked cold baths and they washed every day, but hot baths were also available for foreigners.

Generally his book celebrates the achievements of the Great Khan, and it is written in the tone of a loyal subject. Surprising among all the wealth of detail about individual Chinese cities and about the places Marco Polo saw on his way to and from the court of Kublai Khan is the absence of any mention of the Great Wall of China, or of China tea, or of the fact that the Chinese were already familiar with printing techniques.

A Portable Palace

"Kublai Khan built a huge palace of marble and other ornamental stones. Its halls and chambers are all gilded, and the whole building is marvellously embellished and richly adorned . . . a wall encloses and encircles fully sixteen miles of parkland well watered with springs and streams . . . in the midst of this enclosed park, where there is a beautiful grove, the Great Khan has built another large palace, constructed entirely of canes, but with the interior all gilt and decorated with beasts and birds of very skilful workmanship. It is reared on gilt and varnished pillars, on each of which stands a dragon, entwining the pillar with his tail and supporting the roof on his outstretched limbs. The roof is also made of canes, so well varnished that it is quite waterproof . . . and the Great Khan has had it so designed that it can be moved whenever he fancies; for it is held in place by more than 200 cords of silk. The Great Khan stays at Xanadu for three months in the year, June, July and August, to escape from the heat and for the sake of the recreation it affords. During these three months he keeps the palace of canes erected; for the rest of the year it is dismantled."

from *Marco Polo: The Travels* (translated by R.E. Latham)

Below *Marco Polo saw Mount Ararat, Armenia's highest peak, on his way to Tabriz and recorded the legend that the mountain was the place where Noah's Ark came to rest on dry land when the waters of the Great Flood subsided.*

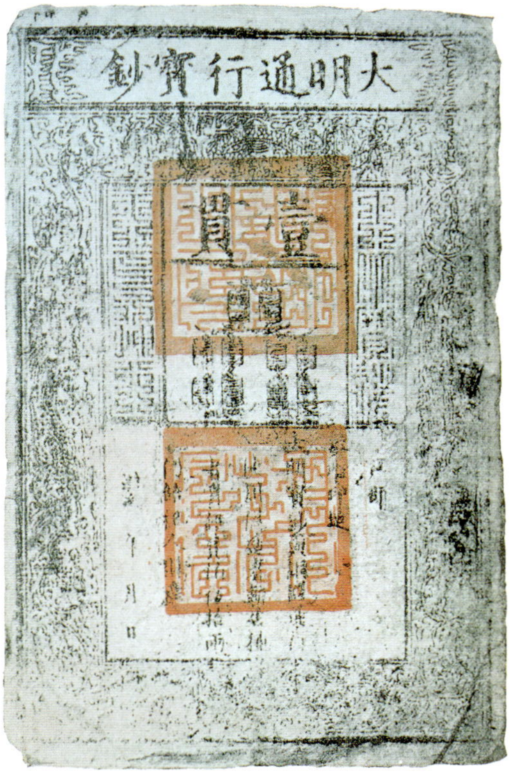

***Right** A bank note issued by the Ming Dynasty. Marco Polo was astonished by the efficiency and luxury of the Chinese empire, with paper money and paperback books, canals, huge and civilized cities and an autocratic civil service.*

The Silk Road

Silks and spices were carried to the west for centuries along trade routes established perhaps more than 3000 years ago. The Ancient Greeks and Romans knew of these precious commodities, but they understood little about their origins, and it was long thought that silk was a vegetable product that grew on trees in the land of the people known to the Romans as Seres. There is evidence of communication by sea between east and west at an early date, but the celebrated route known since the 1870s as the Silk Road ran overland, between oases in the Takla Makan desert, to the town of Kashgar, where merchants from different lands met and did business. It then crossed the Pamir Mountains towards Persia and the west. Marco Polo followed part of the Silk Road himself, and he describes Kashgar as a starting point from which traders would set out, taking their goods to distant parts of the world. It seems that he was not the first European to travel to China – a Chinese document contains a reference to officials apparently sent on a mission by the Roman Emperor Marcus Aurelius in the 2nd century AD.

The slow journey home

When the Khan reluctantly agreed to the Polos' request to leave his court in 1292, after they had been there for 17 years, it was on condition that they act as escorts for a Tartar princess on her way to her fiancé in Persia (modern Iran). Equipped as before with the Khan's golden safe-conduct passes, Marco, his father and his uncle travelled this time by sea in a fleet of 14 four-masted ships. The difficulties of the two-year journey back to Hormuz began with a five-month wait for favourable weather at Sumatra (Sumatera). Here, to avoid the attentions of cannibals, they built a fortified camp surrounded by a defensive ditch and reinforced with wooden lookout towers. Despite feeling a need for these precautions, the travellers appear to have been on good terms with the natives.

From Sumatra the expedition went on to the Nicobar Islands, the Andaman Islands and then to Sri Lanka, where Marco Polo comments on the abundance of precious stones and where, he claims, the king possessed a ruby as thick as a man's arm. From Sri Lanka they sailed to India, but Marco Polo's description of various different parts of the subcontinent is rather confused. He describes only the coastal regions, talking about the shrine of St Thomas, which can still be seen in Madras on the east coast, and also refering to Cape Comorin, the very southern tip of India. He seems to know about Quilon, on the southwestern Malabar coast, where it is so hot that he swears one could boil an egg in any of the rivers. And he describes Gujarat, in the northwest, which was notorious for its piracy and celebrated for its abundance of ginger and pepper. Nowhere in the world, we are told, was there embroidery to match that of Gujarat and it is an observation that Marco Polo was uniquely qualified to make – he had seen more of the world than anyone else alive at the time.

Some 600 men are said to have died in the early stages of this voyage from China, but Marco Polo, his father and uncle survived all the rigours of the journey and returned to Venice from Hormuz, via Trebizond (Trabzon) and Constantinople in 1295. The following year Marco Polo sailed in command of his own ship, in the Venetian fleet campaigning against the Genoese.

In September 1296 the Venetians were defeated and Marco Polo was held in Genoa (Genova) as a prisoner-of-war for some three years. A fellow prisoner, Rustichello of Pisa, was a professional storyteller and the two compiled an account of the things Marco had seen during his 26 years abroad. Marco Polo's account of his journey became known in Italian as *Il Milione* (the Book of Marvels), a title that suggests a concoction of tales, more fantasy than fact.

While there are signs of romantic embellishment – and tales of magicians who could alter the weather in the vicinity of the Khan's palace may seem hardly credible – it is also the case that the book dealt with things that no one in Europe had ever seen before, including such scarcely believeable materials as coal – miraculous 'black stones' that produced lasting fire. Religion, human occupations and natural history are topics to which Marco Polo pays particular attention. He shows considerable interest in architecture, ship design and building techniques, but little concern for music, art and literature.

Scepticism among its readers might be

Biographical Notes

1254
Born in Venice.

1271
Travelled overland with his father and uncle to the court of Kublai Khan. Spent 17 years in the east as diplomat and special envoy acting on behalf of the Khan.

1292
Began return journey by sea.

1295
Arrived back in Venice.

1298
Detained as prisoner-of-war at Genoa. Dictated account of his travels to Rustichello of Pisa.

1324
Died at home in Venice.

explained as European reluctance to believe in the remarkably advanced civilisation that Marco Polo observed. At the end of the 13th century Venice was a proud, cultivated city offering comfort and luxury to those able to afford it. The news that there was a distant land with advanced communication systems, a fire service, well-organised roads and plentiful supplies of hot water, where even the poor had a reasonable standard of living, may have been resented. The language of the lost original manuscript may have been French, Provençal, or a mixture of French and Italian, and there were many subsequent versions and translations. Some editions had magnificent illustrations, and some were edited in a way that suggested the Polos were Christian missionaries.

Marco Polo was released in 1299 and at some stage he married and became the father of three daughters. He died in Venice in 1324. His book, which probably relied chiefly on memories rather than written notes, was to influence many future generations of travellers – it was the first comprehensive account of the east to become available in a Europe that had previously based most of its ideas about eastern geography on stories about Alexander the Great. When Columbus sailed to America in 1492, Marco Polo's *Travels* accompanied him.

The Corte Seconda del Milion is a place ignored by almost all of the thousands of tourists who crowd into Venice each year. A modest courtyard enclosed by buildings of many dates and styles, it deserves to be better known because of its associations with the early history of travel. It was here that the family of Marco Polo lived, and from here in the 13th century that Marco himself set off on one of the most amazing journeys of exploration and discovery made by anyone.

Above *The Polos on their way to China, a detail from the 14th-century Catalan Map, which was drawn for Charles V of Spain. The Venetian merchant's account of his travels helped progress in geography and mapping.*

IBN BATTUTA

In the 14th century Ibn Battuta covered some 75,000 miles during half a lifetime of travel.

It is difficult to be a Muslim and not to be a traveller too. Other religions recognise and respect the concept of pilgrimage, but there is nothing to compare with the solemn obligation in the Koran that requires believers in Islam to complete the *hajj*, the journey to the holy city of Mecca (Makkah).

In 1325, at the age of 21, Ibn Battuta left Tangier (Tanger) for Tunis on the first stage of his first journey to Mecca. Although there is no evidence that he left home with any intention beyond that of performing the prescribed religious observances and going home again to Tangier, the experience of that journey seems to have turned him into an inveterate traveller. He embarked on a sequence of journeys that add up to a total of some 75,000 miles, and which occupied him for almost 30 years.

He came from a noble family and, armed with a good legal education, he left home in the knowledge that, if his religion required him to travel, it also helped him in a way denied to other travellers. He might encounter foreign languages and strange customs, but in any land within the realm of Islam he could expect to be recognised and honoured as an educated man. The language of the Koran would be a language in common, the beliefs and laws of those he met would be familiar and he could expect to find accommodation in the religious schools and colleges associated with the faith. His status as a learned pilgrim would place fellow Muslims of means under an obligation to offer him financial and practical support, and in a sense he should feel equally at home in lands as far apart as India, China and southern Spain.

In the *Rihla*, his account of his extensive journeys, Ibn Battuta makes a number of observations about his reasons for travelling. Near Alexandria, where he stayed for some weeks in 1326 on the way to Mecca, he says that he met a member of the mystic Sufi sect, a branch of Islam that appears to have fascinated him. This shaikh, something of a saint, told him of other Sufi holy men, two in India and another in China, and told the young pilgrim that a dream of his meant that he would travel widely and consult them, too. This was a turning point for Ibn Battuta. He claims that once the idea had taken root in his mind, his wanderings did not cease until he had met all three. He did not quite achieve this feat, but he certainly travelled to the lands in question. As a citizen of a large Islamic world, he seems to have formed an ambition to visit all the major sites of that world and he talks of his reluctance ever to travel the same road twice. Wherever he went, if there was an alternative route, a detour or a more circuitous approach to a place, he would he tempted to take it.

Acquiring a taste for travel

After an overland journey from Tangier to Tunis, where he admits to initial feelings of desperation and loneliness, Ibn Battuta joined a convoy of

Below *The dome of the Rock in Herusalem was built in the 7th century AD. One of the holiest of Islamic shrines, it stands on the spot where, according to Muslim tradition, the Prophet Muhammad ascended into heaven for an audience with God. Ibn Battuta took a side trip to Jerusalem during his first journey to Mecca.*

The Rihla

Ibn Battuta was not an explorer who uncovered previously unknown lands and cultures, but he set himself the task of exploring the known Islamic world, and so gained a unique, comprehensive view of that world. This valuable information was later written down in the form of a *Rihla*, a type of scholarly handbook popular at the time, which placed special emphasis on religious matters. Ibn Battuta wrote his *Rihla* in the middle of the 14th century in collaboration with a scholar called Ibn Juzayy, at the request of the ruler of Morocco. Never lacking in religious detail, it is tantalisingly short on material about the traveller himself. There are references to marriage contracts and to Ibn Battuta's acquiring a wife in one city or another, but these wives seem to have been lost or abandoned with remarkable ease. Similarly, the death of an infant daughter in Delhi is described almost without emotion and seems to be included only because it provides an opportunity to describe the funeral customs of the region. Inconsistencies over dates and routes make it impossible to reconstruct accurately all the details of the travels, but the book remains an impressive document whose history offers a stark comment on the lack of communication between Christian and Muslim cultures. It was only in the 19th century that the book became known beyond the borders of Islam, and an English translation of the entire work is still not complete.

Left *Artist's impression of Ibn Battuta in Egypt.*

other pilgrims and continued along the Mediterranean coast to Alexandria, via Sousse and Tripoli (Tarābulus). With time on his hands before the next pilgrimage season, he explored the Nile delta and spent some time in Cairo before deciding to abandon the safety of the pilgrim convoys and follow a different route south, along the Nile to Luxor and Edfu (Idfu), with a view to taking ship at 'Aydhab and crossing the Red Sea to the Arabian port of Jeddah (Jiddah). This, too, was an established route to Mecca, but it was a dangerous one and, although 'Aydhab itself was a busy port, handling much of the silk and spice trade from India and the Far East, Ibn Battuta arrived to find it in turmoil as a result of rebellion. With little prospect of making the sea crossing, he was forced to retrace his journey back along the Nile to Cairo and rejoin the pilgrims travelling to Mecca via Damascus (Dimashq). He found time for an excursion to Bethlehem and Jerusalem, where he consulted another Sufi and received as a gift a cloak of a sort normally worn by scholars of the sect.

At the beginning of August 1326 he arrived in Damascus, where he spent about a month completing a brief course of study before joining the pilgrim caravan that left the city at the beginning of September. The journey, through barren, semi-desert lands, was a long, difficult one – some 800 miles to the holy city of Medina (Al Madīnah), and then a final, 200-mile stage to Mecca, where Ibn Battuta records that he arrived in mid October. After performing the various religious rituals and spending about a month in the city, he prepared to leave, not for home, but for a journey through Persia (Iran) and Iraq. He went first to Basra (Al Basrah), an important seat of Islamic learning, then to Abādān, where an encounter with another Sufi saint almost persuaded him to opt for the life of a hermit, but he thought better of it and instead travelled on to the Persian cities of Isfahan (Eşfahān) and Shirāz. He seems to have had three companions with him when he reached Shirāz, where he was welcomed as a scholar and a pilgrim.

Below *The Islamic pilgrimage vow is inscribed in the outlines of a cypress tree next to this picture of Mecca in Ottoman times.*

His next destination was Baghdād, where he discovered that the entire royal court of the Ilkhan, or king, of the area known as al-'Iraq, was about to leave the city to return to the northern capital of Sultaniya. The huge royal cavalcade was an astonishing sight and Ibn Battuta quickly found a patron, joined the convoy, took part in a brief mission to Tabrīz, and had an audience with the king himself. He then returned to Baghdād, and, after visiting a number of towns along the River Tigris, including Mosul, set off again for Mecca, where he arrived towards the end of 1327 in a state of exhaustion brought on by chronic sickness. There were other times, too, when he suffered ill health, and it is a sign of his determination that these problems never caused him to abandon his adventuring life. However, he did stay in Mecca for a year or more at this stage.

Left The graceful outlines of the Al Rifai and Sultan Hassan mosques stand out against the evening sky in Cairo, another of the cities that Ibn Battuta visited.

Below Ibn Battuta's complicated web of journeys occupied most of his adult life. He explored much of the Muslim world of the time and he disliked treading the same road twice. Travelling within the confines of Islam, he could feel at home wherever he went.

Through Arabia to Africa and Afghanistan

During the next five years, Ibn Battuta travelled over an extensive area, but some of the claims made in the *Rihla*, notably his references to the Yemeni city of Ṣan'ā, appear to be false and it is impossible to be certain about the details of his route. Unfavourable winds complicated his Red Sea voyage from Jeddah to the Yemen, but he eventually reached the city of Zabīd and then seems to have travelled to the port of Aden, where he joined a ship that took him to Mogadishu (Mugdisho). Here the Muslim ruler received him as an honoured guest and he then sailed on to Kilwe (Kilwa Kivinje) south of the equator. This, too, was a Muslim state that had acquired enormous wealth through control of the gold trade. From here one ship took Ibn Battuta on to the Arabian port of Zafar (Salālah)

The Sultan's Return

"When the Sultan comes back from his journeys, the elephants are decorated, and over sixteen of them are raised sixteen parasols, some brocaded, some set with jewels. . . . Wooden pavilions are built, several stories high, and covered with silk cloths, and in each story there are singing girls, wearing the most beautiful dresses and ornaments . . . In the centre of each pavilion there is fashioned a large tank made of skins and filled with rose syrup dissolved in water, from which all the people, that is to say all comers, natives or strangers, may drink . . . I saw three or four small catapults set up on elephants throwing dinars and dirhams amongst the people, and they would be scrambling to pick them up from the moment when he entered the city until he reached the palace."

from the *Rihla* (quoted in *Adventures of Ibn Battuta*, R. Dunn)

The Caravan Trail to Mecca

Mecca can be visited throughout the year, but for the devout the holy month of Ramadan has always been the preferred time. The Muslim calendar observes lunar months and the time of Ramadan shifts from year to year. By the 14th century, arrangements for pilgrims were highly organised. The dates of the pilgrimage season were communicated to the faithful well in advance and the routes clearly charted. Individuals could set off from distant parts of the Islamic world in the knowledge that they would be able to join vast numbers of fellow believers at one of the great caravan departure points, such as Damascus. As many as 20,000 people might leave Damascus in convoy with all their associated baggage and pack animals at the beginning of the season, all benefiting from companionship and the safety of numbers, as well as from the highly organised infrastructure, which provided food and supplies along the route. The convoys travelled slowly, but they functioned efficiently, operating like cities on the move with their own hierarchy of officials to keep every aspect of life under control. It was as an official, in one of the lesser caravans that would merge with the great gathering in Damascus, that Ibn Battuta left Tunis towards the end of 1325.

Below *Mecca and the sacred shrine in 1882.*

ions on the same route. Again his itinerary is in doubt, but he speaks of Astrakhan, New Sarai and Bukhara, and he seems to have spent some time in the camp of the Khan of Chagatay near Samarkand. Travelling with a merchant caravan, Ibn Battuta safely negotiated the Hindu Kush mountains, paused at Ghazna (Ghazhi) and reached the Indus in the autumn of 1333.

The traveller on official business

Ibn Battuta's circumstances now changed. Mohammed Tughluq, Sultan of Delhi, employed him, as he employed many foreigners, as an official of his court. Ibn Battuta became a judge with a retinue and a generous income, which did not prevent him from accumulating serious debts. He spent eight years as the Sultan's employee before being imprisoned on suspicion of treachery. Soon released and granted permission to become a disciple of a Sufi ascetic, he renounced his possessions and embarked on a five-month period of religious contemplation, which was ended by a call from the Sultan who appeared to trust him once more. 'I have expressly sent for you to go as my ambassador to the King of China,' the Sultan said, 'for I know your love of travel and sightseeing.' The expedition was shipwrecked off the southwest Indian coast and Ibn Battuta then spent two years exploring this region, Sri Lanka and the Maldives, working for part of the time as a judge on behalf of local Moslem rulers. In 1345 he set off for China again, this time on a private expedition that took him by way of Bengal, Burma and Sumatra (Sumatera) (where the Muslim ruler supplied him with a ship and courtiers to keep

and another carried him to Sūr on the Gulf of Oman. He describes a perilous journey overland from Sur to Qalhāt, during which he feared for his possessions and his safety, but, again, he was hospitably received at his destination and the governor accommodated him for six days while he nursed his aching feet back to health. After further complicated wanderings, he arrived back in Mecca, which by now he seems to have regarded almost as a second home.

Perhaps towards the end of 1330 he was travelling again, this time on a Genoese ship, which took him from Latakia (Al Lādhiqīyah) in Syria to Alanya and Antalya in Anatolia on the first stage of a circuitous approach to India. He appears to have travelled widely in Anatolia, visiting such places as Bursa and Iznik, before sailing across the Black Sea from Sinop and apparently making a long detour overland with a royal convoy travelling to Constantinople (Istanbul).

Ibn Battuta was soon heading east again, into the steppes of central Asia, where the extreme cold forced him to wear so many clothes that he says he was unable to climb on to a horse without assistance, presumably from travelling compan-

Above *The Citadel in Cairo with its two slender minarets was built by Saladin in the 12th century and contains the mosque of Muhammad Ali. As an educated man, Ibn Battuta could expect a welcome in the Islamic religious schools and help on his journeys.*

Left *A Muslim pilgrim caravan, from a 13th-century illustration. Mecca was the birthplace of the Prophet and the obligation to visit the shrine there rests on every Muslim. It was the pilgrimage to Mecca that put Ibn Battuta in the way of travelling.*

him company), to Canton (Guangzhou). He was impressed with China, considering it a remarkably safe place for travellers, but he was also unhappy to find that Islam did not dictate the way of life to an extent that would enable him to feel at home. He speaks of visits to Peking (Beijing) and Hangchow (Hangzhou), but there is some doubt over this – Hangchow, of course, was a remarkable city, described in detail by Marco Polo, and Ibn Battuta may have relied on an existing stock description.

The return home and one more journey

Perhaps the very foreign feel of China and an encounter with a fellow Moroccan made Ibn Battuta yearn for home. In 1346 he left China, sailing from Ch'uan-chou (Quanzhou) via Sumatra and the Malabar coast of India, to Zafar and Hormuz (Bandar 'Ahbās), and then travelled overland through Persia, Iraq and Syria (where he made a detour to Aleppo [Halāb]). His journey took him through lands ravaged by the Black Death. He succeeded in his ambition to visit Mecca once more, in November 1348; 12 months later he was in Fez (Fēs), and shortly after that back in Tangier after a 24-year absence. He reports that his mother had succumbed to the Black Death only a few months before his arrival. Showing no desire to settle in one place, Ibn Battuta now made a brief visit to the Moorish kingdom of Granada, in Spain, where he met Ibn Juzayy, the man who was later to write the *Rihla*.

There was still a part of the Islamic world which Ibn Battuta had not seen, and in 1351 he set out to remedy this situation by venturing across the Sahara to the Kingdom of Mali. After crossing the Atlas mountains he joined a merchant caravan for the long trek across the desert to Walata (Qualata), a town where he found adherence to Islamic law and customs distressingly lax. He witnessed greater respect for Islam in the capital of Mali (a city whose location at that time remains a mystery), but the ruler, Sulayman, virtually ignored him. Following some further exploration, including a canoe voyage on the River Niger and a visit to Timbuktu (Tombouctou), Ibn Battuta joined a slave caravan heading for Morocco and returned to Fez in 1354. The *Rihla* was compiled during the next two years, a work of scholarship and record that was to be of incalculable value. Ibn Battuta apparently stayed in North Africa until his death in or around the year 1368.

Biographical Notes

1304
Born Tangier, Morocco.

1325–7
Left Tangier on pilgrimage to Mecca. Travelled to North Africa, Egypt, Palestine, Syria, Iraq and Persia.

1328–30
After prolonged stay in Mecca, travelled in Arabia and explored East African coast as far south as Zanzibar and Kilwa.

1330–3
Sailed from Latakia, Syria, to southern Anatolian coast. Explored Anatolia and crossed Black Sea to enter Crimea. Travelled through Central Asia and Afghanistan, from Astrakhan, via Samarkand to Kabul and Ghazna.

1333–46
Employed as legal official for Sultan of Delhi. Extensive travels along western coastal region of India. Also visited Sri Lanka, the Maldive Islands and crossed Bay of Bengal to Chittagong and Burmese coast. Sailed from Chittagong to Sumatra, through Strait of Malacca, and lands on Chinese coast. Journeyed to Canton and possibly Peking.

1346–9
Travelled from China to Tunis, sailing via Sumatra, Quilon and Zafar to Hormuz, then travelling overland through Shirāz, Isfahan, Baghdād and detouring to Aleppo.

1349–54
Travelled from North Africa to Granada, Mali, and Timbuctu.

1355–6
The *Rihla*, his account of his travels, written at Fez.

1368/9
Died, probably in western coastal region of Tangier.

North and Central America

'O my America! my new-found land'

JOHN DONNE
To His Mistress Going to Bed

Above *Palm trees with their graceful fronds on the north coast of the Dominican Republic. Columbus discovered the island in 1492 and named it 'the Spanish Island' (Hispaniola). Spain ruled the eastern end of the island until the end of the 18th century and for two brief periods in the 19th century, before finally withdrawing in 1865.*

The first people to discover and settle in the Americas were the ancestors of the American Indians, who came from Asia across the Bering Strait, which was then dry land, 20,000 to 30,000 years ago or more. They spread south down the whole length of the Americas, and in isolation from the Old World developed their own ways of life, their languages and religions, city-states and empires, until 500 years ago.

The first Europeans to cross the Atlantic to North America, so far as is known, were Viking sea-rovers. They reached Greenland in the 980s and about the year 1000 Leif Eriksson (son of Erik the Red) and his men explored the north-east coast of what is now Canada and established a short-lived settlement in Newfoundland.

Legendary discoverers

There are other claimants to the honour of reaching America before Columbus. In 1991 the official Chinese news agency proclaimed that the Chinese had discovered Alaska by the 7th century. In 1989 an American academic announced the Jewish discovery of America in the 1st century AD. Taking ship across the Atlantic after the Roman conquest of Judea, Jewish fugitives intermarried with the native inhabitants, which according to this theory accounts for alleged similarities between American Indian and Old Testament words and customs.

These claims met with the same general incredulity as the older, Welsh legend of Prince Madoc, who sailed to the west in the 12th century and found an unknown land where he saw many wonders. He brought the news of this discovery back to Wales, recruited several shiploads of hopeful settlers and sailed away again, never to return. In the 17th century there were reports of white-skinned Indians in North America speaking a language similar to Welsh. They were actually the Mandans of the Missouri River, and excited theorists identified them as descendants of Prince Madoc's people. The story was still alive in 1953, when the Daughters of the American Revolution installed a plaque at Fort Morgan in Mobile, Alabama, to commemorate Prince Madoc's landing in Mobile Bay in 1170.

Columbus, Cabot and cod

Leaving legend aside, the European rediscovery of the Americas in the 15th and 16th centuries was the accidental reward of attempts to reach the East by sailing west. This was clearly a theoretical possibility, given that the earth is round, which all educated people in Columbus's day accepted (the idea that the Church thought the earth was flat is a modern anti-clerical myth). Columbus wildly underestimated the distance to be travelled, but even so, it required great resolution to set out into the vast Atlantic in 1492 in the hope of finding the Orient.

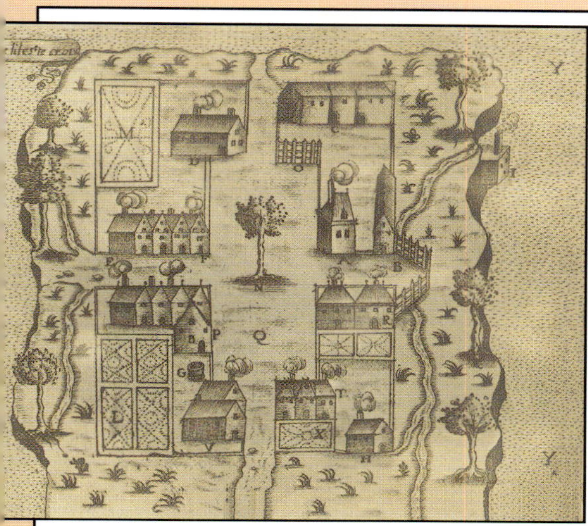

Left A diagrammatic picture of an early French settlement in the New World, on the island of Sainte Croix, where Samuel de Champlain wintered in 1604 while exploring the coast of Nova Scotia and the Bay of Fundy.

What they actually found was the West Indies – the Bahamas, Cuba and Hispaniola (modern Haiti and the Dominican Republic). In three further expeditions Columbus explored more of the Caribbean, touched the mainland of South America and investigated the Central American coast. It was entirely natural for Columbus and everyone else to assume that he had succeeded in reaching the Orient, and it took some time for the truth to sink in.

Meanwhile, another Italian seaman had been fired by the idea of sailing west to the fabled riches of Cathay. This was John Cabot (Giovanni Caboto) who persuaded Henry VII of England and the merchants of Bristol, then England's premier west coast seaport, to finance a voyage. He left Bristol in May 1497 in a tiny ship called the *Mathew*, with a crew of 18. After 52 days at sea they reached land, which they took to be China. In fact, they were somewhere near Cape Breton. After exploring some 400 miles (645km) of coastline Cabot returned in triumph. According to Bristol tradition, America is not named after Amerigo Vespucci, but after Richard Ap Meyrick, who welcomed Cabot home on behalf of Henry VII.

Cabot reported that the waters off 'China' were teeming with fish, so plentiful that they could be caught in quantity simply by lowering baskets into the sea. The news galvanised fishermen and the Newfoundland and Labrador cod fisheries were soon swarming with English, Breton, Basque and Portuguese fishing boats. These probably explored much of the coast without reporting to governments back home that were still avidly preoccupied with gold, pearls, silks and spices.

New Spain

Columbus's voyages founded the Spanish empire in the Americas. The Spaniards swiftly established themselves in Cuba and Hispaniola. In 1513 Vasco Nuñez de Balboa, with hundreds of Spaniards and Indian guides and porters, hacked through 45 miles of jungle and swamp in Panama to set eyes on the glittering Pacific, which he promptly claimed for Spain.

In the same year Juan Ponce de Leon sailed from Puerto Rico to find the land of Bimini, where he hoped to discover the fabled fountain of youth. In reality he discovered Florida, and also the Gulf Stream. In 1517 Hernandez de Cordoba explored the Yucatan coast and brought back the first reports of the ruined Mayan cities in the jungle. Two years later Hernán Cortés left Cuba with a private army of 600 men and 16 horses for an astoundingly rapid conquest of the blood-soaked empire of the Aztecs in Mexico.

Claim to Canada

Kept out of Central and South America by the Spanish and Portuguese, the French and English were forced to look for a passage to Asia further north. Their efforts opened up the eastern seaboard of North America to discovery and settlement, while at the same time Spanish adventurers were probing north from Mexico.

In 1524 a Florentine sea-captain named Giovanni da Verrazzano crossed the Atlantic in *La Dauphine*, a ship of the French royal navy. He was backed by the French government and a group of Italian merchants in France who hoped to open a connection for oriental silks. From the North Carolina coast he sailed the whole way up the seaboard to Newfoundland. On the way he encountered various groups of American Indians, clothed in animal skins and feathers. They were friendly and he found them gentle and courteous. He was the first European to enter New York harbour (where the great bridge named after him stands today).

Below A statue of Christopher Columbus stands in front of the cathedral in Santo Domingo, the capital of the Dominican Republic. Founded in 1496, the city is the oldest surviving white settlement in the New World and the cathedral is one of the places which claims to have the grave of Columbus.

Verrazzano returned to France in no doubt that he had explored the coast of a new continent, but his backers were disappointed that he had found no route to Cathay. He came to a grisly end on an expedition to the Caribbean in 1527, chopped to pieces on a beach and eaten raw by cannibal Caribs.

A Breton captain, Jacques Cartier, explored the Gulf of St Lawrence and the St Lawrence River for the French in the 1530s. He was still in quest of a passage to Asia, but his journeys were the foundation of the French claim to Canada. Local Indians told Cartier he had reached Canada, which was their word for a village, but he thought it applied to the whole region.

Realms of gold

Spanish explorers were meanwhile pressing north of the Rio Grande and up the Pacific coast, lured on by tales of vast wealth – the Seven Cities of Cibola dripping with gold or the Island of California, where a black queen ruled an all-female realm of fighting Amazons, whose weapons and horse-trappings were made of gold.

Francisco de Ulloa explored the Gulf of California in 1539. The following year, Francisco Vasquez de Coronado led a land expedition hundreds strong north into what are now the states of Arizona and New Mexico. One of the party was the first European to set eyes on the splendour of the Grand Canyon. In 1542 Juan Rodríguez Cabrillo, a Portuguese in Spanish service, sailed north up most of the coast of California. He found no black queen, no Amazons and no gold, though unknown to him plenty was waiting inland to set off the Gold Rush of 1849.

Land of lakes and rivers

In the north, though the dream of a passage to Asia was far from exhausted, interest began to grow in settling the new continent and exploiting its wealth in furs and timber. The English claimed Newfoundland in 1583 and in 1607 an English colony was planted at Jamestown in the territory that had earlier been christened Virginia in honour of Elizabeth I, the Virgin Queen. Jamestown was named after her successor, James I, and gave the English their first lasting foothold in North America.

French minds were turning in the same direction. In 1608 Samuel de Champlain founded a colony at Quebec with the backing of the French government. A soldier, he had earlier travelled in Mexico, where he was struck by the idea of cutting a canal across the Isthmus of Panama. He explored the eastern Great Lakes area, discovering Lake Ontario and Lake Huron. He organised the fur trade and made friends and allies among the Huron-Algonquin Indians, fighting with them against their Iroquois enemies. French trappers, settlers and missionaries were now moving in to New France.

***Above** Henry Hudson's ship* The Half-Moon *chaffering with American Indians while anchored in the Hudson River north of New York in 1609. Verrazzano had gone a little way up the river in the previous century, but Hudson was the first explorer to discover its size and importance. He was in Dutch service and Dutch colonists settled in the Hudson Valley.*

***Left** Jacques Cartier and a band of hopeful French colonists are seen landing in Canada in 1542. Cartier had earlier discovered the St Lawrence River and the future sites of both Quebec and Montreal, but this particular colony did not succeed.*

Right The Prospector, *seen as a heroic figure of the American West in a painting by an American illustrator, Sidney Reisenberg. Following in the wake of the early explorers, fur traders and trappers, prospectors for gold, silver and other minerals penetrated into nooks and crannies previously unknown to whites.*

An Englishman, Henry Hudson was meantime failing to find the Dutch a northeast passage to Asia through the Arctic Ocean north of Russia. In 1609 he persuaded his crew to go to America and look for a northwest passage instead. They pushed up what is now the Hudson River for 150 miles (240km) before deciding that it was not going to lead to the East. The exploit gave the Dutch a claim to North America and they later founded their colony of New Amsterdam on the island of Manhattan: eventually to be taken over by the British and renamed New York.

In 1610 Hudson left London with English backing in the 55-ton *Discovery* and sailed into the vast expanses of Hudson Bay. His crew mutinied and set him adrift in an open boat with his son and a handful of loyal men. They were never seen again.

Attempts to find the North-West Passage continued, while French fur-traders and missionaries opened up more of the Great Lakes region and the country to the west and south. Montreal was founded in 1642. Detroit in 1710. A prodigiously energetic and determined ex-fur-trader René-Robert Cavelier de la Salle, travelled down the Illinois River to the Mississippi and then on the whole way down to the Gulf of Mexico, which he reached in 1682. On the way, while noting the friendly helpfulness of the Indians he grandly claimed the entire area for Louis XIV under the Name of Louisiana. He then began on a planned invasion of Mexico, but was murdered in 1687.

In the following century French traders relying on Indian guides explored the Dakotas and the country between Lake Superior and the Rocky Mountains while the British pressed west from their colonies down the eastern seaboard, through the Appalachians to the Mississippi. In 1760 the French were forced to surrender most of their North American possessions but this British triumph was swiftly followed by the revolt of the Thirteen Colonies and the establishment of the United States as an independent power.

Below *A covered wagon has halted for the night, while supper is cooked and the washing hung out to dry: an illustration from* Scribner's *magazine in 1876. From the 1840s on, a growing army of emigrants set out across the Great plains to settle and tame the West.*

The way west

At the other side of the continent, Spanish expeditions sailed up the Californian coast and Junipero Serra a Spanish Franciscan, founded a string of missions in California in the 1770s and 1780s. The Golden Gate and the magnificent harbour of San Francisco were not discovered until 1775, by Juan de Ayala.

Captain Cook sailed up the Pacific coast of Canada to Alaska and the Bering Strait in 1778 and Russian agents moved into Alaska to trade in furs. George Vancouver surveyed the northwestern coast in the 1790s and between 1789 and 1793 a Scots fur-trader named Alexander Mackenzie made two immense Canadian inland journeys: from Lake Athabasca on the plains of Saskatchewan up the river subsequently named after him to the Artic Ocean, and later from Lake Athabasca across the Rockies to the Pacific coast of British Columbia.

In 1804 Meriwether Lewis and William Clark, under orders from President Jefferson to find a land route across the continent to the Pacific, set off on their epic trek from St Louis. With an Indian woman as guide, they crossed the Rocky Mountains and followed the Columbia River to the Oregon coast. They returned with an unprecedented quantity of systematically gathered information, while army officers, fur-trappers and adventurers explored the Rockies and the wide open spaces of the west.

In the 50 years between 1803 and 1853, by purchase, negotiation and force of arms, the United States acquired more than 2 million square miles between the Mississippi and the Pacific. The stage was set for the covered wagons to roll, for the defeat of the American Indians and the European settlement of the West.

CHRISTOPHER COLUMBUS

The European rediscovery of the Americas was one of the major turning points in the history of the world

The most famous voyage ever undertaken began on 6 September 1492, when three diminutive ships left the safety of the Canary Islands (Islas Canarias) and set out westward across the Atlantic into the unknown. The commander was Christopher Columbus and the expedition was one of the most fateful in history. From it followed the European and Christian conquest of the Americas, the subjugation of the original inhabitants, massive immigration from the Old World to the New and the emergence of the United States of America as a great power.

The quincentenary of the voyage in 1992 aroused strong feelings. The view of Columbus as the bold individual pioneer who opened the way to the development of American democracy and liberty was fiercely challenged by those who denounced him as the spearhead of genocide and oppression, forcible conversion to an alien religion, the slave trade and the rape of the world in harmony with nature. An opinion poll in the Unites States in 1991, however, commissioned by the National Italian American Foundation, found that 90 per cent of respondents regarded Columbus's arrival in the New World as a positive rather than a negative event in world history.

Driven by God

The event and its central character have attracted speculative theories in shoals, for much about Columbus and his life is unknown or disputed. Certainly he never thought of himself as Christopher Columbus. His name in Italian was Cristoforo Colombo, in Portuguese Christavão Colom. In Spanish, the language in which he wrote and probably thought for most of his adult life, he was Crístobal Colón. His

Below *The four epoch-making voyages. Columbus's first voyage used the north-east trade winds to sail west from the Canary Islands. He was blown home again, stormily, by the North Atlantic westerlies.*

younger brothers also used the Spanish form of their names, as Bartolomé and Diego Colón.

A seaman of genius, Columbus was also a driven man, a visionary who believed that God had chosen him for a great task. He was a devout Christian and the significance of his first name, Christopher meaning 'Christ-bearer', did not escape him. A man of formidable presence, he was arrogant, avaricious, obstinate, ruthless and despotic, and at times on the edge of madness. Voices from God spoke in his mind, telling him what he wanted to hear and confirming his rightness.

Columbus was born in 1451 or 1452 at Genoa, an independent city-state in Italy, where his father Domenico Colombo was a moderately prosperous weaver. There is a theory that the family was of Spanish-Jewish origin. There is another that Columbus was the bastard son of a Portuguese prince and was subsequently sent off to Spain as an undercover agent for Portugal. Other writers have made him German, French, English, Irish, Greek or Russian, and there is even a notion that he was an American, descended from one of the Norse settlers of 500 years before, who sailed to Europe, took the name of Colón and returned to 'rediscover' his homeland.

Above *There is no authenticated portrait of the great explorer: this engraving dates from 1597.*

The enterprise of the Indies

Little is known about the explorer's youth, but at some point he decided to make his living at sea. Caught in a sea battle in 1476 and washed ashore in Portugal, he went to Lisbon (Lisboa), where his brother Bartolomé was a cartographer. Columbus lived in Portugal and Madeira for nine years. He married and made voyages to Iceland and the west coast of Africa. Meanwhile he meditated on his great plan, which he called 'the enterprise of the Indies'.

The Indies in those days meant Japan, China, southeast Asia and Indonesia. The idea of reaching the Indies by sailing west had already been put forward by a physician in Florence, Paolo Toscanelli. Columbus corresponded with Toscanelli and combed classical and medieval authors for support, but he was mainly inspired by passages in the Old Testament and the Apocrypha, which he interpreted as prophetic of his own mission.

Columbus knew that the earth was round – as all educated opinion in western Europe acknowledged – and he doggedly contrived to underestimate the distance from the Canary Islands to Japan. It so happened, however, that the distance he came up with was approximately the distance from the Canaries to America.

In 1484 Columbus asked King John II of Portugal to back an expedition across the Atlantic to the Indies. The king turned down the idea on the well-founded grounds that the distance across the ocean had been grossly miscalculated. In the following year Columbus moved to Spain, where he canvassed support for his plan. Queen Isabella and King Ferdinand set up a special commission to study the proposal, which after years of dallying produced an unfavourable report in 1490. 'We can find no justification,' it said, 'for Their Highnesses supporting a project that rests on extremely weak foundations and appears impossible to translate into reality to any person with any knowledge, however modest, of these questions.'

With admirable strength of character or reason-proof fanaticism, whichever way you care to look at it, Columbus kept faith in his plan through all these years of discouragement, derision and hostility. He impressed Queen Isabella and at last, after two more years of persistent lobbying, he was given his head. He set his terms high: to be made governor of any territory he discovered and to have 10 per cent of all gold, precious stones and spices produced there, plus a 10 per cent cut of all trade.

To the New World

Matters now moved swiftly and at dawn on 3 August 1492 the 40-year-old explorer sailed from the harbour of Palos de la Frontera on the southwestern coast of Spain with three ships: the *Santa María* of perhaps 100 tons and two caravels of about half the size, the *Pinta* and the *Nina*. In command of the smaller ships were two brothers from Palos, Martín Alonso Pinzón and Vincente Yãnez Pinzón, whose skills and steadfastness would prove invaluable. Ninety men and boys sailed on an expedition that would change the course of history. The names of 87 are known and almost all of them were Spaniards.

On 12 August the ships reached the Canary Islands. They sailed again at dawn on 6 September. On 9 September they passed out of sight of the Canaries and the rest of the world they knew and were alone on the wide, wide sea.

Until 18 September they made steady progress and all went well. They passed through floating clumps of sargasso weed, the winds fell and the ships crawled across the ocean. The sailors had never before been out of sight of land for so long. They began to worry about whether they would ever be able to sail back to Spain (the idea that they were afraid of falling off the edge of the earth is a modern invention). There were frictions, grumbling, fist fights. Columbus and his captains somehow kept the expedition going. He was keeping two different logs, one with his real reckonings and the other false, to pretend to the men that they were not as far from Spain as they really were.

'Land' was spotted more than once, but proved illusory. It became clear that even by the false log they had passed the point at which by Columbus's reckoning they should have reached the Indies, and still there was nothing to be seen but sea. Flocks of birds were seen flying southwest and they altered course in that direction,

Below *Columbus kisses the hand of Queen Isabella, as she and King Ferdinand see the expedition off from the harbour of Palos de la Frontera on 3 August 1492. The queen was more impressed by the explorer than most people in high places in Spain. The imaginative illustration of the scene is by Victor A Searles.*

but a mutiny was only narrowly averted. At last, at 2 o'clock in the morning of 12 October a lookout in the *Pinta* raised the cry of 'land' in the moonlight and this time it was no mistake. They had found an island in the Bahamas group; which one is uncertain. The lookout was subsequently cheated out of the reward money promised for the first sighting; Columbus took it for himself.

Next day they landed on the island, which Columbus named San Salvador (Holy Saviour). Columbus went ashore with his captains, gave thanks to God on his knees and claimed the island for Spain. He believed he was in the Indies and so, when some of the local people cautiously approached, he decided they were Indians. He handed out glass beads and little tinkly bells, which they liked. They were frightened of the cannibal Caribs, who preyed on them, and did not yet understand that worse predators had now appeared. They wore gold nose ornaments, which encouraged Columbus, who noted that, sweet-natured and guileless, they would make useful Christian converts and slave-labourers.

Cuba and Hispaniola

Columbus soon sailed on to find Japan or China, which he assumed must be close at hand. Guided by the Indians, who were skilful handlers of their dugout canoes, he negotiated the Bahamas and on 28 October came to the north coast of Cuba. This must be the southeast corner of China, he decided, though an expedition inland to find the Chinese emperor proved disappointing. The Spaniards were astonished to see the natives putting lighted 'torches' (*tobacos*) to their lips and puffing out smoke. It was the first European sighting of cigars and it introduced tobacco to the western world.

The *Pinta* sneaked off alone to find gold, to Columbus's dismay. He feared that Martín Alonso Pinzón would reach the Chinese emperor first or might sail back to Spain and steal the credit for the expedition. He sailed east along the Cuban coast and on to another island, so

Giving Their Hearts

From Columbus's report on the 'Indians' to King Ferdinand and Queen Isabella of Spain, 1493:

"... they are artless and so free with all they possess, that no one would believe it without having seen it. Of anything they have, if you ask them for it they never say no; rather they invite the person to share it, and show as much love as if they were giving their hearts; they are content with whatever little thing of whatever kind may be given to them. I forbade that they should be given things so worthless as pieces of broken crockery and broken glass, and ends of straps, though when they were able to get them, they thought they had the best jewel in the world; thus it was ascertained that a sailor for a strap received gold to the weight of two and a half *castellanos* ... They believe very firmly that I, with these ships and people, came from the sky ... and this does not result from their being ignorant, for they are of a very keen intelligence and men who navigate all those seas."

from *The Great Explorers*, Samuel Eliot Morison.

Above *The sword and the cross at the opening of a new era in history, as Columbus sets foot in the New World, on the island he named San Salvador: a Currier & Ives print of the 1840s. In the background a cross is being landed from one of the boats, and the advancement of Christianity was one of the explorer's leading motives.*

***Above** In another picture by Victor A Searles, the Admiral of the Ocean Sea is received by the court in Barcelona in 1493 on his return from his first New World Voyage. He has brought several Indians with him and various native products, including potatoes and Indian corn.*

beautiful that he named it Hispaniola, 'the Spanish island' (now Haiti and the Dominican Republic). Friendly contact was made with the local chiefs. The people seemd to have plenty of gold and the women went naked and were free with their favours. Columbus described the natives as 'very cowardly' and 'fit to be ordered about and made to work'.

On Christmas Day the *Santa María* was wrecked on a coral reef and had to be abandoned. Columbus interpreted this as a sign that God meant him to found a colony. A camp called Navidad (Nativity) was built of the *Santa María's* timbers and 38 men were left there with ample food and ammunition. (They afterwards went on the rampage for gold and women and were wiped out by the Indians.)

On 4 January Columbus set sail in Niña. He fell in with the *Pinta* again and there was a furious scene, but the two ships set off together for a laborious and difficult passage back to Europe. At one point, in a towering storm, Columbus wrote out an account of the expedition and put it in a sealed cask which he threw overboard in the hope that if the ship foundered, the cask might float safely to Spain. He reached the Azores (Ilhas das Açôres) on 18 February and Portugal on 4 March. Received with honour by the King of Portugal in Lisbon, he sailed on to a warm welcome in Palos on 15 March.

Admiral of the Ocean Sea

Summoned to court in Barcelona, Columbus arrived with gold and amber and an escort of Indians he had brought back with him, carrying green and yellow parrots in cages. The townspeople were agog and the half-naked Indians were the subject of intense curiosity and excitement. The explorer was greeted by the king and queen with the utmost honour and enthusiasm. Declared Admiral of the Ocean Sea and Viceroy and Governor of the Indies, his fame was assured and he appeared to be on the threshold of colossal wealth. Though he could not know it, he had reached the high point of his life and from now on his path would lead downhill.

A second and much larger expedition of 17 ships was urgently prepared, to settle Hispaniola, explore Cuba and forestall any attempt by the Portuguese to interfere in the Indies. Unfortunately, Columbus could not get on with the royal officials appointed to the expedition. Reports of his high-handedness were sent to court behind his back and began to undermine his credibility.

On 25 September the fleet left Cadiz for the Canary Islands with 1,000 sailors, soldiers, colonists, gold hunters and adventurers on board. Taking a more southerly route than before, on 3 November the Admiral arrived off an island he named Dominica, because it was a Sunday. He went on to take formal possession of Guadeloupe, inhabited by cannibal Caribs.

The fleet sailed on past the small islands of the Leeward and Virgin groups to Puerto Rico and then to Hispaniola, where Columbus learned the fate of Navidad and founded the first European town in the New World, which he named Isabela in honour of the queen. On the north coast of the Dominican Republic, it is now in ruins.

The Admiral went on to discover Jamaica,

which he called Santiago. He explored the south coast of Cuba, which he still believed to be mainland China, though it was disappointing to see no junks or sampans.

In Hispaniola things went badly. Columhus was a far better explorer than colonial governor. Many of the new settlers had one thing in mind only – gold. Greedy and ruthless, they would virtually wipe out the island's native population in the next 50 years. There was conflict with the Indians, hundreds of whom were shipped to Spain as slaves, to Queen Isabella's disapproval. Not enough gold was found to satisfy expectations, and cynics at home doubted if Columbus had discovered anything more than a few islands inhabited by savages. The court sent an official to report on the situation. Columbus, humiliated, sailed back to Spain.

The Garden of Eden

Arriving in June 1496, the Admiral succeeded by sheer force of personality in re-establishing himself in the good graces of the king and queen. In 1498 he set off with yet another expedition to the Indies, which included 30 women for the Spanish settlers to marry. Three ships sailed direct for Hispaniola, while Columbus took three others on a still more southerly course than before, which brought him to an island with three peaks, which he named Trinidad. He sailed on westwards into the Gulf of Paria and landed briefly on the coast of modern Venezuela, on the mainland of South America, on 5 August 1498.

The fact that the local women wore pearl necklaces excited the Spaniards, who took it as proof that they really had reached the Orient. Columbus, however, wrote in his journal that he had found 'a very great continent, until today unknown'. It was an 'other world' where Christianity will have so much enjoyment and our faith in time so great an increase'. He decided that it was the earthly paradise, the Garden of Eden, protruding like a woman's nipple from the very top of the pear-shaped earth.

Leaving Eden and sailing to Hispaniola, Columbus found a rebellion in progress against his brothers. He failed to resolve the situation and a new governor was sent out from Spain to take control. He arrested Columbus and his brothers, put them in irons and shipped them back to Cadiz, where Columbus landed still in chains in October. Ferdinand and Isabella had him set free at once, but they had lost all confidence in him as an administrator. He whiled away his time by contemplating leading a crusade to free Jerusalem from the Muslims.

Bitter end

In May 1502 Columbus set out with four ships on what would prove to be his last voyage, on which he would yet again make remarkable discoveries without understanding what he had found. Strictly forbidden to go to Hispaniola, he crossed from the Canaries to Martinique and then made for Hispaniola, but was refused entry to the harbour of Santo Domingo. He sailed on to explore the shores of the Gulf of Mexico, along the coasts of modern Honduras, Nicaragua, Costa Rica and Panama. He was searching for a strait between 'China' (Cuba) and the continent he had touched in 1498. He thought he was sailing along the Malay Peninsula and was only 10 days journey from the Ganges. Finding no strait, he returned to Spain in November 1504.

His incoherent report on his voyage failed to make a good impression and Queen Isabella, his staunchest supporter, died soon after his return. He had plenty of money, though he complained bitterly that the government had broken its promises to him. Crippled with arthritis, he felt slighted and humiliated as other men made free with 'his' Indies, while King Ferdinand refused to reappoint him as governor.

Christopher Columbus died an embittered man on 20 May 1506 at his house in Valladolid. He was in his mid-fifties. No one from the Spanish court troubled to attend his funeral. It is said that in 1513 his remains were moved to a monastery in Seville and in 1542 the bones of the Admiral of the Ocean Sea crossed the Atlantic for the last time to Hispaniola, to be interred in the cathedral of Santa María in Santo Domingo. There they lie still, or so it is claimed, though both Havana (La Habana) and the cathedral in Seville also claim to have them. It is typical of the man and his story that even his final resting place is disputed.

Calculated Blunders

Columbus's historic first voyage was only made possible by geographical mistakes of remarkable magnitude. The great geographer Ptolemy, writing in the 2nd century AD, had calculated the width of the Euro-Asian landmass as equal to 180° of longitude, or half the surface of the world. An earlier writer, however, Marinus of Tyre, had put it at 225°. This figure suited Columbus much better as it reduced the distance from Europe westwards round the globe to the eastern edge of Asia to only 135°. Columbus then reduced this further still by deducting 28° for Marco Polo's discoveries, 30° for the assumed distance from China to Japan, 9° for starting from the Canary Islands and another 8° more or less for luck. He was left with a mere 60° of longitude between the Canaries and Japan (the true figure is nearer 200°).

Columbus went on to make a second giant miscalculation by figuring the width of a degree as only 40 nautical miles at the latitude where he intended to cross the Atlantic. This enabled him to maintain that the distance from the Canaries to Japan was 2,400 miles (3,860km), when in reality it is 10,600 miles (17,055km).

If Columbus had not made these staggering miscalculations, he would never have set out. And if the Americas had not existed, he and his men would have sailed into the Atlantic Ocean never to be heard of again.

Biographical Notes

1451/2
Born at Genoa, Italy.

1476–85
Lived in Portugal and the Madeira Isles.

1485
Moved to Palos de la Frontera, Spain.

1492–3
First expedition to the New World. Discovered the Bahamas, Cuba and Hispaniola.

1493–6
Second expedition. Discovered Dominica, Guadeloupe, Puerto Rico, Jamaica; explored more of Cuba; founded the first European city in the Americas, on Hispaniola.

1498–1500
Third expedition. Discovered Trinidad, mainland of Venezuela; sent back to Spain in chains.

1502–4
Fourth and last expedition. Explored the Central American coast.

1506
Died at Valladolid, Spain (20 May).

VASCO da GAMA

An epic voyage secures the sea route to India for Portugal

In 1488, acting on instructions from King John II of Portugal, Bartholomeu Dias became the first European to sail from the Iberian peninsula to the southern tip of Africa. Dias named the place he had reached *Cabo Tormentoso* or Cape of Storms and for him the choice was to prove sadly prophetic, because he died there in a storm 12 years later. The king, however, rejected this name as being too gloomy. The rounding of the Cape was a momentous event offering Portugal the promise of a sea route to India and so a more appropriate, symbolic name was needed. The king decided on the Cape of Good Hope.

***Below** An imaginary portrait of Vasco da Gama, who opened the sea route to India to Europeans.*

Surprisingly, nearly 10 years passed before anything was done to exploit Dias's achievement. Wars with Castile and the death of the king delayed plans for an Indian expedition, but despite the delay, no other European power was in India before the Portuguese. Dias himself was responsible for designing two ships that were specially built for the voyage, but he was not given command of the fleet. King Manuel, who had succeeded to the throne in 1495, appointed instead one Vasco da Gama, a man not yet 30 years old who appears to have played no significant part in Portuguese seafaring before that time. Different accounts suggest that he might not have been the King's first choice, but that he inherited a commission intended either for his father, who died before the ships were complete, or for his brother, Paulo, who refused on the grounds of delicate health but who did eventually agree to join the expedition.

When the Portuguese finally set sail for India, it was with the advantage of years spent in careful planning. Dias's expertise and knowledge of the conditions likely to been encountered during the first part of the journey had led him to adapt the design of the traditional caravel, producing two ships which, although slower, would also be stronger and better able to cope with the demands of the journey. The *S. Gabriel* and *S. Raphael* were three-masted vessels of around 100 tons, and they were accompanied by the 50-ton *Berrio* and a 200-ton supply vessel loaded with perhaps as much as three years' rations. There was only one serious miscalculation. Because they knew nothing of East Africa and India, the explorers saw no reason to take valuable gifts with them. Instead, they loaded a supply of worthless trinkets, which were to prove profoundly embarrassing when the affluent rulers of these lands later greeted them with derision.

The voyagers set out

The four ships, carrying a total of 150 to 200 men, left Lisbon (Lisboa) on 8 July 1497 with Vasco da Gama, the Captain-General, aboard the *S. Gabriel* and Paulo da Gama in command of the *S. Raphael*. Nicolau Coelho, a man who appears always to have been da Gama's first choice for the performance of any technical or tricky navigational duties, took charge of the Berrio and Gonçalo Nunes was responsible for the stores ship. Among the crew were a number of convicted criminals, who would be considered more expendable if any particularly risky adventures

were called for. A surviving Roteiró, a diary of the voyage, anonymous but apparently written by someone on board the *S. Raphael*, explains that the king had dispatched the expedition 'to make discoveries and go in search of spices'. Later, when asked what they were seeking, one of Vasco da Gama's men gave the answer 'Christians and spices'. European adventurers were still hoping to make contact with the legendary eastern Christian kingdom of Prester John and, as always, the Portuguese travelled with the intention of recruiting new converts to the Christian faith. They also took with them a supply of *padrãoes* – pillars surmounted by a cross, which were to be planted along the route to indicate Portuguese and Christian conquest.

In the early stages of the voyage, the flagship became separated from the others in fog and there were 10 days of increasing anxiety before the four were reunited in the Cape Verde Islands (Ilhas do Cabo Verde), the place which the Captain-General had earlier designated as a rendezvous should such a problem arise. Then, from 3 August until 4 November, all four ships were out of sight of land as they sailed out into the Atlantic to avoid the difficulties of west African coastal navigation. They named the bay where they eventually anchored just short of the Cape of Good Hope, Santa Helena, stayed there for eight days attending to essential repairs and trying to discover whether any spices could be obtained in the region. After a misunderstanding with some local people, during which Vasco da Gama himself was slightly wounded, they set sail again and on 22 November rounded the Cape. Anchored in the bay of Saint Bras (Mossel Bay) for a fortnight, da Gama decided to break up the store ship and transfer his supplies to the other three vessels before continuing. There were further disputes with the native people here, perhaps because da Gama's men helped themselves to water, which was in short supply. Finally, the Portuguese set up a *padrão* overlooking the bay, but they had barely left before a group of natives arrived to demolish it.

Help and hostility in Africa

The explorers sailed on, calling the extreme southeastern coastal region 'Natal' because they

Left *Vasco da Gama's squadron. The four square-rigged ships carried not more than 200 men all told and large quantities of supplies. Once they had passed the Cape of Good Hope and negotiated the East African coast, the crossing to India was easy enough.*

Below *The Cape of Good Hope was given its encouraging name for morale purposes by the king of Portugal. Da Gama and his ships had trouble in passing it as the winds were difficult, but were able to tack around it on 22 November 1497, more than four months after leaving Lisbon.*

passed it on Christmas Day, and describing the Bantu they encountered further up the coast as the Boa Gente, or good people, because they were friendly to the travellers and helped them restock their ships with water. The visitors noted the abundance of copper in the land of the Boa Gente and named a river after it: Rio Cobre (River Limpopo). During the next stage of the journey many of the men began to suffer from scurvy – a condition that was almost inevitable on any long voyage at this date.

In Mozambique, the voyagers found plenty of evidence of trade with Arabia and India, but, after a promising welcome, there began to be signs of hostility, and when armed men appeared ready to resist da Gama's attempts to go ashore in search of water, he dealt with the problem by firing the cannon at them. According to a pilot whom da Gama took on board here, the visitors

Left *Fort Jesus in the old city of Mombasa, built by the Portuguese in the 1590s, is now a museum. Mombasa was an important harbour when da Gama called there.*

Below *The Portuguese spent 70 years probing their way down the west coast of Africa to the Cape of Good Hope and rounding it. To cross from Africa to India took Vasco da Gama only just over three weeks. Pedro Cabral's voyage was a follow-up to da Gama's.*

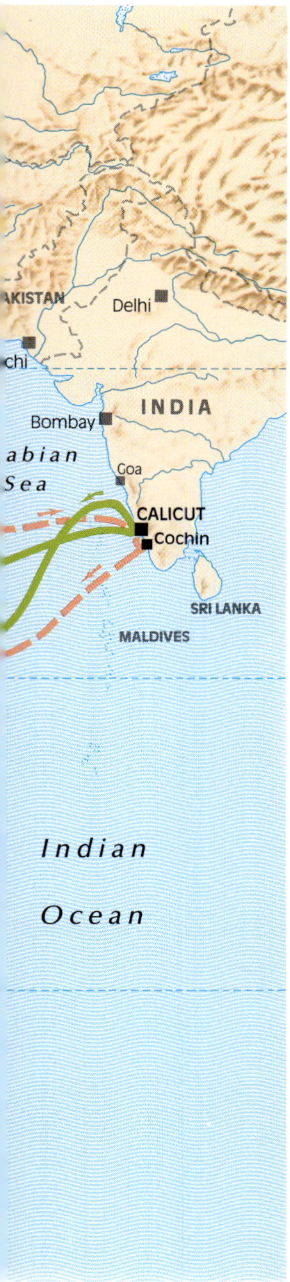

had been welcomed in the belief that they were Moors or Turks. When they were discovered to be Christians, attitudes changed and da Gama's violent reaction did nothing to improve the situation.

Da Gama's local pilot failed to prevent the *S. Raphael* from running aground on shoals near Mombasa at the beginning of April 1498, but the Portuguese still believed this man when he promised them that they had reached a city where they would find a large Christian community as well as a Muslim one. The information turned out to be false and after some apparently friendly approaches from Moors who rowed out to da Gama's ships in dug-out canoes loaded with oranges, the locals organised a more sinister welcome in the form of a ship carrying 100 men armed with cutlasses.

Eventually the King of Mombasa promised the Portuguese that they would be treated hospitably if they came ashore, but da Gama extracted a different story from two captured Moors by dropping boiling oil on to their skin as he questioned them. They revealed that he and his men were to be detained as soon as they entered the port and punished for their behaviour in Mozambique. The sailors keeping watch that night saw in the water what they took at first to be shoals of tuna fish. The writer of the *Roteiró* reveals that they soon realised their mistake: these were groups of men swimming towards the Portuguese vessels and intending to board them. 'These and other wicked tricks were practised upon us by these dogs,' he concludes, 'but our Lord did not allow them to succeed, because they were unbelievers.'

By now the local pilot had made his escape overboard and da Gama needed to find a new one with knowledge of the route to India. As they sailed from Mombasa, he captured a trading vessel in the hope that he would find a pilot on board, but the prisoners he took urged him to go to Malindi, where he would be sure to find someone suitable. The Portuguese appear to have been treated with courtesy at Malindi; they were obviously to be feared because it was known that they had succeeded in capturing a ship and taking prisoners, but da Gama, no doubt suspicious after his experiences in Mombasa, seems to have adopted a heavy-handed attitude towards the ruling sultan. The writer of the *Roteiró* talks of the 'Christian Indians' they met here, but he seems really to be describing Hindus. In less than a week the sultan had produced a pilot. Some accounts of the voyage state that this was a distinguished Muslim navigator called Ibn Majid; others find the suggestion highly unlikely and agree with the author of the *Roteiró* who talks of a 'Christian Indian', probably a seafarer from the northwestern Indian kingdom of Gujarat. Whoever he was, he was efficient. The explorers left Malindi on 24 April and reached Calicut on the southwestern Malabar coast of India on 20 May.

Above *Vasco da Gama refuses to turn back, despite the anxious entreaties of his crew.*

A Sailor's Diet

It is difficult to imagine the many discomforts and trials endured by the average sailor on a voyage from Europe to India at the end of the 15th century, but some details about his diet help to shed a little light on the picture. Vasco da Gama's first expedition to India was well equipped and his store ship is said to have carried lentils, flour, sardines, plums, almonds, garlic, mustard, salt, sugar and honey. Water would be taken on board at every opportunity and fresh fish and meat were obtained wherever possible. In many places it was the custom for the local people to welcome a foreign ship by rowing out in small boats filled with the sort of fresh provisions craved by sailors who had been out of sight of land for weeks on end. The daily ration for da Gama's ordinary seamen is given by one contemporary writer as one and a half pounds of biscuit, one pound of beef or half a pound of pork, two and a half pints of water, one and a quarter pints of wine and a little oil and vinegar. On holy fast days the allocation was a half a pound of rice and a portion of dried fish or some cheese. It was the lack of fresh fruit and vegetables that resulted in a deficiency of vitamin C, causing scurvy.

Slow progress in India

The *Roteiró* records that the first man da Gama sent ashore in India was greeted with the words 'May the Devil take you! What brought you here?'. It was a welcome that gave a reasonable indication of the difficulties to come. The Captain-General's first audience with the local king known as the Zamorin promised well and he was treated as an honoured guest. Soon afterwards, however, both parties began to lose patience with one another. Da Gama was carried in a palanquin to his lodgings and the journey, slowed down by monsoon rains, irritated him. Then he appears genuinely to have offended the Zamorin with his paltry gifts and by failing to keep an appointment, and to have taken offence himself at the suggestion that he should ride a horse without a saddle. After instructions from the Zamorin that they should unload any merchandise they had brought, da Gama and his delegation of men found themselves detained ashore against their will. At last da Gama received permission to return to his ship and for a while relations improved so that he was sufficiently confident not only to allow his men to go ashore in groups of two or three, but also to receive Indian visitors aboard his ships. At the last minute, however, as the Portuguese were preparing to sail, the Zamorin took hostages and demanded a large sum of money as a sort of departure tax. His behaviour seems not to have stemmed from personal antagonism, but to have been provoked by the local Moorish merchants, who had threatened to withdraw all their valuable trade with the region if the Europeans were allowed to have any share in it.

Da Gama reacted to the situation by taking hostages of his own and pretending to sail for home and this was enough to secure the release of his men. The Zamorin also agreed that a *padrão* could be set up in Calicut and he wrote a letter to the King of Portugal offering to trade his country's cinnamon, cloves, ginger, pepper, and precious stones for gold, silver, coral and scarlet cloth. This seemed to be as much as the Portuguese could hope for at this stage and the author of the *Roteiró* announces that on 29 August 1498 'the Captain-General and the other captains agreed that, inasmuch as we had discovered the country we had come in search of, as also spices and precious stones, and it appeared impossible to established cordial relations with the people, it would be as well to take our departure'. They decided to take the hostages with them hoping that they would be useful when they returned to Calicut and they set sail 'greatly rejoicing at our good fortune in having made so great a discovery', but one suspects with feelings of frustration that they had not been able to achieve more.

The voyage home

The weather conditions made it difficult to sail away from the coast, and at first the departing explorers had to fend off a number of marauders. Then calms and opposing winds plagued the journey across the Arabian sea; Mogadishu

***Below** Portuguese ocean greyhounds of the 16th century, from the* Livros das Armadas. *Once Dias had rounded the Cape and da Gama had reached India, the Portuguese swiftly built up a commercial empire in the east. They reached Indonesia by 1512 and China by 1514.*

A Hindu 'church'

"Within the sanctuary stood a small image that they said represented Our Lady. Along the walls, by the main entrance, hung seven small bells. Priests, called *quafees*, wore some threads passing over the left shoulder and under the right arm, in the same manner as our deacons wear the stole. They threw holy water over us, and gave us some white earth, which the Christians of this country put on their foreheads . . . Many saints were painted on the walls of the church, wearing crowns. They were painted variously, with teeth protruding an inch from the mouth, and four or five arms."

from the *Roteiró* author unknown (quoted in Volume 99 of the Hakluyt Society)

Left *St Francis Xavier is seen arriving in Goa, which is shown below, in a 17th-century Portuguese painting in the Museo Nacionale de Arte Antiga, Lisbon. The Portuguese kept their hold on Goa until 1961.*

Old Goa

The Portuguese strengthened their hold on India during the first few years of the 16th century, building a fort at Cochin and appointing their own Viceroy. In November 1510 they captured the former Muslim stronghold of Goa and turned a small town into the Portuguese capital of India. For 150 years it was a place of astonishing magnificence, noted for its wealth and for its many churches and monasteries, but the site proved unhealthy and a new capital was established a few miles away. Visitors to Old Goa today find the ruins of a deserted city of churches where the tomb and shrine of St Francis Xavier, the Jesuit leader who worked here in the middle of the 16th century, still attract large numbers of pilgrims. The region remained a Portuguese enclave until the 1960s, and the effects of centuries of European Christian influence are still very evident today.

(Muqdisho), on the East African coast, was not sighted until 2 January 1499, three months after the departure from India. Again, the travellers were graciously welcomed at Malindi, and allowed to set up another of their pillars, but even generous gifts of oranges and other fresh foods failed to save many of the men who had become ill during the long voyage. So many died that there were no longer sufficient hands to manage three ships and the *S. Raphael* was duly burnt on the shoals where she had run aground on the voyage out. Her figurehead alone was saved and transported back to Lisbon. The depleted company was close to home when Paulo da Gama died and his brother arranged for his burial on an island in the Azores (Ilhas dos Açôres).

Vasco da Gama reached Lisbon in September 1499 and King Manuel lost no time in authorising another expedition. The following year, Pedro Cabral was sent to India with a fleet of 13 ships, which steered so far out to sea from the west African coast that they reached Brazil, which they claimed for Portugal, calling it the Island of the True Cross. They then resumed their journey, hit storms off the Cape of Good Hope, during which Bartholmeu Dias was killed, and limped on to Calicut where their presence led to further conflict with the established Moslem traders. A better welcome awaited them at Cochin, where they set up a trading base, but they did not stay long and only four of the original 13 ships made it back to Portugal. Da Gama went out again in 1502 in charge of a large armed fleet and with instructions to make the whole sea route to India subject to Portugal. After inspecting the Portuguese base at Cochin, setting up some rudimentary defences and arranging for ships to guard the Malabar coast, he returned home in 1503.

Vasco da Gama was given generous allowances and honours as a result of his achievements, eventually receiving the title of 'Count' and acquiring the right to valuable revenues in northern Portugal. In April 1524 he set sail for India for a third time in order to take up the position of Viceroy, but on 24 December of that year, very soon after his arrival, he died. He was buried in the church of a Franciscan monastery in Cochin, where his gravestone can still be seen, but his body was returned to the Belem convent in Lisbon a few years after his death. He has another lasting memorial: the soldier and poet Luis Vaz de Camoes, during a long stay in the east, composed an epic poem, *Os Lusiadas*, celebrating Vasco da Gama's voyage of discovery.

Biographical Notes

c.1460
Born in Sines, Portugal

1497
Left Portugal for India.

May 1498
Arrived at Calicut.

1499
Back at Lisbon.

1502
Second voyage to India.

1503
Returned to Portugal.

1524
Travelled to India to become Viceroy. Died at Cochin soon after arrival.

FERDINAND MAGELLAN

The man who proved the world was round, but died in the attempt

In September 1522 a ship called the *Victoria* docked at Seville (Sevilla), and in doing so became the first vessel ever to have circumnavigated the world. She had left Spain three years earlier, one of a fleet of five with a total crew of 237. Now, after countless dangers, mutinies, desertions, and long periods of near starvation and despair, only 18 men were left and Ferdinand Magellan, the mastermind of the whole ambitious enterprise, was not among them. Magellan had died in the Philippines in April 1521, but not before he had proved what he had set out to demonstrate – that by sailing west from Europe one could find a route to the Spice Islands of the east.

Details of Magellan's early life are sparse. Born to a noble family in an inland district of Portugal around the year 1480, became to Lisbon as a boy to serve as a royal page at the court of King John II. It was a time when a young man could hardly fail to be inspired by Portugal's daring maritime exploits and in 1505 he began his own nautical career, apparently in the modest role of an ordinary seaman, sailing with the fleet commanded by Don Francisco de Almeida on a mission to consolidate and extend Portuguese interests in India and beyond.

Magellan seems to have distinguished himself and won promotion during this long campaign, acting swiftly to rescue some companions at one point and also helping to avert a mutiny. He was still in the east in 1511 and in that year he took part in the Portuguese conquest of the strategically vital port of Malacca (Melaka) under Afonso de Albuquerque. From this new Portuguese base at Malacca, Albuquerque sent exploratory missions out in search of the Moluccas, also known as the Spice Islands. Magellan does not seem to have been involved, but a close friend, Francisco Serrano, settled in the islands, and his subsequent letters may have played a part in encouraging Magellan to seek the islands for himself.

Injury, disgrace and defection

After a year back at the Lisbon court, where Manuel I was now king, Magellan left again in the

Below *The course of the first successful circumnavigation of the globe, with which Magellan's name is always associated, though he did not live to complete it and probably had no intention of sailing the whole way round the world.*

Right *An engraving of Magellan. Though not the first European to set eyes on the Pacific, which was seen by Balboa and his men from Panama in 1513, Magellan was the first to demonstrate the ocean's immense size.*

summer of 1513 on a campaign to suppress Moorish insurgents in Morocco. Here he suffered a serious leg injury that left him permanently lame and he is said to have been accused of trading illegally with the Moors and of returning to Lisbon without receiving official leave to do so. From this point on he seems to have fallen out of favour with the King. Slighted over a matter of salary, and refused permanent employment in the navy, he asked Manuel if he was free to take his services elsewhere and received no discouragement from doing so.

Magellan believed that under the Tordesillas Treaty, which had divided jurisdiction over the world between Portugal and Spain, the Spice islands might belong not in the Portuguese but in the Spanish sector, and after consulting Ruy Faleiro, an eccentric character who was both astronomer and astrologer, he decided at the age of 37 to abandon his allegiance to Portugal and try his luck in Spain. Magellan was sure that a western route to the Spice Islands awaited discovery, but he was reluctant to disclose the exact nature of his plans to the Spanish authorities. After initial rejections and a disagreement with Faleiro, he finally won the support of King Charles V of Castile. A detailed agreement between the King and Magellan survives. The King would provide Magellan with five ships to enable him to 'go with good luck to discover the part of the ocean within our limits and demarcation'. The King undertook to allow no other person to embark on the same course for a period of 10 years from the time of Magellan's departure, and he granted Magellan a percentage of the wealth that might be gained as a result of the expedition.

In search of spice and elusive straits

Magellan's fleet of five ships (the *Santiago*, the *Concepcion*, the *S. Antonio*, the *Trinidad* and the *Victoria*) sailed from Seville in September 1519. Among the company was Antonio Pigafetta, a man from Vicenza in Italy, whose diary of the voyage provides a detailed, eyewitness account of day-by-day progress. Pigafetta describes Magellan, the 'Captain-General', as a discreet and virtuous man, careful of his honour', but comments that the masters and the captains of the other ships did not love him, presumably because they were Spanish and he was Portuguese. The declared intention of the voyage was 'to find the islands of Maluco, from whence the spices come', but Magellan did not go into details at this stage 'so that his men should not from amazement and fear be unwilling to accompany him on so long a voyage'.

Magellan's s flagship was the *Trinidad,* and in this he led the way carrying a burning torch on the poop at night so that the others would not lose contact. The ships took on provisions and supplies of pitch in the Canary islands (Islas Canarias) and then navigated along the West African coast, encountering sharks ('large fishes which have teeth of a terrible kind and eat people when they find them in the sea either alive or dead') and strange, footless birds. On 13 December the ships reached Rio de Janeiro in the country of 'Verzin', where they were received as visitors from heaven because their arrival coincided with the first rain for two months. Pigafetta comments on the curious boats called 'canoos' made from hollowed trees and the 'infinite number of parrots'. Here, in exchange for a small mirror or pair of scissors, the people would give enough fish for 10 men to eat, while 'for a hatchet or for a knife they used to give us one or two of their daughters as slaves, but their wives they would not give up for anything in the world'.

After exploring the River Plate (Rio de la Plata) estuary in the belief that it might be the entrance to the straits he was seeking, Magellan continued the journey south along the uncharted coast, exploring any inlet that might conceivably connect with another sea. Finding nothing, on 30 March 1520 he put in to the port of St Julián for the duration of the Antarctic winter, and immediately faced the threat of rebellion.

Mutiny and shipwreck

There had been trouble earlier in the voyage, and Juan de Cartagena (apparently acting as an agent of the Portuguese king, who wanted the expedition thwarted) had been relieved of his command of the *S. Antonio* for insubordination. Now supplies of provisions were running low, and when Magellan put his men on short rations the order appears to have caused simmering discontent to boil over. The *Victoria*, *Concepcion* and *S. Antonio* all mutinied, but even in the face of such overwhelming disloyalty Magellan's skill and experience enabled him to deal with the situation. He sent an armed boarding party to the *Victoria* and one of the ringleaders of the mutiny, Luis de Mendoza, was knifed and later drawn, quartered and hacked to pieces. Gaspar de Quesada, the captain of the *Concepcion*, who had attempted to supplant Magellan as Captain-General, was then tried and executed, while Juan de Cartagena was abandoned on the Patagonian shore. Thirty-eight men were taken prisoner, sentenced to death, but then reprieved and allowed to rejoin the crew. Complaints about the wisdom of the expedition continued to be voiced, but Magellan's authority was not in doubt. He coped with another emergency – the wreck of the *Santiago* which, under the command of Juan de Serrano, had been sent to look for the elusive straits. Remarkably, all of the crew except one were saved.

Magellan kept his ships at St Julián throughout the severe southern winter. Intrigued by a curious race of giants to be seen in the region, he succeeded in capturing one, or perhaps two of them, and Pigafetta reports how these creatures swallowed barrel-loads of biscuits and ate rats without even bothering to skin them. One report suggests that one of these giants survived the

Penguins and Seals

"We found two islands full of geese and goslings, and sea wolves, of which geese the large number could not be reckoned; for we loaded all the five ships with them in an hour. These geese are black, and have their feathers all over the body of the same size and shape, and they do not fly, and live upon fish; and they were so fat that they did not pluck them, but skinned them. They have beaks like that of a crow. The sea wolves are of many colours, and of the size and thickness of a calf, and the ears small and round. They have large teeth and have no legs, but feet joining close on to the body, which resemble a human hand; they have small nails to their feet, and skin between the fingers like geese. If these animals could run they would be very bad and cruel, but they do not stir from the water, and swim and live upon fish."

from Antonio Pigafetta's chronicle (quoted in Volume 52 of the Hakluyt Society)

entire voyage, and travelled to Seville after being baptised and given the Christian name Paul.

Pacific breakthrough

The ships sailed again in October 1520 and on 21 October a vast cape was sighted, which Magellan called the Cape of the Virgins, taking the name from St Ursula and the 11,000 virgins whose feast day it was. This great stretch of water looked hardly more promising than many others they had explored, but when the *S. Antonio* and the *Concepcion* were sent to investigate they returned with the news that this was tidal salt water, and not another river. They had found the entrance to the straits that had eluded them for so long. Magellan now appears to have given his captains the option of returning to Spain by the known route, pointing out that there was a severe shortage of rations and that the distance they would have to travel if they pressed on was completely unknown. He, however, had no intention of turning back, and the others agreed to continue.

The second part of the strait was far more hazardous than the entrance. They sailed through a narrow, rocky channel between snow-capped mountains. The wind was coming from the west, and they sailed straight into it. At times

Below *Magellan directing operations from a small boat as his ships find a way through the tortuous strait, winding among snow-capped peaks. The strait was subsequently named after him. It took the expedition five weeks to find the way through. From a painting by W O Brierly.*

Above *Two of Magellan's men try out a native sailing pirogue at the 'Isle of Larrons' (which may be Guam): from a manuscript of the account of the epic voyage by Antonio Pigafetta, who sailed on it.*

the wind was so strong that they had to use rowing-boats to tow the ships along. After 38 days they finally passed the headland and were back in open sea again. During the passage of the straits the *S. Antonio* went missing and some time was lost in searching for her. In fact, she had defected and turned for home.

Magellan and his three surviving ships emerged from the straits, which were to be named after him, on 28 November 1520, over 16 months after leaving Seville. Using the same type of navigational instruments as those of Columbus and Vasco da Gama, and hypothetical charts, they sailed on a west-north-west course across the Pacific into the unknown. Magellan, like Columbus before him, greatly underestimated the size of the world, and the distance involved in crossing the Pacific. He believed that it would take them another month at the most to reach the Spice Islands. For three months and 20 days they sailed on, glimpsing only two uninhabited islands (which they named, appropriately, the Unfortunate Islands) and finding no new supplies of food.

The crew lived on old biscuits that had been reduced to a grub-infested powder fouled by rats as they had eaten the good biscuits. The water that they had to drink was yellow and stinking. They removed strips of oxhide from the rigging under the main-yard, and because these had dried out in the sun, they soaked them for four or five days in the sea, then toasted them over a fire for a short time and ate them. They made soup with sawdust from the ship's planks. Rats, which were caught in the hold and sold for half a crown each, were in short supply and were therefore considered a delicacy. Many of the men became desperately ill with scurvy and other ailments, and at least 19 died. At last, on 6 March 1521, they came to some inhabited islands and landed at Guam. They called the islands Ladrones, or Thieves' Islands (the modern Marianas) when the local people tried to steal one of the ships' dinghies. Magellan's reaction was to murder several islanders and burn a number of houses.

Death of Magellan

Restocked with sorely needed supplies of fish, fruit and vegetables, the three ships now sailed on to the Philippines. The King of Cebu Island appeared to be willing to convert to Christianity, but his submission to Spain provoked rebellion on the neighbouring island of Mactan among a faction that refused allegiance to Cebu or to Spain. In attempting to win Mactan for Spain and the Christian Church, on 27 April 1521, Magellan, who had appeared immune to danger and had refused to listen to advice not to become involved in such a raid, was killed. Further disaster followed when the King of Cebu renounced his recently acquired Christian faith and turned on his Spanish guests. The *Concepcion* was burned and the two men who had succeeded Magellan as joint Captain-General were killed. Magellan had not achieved his aim of reaching the Spice Islands via a westerly route, but he had demonstrated that such a route existed, and in future his name would always be associated with the first-ever circumnavigation of the world.

The survivors struggled on, now with only two ships, the *Trinidad* and the *Victoria*, eventually reaching Tidore in the Spice Islands on 8 November 1521. In the end it was decided to send the *Trinidad* on a mission back to South America and only the *Victoria* set course for Spain, arriving at Seville after a voyage that had lasted three years and one month. The mission brought King Charles of Castile no wealth or advantage. However, the world was now recognised as a far larger place than anyone in Europe had previously supposed.

The world is divided into two parts

At the end of the 15th century, the European view of the world underwent a radical alteration. In 1488, Bartholomeu Dias reached the Cape of Good Hope, showing that the way was clear for Portugal to dominate a new, southern sea-route to India and beyond – a route that Vasco da Gama went on to establish in 1498. In 1492, Columbus thought that he had found a western route to the East Indies and claimed it for Spain. The new world picture confirmed that the earth was not flat, but no one had yet guessed at the existence of a Pacific Ocean, or come close to appreciating the true size of the globe. With supreme confidence in his God-given right to deal with the world as he chose, Pope Alexander VI attempted to forestall future conflict between Portugal and Spain by allocating sovereignty over the entire western hemisphere to Spain and over the eastern to Portugal. It was easy enough in theory to draw a boundary on a map of the known world and the Pope promptly did so, but his choice of a line linking points 100 leagues west of the Azores (Ilhas dos Açôres) and the Cape Verde Islands (Ilhas do Cabo Verde) (by no means on the same longitude) brought protests from Portugal. In 1494 the Tordesillas Treaty moved this line of demarcation 270 leagues further west with the result that Brazil now fell under Portuguese jurisdiction. Although this much was clear, notions of what exactly happened on the other side of the globe remained hazy. Portugal had gained Brazil, but did the movement of the boundary line also mean that she had lost the Spice Islands to Spain's western jurisdiction? A Papal ruling in 1514 that Portugal was entitled to all lands reached by sailing east only confused the issue, and the matter was the subject of much wrangling for years. It was in the belief that the Spice Islands might be claimed from Portugal by Spain that Magellan set sail on his Spanish-sponsored journey of circumnavigation in 1519. Although the Spice Islands were within the Portuguese hemisphere, Spain attempted to claim them and Portugal only gained supremacy over them in 1529 on payment of 350,000 ducats to Spain.

Biographical Notes

c.1480
Born at Villa Real in Traz-os-Montes, Portugal.

1505
Sailed with Almeida's fleet to establish Portuguese presence in India.

1511
Took part in conquest of Malacca under Albuquerque.

1513
Campaigned against Moors in Morocco. Suffers serious leg injury.

1515
Request for employment in Portuguese navy turned down by King Manuel.

1518
Signed agreement with King Charles V of Castile. Given five ships with which to seek a western route to the Spice Islands. The fleet sailed the next year.

November 1520
Ships completed passage of the straits (later to be named after Magellan) from Atlantic to Pacific Ocean.

April 1521
Magellan died at Mactan in the Philippines.

September 1522
The *Victoria* arrived back in Spain, the first ship to circumnavigate the world.

***Left** Magellan was in his early forties when he was killed while attempting to seize the island of Mactan in the Philippines for Spain and the Christian faith. His men sailed on to Borneo and then to the Moluccas.*

HERNÁN CORTÉS

A soldier of fortune, Hernán Cortés succeeded in conquering the mighty Aztec Empire in Mexico

The Spanish conquest of Mexico was an epic of courage, endurance, brutality and rapacity, as a few hundred soldiers of fortune mastered an empire about the size of Italy. Their commander was one of history's most effective leaders of men. Hernán Cortés was in his thirties. Shrewd and resourceful, persuasive and determined, he was an engaging personality – cheerful, warm and outgoing, but chillingly brutal if threatened. He had an eye for the dramatic effect and he led from the front.

Cortés was born in 1485 at Medellín, near Mérida in the Spanish province of Extremadura, and came from an impoverished Castilian noble family. Intelligent, mischievous and reckless, he was a constant anxiety to his parents and, as he grew older, an enthusiastic womaniser. (In Mexico he had at least eight Indian mistresses.) Longing for action and adventure, he was fired by news of Columbus's discoveries, but his departure for the Indies was delayed when he was badly hurt falling off a wall while running away from a married woman's home, pursued by her furious husband. He eventually sailed for Hispaniola in 1504, when he was 19.

The Feathered Serpent

Except for contracting syphilis, nothing much happened to the future conquistador for some years, until in 1511 he served under Diego de Veltásquez, who conquered Cuba with 300 men. Cortés was rewarded with a grant of land and Indian slaves to work it. He had a house in the newly founded town of Santiago de Baracoa, of which he was elected mayor.

Cuba disappointed the Spaniards, and Velásquez sent out expeditions in search of richer pickings across the sea to the west. In 1517 Hernandez de Córdoba probed the coast of Yucatan, which the Spaniards mistook for the native name of the area, though the Indian they asked had replied, 'I don't understand you'. In the following year, Velásquez sent his nephew Juan de Grijalva with four ships to follow up. Grijalva sailed along the coasts of Yucatan and Mexico, hearing stories of a rich kingdom under a powerful ruler somewhere in the interior.

The rich kingdom was the Aztec Empire, and the ruler was its Chief Speaker, Moctezuma II, reigning from his capital of Tenochtitlán, where Mexico City stands today. Troubling reports were reaching him from the coast of strange 'temples' seen floating on the sea, containing white men with beards, armed with weapons that breathed out fire and smoke. There were old Indian myths and prophecies about the god-king Quetzalcoatl, 'the Feathered Serpent', who had sailed away from Mexico centuries before, but who would soon be returning from the east to claim his kingdom. Quetzalcoatl was white. Might these white beings in their floating temples be the god and his escort? The possibility would seriously weaken Aztec resistance to the coming Spanish invasion.

In Cuba, knowing nothing of this, Governor Velásquez decided to send an expedition to Mexico, and he put Cortés in command. Cortés energetically recruited ships and men, including many who had sailed with Grijalva, while giving himself such lordly airs as to arouse Velásquez's

__Below__ Cortés and his expedition rounded the coast of Yucatan on the way to the Mexican shore, where Cortés founded the town of Veracruz. Also shown is the route of the later expedition to Honduras, which Cortés led in 1524 to strengthen Spain's sway in central America.

jealousy. Velásquez cancelled Cortés's appointment, but Cortés promptly set sail. He left Cuba on 18 February 1519 with 11 ships, some 500 to 600 soldiers, 100 seamen, 16 horses and a few small cannon. The soldiers were armed with swords, but a few had crossbows and a handful had muskets.

The story of what followed comes mainly from three Spanish sources, which do not invariably agree: the letters Cortés wrote to the Emperor Charles V, who was now King of Spain; a biography of Cortés by his secretary, Lopez de Gomara; and a lively eyewitness account of the whole affair by Bernal Diaz, a soldier who served with both Grijalva and Cortés. He wrote his *History of the Conquest of New Spain* long afterwards, in his seventies.

Doña Marina

The expedition arrived at the island of Cozumel off the Yucatan coast and sailed north along the Gulf shore to an Indian settlement later known as Tabasco. The people there gave the Spaniards a present of 20 slave-women. Cortés gave them an image of the Virgin Mary in return and sailed on. One of the women turned out to speak the local Maya language and also the Aztec language, Nahuatl. She was herself an Indian, sold as a girl to the people further south. She became Cortés's 'tongue', or interpreter, his adviser and expert on Indian affairs, and his mistress. She later bore him a son, Martin. Her grasp of local politics was a crucial factor in Cortés's success. The Spaniards greatly respected her and called her Doña Marina. Mexican historians regard her as a traitor.

A Taste of Chocolate

An eye-witness account of Moctezuma at dinner:

"For each meal his servants prepared him more than thirty dishes cooked in their native style which they put over small earthenware braziers to prevent them from getting cold. They cooked more than three hundred plates of the food the great Moctezuma was going to eat, and more than a thousand more for the guard . . . every day the cooked fowls, turkeys, pheasants, local partridges, quail, tame and wild duck, venison, wild boar, marsh birds, pigeons, hares and rabbits, also many other kinds of birds and beasts . . .

While he was dining, the guards in the adjoining rooms did not dare to speak or make a noise above a whisper. His servants brought him some of every kind of fruit that grew in the country, but he ate very little of it. Sometimes they brought him in cups of pure gold a drink made from the cocoa-plant, which they said he took before visiting his wives. We did not take much notice of this at the time, though I saw them bring in a good fifty large jugs of this chocolate, all frothed up, of which he would drink a little. They always served it with great reverence. Sometimes some little humpbacked dwarfs would be present at his meals, whose bodies seemed almost to be broken in the middle. These were his jesters. There were other Indians who told him jokes and must have been his clowns, and others who sang and danced . . ."

from *The Conquest of New Spain*, Bernal Díaz (translated by J.M. Cohen)

Above *The victor: shrewd, ruthless and an altogether tougher character than this piously romanticised portrait makes him look, Cortés made himself master of the Aztec Empire. However, the Spanish bureaucratic regime brought him down too in the end.*

Left *The vanquished: Moctezuma, the Aztec emperor, depicted by an unknown 16th-century artist. Bernal Díaz, one of Cortés's soldiers, described the Aztec ruler as slightly built, with a long, cheerful face and fine eyes.*

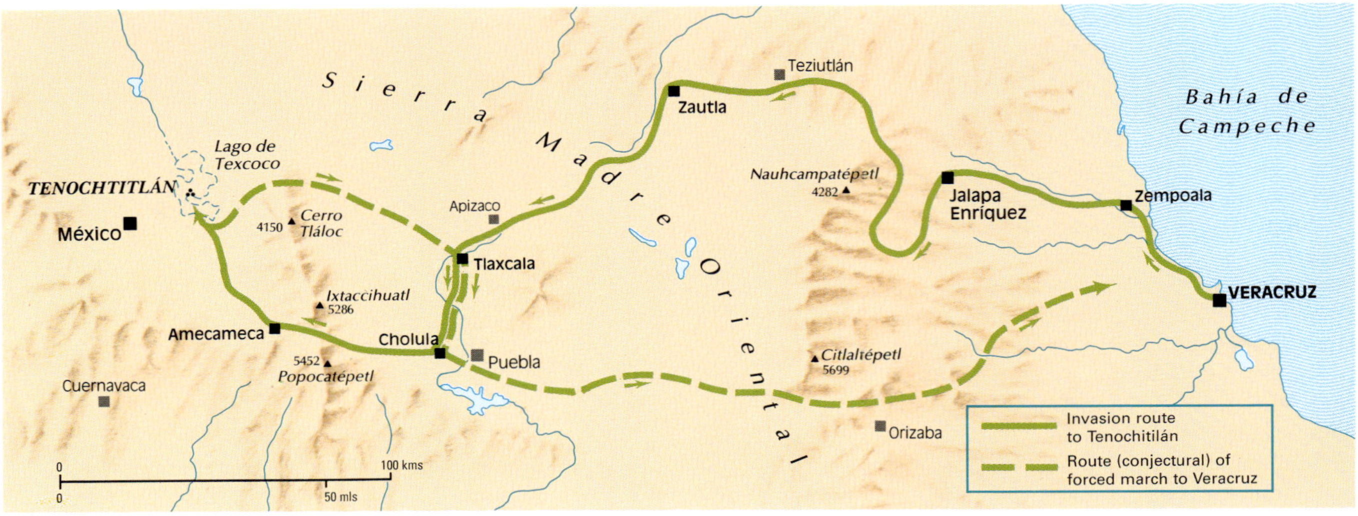

***Above** Aztec ambassadors tried to deter Cortés from marching on Tenochtitlán, the Aztec capital, by saying that the Spaniards would find the passage through the mountains too difficult. As it proved, the route he took enabled Cortés to recruit allies among the subject peoples.*

Cortés sent a message to Moctezuma by swift Indian runners, telling him that the Spaniards suffered from a disease that only gold could cure – which was true enough. Presently a reply arrived with rich presents of gold and silver that brightened the Spaniards' eyes, regretting that Cortés could not come to Tenochtitlán because the journey through the mountains would be too difficult.

For the moment Cortés busied himself with founding the town of Veracruz (True Cross), so that he could have himself elected its captain. This gave him an authority independent of Governor Valásquez in Cuba. Then he moved north up the coast to Cempoala (Zempoala), where the Spaniards were welcomed by the local chief, who complained bitterly of Aztec oppression and allied himself with them.

All through the enterprise, with Doña Marina's help, Cortés shrewdly exploited the subject Indian peoples' resentment of the heavy tribute they were forced to pay to the Aztec regime and the desperate need for blood to feed the Aztec gods, which saw thousands of victims sent to Tenochtitlán every year for sacrifice, their pumping hearts ripped from their living bodies as an offering to the sun. He played astutely on their fears and hopes, while keeping Moctezuma's envoys in doubt about his real intentions.

The Indians, on their side, were impressed and alarmed by the newcomers. They had never seen horses before and the Spanish steeds – snorting and foaming and shaking the ground with their galloping hooves – were frightening. So were their dogs, massive mastiffs that could kill a man. The Indians' obsidian-edged clubs, spears and arrows were no match for Spanish steel, still less for the deafening cannon and muskets that killed bafflingly at a distance. Native artists made pictures of the invaders and their horses and weapons, which were sent to Moctezuma.

Gaining allies

Cortés now discovered a plot against him by partisans of Velásquez. Two of the ringleaders were hanged, one had his feet cut off and other conspirators were flogged. Cortés then had all the Spanish ships scuttled. This action almost provoked a mutiny, but left the men with no choice but to remain in Mexico and either conquer or die.

On 16 August 1519 they set off from Cempoala to conquer an empire – 400 men, 15 horses and three cannon, with 300 Indian warriors and bearers. From the steaming forests of the tropical Gulf coast they had 200 miles to march through the towering, snow-clad mountains. The route was deliberately chosen to take them to the mountain stronghold of Moctezuma's most unruly subjects.

***Right** Armoured horse and rider of the period. The inhabitants of Mexico had never seen horses before Cortés and his army arrived. They found these strange beasts thoroughly alarming and Cortés deliberately exploited their fears.*

The march took them to Jalapa (Jalapa Enriquez), where the people were friendly, and up into the heights of the Sierra Madre Oriental. An icy wind blew from the snowy peaks and the men trudged doggedly through rain and hail. They passed through Xocotlan (Zautla), where they saw huge piles of human skulls and bones heaped up in the town square, and lectured the inhabitants about the superiority of Christianity.

After several skirmishes the Spaniards fought their way into Tlaxcala, whose people were fierce opponents of the Aztec regime. Cortés persuaded them to join him as allies. He moved on with thousands of Tlaxcalan warriors to the ancient city of Cholula, famed then as now for its vast pyramid, a mile in circumference and topped by a temple of Quetzalcoatl. The inhabitants seemed welcoming, but the Spaniards swiftly discovered that an ambush was intended. Cortés took the initiative, attacked with his cannon and killed thousands of Indians before sacking the city. The temple on top of the pyramid was destroyed and replaced by a huge cross, which was visible for miles around. Word of the Spanish victory soon reached Moctezuma's ears and seems to have deepened the pessimism with which he viewed the future.

The entry to Tenochtitlán

Marching on again with their Tlaxcalan allies, the Spaniards negotiated a high pass between the towering volcanoes of Popocatépetl and Ixtacchihuatl, both over 17,000ft (5,000m). Popocatépetl was hurling out stones and ash, to the fascinated amazement of the Spaniards, who had never seen a volcano before.

Ahead as they came through the pass was an even more remarkable sight – the spreading valley of Anáhuac, with broad Lake Texcoco (Lago de Texcoco) studded with islands and ringed with cities. On the biggest of the islands stood the towers of the Aztec capital, one of the largest cities in the world at that time.

Descending to the lake, the Spaniards crossed a causeway to the city, Cortés himself in gleaming armour astride his warhorse. There to meet them was Moctezuma, with his chiefs. The 52-year-old emperor stood beneath a rich canopy of green feathers worked with gold, silver, pearls and jewels. He wore rich robes and his sandals had golden soles.

Received with all honour, loaded with gifts and lodged in one of the royal palaces, the Spaniards spent several days wandering about the city gaping at the magnificent stone buildings, temples and courtyards, the canals busy with swift canoes, the markets, the animals in the zoo, the royal aviary of eagles, parrots and ducks, the gardens with their flowers and sweet-scented trees, their walks and summerhouses. In the temples they were horrified by the grim images of the Aztec deities and by altars caked in human blood on which human hearts were burning as offerings.

Left *This statue of the Aztec earth goddess, Coatlicue, is now in the Anthropological Museum in Mexico City. She has a necklace of human hands, hearts and a skull, and the heads of rattlesnakes form her face. The figure stands 8ft (2.4m) high. Aztec religion horrified the invading Spaniards.*

Blood for the sun

When Cortés came on the scene, the Aztec Empire covered most of central and southern Mexico and Moctezuma II as Chief Speaker ruled a population numbering at least 12 million. The Aztecs had established their city of Tenochtitlán centuries before on an island among the swamps at the western side of Lake Texcoco. They enlarged it by constructing artificial islands, drained the swamps, adorned the city with fine stone temples, pyramids and palaces, and eventually built three stone causeways to connect it to the mainland.

At the same time the Aztecs subjugated their neighbours, who were compelled to supply tribute to the Aztec rulers civil servants and priests. Aztec society was organised for war. Teenage boys were given military training and all able-bodied men served in the army when required. The Aztecs never developed the wheel or writing, but they had a 365-day calendar and notable achievements in engineering and architecture to their credit, as well as fine craftsmen in gold and silver, copper and ceramics, featherwork and basketry.

The Aztec appetite for war was due partly to the need to take prisoners to sacrifice to their gods, whose continued existence required the nourishment of human blood. This was true especially of the god of the sun, which it was feared would grow weak and pale if not supplied with a constant diet of strengthening red blood. The god's victims were spread-eagled over a stone on their backs and held down by four priests while a fifth cut the prostrate body open with a sharp obsidian knife, plunged his hand into the chest and tore out the pulsating heart, to hold it aloft.

Other sacrificial victims were drugged and then burned alive or tied to a rack to be shot to death with arrows. Some were flayed and the priests wore their skins. Children were sacrificed to the rain god in the belief that their piteous tears would stimulate the fall of the gentle, life-giving rain. Besides prisoners-of-war, convicted criminals were sacrificed and the subject peoples were forced to send a steady supply of victims to the capital. It is estimated that by the time the Spaniards appeared, the priests in Tenochtitlán were offering 50,000 victims a year to their gods.

Above *A pair of panels, now in the Museum of America, Madrid, depict the first meeting of Cortés and Moctezuma when the Spaniards came to Tenochtitlán. This one shows the Aztec emperor carried in a litter, and his escort of nobles.*

Years afterwards, Bernal Diaz still vividly remembered the luxury that surrounded Moctezuma, his harem of thousands of woman, and the taboos that hedged him round. No one ever looked directly at him and when he walked, his attendants put cloths down in front of him so that his sacred feet should not touch the ground.

The puppet-master

Wandering about like tourists, the Spaniards went everywhere armed to the teeth, keenly aware that they were virtually prisoners in a city in which they were vastly outnumbered. Cortés now made perhaps the most audacious move of his whole audacious career. He simply seized Moctezuma and carried him off to the Spaniards' quarters, where he was treated as an honoured guest. The enigmatic emperor fatalistically accepted the situation, and when a party of his people killed some of the Spaniards, he allowed Cortés to burn them alive. Moctezuma became, in effect, a Spanish puppet, through whom Cortés began to take control of the empire. The Spanish leader had the images of the Aztec gods removed from the principal temples and replaced by crosses and figures of the Virgin Mary and the saints, to the fury of the Aztec priests.

This curious situation lasted for what must have been a nerve-racking five months until in April 1520 news came that a powerful Spanish force had landed at Veracruz, sent by Governor Velásquez to put Cortés under arrest. Leaving a hundred or so of his men in Tenochtitlán, the conquistador made a forced march to Veracruz. Arriving in the middle of the night, he attacked immediately, forced his opponents to surrender and persuaded many to enlist with him.

Now word came that, with Cortés gone, the Aztecs had risen in wrath in Tenochtitlán and blockaded the Spaniards in their quarters. Cortés and his men hurried back to the city. The Aztecs let them in, but only to trap them inside. The chiefs deposed Moctezuma, who was still a Spanish captive, and chose his brother Cuitlahuac as Chief Speaker in his stead. Then they launched a relentless attack on the Spaniards, hurling spears and stones, firing arrows, setting buildings on fire, staging fake retreats to lure their opponents into ambushes.

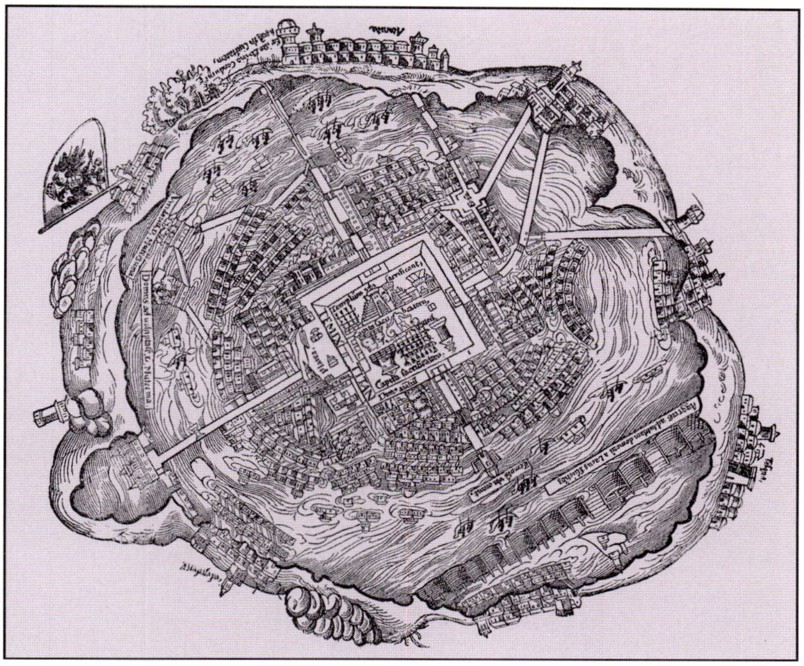

Above *This plan of the Aztec capital city is believed to have been made for Cortés.*

Below *A painting of Cortés and Cuahtemoc, last of the Aztec rulers. Caught trying to flee from Tenochtitlán by canoe, he was taken to Cortés.*

Biographical Notes

1485
Born at Medellín in Castile.

1504
Sailed for the New World

1511
Took part in the conquest of Cuba and settled there.

1519
Sailed from Cuba for Mexico (18 February); entered Tenochtitlán at the head of his troops (8 November).

1520
Escaped from Tenochtitlán on the 'Sad Night' (1 July).

1521
The Aztec capital surrendered to him (13 August).

1524
Led expedition to Honduras.

1540
Final return to Spain.

1547
Died near Seville (2 December).

Brought out by Cortés to reason with the people, Moctezuma was struck by a shower of stones and killed (though there are charges that he died at Spanish hands). The situation was untenable and Cortés resolved on an escape from the city by night over one of the causeways. The retreat was a carnage. Many of the Spaniards and their faithful Tlaxcalan allies were felled by the rampaging Aztecs or shot by archers in canoes. Some of the soldiers were so weighed down by loot that they fell into the lake and drowned or were chased down and captured, to be used as human sacrifices later. The survivors gained the mainland, where an exhausted Cortés sat down under a tree and wept. It was the night of 30 June/1 July 1520, known in Spanish annals as *La Noche Triste* (Sad Night).

Fallen eagle

Cortés was not a man to give up. Retreating to Tlaxcala, he gathered thousands of Indian warriors to his banner and built himself a navy of 13 ships. Meanwhile Cuitlahuac died of smallpox – an early victim of the deadly diseases the Europeans took with them to the New World – and was replaced by his nephew Cuahtemoc, whose name, ominously, meant 'Falling Eagle'.

With his Indian allies and his ships, Cortés laid siege to Tenochtitlán by land and water, and after several weeks, starved of food and riddled with disease, the city was forced to yield. Cuahtemoc was captured, tortured unavailingly to make him reveal the whereabouts of Moctezuma's treasure, and subsequently hanged.

The Aztec Empire had fallen. Cortés lost no time in having Tenochtitlán destroyed and a new capital built on its ruins. Named Governor and Captain-General of New Spain by Charles V, he sent armed expeditions to the west and the south to secure his hold and bring what are now Guatemala and El Salvador under Spanish sway. He himself led an expedition to Honduras. He also sent to Spain for friars to come and convert the Indians to Christianity and help protect them from the ruthless rapacity of the Spanish colonists and officials.

Though Cortés had mastered the Aztecs, he was no match for the suspicions, jealousies and intrigues of the regime in Spain. Assuming that he must intend to set himself up in New Spain as an independent ruler, the government established its own bureaucracy in Mexico to undermine him. He returned to Spain in 1528 and again in 1540, but though he was treated with every mark of respect, his governorship of New Spain was not confirmed. He spent some time at Cuernavaca, south of Mexico City, where he built himself a palace, which is now a museum.

The conquistador's final years were spent miserably in Spain, where he was largely ignored. Embittered and resentful, he died near Seville in 1547, aged 62. His body was shipped to Mexico City for burial in the Hospital de Jesus. There are no statues of Hernán Cortés in Mexico today.

South America

'Guiana is a country that hath yet her maidenhead . . .'

SIR WALTER RALEIGH
The Discovery of Guiana

Above *The Orinoco, one of the major rivers of South America, was discovered by Columbus in 1498 and later offered a route into the interior for explorers in search of the gold of El Dorado. Among them was Sir Walter Raleigh.*

When Christopher Columbus's ships sailed into the Gulf of Paria in August 1498, dangling brass chamber-pots over the sides to conciliate the local inhabitants, South America had been settled for thousands of years by the descendants of people who came originally from Asia. The main indigenous civilisations developed down the western side of the continent, along the coast and on the high plateaux among the Andes Mountains. On that fateful day in 1498 the Incas were ruling from their capital at Cuzco an empire that stretched for more than 2000 miles from modern Ecuador to Chile. Before long it would fall into Spanish hands like a ripe plum.

The European discovery and colonisation of South America was carried out almost entirely by the Spaniards and the Portuguese. The early explorers showed remarkable courage and tenacity in overcoming peoples who vastly outnumbered them and conditions ranging from the snows of the high Andes to the fetid tangles of the Amazon jungle. Exploiting the native inhabitants with ruthless greed and cruelty, they built themselves profitable empires.

Amazon and Ganges

Columbus was swiftly followed to the north coast of South America by Spanish adventurers eager for profit and slaves in an area still believed to be part of Asia. In 1499 an expedition arrived on the Guiana coast under Alonso de Ojeda, a former captain under Columbus and a bold, brutal and unscrupulous character even by the standards of the time. The ships travelled west along the shore to the Gulf of Paria and the island of Curaçao, raiding and killing, in search of pearls. At one point they saw a native village built out over the water on stilts. They called it Venezuela – 'little Venice' – and the name stuck.

Travelling with the expedition was an Italian named Amerigo Vespucci. A Florentine working in Spain for the Medici family financial firm, he knew Columbus personally. He was also a skilful writer and a gifted self-publicist. He apparently detached himself from Ojeda and sailed south with two caravels, discovering the mouth of the Amazon while believing he was coasting along the eastern edge of Asia. Retracing his steps, he rejoined Ojeda and after raiding in the Bahamas for slaves, they returned to Spain in 1500.

Late in 1499 meanwhile, Vicente Yañez Pinzón, captain of the *Niña* on Columbus's historic first voyage, had set out with four caravels from his home port of Palos de la Frontera for the South American coast. Blown across the Atlantic at a record speed of 20 days in a ferocious gale, the fleet gained the Brazilian coast near modern Recife in January 1500 and spent months going northwards along the shore. On the way, Pinzón

Right *Traditional palm-thatched houses stand on piles in a Venezuelan lagoon. Houses like this put early European explorers in mind of Venice, hence the name Venezuela. The area remained under Spanish rule until early in the 19th century.*

sailed 50 miles up the Amazon, which he seems to have identified as the Ganges. Another Spanish expedition under Rodrigo Bastidas was exploring the north coast of modern Colombia meantime.

Amerigo, America

Next the Portuguese took a hold. In March 1500 a substantial fleet left Lisbon under Pedro Alvarez Cabral to sail to India around the Cape of Good Hope on the route pioneered by Vasco da Gama. Venturing well out into the Atlantic to take advantage of the prevailing winds – as ships have been doing ever since – they bumped into the coast of Brazil. Cabral claimed the territory for Portugal, made friends with the local Indians – he did not realise they were cannibals – and sent a ship back to Lisbon with the news, before resuming his voyage to India round the Cape of Good Hope.

The new territory belonged to Portugal under the Treaty of Tordesillas of 1494, which had divided the world between the Spanish and the Portuguese. Amerigo Vespucci now reappeared accompanying a Portuguese expedition intended to penetrate the Indian Ocean by sailing west. The ships reached the Brazilian coast and steered south to the Bay of Rio de Janeiro, which they named in January 1502. They probably sailed on southwards to the River Plate (Rio de la Plata) and down the Patagonian coast before returning to Europe. At one point they sent a young man ashore to talk to a crowd of Indians, but while the warriors fired arrows to keep the rest of the Europeans back, the women seized the young man, cut him up, roasted him on a fire and ate him with evident enjoyment.

Vespucci gave vivid, self-boosting accounts of his travels in letters published after his return to Europe. It began to look as if what had been found across the Atlantic was not Asia but a new continent. So it seemed to a German geographer named Martin Waldseemüller, who in 1507 suggested that the new land should be called America as a salute to its discoverer. So an honour that should have gone to Columbus if to any European, went instead to a lesser man. Vespucci died in Seville in 1512 and was buried in his native Florence.

Around the world

Many people in Europe were still not convinced that a new world lay across the Atlantic, but in 1519 five ships left Spain under Ferdinand Magellan, a tough and experienced Portuguese captain in Spanish service. In an epic voyage punctuated by savage mutinies and equally

Below *An idealised 16th-century portrait of Amerigo Vespucci, the Italian explorer in whose honour America was named. The Spanish government appointed him its pilot major, which meant that he was the principal examiner of pilots for Spanish voyages to the Americas.*

Above *A stretch of the Amazon in Peru. The world's second-longest river, at 4,080 miles (6,570km), it runs from the Andes Mountains in Peru across Brazil to the Atlantic. Discovered by Vespucci, the river was named after the warrior women of Greek mythology, when later explorers brought back tales of redoubtable female warriors in the jungles.*

savage executions, Magellan sailed down the east coast of South America and found a way through the maze of channels north of Tierra del Fuego by the narrow and dangerous strait that now bears his name. On 27/28 November 1520 he and his crew emerged into an ocean so smooth and placid that they called it the Pacific. They sailed some way up the western coast before heading out across the vast breadth of the ocean to the Philippines – where Magellan was killed in a fight with the natives – and on to Indonesia and the Indian Ocean. The single ship that finally limped home to Spain was the first ever to sail around the world.

The result of this historic voyage from the Spanish government's point of view was distinctly disconcerting. South America was clearly not part of Asia, but separated from it by a substantial ocean. A route to Asia by sailing west had been discovered at last, but the voyage was too long and too difficult to be commercially useful. Spain would find ample compensation, however, by exploiting the resources of South America herself.

A silver mountain

The Spaniards in Panama heard rumours from the Indians of a land immensely rich in gold somewhere to the south. They set out to look for it, probing down the west coast of Colombia. In 1531 an aging and ruthless soldier of fortune named Francisco Pizarro sailed from Panama down the coast and struck inland with a tiny force to conquer and plunder the empire of the Incas. He had the Inca ruler executed and entered Cuzco in triumph. Civil war among the Spanish conquerors followed, and in 1541 Pizarro was assassinated. Four years later an entire mountain of silver was discovered at Potosi in Bolivia and Spanish settlers came pouring in.

Meanwhile, Francisco de Orellana had completed an astonishing journey from Ecuador eastwards down the Napo and Amazon rivers for 3,000 miles (4,830km) all the way across the continent to the Atlantic coast. Pizarro's subordinates had also begun to push south into Chile, against determined resistance from the Araucanian Indians. 'Few nations,' wrote an admiring Spaniard, 'have shown such bravery and fortitude in defending their land . . .'

The lure of El Dorado

Other Spanish adventurers had been hunting for gold in the high country of Colombia, where Bogotá was founded in 1538. They had heard of El Dorado, 'the golden man', and of the ceremonies at Lake Guatavita, 10,000ft (3,000m) up in the Andes. On the accession of a new ruler, a raft laden with gold and emeralds was paddled out into the lake, bearing the chiefs and the ruler, whose body was oiled and then powdered with gold dust to give him a second, golden skin. The gold and jewels were thrown into the lake as offerings to the gods and the ruler himself dived in to wash off the gold dust.

The Spaniards found the lake and made earnest but vain attempts to drain it. The name El Dorado somehow became transferred from the man to a place, a mysterious realm of fabulous riches that was always just a little further away, beyond the next mountain range. Antonio de Berrío tried to find it in Guiana and along the Orinoco and its tributaries, and in 1595 Sir Walter Raleigh arrived from England and went up the Orinoco by canoe in search of the land of gold, in the country which, as he said, still had its maidenhead – a revealing phrase. He made a second unsuccessful voyage in 1617.

Rounding the Horn

Over on the Atlantic coast, meanwhile, the Portuguese had established a few small camps for cutting the valuable brazil-wood at places like Pernambuco (Recife). Further south, in 1535 Pedro de Mendoza arrived from Spain with orders to found a colony and open up a route across the

continent to Peru. His ships, laden with colonists, horses, cattle and pigs, have been likened to 'floating barnyards'. A settlement was founded where Buenos Aires stands today. It had to be abandoned in the face of Indian attacks, but not before an expedition had penetrated far inland to build a fort at Asuncion, today the capital of Paraguay. When the colonists deserted Buenos Aires, they left their horses behind, and the local Indians soon became masterly horsemen.

The entire South American coastline had been explored by this time, except in the extreme south, below the Strait of Magellan. The Falkland Islands were discovered in the 1590s, but it was not until 1616 that a Dutch ship under Willem Schouten, dodging about to avoid sailing into the innumerable whales in the water, sighted and named Cape Horn (after Hoorn, the Dutch town that Schouten came from). The crew all had three cups of wine to celebrate. They had established that there was an open sea passage from the Atlantic to the Pacific, though at first no one would believe them.

Left *The fate of Colonel P. H. Fawcett and his two companions, who disappeared in the Matto Grosso area of Brazil in 1925, aroused much concern, but still no one knows what happened to them. The Amazon jungles remain one of the world's most dangerous areas.*

Lost worlds

The routes into the interior of the continent lay along the three great river systems of the Plate, the Amazon and the Orinoco. From the mid-16th century, Jesuit and Franciscan missionaries moved into the interior to convert the Indians, for whom they did their best to protect them from enslavement by the colonists. A Jesuit from Czechoslovakia, Father Samuel Fritz, ranged the Upper Amazon by canoe for almost 40 years until his death in 1723.

The natural wonders of South America were now attracting serious attention. A scientific expedition under a Frenchman, Charles-Marie de la Condamine, travelled down the Amazon by canoe and raft in the 1730s. In 1799 a redoubtable German naturalist, Baron Alexander von Humboldt, arrived in Venezuela. With infinite pains and inexhaustible curiosity he spent five years exploring and risking his life in the northern part of the continent, climbing peaks in the Andes, carrying out alarming experiments with curare and electric eels, and collecting vast quantities of plant specimens. Other naturalists were drawn to South America, notably Charles Darwin, cruising the Atlantic and Pacific coasts in *HMS Beagle* in the 1830s. It was this journey that inspired the theory of evolution.

'Lost cities' replaced El Dorado as a lure. Hiram Bingham, an American academic, was fascinated by stories of hidden cities in the Andes where the last Incas had taken refuge. In 1911 he discovered the spectacular ruins of Machu Picchu perched high up among the mountains. In 1925 a British army officer, Colonel Percy Fawcett, was searching for a lost city that he believed to be concealed deep in the forests of the Matto Grosso. He and his two young companions vanished without trace and were never seen again.

Even after World War II, adventurous travellers were exploring some of the last unrevealed places on earth. In 1957 two young Britons, Richard Mason and Robin Hanbury-Tenison, took a jeep across South America at its widest point, from Recife to Lima. Their basic diet on the way was porridge. Mason was ambushed and killed by Indians in central Brazil in 1961, but in 1964 Hanbury-Tenison spent months travelling by inflatable rubber dinghy from the Caribbean down the Orinoco, Amazon and Paraguay river systems to the Atlantic at Buenos Aires. He was greeted there as 'El Intrepido', a title he could share with many before him.

Below *High up in the Andes stand the spectacular ruins of Machu Picchu. Hiram Bingham, who rediscovered the site in 1911, identified it as the lost Inca city of Vilcabamba, where the Inca rulers took refuge after the Spanish conquest, but Machu Picchu is now thought to have been an important religious centre rather than a city.*

FRANCISCO PIZARRO

Lured by stories of Inca gold, Francisco Pizarro vanquished the empire of the Incas and claimed Peru for Spain.

Eight years after Mexico fell to Hernán Cortés, the empire of the Incas in South America, with a population approximately equal to that of Spain, was conquered by a handful of Spanish soldiers of fortune led by Francisco Pizarro. As in Mexico, the conquest of Peru was a feat of extraordinary audacity by daring and unscrupulous adventurers who took advantage of their superior weaponry and determination, and of a local political crisis – in this case a power struggle between rival claimants to the Inca throne.

Francisco Pizarro was a hard man and one of the most ruthless of his ruthless breed. Withdrawn, taciturn, vengeful, suspicious, he lacked the engaging charm of Cortés and he seems to have been more respected than liked. He came from the same region of Spain as Cortés, the high, bleak tableland of Extremadura. He was born in 1476, the illegitimate son of an army officer and a peasant girl. He had no schooling and never learned to read and write. In his early twenties he fought as a soldier in Italy and in 1502 he sailed for Hispaniola to seek his fortune in the New World.

Left *Francisco Pizarro in his finery. A bastard in more senses than one, he was a veteran in his fifties when he led his tiny force of Spaniards to the conquest of Peru.*

The dauntless thirteen

Pizarro sailed with the piratical Alonso de Ojeda in 1509 to the northern coast of what is New Colombia and went on with Balboa to colonise Panama. In 1513 he was one of the first Europeans to set eyes on the Pacific, when Balboa surveyed the gleaming ocean from a high hill in Panama. Pizarro was one of the party that went down to the shore, brandishing a banner of the Virgin Mary, to scoop up the water in their hands and taste it to see if it was salty.

Years later in 1519, the governor of Panama had Balboa arrested on trumped-up charges and beheaded. The officer who arrested his former leader was Francisco Pizarro.

Pizarro was now in his forties and comfortably ensconced in Panama City, with a substantial estate and Indian slaves to work it. The Spaniards in Panama had long heard rumours of a country to the south – Biru or Peru – that was rich in gold. Balboa had sent several expeditions to probe down the Pacific coast. Pizarro now became sufficiently interested to set up an expedition of his own. His right-hand man was Diego de Almagro, a cheerful, boastful and gregarious personality and a capable organiser, who had started life as an abandoned foundling, named after the town from which he came.

Their first voyage, in 1524, made little progress and Almagro lost an eye in a fight with local Indians. A second expedition, launched late in 1526, penetrated further south, though the winds and currents were difficult, the coast was swampy and unhealthy, and the natives often hostile. One of the ships intercepted a big native sailing raft, constructed of reeds, with wooden masts and cotton sails. On board were traders with a rich cargo of gold and silver ornaments, clusters of rubies, silver cups and little bags of emeralds.

This news brought a gleam to Spanish eyes, but the main body of the expedition was at this point resting on Gallo Island, an uninhabited island in the Tumaco estuary. A ship arrived from Panama and most of the men, sick and weary, decided to go back home on it. The story goes that Pizarro drew a line in the sand with his sword. On one side, he said, lay Peru and all its riches, on the other Panama and poverty. He knew which side he had chosen. Thirteen dauntless volunteers stepped across the line to join him and it was their decision that led in time to the conquest of Peru.

Early in 1527 Pizarro and his gallant few pressed on south to the Gulf of Guayaquil (Golfo de Guayaquil) and the town of Tumbes. With

Right *The first stage of Pizarro's route into the interior took him and his men from the coastal plain up to Cajamarca, high in the Andes, where he seized and executed the ruling Inca. The Spaniards then marched south down the Andes range to take the Inca capital of Cuzco.*

Below *A decorated Inca drinking vessel carved in wood in the form of a puma's head.*

such a small force they were pleasantly treated. There was an encouraging amount of gold and silver to be seen and Pizarro and Almagro felt sure that they were on the fringe of a rich, advanced civilisation based further inland among the mountains – the Inca Empire.

Viper's brood

Returning to Panama, the explorers decided to send Pizarro to Spain, to get authority direct from Charles V. He arrived at court in Seville at the same time as Hernán Cortés, blazing with glory from the subjugation of Mexico. Pizarro

Right *It was rumours of gold in the highlands of the interior that drew the Spaniards to Peru. This golden ceremonial knife, decorated with turquoises, dates from the earlier Chimu culture and represents a deity.*

duly obtained an appointment as Governor and Captain-General of Peru – which cost the government nothing – and returned to Panama, where Almagro was busy drumming up money, ships and men. Pizarro brought reinforcements with him from Spain, including his three younger half-brothers, all by different mothers. Hernando, Gonzalo and Juan Pizarro were as hard-bitten and unscrupulous as their elder brother – 'a viper's brood', they have been called.

Accounts of what followed were written by several of those who took part, including Hernando Pizarro, the only legitimate and literate member of the brood, and Pedro Pizarro, a young cousin. After the conquest, Spanish writers also gleaned information from the Indian side.

Different accounts supply different numbers for the party that left Panama at the end of 1530: 177 men and 67 horses is one figure, 185 men and 27 horses another. At any rate, it was a diminutive army. Putting in to San Marcos Bay, they made a slow and difficult march down the coast through swamps and dense forest until they reached Tumbes, which they found in ruins. They moved on south and established a base, which they named San Miguel (Amotape). They remained there, exploring the surrounding country, for many months.

The Spaniards discovered that a savage war had broken out between two of the sons of Huayna Capac, the Inca emperor who had died a few years before in an epidemic (possibly of smallpox). His throne was disputed by two claimants. Huáscar was his child by his sister and queen – like the pharaohs of Ancient Egypt, the Inca emperors married their sisters – and Atahuallpa was his son by a concubine. They had divided the empire between them for a time, Huáscar ruling from the old Inca capital of Cuzco and Atahuallpa from Quito in the north. Then the arrangement had broken down in civil war, and Spanish reconnaissance parties found trees festooned with the dangling bodies of Indians caught on the wrong side. They learned that Huáscar had been defeated in battle and taken prisoner by Atahuallpa, who was now camped at the inland town of Cajamarca.

The march to Cajamarca

On 24 September 1532, Pizarro moved out from San Miguel for Cajamarca at the head of his tiny army of fewer than 200 men with a few small cannon and muskets. They moved along the Piura River through a peaceful area rich in wildflowers, orchards and fields of grain. At Sarran messengers arrived from Atahuallpa with modest presents and an invitation to visit the Inca's camp. Pizarro gave the messenger a shirt and two glass goblets in return and told him to tell Atahuallpa that the Spaniards were coming to offer him their services.

Moving on southwards to Motupe and Zaña, the invaders turned inland to confront the towering barrier of the Andes Mountains. Pressing on through narrow gorges and passes, always alert for an ambush, the small force climbed higher and higher, as the weather grew fiercely cold, to a bleak windswept plain some 13,500ft (4,100m) up. On 15 November, with rain and hail falling, they came to Cajamarca in its mountain valley, known then as today for its hot springs.

The Spaniards occupied the buildings round the central square and Pizarro sent a detachment of horses under his brother Hernando and Hernando de Soto to parley with the Inca, who was outside the town at the hot springs with his army, his court and his harem. Atahuallpa was about 30 years old. De Soto tried to impress him with a spectacular show of horsemanship, but the Inca, though he had never seen a horse before, remained blank-faced and impassive. Through an interpreter he told the Spaniards he would visit their leader in town the next day. It proved to be a profoundly misplaced display of self-confidence.

The next day came, 16 November, and the Inca delayed his appearance. The anxious Spaniards sent messengers to assure him that he need not fear, not that he showed any sign of it. Late in the afternoon he rode in, carried high on a litter, on which was a golden throne. Round his neck was a collar of emeralds and golden ornaments glistened in his hair. With him came an

Right *A dramatic canvas by the English painter Millais shows Pizarro seizing Atahuallpa in Cajamarca, while the Spanish priest, Father Valverde, holds a crucifix aloft and the Indians look on in bewilderment.*

Down the Amazon

In 1540 Francisco Pizarro ordered his brother Gonzalo to explore the unknown area to the east of Quito, in modern Ecuador. Making its way through the high Andes, the expedition struggled on for months through dense jungles, running short of food and harassed by local Indians. Coming to a big river, Gonzalo Pizarro had a wooden boat built, which took many weeks, and put it under the command of his boyhood friend from Trujillo, Francisco de Orellana. Orellana took some 60 men in the boat to go ahead, collect provisions and return.

Orellana and his men never did return. They said afterwards that they had been unable to get back against the current, but Gonzalo Pizarro believed that they had deliberately deserted him. He eventually led his party back to Quito, where they reappeared in June 1542, looking like walking skeletons.

Orellana and his men, meanwhile, were carrying out one of the most remarkable journeys on record. They drifted with the current down the Napo River, which took them into the Amazon (Amazonas), and then all the way down the Amazon to the Atlantic Ocean. Taking food by force from villages on the way, they survived ferocious attacks by hostile Indians in canoes, and they often heard the ominous throbbing of the war drums in the jungle. Some of the Indian war parties included women, and the Spaniards persuaded themselves that there must be a kingdom of Amazons, the warrior women of Greek mythology.

After nine months of desperate danger and hardship, in August 1542 they emerged at the mouth of the Amazon after a journey of 3,000 miles (4,825km). Orellana took a ship to Spain, where he enthralled the court with tales of gold and Amazons – hence the name of the river. He organised an expedition to return, but his ship capsized near the Amazon's mouth and he was drowned.

escort of upwards of 3,000 soldiers, armed with clubs and slings.

A Spanish priest stepped forward and urged the Inca to accept Christianity. Atahuallpa brushed him aside, at which Pizarro gave the prearranged signal and the Spaniards, yelling a battle cry and firing their cannon and muskets, hurled themselves on the astonished Indians. Killing them in hundreds and driving the rest in flight, they seized Atahuallpa and shut him in one of the buildings. That night Pizarro entertained his rueful captive to dinner.

A king's ransom

Atahuallpa did not seem unduly perturbed. Presumably it did not occur to him that a handful of white men intended to take his whole empire from him. He offered them a colossal ransom, enough gold to fill a room 22ft (6.7m) long by 17ft (5m) wide to as high as he could reach standing on tiptoe, and enough silver to fill it twice over (the supposed ransom room is shown in Cajamarca today). Messengers were sent out with Atahuallpa's orders to collect the ransom and with instructions to his generals not to intervene, or he would be killed. He also gave secret orders for the execution of his half-brother Huáscar.

Through the early months of 1533 gold and silver objects poured into Cajamarca. Atahuallpa seemed affable enough. He was allowed to have some of his attendants and women with him and the Spaniards taught him to play chess. Three Spanish soldiers went with Indian guides and bearers to Cuzco, where they took crowbars and prised the gold plates off the walls of the great temple of the sun, returning with llamas laden with gold. Almagro now arrived with a reinforcement of 150 men, which almost doubled the Spanish strength. An Inca prince arrived too, and put himself under Pizarro's protection. He was Huáscar's younger brother, Tupac Huallpa.

The gold and silver was melted down and divided among the Spaniards. It was enough to make them all rich for life, provided they survived. Atahuallpa had served his purpose and Pizarro had him garrotted with a piece of rope: after kindly having the Inca baptised, so that his soul should not burn for ever in hell. All the Spaniards attended his funeral. They were deeply shocked when his sisters and women came and asked to be buried alive with him, as the custom was. Permission was refused.

The taking of Cuzco

The Spaniards now prepared to march on Cuzco, 700 miles (1,125km) away as the condor flew, in the guise of liberators who had executed the false usurper of the Inca throne. They had Tupac Huallpa crowned as emperor and set out from Cajamarca on 11 August. Taking their time, and welcomed by the Indians along the way, they went south by the deep Huaylas Valley between steep mountains and up by a snow-covered pass to a high, bare plateau where the men suffered from altitude sickness. They reached Jauja on 12 October, routing an Indian force that opposed them. Here the young Tupac Huallpa died of an illness, to the dismay of the Spaniards, who had meant him to be their puppet.

The last stage of the journey took them through spectacular scenery of mountains and deep gorges, across rivers and over heights so dizzying that it looked impossible for birds to negotiate them, let alone men, but the Inca road zigzagged doggedly up them. Hernando de Soto led an advance guard of 50 horsemen and dashed on to try to take Cuzco himself, but was fiercely attacked at Vilcaconga by thousands of Indians hurling javelins and stones. He drove them off and waited for Pizarro to catch up.

The Spaniards paused to burn a captive Inca general alive, after he had refused conversion to Christianity, and welcomed another Inca prince, Manco, who rode in to join them. Then they drove on, defeated another Indian attack and, on 15 November, entered the capital city of Cuzco, with its mighty fortress of Sacsahuaman. Even the Spaniards were amazed at what they they had achieved.

Thieves fall out

The Inca capital was taken and the conquerors consolidated their hold on the empire, but the leaders fell out among themselves. Pizarro moved to the coast, where he founded Lima as the Spanish capital. In 1536 Manco Inca rose against his Spanish masters and came close to

Below *The puma had sacred and symbolic significance for successive South American civilisations. The Inca capital city of Cuzco was built in the shape of a giant puma's head, with the mighty walls of the fortress of Sacsahuaman representing the animal's teeth. This golden puma is of an earlier period. The repoussé work on the body represents a double two-headed snake.*

Sheep Like Camels

A Spanish writer on the beasts of burden of the Andes:

"It appears to me that in no part of the world have sheep like those of the Indies been found or heard of . . . These sheep are among the most excellent creatures that God has created, and the most useful. It would seem that the Divine Majesty took care to create these animals that the people of this country might be able to live and sustain themselves, for by no other means could these Indians (I speak of the mountaineers of Peru) preserve their lives without these sheep . . .

The natives call these sheep *llamas*, and the males *urcos*. Some are white, others black, others grey. Some of them are as large as a small donkey, with long legs, broad bellies, and a neck of the length and shape of a camel. Their heads are large, like those of Spanish sheep. The flesh of these animals is very good when it is fat, and the lambs are better and more savoury than those of Spain. The *llamas* are very tame and carry . . . weight very well. Truly it is very pleasant to see the Indians of the Collao go forth with beasts, and return with them to their homes in the evening laden with fuel. They feed on the herbage of the plains, and when they complain they make a noise like the groaning of camels."

From *Chronicle of Peru*, 1553, Pedro de Cieza de Leon (translated by C.R. Markham)

Left The ruined fortress of Sacsahuaman in Cuzco. Many of the Spanish soldiers said they had never seen a stronger fortress, even in Europe. It was built on solid rock with such massive stones that it was proof against their artillery.

Below left The Inca ruling family claimed descent from the god of the sun, and the emperor, the Sapa Inca himself, was revered as a deity walking the earth: Inca mask of beaten gold.

throwing off their yoke. Juan Pizarro was killed in the fighting. Manco and his successors maintained an independent regime high in the Andes until 1572.

Diego de Almagro was dissatisfied with his share of the spoils. He seized Cuzco from Hernando Pizarro in 1537 and crowned his own puppet Inca, but in 1538 Hernando defeated him in battle and had him garrotted. Almagro's son and his supporters carried on the quarrel and in 1541 they assassinated Francisco Pizarro in Lima. The old conquistador went down under a rain of sword thrusts. Crying 'Jesu!', he traced a cross in blood on the ground before a final blow dispatched him. A glass coffin in Lima Cathedral today houses the shrivelled mortal remains of the conqueror of Peru.

Welfare state

When Pizarro and his men marched in Cajamarca, the Inca Empire stretched down the Andes from modern Ecuador through Peru and Bolivia to central Chile. It was held together by a highly developed system of roads, along which troops moved rapidly to quell any trouble and swift runners carried orders and messages in relays.

The ruling family claimed to be descended from the sun god, and the emperor, the Sapa Inca, was revered as a god walking the earth. Surrounded by his harem and his immediate family and advisers, he controlled a vast bureaucracy that regulated every aspect of his subjects' lives. There was no writing, but the records required by officialdom were kept on *quipus* – coloured strings knotted at intervals to denote numbers.

The peasants were not allowed to have private property. Agricultural collectives built the irrigation canals and terraced the hillsides. They paid tribute of crops and produce to support their rulers, who operated a rudimentary welfare state food surpluses were stored to be distributed in times of shortage and to the sick and the old.

The peasants wore a uniform issued by the state. As there were no wheeled vehicles, they and the llamas were the beasts of burden. They were conscripted to work in the mines and build temples, palaces, fortresses and the roads that tunnelled through mountains and crossed chasms on osier (willow) suspension bridges.

The Spaniards took full advantage of the civil war they found raging in the empire, but the ease of their conquest does not suggest that the majority of the Incas' subjects felt much affection for the system that enslaved them.

Biographical Notes

1476
Born at Trujillo, Spain.

1502
Sailed for Hispaniola.

1513
With Balboa, discovered the Pacific Ocean.

1524–7
Led expeditions down the Pacific coast of South America.

1530
Led an expedition to Peru.

1532
Left San Miguel for Cajamarca (24 September); seized Atahuallpa in Cajamarca (16 November).

1533
Execution of Atahuallpa (26 July); fall of Cuzco (15 November).

1535
Founded city of Lima.

1541
Assassinated in Lima (26 June).

SIEUR DE LA SALLE

A determined explorer, La Salle travelled down the Mississippi River and claimed Louisiana for France

French traders, missionaries and settlers played a major part in the European exploration and opening up of Canada, the American mid-west and the Mississippi River. This exploration progressed from fishing off the northeast coast to fur-trapping and trading with the Indians of the interior, and then to colonisation and the creation of a potential empire.

The formidable Samuel de Champlain, who founded Quebec in 1608, explored the eastern Great Lakes area to find fresh sources of furs, but also in the hope of discovering a route to the Pacific and so to China and Japan. Tough and resourceful French frontiersmen, the *coureurs des bois* (literally 'runners of the woods') probed further into the interior. They paddled along the rivers Indian fashion in canoes, which had the advantage of being light to carry between navigable rivers and easily repaired with birchbark, which was readily available along the way. In winter they used snowshoes, again in Indian style.

The Indians were eager to trade furs for European goods, especially guns. Marten and beaver commanded particularly high prices in Europe and in the next 200 years the beaver was almost wiped out in North America to supply Europeans with felt hats.

The Great River

Commerce inevitably involved politics, for the English were trying to increase their share of the fur trade. In 1634 a *coureur du bois* named Jean Nicollet was sent to make allies for the French among Indian tribes to the west. He travelled from Lake Huron to Lake Michigan and on to an Indian village near modern Green Bay in the American state of Wisconsin. He succeeded in his mission, though at first he optimistically mistook the local Indians for Chinese. From them he brought back word of the Sioux nation further west and of a mighty river leading to a distant ocean, which it was not unreasonable for the French to think might he the Pacific.

Missionaries were also active, zealous to convert the Indians to Christianity, and colonists were coming to settle in New France. Montréal was founded in 1642 as a religious colony and base for missionary work and was dominated by the Sulpicians, a religious order from Paris. It swiftly became the headquarters of the fur trade and a boisterous frontier town.

By the 1670s the full extent of the Great Lakes had been established by frontiersmen and missionaries, and more reports had come in of the 'Great River' in the west. In 1671 at Sault Ste

Right *'The manner of their attire and painting themselves . . .' This watercolour of 1587 by John White shows an Indian of North America with his hunting bow, quiver of arrows, loincloth, necklace and bracelets. White encountered his subjects in Virginia.*

Marie on Lake Superior a representative of the governor of New France, with 14 Indian tribes solemnly assembled, took formal possession of the whole of the American West – discovered and to be discovered – for Louis XIV of France. In the following year a French Canadian called Louis Jolliet was put in command of an expedition to follow the Great River and discover where it reached the sea.

With his Jesuit companion, Father Jacques Marquette, Jolliet led a small party from Green Bay across the land between the Fox River and the Wisconsin to the broad, majestic waters of the river the Indians called the Mississippi. They were the first Europeans to see it. They travelled down it past the stretches where the river is joined by the Missouri and the Ohio, almost to the confluence with the Arkansas. At this point, some 400 miles (640km) from the river's mouth, it was clear that the Mississippi was not headed for the Pacific, but for the Gulf of Mexico. Reluctant to venture into the Spanish zone of influence to the south, Jolliet and his men turned back. The feat of travelling all the way down the

Mississippi to the Gulf was to fall to a young man of larger ideas altogether, who had come to Montréal some years earlier.

Norman conqueror

René-Robert Cavelier, Sieur de La Salle, was born in Normandy in 1643. His father, a well-to-do citizen of Rouen, had the boy trained for the Jesuit priesthood. The effect was to instil in him a lifelong detestation of Jesuits. He broke away in his early twenties and emigrated to New France, where his elder brother, a member of the Sulpician order, had already settled, to seek his fortune there. The order gave La Salle land near Montréal, which he farmed. He also set himself up as a fur-trader, which brought him into direct contact with Indians. He learned their languages and heard their stories of the west, and an ambition grew in his mind to be the one who would find a route to the East by way of the western rivers. His estate near Montréal was afterwards nicknamed La Chine in sardonic reference to his hopes of using it as a springboard to China.

Restless and adventurous by temperament, La Salle soon sold his farm and in 1669 joined a Sulpician missionary expedition travelling with Seneca Indian guides by canoe to Lake Ontario and into the country to the south, where they happened to encounter Luis Jolliet. They came close enough to the Niagara Falls to hear their

***Below** La Salle's journey took him down the river the Indians called the Mississippi, past the future sites of St Louis, Memphis, Vicksburg, Baton Rouge and New Orleans.*

Above *The first person to describe the splendour of the Niagara Falls was La Salle's chaplain, Father Hennepin. By the early 19th century the falls were a tourist attraction and famous all over the world, and in 1859 the French acrobat, Blondin, crossed them on a tightrope.*

thunder, but did not go to look at them. This seems extraordinary now, but a taste for spectacular wild scenery had not yet been born in Europe. La Salle parted from the missionaries and seems to have spent the next few years wandering about and learning from the Indians how to live off the country. He later claimed that during this time he discovered the Ohio River.

First ship on the Great Lakes

In 1672 a new governor of New France was appointed. This was the colourful, extravagant and vigorous Comte de Frontenac. It was he who sent Louis Jolliet to the Mississippi. A close sympathy developed between Frontenac and La Salle. Both men shared a determination to create a French empire in North America and shut the English out of the fur trade.

Frontenac sent La Salle to France as his emissary to the royal court, and put him in command of the newly built Fort Frontenac on the north shore of Lake Ontario, where the Canadian town of Kingston stands today. The fort was placed there to intercept much of the fur traffic flowing into Montreal, to the vexation of the Montreal merchants and their supporters among the Jesuits.

Presently La Salle was sent on a second visit to the French court. Intelligent and persuasive, he made a good impression and returned in 1678 with the grant of a potentially lucrative monopoly over trade in buffalo hides and authority to explore the western area of New France and build forts there. To finance this strategy he borrowed large amounts of money in Paris and Montreal. The debts would soon become a millstone around his neck.

La Salle brought back with him a young Italian soldier named Henri de Tonti, who became his faithful right-hand man. Tonti came from a Neapolitan family settled in Paris, where his father was the inventor of the tontine variety of insurance annuity. Tonti had lost his right fist in an explosion. He had a metal one, worn in a glove, and was known as 'the man with the iron hand'. He sometimes used it to effect on recalcitrant Indians.

La Salle intended to use ships on the Great Lakes and the western rivers rather than canoes, and a start was made by building a vessel called *Le Griffon* on the Niagara River, near present-day Buffalo. Father Luis Hennepin, La Salle's Franciscan, chaplain, went to see Niagara Falls, of which he left the earliest published account.

Of some 60 tons (61 tonnes), armed with seven cannon, *Le Griffon* was the first ship ever to sail on Lake Erie. La Salle took her on through Lake Huron to Lake Michigan and Green Bay.

From there *Le Griffon* was sent back with a massive cargo of furs to pay La Salle's creditors in Montréal, but unfortunately the ship and the furs disappeared and were never seen again. No one knows what happened to her, but the creditors remained unsatisfied.

La Salle now tried to carry out his plan of building forts in the area southwest of Lake Michigan. He and a small party set off by canoe along the shore of the lake and past the open country where the skyscrapers of Chicago would one day rise to the heavens. They penetrated down the St Joseph River to a point near the present city of South Bend, Indiana – where a monument to La Salle would later be erected – and southwest by the Kankakee and Illinois rivers. Forts were constructed at various places, one being Fort Crévecoeur, or 'Heartbreak', on the Illinois, where an attempt was made to build a second boat.

At one stage La Salle made an astonishing journey of 1,000 miles (1,600km) in 65 days over an unknown route to Fort Frontenac to arrange for supplies, which his creditors were holding up. Returning to the Illinois country, he discovered that his enterprise had disintegrated, hostile Iroquois Indians had destroyed his forts and his men had drifted away. After searching in vain for the vanished Tonti, he went back to Fort Frontenac again.

A lesser man might well have given up at this point, but La Salle was not a lesser man. Doggedly returning to Illinois in the summer of 1681, to his great relief and delight he found Tonti, who

Above *'The life I am leading has no other attraction for me than that of honour; and the more danger and difficulty there is in undertakings of this sort, the more worthy of honour I think they are': the Sieur de La Salle.*

Below *This Indian village inside its stockade was portrayed by John White.*

An Indian Welcome

La Salle and his party meet friendly Indians on their way down the Mississippi.

"For several days more they followed the writhings of the great river on its tortuous course through wastes of swamp and canebrake, till on the thirteenth of March they found themselves wrapped in a thick fog. Neither shore was visible; but they heard on the right the booming of an Indian drum and the shrill outcries of the war-dance. La Salle at once crossed to the opposite side, where, in less than an hour, his men threw up a rude fort of felled trees. Meanwhile the fog cleared; and from the farther bank the astonished Indians saw the strange visitors at their work. Some of the French advanced to the edge of the water, and beckoned them to come over. Several of them approached, in a wooden canoe, to within the distance of a gun-shot. La Salle displayed the calumet [peace pipe], and sent a Frenchman to meet them. He was well received; and the friendly mood of the Indians being now apparent, the whole party crossed the river.

On landing, they found themselves at a town of the Kappa band of the Arkansas, a people dwelling near the mouth of the river which bears their name. 'The whole village,' writes Membré to his superior, 'came down to the shore to meet us, except the women, who had run off. I cannot tell you the civility and kindness we received from those barbarians, who brought us poles to make huts, supplied us with firewood during the three days we were among them, and took turns in feasting us.' "

from *France and England in North America*, Francis Parkman

had wintered at Green Bay. At the end of the year they set out from Fort Crêvecoeur on the journey down the Mississippi that was to write La Salle's name in the history books.

Down the Mississippi

The expedition set off down the Illinois River around Christmas, nearly 50 strong, roughly half Frenchmen and half Indians. Besides Tonti, La Salle had a missionary with him, a Franciscan friar named Zenobe Membré. Both Tonti and Membré wrote accounts of the journey.

The river was frozen solid, so they loaded their luggage on canoes and dragged them along the ice until they came to open water below Lake Peoria. From there they floated with the current southwards between the bare forests on either bank until on 6 February they reached the Mississippi. The great river was full of floating blocks of ice, which made things difficult, but they went on past the mouth of the Missouri, bringing its muddy torrent in from the right, and past the future site of the city of St Louis and the mouth of the Ohio River on their left.

On 24 February they landed close to the spot where Memphis, Tennessee, stands today and some of the party went hunting. There was a delay of several days while they searched anxiously for one hunter who failed to return, but he eventually turned up exhausted and half-starved. Travelling on southward down the river with the current as it made its leisurely way in vast loops and bends along what is now the border of the state of Mississippi, they encountered pleasing signs of spring as the weather grew warmer. They met some Arkansas Indians, who welcomed them hospitably and entertained them with dances and ceremonies. La Salle, Tonti and their followers marched with proper gravity to the centre of the Indian village and erected there a cross bearing the arms of France. Father Membré sang a hymn, the French shouted 'Vive le roi!', and La Salle announced that he was taking formal possession of the whole country for Louis XIV. Membré then did his best to convey the rudiments of Christianity in sign language. The Indians watched it all good-humouredly and their chief said something that was understood as a pledge of fealty to the King of France.

Below An illustration by Howard Pyle in Harper's Monthly in 1904 shows La Salle formally claiming the whole Mississippi Valley for Louis XIV of France. Behind him stands Father Membré and in the background is the blue water of the Gulf of Mexico.

The explorers voyaged on down the river, taking two of the Arkansas Indians as guides. Passing the site of modern Vicksburg and killing the occasional alligator, they came to a swampy area on the western bank in what is now Louisiana. Their guides told them there was an important Indian village nearby. Tonti and Membré took a party to visit it, carrying a birch-bark canoe through the swamp and launching it again on a lake. They presently came to the village, of huts built of mud and straw. In the largest hut they were politely received by the chief, three of his wives and his elders, wearing white cloaks made of mulberry bark. They were shown a temple where the chiefs ancestors were honoured and enemy captives sacrificed. The chief came to visit La Salle next day.

On again down the river they went, kindly treated by Natchez and Coroa Indians on the way. They only met one group of hostile Indians, whom they ignored, paddling on down the stream. By 6 April they reached the Mississippi delta and they went on down to the heaving water of the Gulf. On 9 April at a spot near the river's mouth they erected a column bearing the arms and titles of Louis XIV and the date, with volleys of musket fire and the singing of a *Te Deum*. Then La Salle in his best scarlet coat solemnly announced that he took possession for France of the entire watershed of the Mississippi and its tributaries under the name of Louisiana.

'On that day,' as the great American historian Francis Parkman wrote, 'the realm of France received on parchment a stupendous accession. The fertile plains of Texas; the vast basin of the Mississippi, from its frozen northern springs to the salty borders of the Gulf; from the woody ridge of the Alleghenies to the bare peaks of the Rocky Mountains – a region of savannahs and forests, sun-cracked deserts, and grassy prairies, watered by a thousand rivers, ranged by a thousand warlike tribes, passed beneath the sceptre of the Sultan of Versailles; and all by virtue of a feeble human voice, inaudible at half a mile.'

***Left** A highly imaginative picture of La Salle's murder by his own men, near the Brazos River in Texas. According to one who served under him, La Salle's intolerable arrogance was the real cause of his death.*

In His Defence

In a letter La Salle defends himself against the accusation of being harsh to his men:

"The facility I am said to want is out of place with this sort of people, who are libertines for the most part; and to indulge them means to tolerate blasphemy, drunkenness, lewdness, and a license incompatible with any kind of order. It will not be found that I have in any case whatever treated any man harshly, except for blasphemies and other such crimes openly committed. These I cannot tolerate: first because such compliance would give grounds for another accusation, much more just; secondly, because, if I allowed such disorders to become habitual, it would be hard to keep the men in subordination and obedience, as regards executing the work I am commissioned to do; thirdly, because the debaucheries, too common with this rabble, are the source of endless delays and frequent thieving; and, finally, because I am a Christian and do not want to bear the burden of their crimes."

quoted in *France and England in North America*, Francis Parkman

Death on the Trinity

La Salle had a vision of a vast new French imperial province with himself as its proconsul, independent of the authorities in Canada. For a time it must have seemed that the vision would become a reality. He returned to France late in 1683 to be treated with honour and discover that the government had hatched a plan to drive the Spaniards out of Mexico. The spearhead was to be a French base at the mouth of the Mississippi and La Salle was given command of a substantial expedition that sailed from La Rochelle in July 1684.

Everything that could go wrong went wrong. La Salle quarrelled with his naval commander, vessels were lost to shipwreck and buccaneers, and worst of all the expedition somehow contrived to miss the mouth of the Mississippi. Sailing on by without identifying it, they made landfall in Matagorda Bay, 500 miles (800km) too far west.

La Salle landed his people and built a fort. The expedition was hopelessly lost and months dragged by as attempt after attempt was made in vain to find the Mississippi. On the last of these expeditions La Salle led a party northward early in 1687. They crossed the Brazos River and had reached the Trinity, south of present-day Dallas, when his men finally went out of control, mutinied and shot their commander. They stripped the body and left it for the buzzards and the wolves.

Father Membré, left behind at the fort, was never heard of again. Tonti, who had not joined the final expedition, travelled down the Mississippi in 1686 to rendezvous with La Salle, but could not find him. He later joined the infant colony at New Orleans, and died in his bed in 1704.

La Salle was only 43 when he was murdered. Membré and others paid tribute to his driving energy, his courage and his indefatigable pursuit of his objectives. However, he was also reserved, arrogant, harsh and unpopular with his men. When he reached the mouth of the Mississippi, there seemed to be every possibility of a French empire stretching from Canada to the Gulf of Mexico, but it was not to be.

Biographical Notes

1643
Born at Rouen, France.

1666
Emigrated to Canada.

1673
In command at Fort Frontenac.

1679
Launch of *Le Griffon*.

1681
Start of the journey down the Mississippi (December).

1682
Took formal possession of 'Louisiana' (9 April).

1684–7
The final expedition.

1687
Murdered in Texas (19 March).

Australasia and the Pacific

'The first love, the first sun-rise, the first South Sea island, are memories apart, and touched a virginity of sense.'

ROBERT LOUIS STEVENSON
In the South Seas

Above *An oasis in the desert, Alice Springs symbolises the drive to conquer the Australian outback.*

Occupying about one-third of the surface of the earth, the Pacific Ocean is the biggest single element in the geography of the globe. The earliest explorations of this huge expanse of water and its thousands of islands were carried out long before any European set eyes on the Pacific, by people whose ancestors came originally from southeast Asia.

The first human beings in Australia arrived there 40,000 years ago or more, at a time when it was still possible to walk from New Guinea to Australia and plod on dry-shod all the way to Tasmania. More people arrived in successive waves over many thousands of years. Later, from the western (Asian) side of the Pacific, intrepid voyagers in outrigger canoes ranged across the ocean, discovering and settling island after island as the centuries wore on. Some of their vessels were larger than the ships of the European discoverers, and were capable of voyages over thousands of miles. The Fijians, for instance, had double-hulled canoes 100ft (30m) long.

The Stone Age

These voyages depended on remarkable feats of seamanship and skill in navigation by the stars, winds and currents, but practically nothing is known about them. All the peoples of the Pacific were still in the Stone Age when the first Europeans encountered them. They had no written history, and only a few stories handed down for generations by word of mouth have survived. The Maoris in New Zealand, for example, have a tradition that their ancestors came from somewhere near Tahiti in 'the great fleet' of seven long canoes, led by Tama Te Kapua. This happened in the 14th century AD. It is clear from archeological investigations, however, that Polynesians settled in New Zealand long before that.

Thor Heyerdahl's voyages in his raft, the *Kon-Tiki*, in the 1940s and 1950s demonstrated that Easter Island and the Polynesian islands could have been populated from South America. The weight of academic opinion, however, remains convinced that the Pacific was settled from the west, not the east.

Terra Australis

The first Europeans to sail out onto the broad expanse of the South Sea (South Pacific), as they called it, were Ferdinand Magellan and his men in 1520, during the first circumnavigation of the

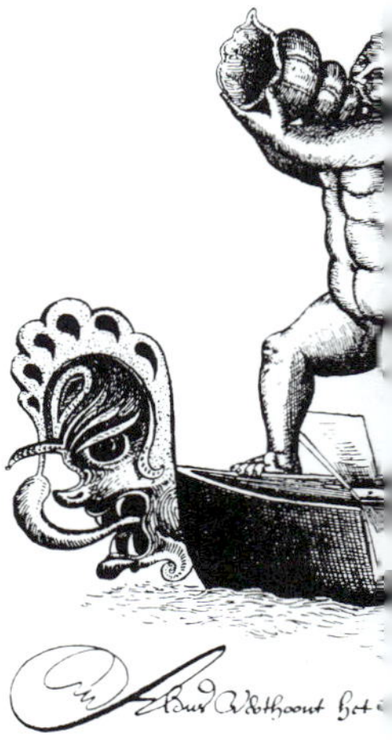

globe. Magellan's voyage revealed the daunting size of the Pacific. It was many years before European knowledge of the ocean was anything more than extremely scanty, and navigational difficulties meant that when a group of islands was discovered by Europeans, they might not be able to find them again.

In 1527 Hernán Cortés sent an expedition across the northern Pacific from Mexico and in time regular communication was established between New Spain and the Philippines, where Manila was founded in 1565. Once the Spanish Empire was established in Peru, adventurers there began to eye the Pacific, not to find a path to the trade of the Far East, but in the hope of finding new lands of vast wealth that might harbour both King Solomon's fabled mines and also a spiritual hoard of souls to be brought to Christ. There were Inca stories of rich islands far away in the western sea and European geographers believed that a huge unknown southern landmass – *Terra Australis Incognita* –must exist in the southern ocean to balance the continents of the northern hemisphere.

Acting on orders from the Governor of Peru, Alvaro de Mendaña sailed in 1567 with three ships and several Franciscan friars aboard on conversion duty. Wandering about haphazardly for two years and 7,000 miles (11,260km), he did by chance bump into islands far in the west. These were hopefully christened the Solomon Islands. They hid no fabulous diamond mines, and it would be 200 years before any European would find them again, but Mendaña was encouraged enough to contemplate another voyage.

Meanwhile, however, in 1578 the piratical Englishman, Francis Drake – to Spaniards *El Draco*, 'the Dragon' – appeared in his 100-ton (101 tonnes) ship *Golden Hind* with a crew of about 80, to burn and plunder his way up the whole Pacific coast of South America, attacking ships, raiding settlements and carrying off loot whose value in modern currency has been estimated at £25 million (c.$42 ½ million). Rich for life, he needed to find his way home and sailed on up the North American coast looking for a strait to take him back to the Atlantic. Not finding one, he paused to refit somewhere on the Californian coast – formally claiming the country for Queen Elizabeth as New Albion – and then set out across the Pacific for what would prove to be the second circumnavigation of the globe. The *Golden Hind* arrived safely back in Plymouth in 1580, the backers of the enterprise cleared almost 5,000 per cent on their investment and Drake was knighted by his gratified queen.

***Above** Sir Francis Drake, in an 18th-century engraving. This daring Elizabethan seadog, who completed the second circumnavigation of the globe in 1580, would later play a leading role in the defeat of the Spanish Armada's attempt to invade England.*

Alvaro de Mendaña, who was much more high-minded, did not fare as well. In 1595 he was at last able to start his second voyage and came to the Marquesas Islands. Since their inhabitants were menacing, heavily tattooed cannibals armed with massive clubs, he sailed on to Santa Cruz. There he tried to establish a colony, but his followers massacred the natives and fought among themselves. Mendaña died and the Portuguese pilot, Pedro Fernàndez de Quiros, took the survivors safely to the Philippines.

Quiros grew convinced that he was the second Columbus, with a God-given mission to find the great southern continent and bring it into the Christian fold. Setting out with three ships in 1605, he got so hopelessly lost that he decided to let the vessels go where they would, under the good guidance of God. This policy brought him to the island he called La Australia del Espiritu

***Left** Natives of New Guinea with an outrigger canoe, after a drawing made by the Dutch navigator, Abel Tasman, in the 1640s. The people of the Pacific were skilled seamen and navigators, capable of finding their way across thousands of miles of ocean.*

Santo (in the New Hebrides), where he founded a town named New Jerusalem and organised a plethora of religious festivals. This New Jerusalem, however, lacked the gold and pearls and precious stones of its Biblical archtype, and his men were unhappy. Quiros sailed away to Mexico and the rest ended up in the Philippines.

Going Dutch

In the following years it was the Dutch East India Company, from its base at Batavia (Jakarta) in Java, that discovered the real Australia instead of the mythical one, while hoping to find gold in New Guinea. Captain Willem Jansz in a ship named Duyfken (Little Dove) made the first known European landing on Australian soil, in 1605, in the Gulf of Carpentaria on the north coast. Over the next 20 years several more Dutch vessels reached or were wrecked on the shores of what they called New Holland.

In 1642 Anthony van Diemen, in charge at Batavia, sent Abel Tasman, an experienced Dutch seaman, to look for the South Land by sailing east from Mauritius. He discovered Tasmania, which he named Van Diemen's Land, and sailed on to another unknown shore, where four of his men were attacked and killed by natives. The natives were Maoris and the place was New Zealand. Tasman, who was a peaceable man, named the spot Murderers Bay and sailed on. He came to Tonga, where the people were friendly, and made his way through the Fiji Islands without stopping on the way back to Batavia. In 1644 he made a second voyage, along Australia's northern coast.

The Dutch were not pleased with Australia, which seemed to have nothing they wanted. When Dutch captains showed the Aborigines gold or silver or spices, they not only displayed no recognition but not the slightest flicker of interest. William Dampier, the English buccaneer who went looking for the southern continent at the end of the century, was similarly unimpressed. However, his book about his adventures aroused English interest in the Pacific.

Still looking for the South Land, Jacob Roggeveen led an expedition from Holland in 1721. Rounding Cape Horn, he discovered Easter Island with its mysterious giant statues. He also discovered Samoa on his way to Batavia.

Island paradise

The 1760s saw British and French ships finding their way across the Pacific, after the two countries had stopped fighting each other in North America and India. Both powers were interested in the commercial and colonisation possibilities. Captain Wallis discovered Tahiti, Captain Carteret discovered Pitcairn. In 1768 a French expedition commanded by Louis Antoine de Bougainville reached Tahiti, to be greeted by hundreds of the inhabitants in canoes with gifts of chickens, coconuts, fruit and naked women. The descriptions of Tahiti which went back to Europe fixed firmly in western minds the image of the lush South Sea island with its coral reefs and palm-fringed lagoons as an erotic paradise. Bougainville called Tahiti New Cythera, the domain of the goddess of love. Unfortunately, the early European contacts infected Venus's realm with syphilis.

Sailing westward, Bougainville came almost in sight of the eastern coast of Australia, which no white explorer had yet seen, but was forced north by the Great Barrier Reef. Returning to Europe, he completed the first French circumnavigation of the world.

At this stage, the European concept of the Pacific was like a half-finished jigsaw puzzle with no master picture. The explorer who completed most of the puzzle was Captain Cook. His first voyage in the *Endeavour* took him round Cape

Above *Several geographical features in New Zealand are named after Captain Cook, including Mount Cook, seen here across Lake Pukaki. The highest peak in New Zealand at 12,350ft (3,764km), it was first climbed on Christmas Day in 1894.*

Horn in 1769, across to Tahiti and on to New Zealand, where he sailed around both islands. He went on to the east coast of Australia, investigated and named Botany Bay, sailed the whole way up the east coast and claimed it for Britain under the name of New South Wales. On his second voyage he revisited New Zealand, twice crossed the Antarctic Circle, went to Easter Island and rediscovered the Marquesas. On his third expedition Cook discovered the Hawaiian Islands, where he was killed in 1779.

All the major Pacific discoveries had now been made. Extensive journeys by French and Spanish expeditions in the 1780s and 1790s filled in the details, but the emphasis was shifting from discovery to commercial exploitation and settlement. The whalers descended on the South Pacific. Merchant ships went trading from island to island. Missionaries appeared, to convert the natives not only to Christianity but to puritanical morals and western ways. The first boatload reached Tahiti in 1797.

Before this, the British government had decided to use New South Wales as a penal settlement for convicts sentenced to transportation. In January 1788 the 11 ships of 'the first fleet' arrived in Botany Bay, carrying more than 700 jailbirds with supplies for two years. A settlement was established on Sydney Cove, shipments of convicts continued and by 1800 about 5,000 people were living in and around Sydney. The foundations of a great new nation had been laid.

Sturt and Eyre

The early settlers were too busy trying to survive to have much appetite for exploration, and besides, they were hemmed in along the coast by the Blue Mountains. The French were taking an unwelcome interest in the new country, however. Napoleon sent an expedition under Thomas-Nicholas Baudin in 1801, which explored much of the coast. The British response was a complete survey of the whole coast, involving the circumnavigation of the continent, which was carried out by Matthew Flinders and completed in 1803. It was Flinders who called the continent Australia, and the name caught on.

With the French threat in the background, new settlements were established at Newcastle and Hobart in Tasmania. Parties probed out from Sydney looking for fresh pastures for cattle and sheep. The Blue Mountains were crossed in 1813 and voluntary immigrants began to arrive from Britain.

Below *The first Europeans to discover Easter Island were Dutchmen under Captain Jacob Roggeveen in 1722, searching for the great southern continent. They observed the massive enigmatic statues for which the island has ever since been famous. The statues stand anything up to 32ft (9.8m) high.*

In the 1820s and 1830s new settlements were founded on the coast at Brisbane, Perth, Melbourne and Adelaide.

The leading figure of the early days of inland exploration was an English army officer named Charles Sturt. After a trek north to the Darling River in 1828, which he discovered and named, he led a party west along the Murrumbidgee and the Murray the following year. There was an alarming encounter with hundreds of Aborigines, who seemed just about to attack when a new arrival calmed them down and they became good-humoured. One of the party's two boats sank and they lost all their supplies except flour, sugar and tea. They eventually reached the sea at Encounter Bay and then had to battle their way back, rowing against the current, before

Left *Dutch trading vessels of the 1640s. The Dutch East India Company built up a vigorous trading empire in Indonesia. They established a base at Batavia (modern Jakarta) in 1619 and made the first tentative probings of the Australian coast.*

their scanty provisions ran out, with each man rationed to 1lb (450g) flour and a few mouthfuls of tea a day.

By 1840 much of southeastern Australia had been explored and settled by whites. All efforts now concentrated on opening up land connections between settlements separated by miles of sea and penetrating the unknown interior.

In February 1841 a tough English immigrant sheepfarmer and drover named Edward Eyre left Adelaide in the summer heat, with another European and three Aborigines, to attempt the long trek along the coast to Albany, south of Perth. Carrying their supplies on horseback, they marched along the beach or the top of the cliffs as opportunity offered. They crossed the scrub and saltbush of the Nullarbor Plain, where they went for 135 miles (220km) without seeing a single drop of water. Their food ran short and they started to eat the horses and throw away their equipment. Two of the Aborigines killed the other European and ran away. Eyre went on with Wylie, the other Aborigine, and shot a kangaroo, which gave them some meat. In May the weather turned cooler, which was a relief, and at Rossiter Bay they were lucky to find a French whaler, which fed and supplied them. They reached Albany in July after a journey of more than four months, which confirmed Eyre's opinion that the land route was useless for livestock.

Above *An aborigine elder in front of Ayers Rock. Rising abruptly from the level plain, this giant hump of rock is 1,150ft (335m) high, changes colour dramatically as day wears on, and is a sacred place to the Aborigines. It was first reported by white explorers in the 1870s and was named after Sir Henry Ayres, Prime Minister of South Australia.*

Left *John MacDonall Stuart, about 1863. One of the most successful explorers of the Australian interior, he was born in Scotland and emigrated to South Australia as a young man in 1839. The overland telegraph line was built largely along the route he pioneered across the continent.*

Eyre was noted for his unusual sympathy for the Aborigines (though he ended his career as a brutal governor of Jamaica). The native Australians were sometimes friendly and helpful to explorers, sometimes fiercely hostile. White settlers often treated them as animals and the effect of the white incursion was to destroy Aboriginal culture except in the centre and north of the continent. The Aborigines in Tasmania were exterminated altogether.

New Zealand shores

Settlement in New Zealand was a by-product of the colonisation of Australia. Late in the 18th century whaling stations were set up along the coasts and the newcomers sold the Maoris guns – which they used against each other in tribal wars – and infected them with measles and other European diseases against which they had no built-in resistance.

Presently, missionaries began to arrive. The first was a Yorkshire clergyman, Samuel Marsden, who crossed from New South Wales in 1814 and conducted the first Christian service in New Zealand on the shore of the Bay of Islands, on the North Island. He established a successful mission station there, protected by the local Maori chief, and he and other missionaries made exploratory journeys into the interior.

Late in the 1830s a company was formed to promote immigration from Britain. In 1840 the British government formally proclaimed its

sovereignty and signed a treaty with 45 Maori chiefs. Auckland was the capital initially and settlements were soon founded at Wellington, New Plymouth and Nelson. The early explorations of the South Island were carried out by surveyors working for the New Zealand Company, with Maori guides.

The heart of the matter

In Australia meantime, attention had focused on penetrating the heart of the continent, which it was thought might contain an inland sea. What it proved to contain was scarcely any water at all – a desert of scrub, spiny grass, tussocks and boulders, broken by mountain ranges.

The intrepid Charles Sturt left Adelaide in 1844 for the centre of the continent, going north to Cooper Creek and the Diamantina River. He and his men were trapped by an interminable drought – from November to July no rain fell – and spent six months cooped up at a waterhole. They had to dig themselves an underground burrow to shelter from the pitiless sun and to allow Sturt to write his notes, because outside the ink evaporated as soon as it touched the pen. When rain came at last, Sturt made repeated efforts to go further north, but each time had to turn back. Desperately ill with scurvy and unable to ride, he had to be carried slowly back to Adelaide in a cart.

A German explorer, Ludwig Leichhardt, completed a tremendous journey through the north-east in 1844–5, from near Brisbane to the Gulf of Carpentaria and then on across Arnhem Land to the coast at Port Essington. Three years later he set out on another expedition, disappeared and was never seen again. In the 1850s Augustus Gregory, searching vainly for traces of Leichhardt, cross the Northern Territory in the opposite direction, west to east.

Tragedy also attended the first crossing of Australia from sea to sea, south to north, by Robert Burke and William Wills, who left Melbourne in 1860 with a party provided with camels. The two leaders reached the coastal swamps of the Gulf of Carpentaria, but died on the way back after enduring dreadful hardships.

Another heroic crossing was made by John MacDonall Stuart, a Scots surveyor who had served with Sturt in the 1840s. In 1860 he went north, discovered and named the MacDonell Ranges and camped at what he calculated to be the exact centre of the continent. He pressed on north until an attack by Aborigines forced him to turn back. He tried again the following year and got further north before lack of water defeated him. At last, on a third expedition and despite appalling heat and Aboriginal hostility, Stuart and his companions struck the Adelaide River and followed it all the way to Van Diemen's Gulf on the north coast, which they reached on 24 July 1862. Stuart almost died on the way back and had to be carried on a litter slung between two horses. He won the South Australia parliament's £10,000 prize for the first man to cross the continent, but his health was shattered and he died four years later at the age of 50.

These expeditions demonstrated that the Australian outback was not a suitable place for settlement, which was confirmed in the 1870s when explorers crossed the deserts of Western Australia. There were still blank spaces on the map to he filled in. Donald Mackay, who did a 240-day round Australia tour on a bicycle in 1900, took to the air in the 1930s and organised aerial surveys of the central region. Even today in Australia there are places that may seldom, or never, have felt the tread of a white foot.

***Left** Milford Sound is a spectacularly beautiful fiord running deep into the mountains on the north coast of New Zealand's South Island. It is believed to have been named by a Welsh sealer after Milford Haven in his native Wales. The first settlers in the area built huts here in the 1870s.*

WILLIAM DAMPIER

At the end of the 17th century William Dampier sailed round the world with a group of buccaneers, and for this reason his name tends to conjure up images of piratical adventures on the high seas. The truth is more complex. Dampier travelled among pirates and admitted that he saw nothing wrong with such a life at the time, but he himself was an explorer by inclination and a keen collector and recorder of scientific data. As such, he was in many ways ahead of his time and some of his scientific observations continued to be regarded with respect long after his death. His published accounts of his journeys around the world made a considerable contribution to literature, providing both Daniel Defoe and Jonathan Swift with material for their own fictional accounts of travels to strange and unknown lands.

A skilled navigator, keen explorer and dedicated scientist, William Dampier is best known as a buccaneer

***Below** Dampier's voyage in 1699 to New Holland (Australia) and New Guinea went badly, but the explorer left his name to Dampier Island on the northwest coast of Australia and to Dampier Strait between New Guinea and New Britain.*

Early life

Dampier was born in Somerset, probably in 1651. His parents died when he was still a boy, but he seems to have received a good education before being apprenticed at 18 to a shipmaster at the port of Weymouth. This was his own choice, and it was in keeping with what he describes as 'the inclinations I had very early of seeing the world'. His scientific inclinations were also expressed early in his life, and we know that, as a boy, he made a careful comparative study of the different types of soil to be found in Somerset.

Dampier took part in a number of trading voyages and, after experiencing the severe cold weather of Newfoundland, he apparently declared that he would only head for warm destinations in the future. His first voyage after completing his apprenticeship was as a foremast

Right *Captain William Dampier, from the portrait now in the National Portrait Gallery in London. Born at East Coker in Somerset, he made three voyages round the world and wrote a bestselling account of his adventures.*

hand on a year's voyage to Bantam in the East Indies. There followed a brief period of service in the Royal Navy during the Third Dutch War, but at this point he fell ill and returned to his brother's home in Somerset to convalesce. Then, after travelling to Jamaica and finding that the offer of a job on a sugar plantation threatened to be a form of near-slavery, he moved to the Bay of Campeachy on the Gulf of Mexico to work as a logwood cutter. It was here that he first fell in with bands of buccaneers and set up in business as a trader. This enterprise looked promising at first, but it was ruined by a hurricane in 1676. Dampier was to write in detail later about hurricanes and typhoons, and he no doubt made notes about this one even while it was depriving him of his livelihood.

After this violent setback, he returned to England, married, purchased some land and for a while it seemed that he might settle in Dorset, but by 1679 he was at sea again.

Around the world in 12½ years

When Dampier left England in 1679 he was planning to go again to Bahía de Campeche as a trader and logwood cutter. Instead, he became involved with a huge privateering expedition numbering about 500 men in nine ships. His decision to join the buccaneers was the beginning of a sequence of journeys that would take him around the world over the next 12½ years and change his life dramatically.

The buccaneers sacked the the town of Porto Bello and then left their ships while they went overland to raid the American isthmus (the land of Darien, as it was known). Dampier then spent 13 months in Virginia before moving off again, rounding Cape Horn (he was already proving a valuable navigator and he advised his ship's captain against tackling the Magellan Straits without adequate charts) and calling at Juan Fernando, a desert island where a Moskito Indian, possibly the prototype of Defoe's Man Friday, had been abandoned three years before. The adventurers sailed along the coasts of Peru, Chile and Mexico and then on to the Philippines and Formosa before approaching New Holland, the name given in 1606 by the Dutch explorer Janszoon, to the northern coast of the as-yet-unexplored and largely unknown continent of Australia. In May 1688, Dampier and seven others parted company from the majority of the buccaneers in the Nicobar Islands and travelled by canoe to Sumatra. From here Dampier made his own expeditions to India and Tonquin in Indo-China. He served briefly in an English fort on Sumatra and finally joined a ship that brought him back to England via the Cape of Good Hope in 1691.

The Buccaneers

Above *A buccaneer, as imagined by Howard Pyle.*

The word buccaneer comes from *boucanier*, a term used in the Caribbean for the hunters who roasted and dried the flesh of the creatures they caught on a *boucan*, a type of grill or barbecue. This hunting of animals was generally a lawless activity, and by association the lawless pirates of the region also seem to have become known as buccaneers. In a sense, the Caribbean was a free for all, an area beyond the reach of law, where other nations refused to recognise Spain's claim to supremacy (allocated by the Pope under the Treaty of Tordesillas) and therefore also refused to discipline their own subjects should they choose to attack Spanish vessels. Buccaneers and privateers were pirates, but many had support and finance from wealthy citizens and city corporations, which gave them vague claims to respectability.

Dampier had a thorough training in the buccaneering way of life, taking part in raising expeditions, capturing ships and sometimes fighting for his life, but at every possible opportunity he was also making notes, taking observations, and studying plant and animal life, although it has to be said that his interest in the latter was often of a gastronomical nature. He protected his pages of notes by rolling them up and inserting them into watertight bamboo canes and guarded them with his life. In 1697 the result of all this work was published as *A New Voyage Round the World*, a journal full of detailed accounts of the strange plants, mammals, fishes, reptiles and human beings encountered across the globe. Dampier also gave information about winds and weather conditions, he observed how compass declination (deviation east or west of true north) varies in different places and he criticised the inaccuracy of many existing maps. The book became an immediate bestseller, going through four editions in two years.

Not only was Dampier famous, he had also won the approval of the Royal Society, to whose president, Charles Montague, the book was dedicated. The writing has a strictly matter-of-fact tone and the author made no attempt to exploit the more sensational aspects of his adventures – indeed it is often difficult to imagine him living the life of a pirate. In his diary for August 1698, John Evelyn writes about a dinner with Dampier and Samuel Pepys, saying that Dampier 'seemed a more modest man than one would imagine by relation of the crew he had assorted with. He brought a map of his observations of the course of the winds in the south seas and assured us that the maps hitherto extant were all false as to the Pacific Sea.'

Below *Dampier's ship* Roebuck *is attacked by the natives of New Ireland. This island lies immediately east of New Britain, though Dampier assumed they were both part of the same landmass off the eastern end of New Guinea.*

An official expedition to New Holland

The book also brought Dampier to the attention of the Government, secured him a job at the Customs House, and won him recognition as an expert whose advice was sought by the Council of Trades and Plantations. The First Lord of the Admiralty was sufficiently impressed to invite him to suggest a destination and lead a type of expedition that was virtually unique at the time – a government sponsored scientific voyage of discovery. Dampier chose New Holland and New Guinea. During his inspection of part of the coast of New Holland in 1688, he had observed the Aborigine communities. Since then, in 1694, an account of Abel Tasman's 1642 discovery of Van Diemen's Land (later Tasmania) and the west coast of New Zealand had been published and this, along with his own experiences, encouraged Dampier to believe that there was more to be discovered and perhaps claimed for Britain.

He was given command of a ship called the *Roebuck* with a crew of 50 men and boys and asked to make a collection of plant specimens and to bring home any native who might be willing to travel with him. He sailed at the beginning of 1699 on what should have been a mission of great distinction but he appears to have been a man promoted beyond the level of his own ability. As a navigator he was little short of a genius; as a captain he was a disaster. He set off with an incompetent crew and he soon began to suspect that his First Lieutenant, George Fisher, was encouraging the men to mutiny. They called first at Tenerife, where there were a number of arguments, and then sailed for Brazil. On landing at Bahía de Campeche Dampier had Fisher removed from detention on board and thrown in prison. Later, he would face a court martial for striking and imprisoning an officer.

On 23 April 1699, the *Roebuck* left Brazil and began the 7,000-mile (11,265km) journey to New Holland. Over three months later, on 1 August, they sighted the west coast of Australia

Above *A mask from Papua New Guinea. The island was earlier known as Magna Margarita and much of the south coast was surveyed in 1606 by a Spaniard, Luis de Torres, who left his name to the Torres Strait. The interior, however, remained largely unknown to the outside world well into the 19th century.*

Journal Extracts

"January 1688: New Holland is a very large tract of land. It is not yet determined whether it is an island or a main continent, but I am certain that it joins neither to Asia, Africa, nor America. This part of it that we saw is all low, even land, with sandy banks against the sea; only the points are rocky and so are some of the islands in the bay."

In Madras, Dampier acquired Jeoly, a 'painted prince', a son of the Raja of Meangis Island who had been enslaved in India:
"He was painted all down the breast, between his shoulders behind; on his thighs (mostly) before; and in the form of several broad rings or bracelets round his arms and legs."

Dampier took Jeoly to England where he was exhibited as a curiosity:
"When he was shown for a sight in England they reported that this paint was of such virtue that serpents and venomous creatures would flee from him . . . but I never knew any paint of such virtue, and as for Jeoly, I have seen him as much afraid of snakes, scorpions or centapees as my self."

After a few months Jeoly developed smallpox and died.

from *A New Voyage Round the World*, William Dampier

– Dampier's navigation and reading of the winds could not be faulted, but, in difficult circumstances, his next decision was a bad one. Anchoring in Shark Bay, a barren place without fresh water, and faced with the problem of a crew sickening with scurvy, he turned north, back towards the far-from-appealing region he knew from his visit in 1688. This northwestern, near-desert area became known as Dampier Land. Had he risked turning south instead, he would have found the far more hospitable and hitherto unknown region of southwestern Australia and his expedition would have been judged a tremendous success.

After five weeks the *Roebuck* sailed on via Timor, to reach eastern New Guinea at the beginning of 1700. Dampier gave the name New Britain to an island here, and the previously unknown strait between this island and New Guinea later became Dampier Passage. By now the ship was giving serious cause for concern and proving almost beyond repair. Although some essential work was done at Batavia (Jakarta) in the Dutch East Indies, it was not enough to get the *Roebuck* home. She began to founder near Ascension Island and the crew had to salvage what they could and camp out on this rocky outcrop for several months. Dampier did not reach England until August 1701, where he immediately faced a court martial over his treatment of Fisher.

Back with the buccaneers

When Dampier set out in the *Roebuck* he was an admired celebrity. On his return, his fortunes were reversed. The court martial pronounced him guilty and imposed a heavy fine, and he soon had to turn again to the buccaneering way of life to find an income. Despite his troubles, he never lost his commitment to science and discovery. Somehow he had salvaged his collection of plant specimens and his notes from the shipwreck, and in 1703 he published *A Voyage to New Holland*. This book contained numerous observations that led later generations of scientists to view his expedition as a valuable one. He was, for example, only the second European ever to describe a marsupial.

Dampier appears next buccaneering again in the South Seas. He was captain of the *St George*, a Bristol privateer, and this voyage too, throws doubt on his ability as a leader of men. He wrote

no account of the expedition himself, but one William Funnell did, imitating Dampier's style and speaking of disagreements and mismanagements, which defeated the participants' 'most promising hopes'. Dampier joined with other privateers and had some limited success in capturing Spanish vessels, but Funnell has little to say in his favour, although he does remark on his 'very exact' descriptions of places and his 'very extraordinary' account of winds and currents.

Feuds and disputes were an inevitable part of the buccaneering way of life, but this expedition saw a remarkable one that resulted in a demand by a crew member, Alexander Selkirk, that he be left ashore on the island of Juan Fernandez off the coast of Chile. His experiences lie behind Defoe's story, *Robinson Crusoe*.

Like all buccaneers, those on the *St George* hoped to capture the supreme prize vessel: the Manila galleon as she approached Acapulco on her way from China with a cargo rumoured to be worth 16 million pieces of eight. Again, Dampier's technical skill was not in doubt – he managed to be in the right place at the right time to intercept the ship, but she escaped, apparently because of incompetence and mismanagement. Mutiny inevitably followed and Dampier was left with a disintegrating ship and a much reduced crew. He reached England again at the end of 1707 after circumnavigating the world for a second time, and later said it was a miracle that he got home at all.

The fourth voyage

The year 1709 saw publication of a sequel to Dampier's account of the voyage to New Holland, indicating his, and his public's, continued interest in news of remote lands. He was not in England when it appeared – in 1708 he had set off again on what was to be his third and last voyage round the world – this time as pilot rather than captain. There were two ships, the *Duke* and the *Duchess*, and the captain of the *Duke*, Woodes Rogers would not stand for any trouble. The expedition has been described as one of the most carefully planned and best organised privateering expeditions that ever put to sea. After the usual call at the Canary Islands, the two ships sailed to Grande on the Brazilian coast, completed a perilous rounding of Cape Horn, and then approached Juan Fernandez where, to everyone's surprise, there were signs of a fire burning. It was, of course, a signal fire lit by Alexander Selkirk. Despite his four years of isolation Selkirk is said to have been reluctant to join a ship that had Dampier on board. Remembering the disasters of Dampier's captaincy of the *St George*, he had to be assured that, this time, Dampier was not in command. Once this

Above *Lake Toba is the largest mountain lake in Sumatra. The Portuguese established a trading post on Sumatra early in the 16th century, but were driven out by the Dutch. The English also established a foothold. Dampier reached Sumatra in 1688, seriously ill with fever but unable to bleed himself because his penknife was too blunt for the task. He served for a while as master gunner of the English fort at Benkulen.*

Defoe and Swift and the Fictional Traveller

Dampier's accounts of his voyages found an eager audience, and there is no doubt that they contributed to the work of both Daniel Defoe and Jonathan Swift. Swift's Gulliver (who was said by Sir Walter Scott to have the character of Dampier, or any other sturdy nautical wanderer of the period) pays two visits to New Holland, as did Dampier, and this same territory also features in Swift's *Tale of a Tub*. In a letter at the opening of *Gullivers Travels*, Swift actually has Gulliver refer to Dampier. Moreover, both Gulliver and Dampier undertook four major voyages, the dates of two of which almost coincide. The Captain Pocock of Bristol whom Gulliver meets in Tenerife is a man going to *Campeachy* to cut logwood and must surely be based on Dampier.

***Above** Robinson Crusoe and 'family' in an illustration of 1903.*

The link with Defoe is to be seen in the Alexander Selkirk story (although this was widely reported elsewhere), and in the very nature of Crusoe's narrative, which goes into detail about the practicalities of life and work on the island in a style reminiscent of Dampier. Defoe's little-known last work has a name just like Dampier's first: *A New Voyage Round the World, by a course never sailed before*. It tells of a journey of circumnavigation dedicated to buccaneering, trade and discovery.

was established, however, the two appear to have got on well together for the rest of the voyage.

This well-disciplined expedition also hoped to capture the Manila galleon, and they almost succeeded. The true galleon escaped after a tough fight, but they did trap the *Encarnacion* – a similar but smaller vessel loaded with costly Chinese silks, fine porcelain and spices. Dampier's navigation brought the ships safely to Amsterdam in July 1711, and he retired to London and died in March 1715.

Dampier's achievements

Despite his many failures, William Dampier succeeded in producing a body of written work that reached a large audience and commanded respect in academic circles. He wrote from experience, and this was usually superior to the received opinion of the day. (He said, among other things, that both the Indian Ocean and the Atlantic were smaller than commonly believed, and he was right – at the time the Atlantic was said to be between 62° and 70° broad. It actually measures about 44°.)

Compendium volumes of *Dampier's Voyages* with maps by the famous cartographer, Herman Moll, were reprinted many times, and the *New Voyage Round the World* and another volume of *Voyages and Descriptions* were soon translated into Dutch, German and French. *Voyages and Descriptions* was particularly valuable for its supplement entitled 'A Discourse of Trade Winds, Breezes, Storms, Seasons of the Year and Currents of the Torrid Zone throughout the World'. This showed Dampier's instinctive ability to understand natural phenomena, and it has been called a classic of the pre-scientific era.

Although the celebrated scientist Edmund Halley was also studying wind patterns at the time, it seems that Dampier's rather than Halley's work provided the basis for cartographic representation of trade winds during the 18th century. It is this ability of Dampier to approach the achievements of notable trained scientists, and in some cases to anticipate their findings, which is most striking. He was not a successful captain and he made many mistakes, but an authoritative mid-19th-century German book on meteorology (*Lehrbuch der Meterorologie*, 1860, Leipsig – a volume of the *Allgemeine Encyklopädie der Physik*) cited Dampier many times and said that in some cases there was little to add to his remarks, while his description of a typhoon was still being used in a manual of meteorology published in Britain in the middle of the 20th century. His picture hangs in the National Portrait Gallery in London and it carries the inscription 'Pirate and Hydrographer' – which is accurate, but is very far from being the whole truth.

Biographical Notes

c.1651
Born in Somerset.

1662
Apprenticed to shipmaster at Weymouth.

1679–91
First voyage round the world.

1699–1701
Second voyage, to New Holland (Australia).

1703–7
Third voyage, to South Seas and around the world.

1708–11
Fourth voyage, to South Seas and around the world.

1715
Died, probably in London.

CAPTAIN JAMES COOK

In his search for a great southern continent, Captain Cook explored the world's oceans more extensively than anyone before him

It has been said of Captain James Cook that no man ever did more to alter and correct the map of the earth. At the age of 40, with over 20 years' practical experience of seamanship behind him, he set off on the first of three momentous voyages, any one of which would have earned him lasting fame. In Cook's day there were some fundamental questions about world geography still to be answered, and he was the man who produced most of the solutions, demonstrating that there was no such thing as a northwest passage south of the Arctic between the Atlantic and the Pacific, and that the vast *Terra Australia Incognita* that cartographers had been putting on maps for centuries in the belief that the southern hemisphere must have landmasses similar to those of the northern, did not actually exist. The journals that he kept during his voyages give precise information about day-to-day progress and reveal the perceptive character of this man who brought new standards of accuracy to the techniques of surveying and charting, and proved that it was not inevitable for sailors on long voyages to fall victim to scurvy.

An education in seamanship

James Cook was born at the village of Marton in Yorkshire on 27 October 1728, one of seven children of a day labourer. He received a basic education at the village school and was then sent to work for a grocer at the nearby fishing village of Staithes. Here he developed a fascination for the sea and in July 1746 became an apprentice to the Walker family of ship-owners at the port of Whitby. Coal from the region was transported along the coast in small colliers known as Whitby cats, which were noted for their shallow draught and sturdy construction. Designed to carry coal in large quantities, they provided ample storage space for a long voyage. Over the next few years Cook became expert at handling these boats and he used them on his three major voyages of exploration.

While based at Whitby, Cook educated himself in mathematics and navigation and by 1755 he had impressed his employers sufficiently for them to offer him the command of one of their ships. For some reason Cook refused and instead joined the Royal Navy as an ordinary seaman. A deliberate choice of such reduction in rank has led to speculation as to whether Cook suffered some disgrace at this stage in his career, but there is no evidence of this, and he may simply have felt that his long-term prospects would be better in the Navy. He saw active service during the Seven Years War and soon received promotion. By 1757 he was master of his own ship, the *Pembroke*, and on 15 September 1759 he was in attendance during Wolfe's capture of Québec. He made it his business to learn all there was to know about navigation on the St Lawrence River and his work was rewarded in 1761 when he received a £50 bonus payment, for 'indefatigable industry in making himself Master of the pilotage'. He returned to England in 1762 and married, and the following year saw him surveying the coasts of Newfoundland and Labrador, this time in command of the schooner *Grenville*. The charts that he compiled and his detailed report on an eclipse of the sun in August 1766 left no doubt as to his great competence and potential and made him an obvious candidate for high office in the future.

The first voyage

It was predicted that on 3 June 1769 the planet Venus would cross in front of the sun, and astronomers believed that detailed observations taken in different parts of the world at this time would enable them to calculate the distance of the sun from the earth. The Royal Society proposed that observers should be sent to the north of Norway, to Hudson Bay and to an island in the Pacific, and Cook was chosen to lead the official British expedition to this last destination. His ship was a Whitby collier named *Endeavour* with a crew of about 80 and a team of 11 scientists, including Charles Green, Assistant to

Below *A model of the* Endeavour, *in the National Maritime Museum at Greenwich. The ship was a slow, but sturdy and spacious Whitby collier of 370 tons (375 tonnes), adapted to carry a crew of about 80, which was more than normal.*

***Right** A portrait of Cook by William Hodges, who sailed round the world with the great explorer in* Resolution *on the second voyage. The painting was discovered, neglected and dirty, in a country house in Ireland in 1986. It is now in the National Maritime Museum, Greenwich.*

the Astronomer Royal, and Joseph Banks, a young Fellow of the Royal Society who supplied numerous scientific instruments of his own. The observation point selected was George III Island, discovered by the British navigator, Wallis, only a few months earlier and later named Tahiti. However, when Cook sailed he did so with a set of sealed instructions that would reveal another motive for the expedition, although this was hinted at publicly before he left England.

Leaving Plymouth at the end of August 1768, the *Endeavour* sailed first to Madeira and then, in November, reached Rio de Janeiro, where there was a delay because she was regarded as a pirate vessel and some of the crew were arrested. By January 1769 the misunderstanding had been dealt with and the *Endeavour* was on her way to Cape Horn (Cabo de Hornos), which she rounded in surprisingly good weather during February. By the beginning of April the ship was within sight of the Tuamotu Archipelago (Îles Tuamotu), and on the 11th she anchored in Matavai Bay (Tahiti). The transit of Venus was observed on 3 June and Cook was now entitled to open his sealed instructions, which revealed that he was 'to proceed southward' as far as latitude 40° in search of the elusive *Terra Australia Incognita*. If this course resulted in nothing, he was to turn west and search between latitudes 40° and 35° until he discovered the unknown land or came to 'the eastern side of the land discovered by Tasman and now called New Zealand'. Cook did not sail south at once – the crew that he had protected from scurvy had become ill with a form of venereal disease instead, and he thought that they should have time to recover from the immediate acute effects. Cook claimed in his journal that before leaving England he had taken great care to select a crew free from disease – was it possible, as many have argued, that his expedition was to blame for the devastating introduction of syphilis to the islands of the Pacific? Cook says the natives agreed that his men had not brought the disease but had themselves been infected by a condition already present on Tahiti. This was seen as the legacy of some other mysterious voyagers whose two ships had visited the island about a year earlier.

After making a detailed survey of the Leeward Islands, Cook began to sail south in the middle of August, but severe weather forced him to turn northwest at the beginning of September. He had reached 40° S and found no sign of the imagined *Terra Australis* and his instructions now took him on to New Zealand, where he arrived at what he was to call Poverty Bay early in October. Here, the initial reaction from the Maoris was hostile and Cook expressed remorse for having fired in self-defence and killed two or three people. From Poverty Bay he sailed south, first to another bay, which he named after Hawke, the First Lord of the Admiralty, and then, finding little of interest,

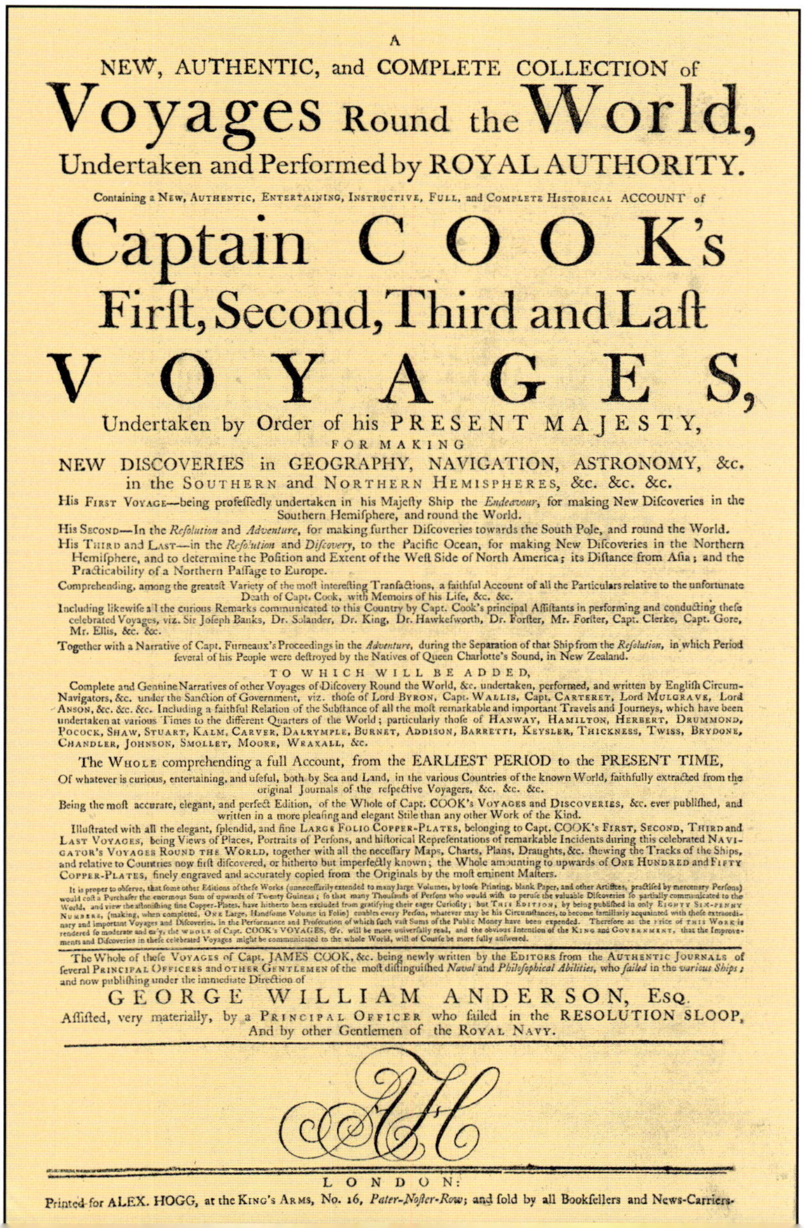
A

NEW, AUTHENTIC, and COMPLETE COLLECTION of

Voyages Round the World,

Undertaken and Performed by ROYAL AUTHORITY.

Containing a NEW, AUTHENTIC, ENTERTAINING, INSTRUCTIVE, FULL, and COMPLETE HISTORICAL ACCOUNT of

Captain COOK's

Firſt, Second, Third and Laſt

VOYAGES,

Undertaken by Order of his PRESENT MAJESTY,

FOR MAKING

NEW DISCOVERIES in GEOGRAPHY, NAVIGATION, ASTRONOMY, &c. in the SOUTHERN and NORTHERN HEMISPHERES, &c. &c. &c.

His FIRST VOYAGE—being profeſſedly undertaken in his Majeſty Ship the *Endeavour*, for making New Diſcoveries in the Southern Hemiſphere, and round the World.

His SECOND—In the *Reſolution* and *Adventure*, for making further Diſcoveries towards the South Pole, and round the World.

His THIRD and LAST—in the *Reſolution* and *Diſcovery*, to the Pacific Ocean, for making New Diſcoveries in the Northern Hemiſphere, and to determine the Poſition and Extent of the Weſt Side of North America; its Diſtance from Aſia; and the Practicability of a Northern Paſſage to Europe.

Comprehending, among the greateſt Variety of the moſt intereſting Tranſactions, a faithful Account of all the Particulars relative to the unfortunate Death of Capt. Cook, with Memoirs of his Life, &c. &c.

Including likewiſe all the curious Remarks communicated to this Country by Capt. Cook's principal Aſſiſtants in performing and conducting theſe celebrated Voyages, viz. Sir Joſeph Banks, Dr. Solander, Dr. King, Dr. Hawkeſworth, Dr. Forſter, Mr. Forſter, Capt. Clerke, Capt. Gore, Mr. Ellis, &c. &c.

Together with a Narrative of Capt. Furneaux's Proceedings in the *Adventure*, during the Separation of that Ship from the *Reſolution*, in which Period ſeveral of his People were deſtroyed by the Natives of Queen Charlotte's Sound, in New Zealand.

TO WHICH WILL BE ADDED,

Complete and Genuine Narratives of other Voyages of Diſcovery Round the World, &c. undertaken, performed, and written by Engliſh Circum-Navigators, &c. under the Sanction of Government, viz. thoſe of Lord BYRON, Capt. WALLIS, Capt. CARTERET, Lord MULGRAVE, Lord ANSON, &c. &c. &c. Including a faithful Relation of the Subſtance of all the moſt remarkable and important Travels and Journeys, which have been undertaken at various Times to the different Quarters of the World; particularly thoſe of HANWAY, HAMILTON, HERBERT, DRUMMOND, POCOCK, SHAW, STUART, KALM, CARVER, DALRYMPLE, BURNET, ADDISON, BARRETTI, KEYSLER, THICKNESS, TWISS, BRYDONE, CHANDLER, JOHNSON, SMOLLET, MOORE, WRAXALL, &c.

The WHOLE comprehending a full Account, from the EARLIEST PERIOD to the PRESENT TIME,

Of whatever is curious, entertaining, and uſeful, both by Sea and Land, in the various Countries of the known World, faithfully extracted from the original Journals of the reſpective Voyagers, &c. &c. &c.

Being the moſt accurate, elegant, and perfect Edition, of the Whole of Capt. COOK's VOYAGES and DISCOVERIES, &c. ever publiſhed, and written in a more pleaſing and elegant Stile than any other Work of the Kind.

Illuſtrated with all the elegant, ſplendid, and fine LARGE FOLIO COPPER-PLATES, belonging to Capt. COOK's FIRST, SECOND, THIRD and LAST VOYAGES, being Views of Places, Portraits of Perſons, and hiſtorical Repreſentations of remarkable Incidents during this celebrated NAVIGATOR's VOYAGES ROUND THE WORLD, together with all the neceſſary Maps, Charts, Plans, Draughts, &c. ſhewing the Tracks of the Ships, and relative to Countries now firſt diſcovered, or hitherto but imperfectly known; the Whole amounting to upwards of ONE HUNDRED and FIFTY COPPER-PLATES, finely engraved and accurately copied from the Originals by the moſt eminent Maſters.

It is proper to obſerve, that ſome other Editions of theſe Works (unneceſſarily extended to many large Volumes, by looſe Printing, blank Paper, and other Artifices, practiſed by mercenary Perſons) would coſt a Purchaſer the enormous Sum of upwards of Twenty Guineas; ſo that many Thouſands of Perſons who would wiſh to peruſe the valuable Diſcoveries ſo partially communicated to the World, and view the aſtoniſhing fine Copper-Plates, have hitherto been excluded from gratifying their eager Curioſity; but THIS EDITION, by being publiſhed in only EIGHTY SIX-PENNY NUMBERS, (making, when completed, ONE Large, Handſome Volume in Folio) enables every Perſon, whatever may be his Circumſtances, to become familiarly acquainted with theſe extraordinary and important Voyages and Diſcoveries, in the Performance and Proſecution of which ſuch vaſt Sums of the Public Money have been expended. Therefore as the Price of THIS WORK is rendered ſo moderate and eaſy, the WHOLE of Capt. COOK's VOYAGES, &c. will be more univerſally read, and the obvious Intention of the KING and GOVERNMENT, that the Improvements and Diſcoveries in theſe celebrated Voyages might be communicated to the whole World, will of Courſe be more fully anſwered.

The Whole of theſe VOYAGES of Capt. JAMES COOK, &c. being newly written by the EDITORS from the AUTHENTIC JOURNALS of ſeveral PRINCIPAL OFFICERS and OTHER GENTLEMEN of the moſt diſtinguiſhed *Naval* and *Philoſophical Abilities*, who *ſailed* in the *various Ships*; and now publiſhing under the immediate Direction of

GEORGE WILLIAM ANDERSON, ESQ.

Aſſiſted, very materially, by a PRINCIPAL OFFICER who ſailed in the RESOLUTION SLOOP, And by other Gentlemen of the ROYAL NAVY.

LONDON:

Printed for ALEX. HOGG, at the KING's ARMS, No. 16, *Pater-Noſter-Row*; and ſold by all Bookſellers and News-Carriers.

***Below** Cook's achievements brought him fame and admiration at home and in Europe. This is the title page of a book describing his three great voyages.*

***Right** Cook watches impassively as a shipmate carves Endeavour's name on a tree at Botany Bay. Cook considered it a good place for a colony and his opinion afterwards influenced the decision to plant a convict settlement there.*

turned north again. He spent four months circumnavigating North Island in a counter-clockwise direction, then a further seven weeks sailing clockwise round South Island, and the result was a chart of remarkable accuracy.

On 1 April 1770 Cook left New Zealand, intent on finding the east coast of New Holland (Australia), which no European had yet visited. The first sighting of land was made by a Lieutenant Hicks and Cook duly named it Point Hicks (it was later renamed Cape Everard). From here they sailed north, and anchored on 29 April in what Cook originally called 'Stingray' Bay, and then, in view of the huge number of unknown plant specimens found there, Botany Bay. Two Aborigines resisted

their landing and fired darts, which Joseph Banks feared might be poisoned, but Cook eventually scared them off with musket fire and met no more serious conflict during a week of exploration in the vicinity. On 7 May they sailed again, travelling north and glimpsing the approach to what was to become Sydney harbour. Failing to investigate it, they landed at Bustard Bay and then, on 11th June, suffered near shipwreck on the Great Barrier Reef. After a tremendous struggle the *Endeavour* was refloated, and despite her seriously leaking hull, she was brought safely into Cook Harbour near modern Cooktown. For two months Cook stayed here, observing and shooting kangaroos and doing all he could to patch up the damaged hull, but when they sailed it was in a still-leaking ship, and they had to resume their journey through one of the most perilous stretches of water in the world. By 21 August they had come in sight of the tip of Australia's north-eastern promontory, which Cook named York Cape, and he then turned west, found and named the Endeavour Strait between the mainland and Prince of Wales Island. On 22 August he claimed Eastern Australia as British territory and named it New South Wales, before continuing westwards and proving that there was a sea route between Australia and New Guinea.

After another near shipwreck, the *Endeavour* limped into Batavia (Jakarta) at the beginning of

***Below** Captain Cook was a navigator of genius and one of the first great scientific explorers. His three epic voyages put him in the class of Columbus and Magellan, and he charted his discoveries with meticulous accuracy.*

October and remained there until 27 December, undergoing repairs. Here the previous record of good health failed. Some of the crew fell sick and Cook blamed the unwholesome climate. Many more were to die before the *Endeavour* reached England, via Cape Town, on 13 July 1771. Cook summed up the voyage as follows: 'I have made no very great discoveries yet I explored more of the Great South Sea than all that have gone before me, so much that little remains now to be done to have a thorough knowledge of that part of the globe'. While Cook was promoted to Commander and had an audience with the King, Joseph Banks attracted even more attention for his extraordinary collection of botanical and geological specimens.

The second voyage

Cook did not believe in the existence of a great southern continent, but he had not demonstrated conclusively that it was a fiction and other nations were still dispatching expeditions to search for it. To answer the question once and for all, another official voyage was planned almost immediately. This time Cook would have two ships, colliers named *Resolution* and *Adventure* (built at Whitby, like the *Endeavour*, by a Mr Fisburn), in which he planned to circumnavigate the world in the high latitudes of the Antarctic. This too was intended to be a scientific expedition, again with Joseph Banks aboard, but there was a dispute over the number of people Banks wished to take with him and in the end he withdrew. Other scientists, however, did join the voyage, including two astronomers. One of their tasks was to improve upon the calculation of longitude – a problem that had troubled explorers for centuries. They took four chronometers (instruments for measuring time against astronomical observations) with them and one proved so accurate that they were able to establish a reliable and easy method of calculation.

They sailed from Plymouth in the summer of 1772, only a year after the return of the *Endeavour*, and a number of Cook's earlier crew chose to accompany him a second time. From Cape Town they continued south, crossing the Antarctic Circle on 17 January 1773. Then, forced by ice to turn north, they reached Dusky Bay on the southwest coast of New Zealand's South Island in March. Cook then returned to Tahiti and also investigated the Tongan Islands (named by Cook the Friendly Islands). In October, on their way south again, the two ships became separated and the *Adventure* sailed home. Cook continued south, travelling as far as latitude 71° 10′S, and, finding nothing but ice, felt entitled to claim that the great southern

The Scourge of Scurvy

Scurvy was a dread disease that weakened and killed thousands of sailors on long voyages of discovery. A serious problem in the days of Vasco da Gama, it was still defying both treatment and prevention in the middle of the 18th century despite the fact that in 1605 one Captain James Lancaster had cured an outbreak of the disease by giving his men lemon juice to drink. In 1617, in a book called *The Surgeon's Mate*, James Woodall stated that lemon juice was the answer to the disease, but this information still failed to reach the majority of seafarers. Captain Cook witnessed scurvy on some of his early travels and took advice from various authorities in planning his major voyages. He probably consulted the papers of James Lind, a Royal Navy physician who had demonstrated scientifically the benefits of orange and lemon juice, and his decision to combine a number of supposed treatments was so successful that his men were able to survive a three-year voyage without any outbreak of the disease. As well as citrus juices, sauerkraut and carrot marmalade were included in Cook's armoury and, on the advice of a Mr Pelham, the Secretary to the British Commissioners of Victualling, he also carried large supplies of a remedy based on an infusion of malt.

Later the name 'limey' came to be used of British sailors and their ships, and even of the British in general, because of the Royal Navy's regular issue of lime juice to its men.

Below *Late in August 1770 Cook went ashore in Australia for the last time to take formal possession of the eastern coastline for Great Britain under the name of New South Wales. Apparently the name was chosen because the country resembled the Glamorgan coast of South Wales.*

continent was a myth. Sailing north again, he called at Easter Island in March 1774, at the Marquesas Islands (Isls Marquises), the New Hebrides (Vanuatu) and New Caledonia, before making for Cape Horn, claiming the island of South Georgia as British, and returning to Plymouth via Cape Town in July 1775. Again, Cook had shown that disease could be avoided by careful attention to diet and hygiene, only four men out of 112 on the *Resolution* died during the voyage, not one of scurvy.

The third voyage

Another mystery remained to be solved, and Cook could not resist tackling it. In the summer of 1776 he sailed again in the *Resolution*, intending to search for a western approach to the supposed northwest passage, while a sister ship, the *Discovery*, was to look for the approach from the east. After pauses in New Zealand and Tahiti and a return to the Friendly Islands, Cook sailed north and discovered the Sandwich Islands (Hawaiian Islands) in January 1778. After sighting the northwest coast of North America, he had to put in to Nootka Sound on Vancouver Island (named after George Vancouver, a member of the party) for repairs. From there they continued north and investigated the Bering Strait but found, in August, that ice prevented any progress beyond latitude 70° 44′N. All they could do was return south, and Cook chose to take another look at the newly discovered Sandwich Islands.

The *Resolution* anchored in Kealakekua Bay and Cook seems to have been regarded as some sort of god by the islanders. Relations were so good that he and his men stayed for several weeks, but this additional strain on the islanders' food supplies gradually led to a build-up of tension and, on 4 February 1779, perhaps with a sense of having stayed too long, Cook left with plans to find another anchorage before going on to explore the northeast coast of Asia. They had travelled only a short distance when the ship suffered serious damage and Cook was forced to return to the bay he had just left. There has been endless speculation about what happened next and why. It is clear that the returning visitors were no longer welcome.

On 14 February a misunderstanding arose over the fate of a local chief and there were rumours that he had been killed by the Europeans. In the confusion, Cook, who seems not to have been the aggressor, was struck from behind while standing on the shore and then stabbed. In spite of this, the Hawaiians still seemed to regard him as a god and treated his body with reverence. A decision was taken to continue the exploration as planned, but the man appointed to succeed Cook became ill and died, morale was understandably low, and no more was achieved. The *Resolution* and the *Discovery* returned to Britain in August 1780.

Above *An artist named John Webber accompanied Cook on his third and final voyage, which left Plymouth in July 1776. This is Webber's picture of* The Resolution *and the* Discovery *in Nootka Sound on the Canadian Pacific coast, where they stayed for almost a month while replacing* Resolution's *mizzen mast.*

Left *Cook landing in Tasmania in the course of his last voyage. His explorations left little of importance still to be discovered in the Pacific.*

A Bitter Remedy

Sauerkraut was one of Cook's anti-scurvy preparations. He explains how he got his men to eat it:

"The Sour Krout the men at first would not eat until I put in practice a method I never once knew to fail with seamen, and this was to have some of it dressed every day for the cabin table, and permitted all the Officers without exception to make use of it and left it to the option of the men either to take as much as they pleased or none at all; but this practice was not continued above a week before I found it necessary to put everyone on board to an allowance, for such are the tempers and dispositions of seamen in general that whatever you give them out of the common way, although it be ever so much for their good yet it will not go down with them and you will hear nothing but murmurings gainst the man that first invented it; but the moment they see their superiors set a value upon it, it becomes the finest stuff in the world and the inventor an honest fellow."

from *The Journals of Captain Cook*, edited by J.C. Beaglehole

Biographical Notes

1728
Born in Yorkshire.

1763–7
Surveyed the Newfoundland and Labrador coasts.

1768–71
First voyage: to Tahiti, New Zealand, Botany Bay.

1772–5
Second voyage: crossed Antarctic Circle.

1776–9
Third voyage: in search of a northwest passage.

1779
Killed on Hawaii.

ALEXANDER VON HUMBOLDT

Forsaking a life of leisure, von Humboldt led gruelling scientific expeditions through the jungles and across the mountains of Central and South America

Alexander von Humboldt and his brother Wilhelm were once described by Goethe as the 'sons of Zeus'. The image is a romantic one, but there is a suggestion of truth in it – both were men of outstanding ability: Wilhelm von Humboldt founded the University of Berlin in 1810 and published important work on language studies, and Alexander's record of achievement in a number of areas was little short of superhuman. He lived to the age of 90, withstood disease in unhealthy climates and survived a variety of perilous, self-inflicted experiments including a series of shocks from an electric eel, and a drink of the Indian poison curare, which he swallowed to demonstrate his belief that it was only fatal when it entered directly into the bloodstream. He is said to have described over 8,000 species of plants, at least half of which were previously unknown in Europe. He was a man for whom life equalled work and, according to his brother, he never allowed anyone or anything to deflect him from his chosen course. Apart from his many valuable contributions to international understanding of some of the most isolated regions of Latin America, his social concern prompted him to establish and finance the first free workers' education institution in Germany and he formulated a holistic theory about the way the earth functions that anticipated present-day ecological concerns by more than 100 years.

Early life in Prussia

Growing up in a well-to-do family in Prussia during the second half of the 18th century, Alexander von Humboldt showed an interest in natural history and the sciences from an early age. He was educated at home at first, by private tutors, and then went to the University of Göttingen to study science. Here he met Georg Forster, a man who had been an official botanical draftsman on Captain Cook's second voyage – the circumnavigation of the world in the Antarctic latitudes – and who had published a book about his experiences in 1777. Forster no

***Below** Alexander von Humboldt, seen in his library in 1856, towards the end of a long and heroically productive life, in which he contributed substantially to the world's store of informative books.*

doubt provided Humboldt with an example of the sort of life dedicated to exploration and experiment that he himself would like to lead, but, feeling bound to obey the wishes of his widowed mother, he left Göttingen after a year and enrolled as a student of economics at the Hamburg School of Commerce and then moved to the Freiberg Mining Academy, where he studied geology. He worked almost unceasingly and his outstanding academic record led directly to a good civil service job as Assistant Inspector in the Prussian Department of Mines and to rapid promotion to Chief Inspector.

Very soon, he had embarked on what was to be a 3,000-mile (4,800km) official tour of the salt mines of Austria and Poland. As a direct result of this he recognised that there was an urgent need for miners to be offered an education and, in 1793, he opened a mining institute at the town of Steben where teaching was available free of charge to those over the age of 12. Humboldt financed the foundation himself, and when the government recognised his achievement and offered to reimburse him he refused the money, requesting instead that it be given directly to needy miners. His concern about the dangers of mining led him to investigate the possibility of introducing new safety devices, and he developed breathing apparatus and lamps that have been seen as forerunners of Sir Humphry Davy's safety lamp. The year 1793 also saw publication of his account of the plant life of the Freiberg area, a serious, scientific study that attracted acclaim and brought Humboldt to the attention of Goethe. His intellectual curiosity was insatiable and he had changed from being a sickly child

Above right *Humboldt in the portrait gallery of an improving 19th century 'weekly instructor'. An intrepid scientific explorer of inexhaustible energy and courage, he pursued interests in electricity, plants, wildlife and social reform.*

Right *Humboldt and his companion, the French botanist Aimée Bonpland, set off down the Orinoco River in 1880 into almost unknown territory deep in the interior of Venezuela.*

and youth to an adult of apparently limitless energy. His work as a civil servant was never neglected, but he supplemented it with countless experiments of his own, including an estimated 4,000 into the phenomenon of galvanism (electricity developed by chemical action). Here Humboldt was to experience a rare failure for, despite all his efforts, he could not make the imaginative leap that later led the Italian, Volta, to the invention of the battery.

At the end of 1796 Humboldt's mother died and in February of the following year he did what he had always declared he would – he resigned from the secure career in which he had already achieved considerable status, intent on becoming an independent travelling scientist. In preparation, he made a special study of astronomy and the techniques of taking bearings, and in Paris in 1798, he met another eager traveller, the botanist Aimée Bonpland.

The great American journey

Both Humboldt and Bonpland had expected to take part in an ambitious French expedition that was planned to last five years and include a voyage to the South Pole. Almost on the eve of departure the French government abandoned the scheme and the two disappointed explorers discussed the possibility of organising their own expedition. They began by travelling to Marseilles and walking from there to Madrid in the space of six weeks at the end of 1798. All the way Humboldt used his instruments to measure altitude. He used his data to produce the first accurate sectional diagram of the Iberian peninsula, showing the uniformity of the central plateau.

By chance, in March 1799, Humboldt secured an introduction to King Carlos IV of Spain and Queen Maria Luisa and immediately impressed them with his ability to speak to them in their own language. They were also impressed with his eagerness to explore the Latin American countries then under Spanish rule, and in a very short time both Humboldt and Bonpland had been issued with passports of a sort that were not commonly available to non-Spanish citizens. Rather like the golden tablets granted by the Great Khan to Marco Polo, these passports, bearing the royal seal, required the King's subjects on the other side of the Atlantic to give the two travellers any assistance they might need.

On 5 June 1799 Humboldt and Bonpland sailed from La Coruna, taking with them a formidable number of scientific instruments. After a few days on Tenerife, during which they climbed the extinct volcano, Mount Teide, the journey proper began, with Humboldt taking readings all the way. Their intended destination was Havana, but an outbreak of typhoid on the boat persuaded them to disembark instead at Cumana in Venezuela in the middle of July. It was not a decision they regretted: the wealth of exotic plant and animal life entranced them and they believed they were living in a place little short of paradise. An expedition to the monastery of the Capuchin mission at Caripe in the mountainous territory of the Chayma Indians left Humboldt grateful for the monks' hospitality but saddened by the effect that the introduction of Christianity was having on the native population. One belief that the Indians still clung to was the idea that the spirits of their dead ancestors went to live in the cave of the guacharo or 'oil bird', and Humboldt and Bonpland went to see this cave for themselves, finding native guides who were prepared to show them the way. After the 'paradise' of Cumana, Humboldt said the 500-yard (450m) passage into the cliff, echoing with the shrieks of the thousands of birds who roosted within, was like the approach to hell. Their Indian guides eventually took fright and fled, but not before the visitors had shot two specimens of this bird, which was then totally unknown in Europe.

__Below__ Humboldt explored this 'oil bird' cave in Venezuela. He was interested in everything he came across, including the beliefs of the local Indians, who thought that the souls of their ancestors lived in the cave.

Into the interior

Humboldt and Bonpland sailed from Cumana to Caracas in November and, after waiting for the end of the rainy season, in February of 1800 they embarked on an ambitious journey into the virtually unknown interior region of Venezuela. Two centuries earlier, Sir Walter Raleigh had sailed along the River Orinoco in search of El Dorado and he had produced a map on which the Amazon and the Orinoco appeared to run parallel to one another. No connection between the rivers was indicated, but Raleigh had shown a huge lake separating the two and there had been international arguments over the true relation of the rivers to one another ever since. One theory held that a third river or canal linked the Amazon and Orinoco, but this was an idea so alien to

***Above** The Canaima Falls on the River Carrao, a tributary of the Coroni, which itself flows into the Orinoco further north. Humboldt found the link between the Orinoco and Amazon river systems, though the source of the Orinoco itself still remained a mystery. These remote regions are still not easy for outsiders to penetrate today.*

established thinking on geography that many dismissed it as ludicrous. Humboldt and Bonpland decided to go in search of the truth, apparently undaunted by the fact that a Spanish expedition to the same region in 1754 had started off with 325 members, of whom only 13 returned alive.

The first stage of the journey took them through rich agricultural territory to Puerto Cabello, but after that life became far tougher as they made the long trek across the *llanos*, huge, barren, desperately hot and waterless plains that were home to thousands of cattle and very, very few human beings. They paused at Calabozo, the only possible place to pause, and it was here that Humboldt made his experiments with electric eels and suffered the after-effects for several days. Having survived the *llanos* and the eels, they arrived at the end of March at San Fernando de Apure, the centre of the Capuchin mission on the Rio Apure, a tributary of the Orinoco, and prepared to take to the water in a large canoe paddled by a team of Indians.

They travelled along the Apure to the Orinoco, tormented by insects, but fascinated by the variety of wildlife, some of which, such as the alligators and jaguars, posed a serious threat to their survival. Once on the Orinoco, they travelled south towards what were known as the Great Cataracts. They survived a capsize at a point where the river was several miles wide and, as it grew gradually narrower, they had to exchange their large canoe for a smaller one, which offered very little space for their books, instruments and selection of animal and bird companions. The discomforts of the journey were considerable. With great skill and endurance the Indian crew paddled the canoe through ferocious rapids as far as the Great Cataracts, at which point they had to leave the river and carry the boat overland, before relaunching again on the waters of the Upper Orinoco beyond the Maipures Rapids. They struggled on up river and at San Fernando de Atabapo joined a tributary of the Orinoco, the Rio Atabapo, where climate and conditions immediately became more hospitable. Again the canoe had to be taken overland some of the way, but at last, at the beginning of May, they reached the Rio Negro and the settlement of San Carlos.

They lost little time in searching for, and finding, the mouth of the Casiquiare River (or canal). Humboldt determined its position in terms of degrees longitude and latitude and then began a dangerous, week-long journey along the

Facts and figures

Humboldt's discoveries during his great American journey filled 33 books: 16 volumes on botany; 4 on astronomical and geophysical data; 2 on zoology and comparative anatomy, and 10 devoted to an account of the journey itself and the geography of the places visited.

Humboldt wrote a single volume on the geography of plants, in French originally (*Essai sur la géographie des plantes*), and translated it into German as *Ideen zu einer Geographie der Pflanzen*. This has been called his greatest work; the German edition was dedicated to Goethe, who had himself written a book on the *Metamorphosis of Plants* and who contributed an illustration to Humboldt's work.

As well as the famous Humboldt Current off the Peruvian coast, there is a Pico de Humboldt near Merida in Venezuela and a Humboldt Peak in Colorado, a Humboldt Range, River, Salt Marsh and Reservoir in Nevada, and some eight Humboldt cities and three Humboldt counties in the USA and Canada.

Above *One of the great volcanic peaks of the Andes range, in Ecuador, Mount Chimborazo was believed to be the highest mountain in the world in 1802, when Humboldt climbed most of the way up it.*

200-mile (300km) waterway, during which they suffered near-starvation and the dog that had accompanied them this far was eaten by a jaguar. Conditions were terrible, but Humboldt characteristically continued with his scientific work and was later able to produce a superb map showing the watercourse whose existence many Europeans had denied, simply because the notion of a natural channel across the watershed between two river systems was previously unheard of.

They now rejoined the Orinoco and Humboldt had hoped to trace this river to its source, but this part of his plan was abandoned. They travelled no further east than La Esmeralda and then went down the Orinoco as far as Angostura (Ciudad Bolívar) where they were forced to stay for a month while Bonpland recovered from a fever. At this stage, they decided to brave the *llanos* again, travelling overland to New Barcelona, and then by sea back to Cumana.

Pioneer mountaineers

In travelling to the Casiquiare, Humboldt explored uncharted territory and produced accurate maps of a hitherto unmapped region. His travels continued and in 1801 he made an extensive study of Cuba and sailed along the Rio Magdalena in Colombia to Bogota. The next year saw him and Bonpland in Ecuador, where he spent six months in Quito and once more demonstrated his enthusiasm for climbing volcanoes. After attempts on a number of lower peaks, during which he discovered something of the effects of altitude on the human body, he decided to climb Chimborazo which, at nearly 21,000ft (6,310m) was considered at the time to be the world's highest mountain. With Bonpland and two other companions he climbed in June 1802 to a height of over 19,000ft (5,610m) before having to turn back. There was no record of anyone ever having climbed higher and the achievement caught the public imagination and won huge acclaim. Humboldt, of course, did not climb mountains simply because they were there. Wherever possible, he carted his instruments with him and used his unique vantage points to collect data and rewrite geographical and geological theory.

After a short stay in Peru (where Humboldt noted the high value placed on the amalgam of bird droppings known as *guano* and took samples that were to draw European attention to the use of this substance as a fertiliser), the two travellers took ship for Guayaquil and Acapulco. As ever, Humboldt lost no opportunity for taking scientific measurements, and on this occasion he measured the temperature of the cold current that was well known to flow along

the Peruvian coast. As a result of this work, the current was named after him.

Most of 1803 was spent in Mexico on research and exploration and the following year Humboldt returned briefly to Cuba before travelling to the United States and spending three weeks as a guest of the scientifically minded President Thomas Jefferson, during which time they shared their scientific observations.

In Europe again

In July 1804, Humboldt and Bonpland left Philadelphia for Europe, bringing thousands of plant specimens with them and hoping desperately that further huge quantities of material they had sent on ahead had arrived safely. Their ship reached Bordeaux at the beginning of August and the reception that awaited them in Paris was such that it is even said to have angered Napoleon because it distracted attention from his coronation.

Humboldt made Paris the base for his academic work – after five years of travelling, the 35 year-old scientist had enough material to keep him writing for the next 30 years, and although he was rapidly appointed a member of the Prussian Academy of Science he did not return permanently to Berlin until 1827. When he did return it was with a sense of disappointment after a visit to London during which he had tried, without success, to win the support of the British East India Company for a visit to the Himalayas and Tibet.

Frustrated in his wish to compare the Himalayas with the Andes, Humboldt formed another scheme, to set up a pan-American institute of science in Mexico, but this too came to nothing. He undertook only one more major expedition and that was of a technical nature when he went, in 1829, to Siberia as one of a delegation of scholars who were studying the geology of the region and assessing its potential as a future mining area.

Despite these disappointments he continued as a prolific worker, giving lectures to vast audiences, regularly re-visiting Paris, and undertaking diplomatic duties on behalf of the Prussian king. As he grew older he devoted great energy to the compilation of a work he called *Kosmos*, a visionary, philosophical and scientific treatise in which he tried to distil contemporary knowledge in a way that would be appreciated by a large, non-specialist audience. He also pleaded for a universal view of mankind, pointing out that all forms of life were inter-related and interdependent. He presented his case with all the conviction of a man who had seen slavery and exploitation at work and found it repellent. The first volume of the *Kosmos* did indeed find a large readership and was an instant bestseller. Another four volumes followed, and the work was unfinished at the time of Humboldt's death a few months short of his 90th birthday in early May 1859.

Below The condor of the Andes, as depicted by Humboldt, who observed the birds high on Mount Chimborazo. One of the world's largest birds, with a wingspan of 10ft (3m) or more, the condor is a type of vulture. It builds nests of a few sticks high on inaccessible ledges of the mountains.

Beautiful Indian World

Von Humboldt's letters reveal his delight in the new world he encountered on arrival in South America.

"Their huts are made of bamboo and are covered with the leaves of the coconut palm. I went into one of them. The mother was sitting with her children, not on chairs, but on pieces of coral thrown up by the tide. They all had coconut shells before them instead of plates and were eating fish out of these."

"What a great number of plants there must be which have not yet been noticed and recorded. And what colours there are here – the birds, the fish, even the crabs which are sky blue and yellow!"

"Up to now we have been running around like mad things and in the first three days were unable to make any clear observations because we tended to drop one thing in order to grasp the next."

"I am returning with 30 packing cases and botanical, astronomical and geological treasures and shall need years to prepare the publication of my great work . . . My heart was heavy at leaving this beautiful Indian world."

quoted in *Alexander von Humboldt 1769–1969*, A. Meyer-Abich

Biographical Notes

1769
Born in Berlin on 14 September.

1792
Joined Prussian Department of Mining.

1799
Began extensive travels in Latin America.

1804
Returned to Europe via North America.

1805–34
At work on 35-volume account of his studies; also gave lectures, and travelled to Russia and Siberia.

1859
Died in Berlin on 6 May.

Naturalists and Plant Hunters

'In Nature's infinite book of secrets
A little I can read.'

WILLIAM SHAKESPEARE
Antony and Cleopatra

In the ancient world and all through the Middle Ages in Europe, travellers' tales of exotic animals and fabulous plants could always command an audience, and the weirder and more wonderful the tale, the better. The Renaissance, which set modern science on its path, stimulated curiosity about the natural world. Wealthy aristocrats formed natural history collections and assembled objects which could divertingly be shown off in a 'cabinet of curiosities' – shells, fossils, animal bones, oddly shaped plants or stones, things that could be labelled 'unicorn's horn' or 'mermaid'.

Already in the 16th century, interest in natural history was a motive for travel or a worthwhile accompaniment to it. Pierre Belon, a pioneering French student of botany, birds and fish, made a scientific journey though Greece, Asia Minor, Egypt, Arabia and Palestine in the 1540s, paid for by a cultivated Roman Catholic cardinal.

In 1629 a ship bringing an Englishman named Thomas Herbert back from Persia – he was the first person to publish a description of the ruins of Persepolis – called at the uninhabited island of Mauritius in the Indian Ocean. Herbert went ashore and made notes on the island's remarkable fauna, including the fat and flightless bird called the dodo, which he said had 'a melancholy visage', as well it might, for it was soon to be extinct.

Lapland and a vulture

It was in the 18th century that the tide of scientific exploration really began to roll. As a young man in 1732, Carl Linnaeus, the great Swedish botanist, made a journey to Lapland, commissioned by the Uppsala Academy of Sciences to investigate the wildlife of a region then almost entirely unknown to the outside world. He set off

Above *The breadfruit: the mutiny on the* Bounty *prevented the first attempt to transplant it to the West Indies.*

Below *Botany Bay in Australia was named by Captain Cook for the excitement it aroused in his accompanying botanists.*

Left *Sir Joseph Banks, President of the Royal Society from 1778 until his death in 1820, sailed to Australia with Captain Cook. A wealthy amateur of natural history, he was the principal driving force behind English scientific exploration in his time.*

boldly with sword and gun, and kept a diary of his 4,000 miles (6,400km) of travel on horseback, by boat and on foot, with notes of his observations and sketches of flowers, birds and insects, and occasionally Lapps. It was hard work and dangerous, and although Linnaeus liked to be admired in his Lapp costume after his return, he took care never to go anywhere as alarming again. He left it to his more adventurous pupils to risk their lives in faraway places.

One of them was Daniel Solander, who became the colleague and employee of Sir Joseph Banks, the uncrowned king of the study of natural history in 18th-century England. Banks,who had ample private means, made his first expedition in 1766, to Newfoundland, returning with a haul of plant and insect specimens. In 1768 he joined Captain Cook's voyage to the Pacific in the *Endeavour*. He took Solander and artists to draw landscape and natural history discoveries.

The *Endeavour* anchored for a week in Botany Bay on the southern coast of Australia, where Banks and Solander were excited to see a kangaroo and enthusiastically gathered plants in such quantities that Cook afterwards christened the place Botany Bay. The expedition was not without its perils. Ashore in South America at one point, Banks and his party were in severe danger of frostbite and had only one small vulture to eat between 10 of them.

Banks and Solander later made an expedition to Iceland, and in 1778 Banks became President of the Royal Society. He remained its autocrat until his death in 1820, when his books and collections went to the British museum.

Breadfruit and boiled sea-cow

Cook's second Pacific voyage was accompanied by an officer who became known in the Royal Navy as 'Breadfruit Bligh'. The breadfruit was discovered in Tahiti and in 1787, at Banks's suggestion, Bligh was sent to the South Seas in command of HMS *Bounty* to collect plants to take to the West Indies, where they would be acclimatised to provide nourishing food for the slaves on the plantations. Unforeseen events interfered with this mission, but in 1791 Bligh was sent to the Society Islands, again on the same errand. This time he delivered the plants safely, but the experiment failed. The West Indians did not like breadfruit.

Banks had a finger in many pies, including the botanic gardens developed by the royal family at the palace of Kew, outside London. At his suggestion, in the 1770s Kew sent its first plant-hunter abroad. He was Francis Masson, a young Scots gardener who went dutifully off to the Cape of Good Hope to collect plants and bulbs. He sent back 60 or more mesembryanthemums, several kinds of arctotis and 40 stapelias (described as 'cactus-like plants with an indecorous smell').

Masson later made another botanical trip to the Cape and Linnaeus named the genus Massonia after him. In France, meanwhile, Louis XV had appointed Philibert de Commerson his Royal Botanist and packed him off with Louis Antoine de Bougainville in the 1760s to search the Pacific for exotic flowers.

The ends of the earth exerted an irresistible attraction on naturalists in eager quest of species unknown to science. A German doctor, Georg Wilhelm Steller, attached himself as botanist to Vitus Bering's second Siberian expedition in 1741. Bossily interested in everything, he collected plants and made accurate observations of Arctic foxes, seals and sealions. He liked to live not only off the country, but in it, digging himself burrows, eating whatever was offered and trying out peculiar recipes. He left his name to Steller's eider duck and Steller's sea-cow, a species of giant manatee that was wiped out by sealers and whalers within 30 years.

Below *The dolorous dodo, depicted in Le Clerc and Buffon's* Natural History *in 1828. Observed in Mauritius in the 16th and 17th centuries, it was extinct by 1681. This flightless bird was unable to survive the arrival of human beings and pigs on the island.*

***Above** A giant tortoise on the Galápagos Islands rumbles across its territory like an animated tank. The islands lie in the Pacific, some 600 miles (965km) west of Ecuador, and their name is the Spanish word for tortoise* (galápago). *Darwin visited them in 1835.*

The American Wild

In North America, one of the objects of the Lewis and Clark expedition to the Pacific in 1804 was the gathering of scientific information. Meriwether Lewis and William Clark were both keen naturalists and their journey introduced to science the grizzly bear, the coyote, the mountain goat, the jackrabbit and the prairie dog.

Another pioneering naturalist was the American artist John James Audubon, who wandered down the Ohio and the Mississippi and through the South, shooting birds for specimens and drawing them in their native habitats. His great work, *The Birds of America*, began appearing in 1827. He later travelled up the Missouri River for his book on North American quadrupeds and was sickened by the carnage being wrought by hunters among the buffalo herds.

David Douglas, a youthful gardener at the Glasgow Botanic Garden, arrived in the United States in 1822 on a mission to collect specimens of American fruit trees for the Royal Horticultural Society in England. The following year he was sent to the Pacific Northwest by way of Cape Horn, and made a collection of Brazilian orchids on the way. He climbed Rocky Mountain peaks and crossed Canada to Hudson Bay, indefatigably gathering specimens in defiance of hostile or astonished Indians, irritable grizzly bears, biting ants, avalanches and tumbles off precipices. He went back to the West again in 1829 and eventually to Hawaii, where he was gored to death by a bull in 1834 while still only in his thirties. He discovered the ribes, or flowering currant, which is now a familiar garden plant, and the Douglas fir is named after him.

***Below** Charles Darwin in his old age. The theory of evolution relied heavily on his observations during the cruise of HMS* Beagle *in the 1830s. The entire first printing of* The Origin of Species *sold out on the day it came out in 1859 and the book aroused a storm of controversy.*

South American Wonders

South America was another magnet to naturalists urgent to discover, examine and categorise its teeming and remarkable wildlife. The brilliant Baron von Humboldt, said to be the second most famous European of his day (the most famous of all being Napoleon Bonaparte), gathered plants and information in heroic quantities among the Andes peaks and in northern Amazonia in the opening years of the 19th century. A figure to be yet more famous appeared on the scene in 1831, when HMS *Beagle*, a brig of 235 tons (239 tonnes), left Plymouth Sound on a five-year surveying voyage round the world for the British Admiralty. On board was a seasick 22-year-old naturalist named Charles Darwin.

It had been agreed that Darwin would be given plenty of time for exploring ashore as the ship made its way round the South American coasts. He had a rapturous time collecting fossils, geological specimens and butterflies and shooting birds and lizards, though he did not much enjoy meeting the inhabitants of Tierra del Fuego, who apparently used to cook and eat some of their women to get through the winter. When asked why they did not eat their dogs instead, they pointed out that dogs were useful for catching otters. On the Galápagos Islands, Darwin admired the giant tortoises and the cactus-eating lizards and diligently collected new species of birds, fish, shells, flowering plants and beetles.

***Below** One of the 'indecorous' stapelias that Francis Masson first sent back to Kew Gardens in the 18th century.*

The voyage bore epoch-making fruit years afterwards in the theory of evolution and *The Origin of Species*, published in 1859. The same conclusions had been reached independently by Alfred Russell Wallace, a schoolmaster who became passionately addicted to beetles. He took up a new career as a professional collector for museums with his friend, the entomologist and butterfly expert Henry Walker Bates, afterwards celebrated for his work on mimicry in the insect world. The two set off to South America in 1848 and travelled far up the Amazon, enthralled by the luxuriance and colour of life in the jungle. Bates would eventually harvest 14,000 species of insects, of which more than half were previously unknown to science.

Natural history societies, museums, botanic gardens and enterprising nurserymen were all hungry for specimens. Wallace and Bates were soon joined by an intrepid Yorkshire botanist named Richard Spruce, who had begun by collecting mosses in Yorkshire and the Pyrenees. He was sent to the Amazon to hunt for plants by a group of influential English botanists and spent 15 years in South America, travelling 10,000 miles (16,000km) by canoe, often in danger, diligently collecting and dispatching mosses, lichens, ferns and flowering plants: more than 30,000 specimens all told, which found their way to the leading European collections. Among other achievements, he discovered 200 new species of fungi and recorded the vocabularies of 21 Indian peoples. He finally returned to England, with his health in tatters, to spend the last 27 years of his life working on his collections, most of the time while lying down. He died in 1893.

By land and sea

Plant and insect collectors gathered their prey in thousands, but the discoveries that aroused greater public excitement were of previously unknown animals. By far the most exciting was the gorilla, long rumoured in travellers' tales, but not apparently seen face to face by any white man before Paul de Chaillu, an American explorer who returned from Africa in 1859 with hair-raisingly overheated and wildly inaccurate accounts of the beast. 'He stood about a dozen yards from us,' he wrote, 'and was a sight I think I shall never forget. Nearly six feet high, with immense body, huge chest, and great muscular arms, with fiercely glaring large deep grey eyes and a hellish expression of face, which seemed to me like some nightmare vision; thus stood before us this king of the African forest.'

Du Chaillu fed popular appetites with all sorts of nonsense about gorillas – that they lurked in trees to strangle passing Africans and carried off women – and he was the first European known to have killed one.

Less sensationalism attended the discovery of the white rhino in Africa by W.J. Burchell or of Thomson's gazelle by an amiable Scotsman, Joseph Thomson, who used to endear himself to the locals by taking his false teeth out and putting them back in again. In 1865 a French missionary, Pére Armand David, daringly scaled the wall of an imperial hunting park outside Peking to see a herd of the deer that were subsequently named after him. In 1900 the elusive okapi, reported to H. M. Stanley by Congo pygmies years before, was seen by Sir Harry Johnston, a colonial administrator in Uganda, to the glee of zoologists.

The day of the all-round amateur naturalist seemed virtually over by this time, with the accumulation of knowledge, the growth of specialisation and the development of professional techniques. The discovery of new species has proceeded steadily all through the 20th century, however, as more and more of the natural world has been revealed to the scientific eye. The development of diving equipment and the submarine opened up a vast undersea preserve to explorers like the American biologist William Beebe, who in 1930 descended 3,000ft (900m) deep in a steel bathysphere off Bermuda to observe the denizens of the deep, or more recently the Frenchman Jacques Cousteau, whose underwater cameras displayed a new realm of wonders to television audiences all over the world. Photographic and television techniques have today brought the world's wildlife into the world's living-room.

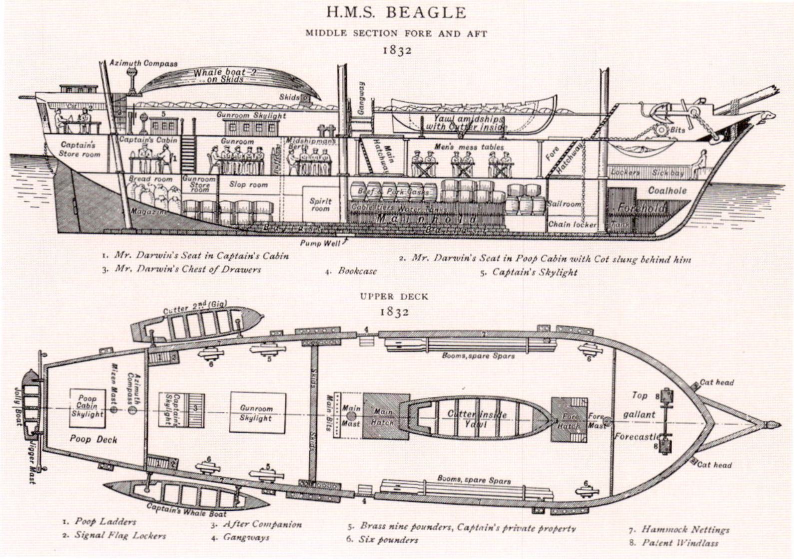

Above *Diagram of HMS* Beagle, *on which Darwin sailed as the expedition's official naturalist. The ship surveyed the south American coast and went on to visit the Galápagos Islands, Tahiti, New Zealand, Australia, Tasmania, the Maldives and Mauritius.*

Below *A 19th-century illustration of 'Gorillas at home'. The false impression of the 'king of the African forest' given the Western public by Paul de Chaillu, the first white man to see one, lasted for years and influenced films like* King Kong.

LEWIS AND CLARK

The Lewis and Clark expedition paved the way for the American conquest of the West

'I set out at 4 oClock P.M., in the presence of many of the neighbouring inhabitents, and proceeded on under a jentle brease up the Missouri . . .' Thus in pouring rain and the erratic spelling of William Clark's diary for 14 May 1804 began one of the great journeys of history. In the next 2½ years the Lewis and Clark expedition would travel 8,000 miles (12,870km) across North America through territory largely unexplored by whites: from St Louis up the Missouri River, through the Rocky Mountains and by canoe down the Columbia River to the wide Pacific, and then back to St Louis again. It was the journey that provided the final pages of the saga begun with Columbus's discovery of the New World 300 years earlier, the story of the attempt to reach the East by travelling west.

The looming Rockies

During the 18th century, as the huge region west of the Great Lakes and the Appalachian Mountains was increasingly opened up by trappers, traders and adventurers from Canada and the eastern seaboard, the question of what lay beyond the Mississippi was for long an enticing mystery. Only in the second half of the century did it become clear that a massive obstacle lay across the westward path, the barrier of the Rocky Mountains, stretching for 3,000 miles (4,800km) from Canada down to Mexico, 400 miles (650km) across at the widest point and rising to heights of 14,000ft (4,000m) (the highest point is Mount Elbert in Colorado at 14,433ft (4,399m)). At this stage, however, no one knew how big an obstacle it was and there were still strong hopes of finding a swift passage by river to the Pacific.

The first European to cross the barrier, north of Mexico, and travel all the way to the Pacific was a Scotsman named Alexander Mackenzie. Born in the Outer Hebrides, at Stornoway on the Isle of Lewis, he emigrated to Montreal and went to work for the North West Company, a leading and aggressive concern in the fur trade. In 1789 Mackenzie set out from a trading post at Lake Athabasca, in rich beaver-pelt country in what

***Below** Starting from St Louis in May 1804, the expedition wintered with the Mandan Indians in what is now North Dakota before setting out again to cross the rockies, finally reaching the Pacific in November, 1805.*

Left *Thomas Jefferson, third President of the United States, sent Lewis and Clark to find a swift route across the continent to the Pacific. Meriwether Lewis, a fellow Virginian, was Jefferson's secretary and confidant.*

is now the Canadian province of Alberta, to follow the river, afterwards named for him, to the western ocean. To his great chagrin, it took him to the Arctic Ocean instead.

Nothing daunted, in 1792 Mackenzie led a party of French Canadians and Indians on a second expedition, along the Peace River, across the Rockies and to the Fraser. They found the raging waters of the Fraser impossible to negotiate by canoe, so they went on by the Blackwater instead and made a long traverse overland to reach the Pacific coast at Bella Coola on a deep inlet from Queen Charlotte Sound in modern British Columbia. They arrived there on 22 July 1793 and Mackenzie painted his name and the date in bright red letters on a rock.

Mackenzie was knighted in 1802 and afterwards retired to Scotland, where he spent his last years until his death in 1820. Lewis and Clark took with them a copy of his book about his travels.

Shooting a Grizzly

One Sunday morning in May on the outward journey Clark shot and killed a gigantic grizzly bear, an animal then unknown to science. Lewis wrote in his diary.

"It was a most tremendous looking animal, and extreemely hard to kill notwithstanding he had five balls through his lungs and five others in various parts he swam more than half the distance across the river to a sandbar, & it was at least twenty minutes before he died; he did not attempt to attack, but fled and made the most tremendous roaring from the moment he was shot. We had no means of weighing this monster; Capt. Clark thought he would weigh 500 lbs. for my own part I think the estimate too small by 100lbs. he measured 8 Feet 7½ Inches from the nose to the extremety of the hind feet, 5 F. 10½ Ins. arround the breast, I F. 11 I. arround the middle of the arm, & 3 F. 11 I. around the neck; his tallons which were five in number on each foot were 4 3/8 Inches in length. he was in good order, we therefore divided him among the party and made them boil the oil and put it in a cask for future uce; the oil is as hard as hogs lard when cool, much more so than that of the black bear. this bear differs from the common black bear in several respects; its tallons are much longer and more blont, it's tale shorter, it's hair which is of a redish or bey brown, is longer thicker and finer than that of the black bear; his liver lungs and heart are much larger even in proportion with his size; the heart particularly was as large as that of a large Ox. his maw was also ten times the size of black bear, and was filled with flesh and fish."

from *The Journals of Lewis and Clark* (edited by Bernard de Voto)

Western promise

Mackenzie's success in reaching the Pacific was seen in America at the time as the possible harbinger of a shorter trade route to the Far East. It would be considerably shorter than the route to China round Cape Horn that enterprising Yankee skippers had already established. It also awoke the United States government to the disagreeable possibility of British fur-traders and British imperialism taking over the whole area beyond the Mississippi.

In 1801 Thomas Jefferson became President of the United States. Jefferson believed that the West held America's destiny. He also wanted to discover a route through the Rocky Mountains to the Pacific that would clear the way for direct trade with the East and so liberate the New World

Above left *Red-haired and outgoing, William Clark was another Virginian. He fought Indians on the frontier in his youth and gained a deep respect for them, which they returned. He spent the last years of his life at St Louis in charge of Indian affairs*

Above right *Kansas City, seen across the Missouri River. This was all open country when Lewis and Clark passed by in 1804.*

from economic dependence on the Old World of Europe. He persuaded Congress to grant money for an expedition, though in diplomatic deference to the Spanish government, which still had a claim to ownership of the territory to be explored, it was disguised as a journey for purely scientific purposes. In command was Captain Meriwether Lewis of the US Army, who was President Jefferson's secretary. Associated with him was Lieutenant William Clark.

The two leaders

Meriwether Lewis and William Clark, both in their early thirties when the expedition set off, were Virginians of good family. Neither of them was particularly well educated, and certain neither of them could spell, but correct spelling was not required for the task. In the qualities that mattered, they were formidably well equipped. They were experienced soldiers and outdoorsmen, accustomed to organise and command, resourceful and determined, intelligently interested in the world about them. They both had a remarkable gift for finding their way in unknown and difficult country, indeed Clark has been called a pathfinder of genius. Both men got on well with Indians. They also got on well with each other, and the expedition proceeded in a harmony between the leaders that was extremely rare in the annals of exploration. Lewis was the more thoughtful and introverted of the two, the red-haired Clark was more dashing, quick-thinking and adventurous.

Lewis was born in 1774. Named after his mother, Lucy Meriwether, he came from one of the leading families of Virginia and he grew up as the neighbour of Thomas Jefferson. He was brought up to ride and hunt, and he showed an early interest in wildlife and the natural world. There is a nice story that as a boy, when he was taught that the earth turns on its axis, he jumped high in the air and was irritated to come down on the same spot. He demanded to know why and it had to be explained to him that he moved with the turning earth.

Lewis joined the army when he was 20 and spent time at posts in Tennessee and Michigan, where he learned Indian languages and customs. As soon as Jefferson became President, Lewis joined him as his secretary and during the next two years at the White House in Washington, Jefferson's long-contemplated plan for a transcontinental expedition to the Pacific was frequently discussed. When Jefferson put him in command, Lewis asked for Clark, whom he knew from the army, as his right-hand man.

Clark was four years older. Brought up on plantations in Virginia and Georgia, he too grew up to know horses and hunting and the ways of wild animals and birds. He also showed a talent for drawing and making maps. When he was 14, his family moved to Kentucky and, as a teenager and later in the army, which he joined at 21, Clark was involved in much Indian fighting on what was then the frontier. He had a profound respect for Indians and their ways, and a straightforwardness in dealing with them, which earned him their liking and trust.

To the Mandans

In the winter of 1803–4 Lewis and Clark assembled their 'Corps of Discovery', some 40 to 45 strong, on the Mississippi-Missouri opposite St Louis, where they trained their men. The expedition was carefully and skilfully prepared, so much so that in the course of it only one member of the party was killed. The men included soldiers, young bloods from Kentucky, French Canadian watermen and Clark's black servant, York. Lewis's Newfoundland dog, Seaman, also made the trip. Both leaders kept diaries, and so did other members of the expedition.

Setting off up river in May, they travelled in three boats, a keel-boat 55ft (16.75m) long and

Below *Meriwether Lewis on 13 June 1805 at the Great Falls of the Missouri River, which he described as 'the grandest sight I ever beheld', where the river drops 400ft (120m) over five cataracts. This area had only just become part of the United States, under the Louisiana Purchase of 1803, and Lewis and Clark were the first whitemen to explore the Missouri all the way to its source in the Rocky Mountains.*

drawing 3ft (90cm) of water, propelled by oars and a sail, and two small open sailing boats called pirogues. Horses accompanied the expedition along the bank. Clark generally commanded the boats,while Lewis spent much time roaming the shore, making notes on the terrain and the flora and fauna.

They moved slowly northwest up the Missouri, past the sites of present-day Kansas City and Sioux City. It was fiercely hot and everyone complained about the mosquitoes and ticks. Discipline was implanted in these early stages by harsh floggings. In September they saw their first prairie dogs, which they called 'barking squirrels', and vast herds of buffalo grazed the prairie. Trouble was feared with the Sioux, but by keeping their nerve and with a mixture of firmness and bluff the expedition got through without fighting.

In October they came to the Mandan villages on the upper Missouri, near modern Stanton, North Dakota. The Indians were friendly and the expedition settled in here to see out a freezing winter, building cabins and a fort and dugout canoes to replace the keel-boat, which was too big to go any further upstream. Much information was gained from the Indians about the country further west, where the expedition would need to obtain horses from the Shoshoni, or Snake Indians, and the party had the good fortune to acquire a young Shoshoni woman as guide. Her name was Sacajawea and she had been carried off from her own people by a hostile Indian raiding party and sold to a French Canadian trader named Toussaint Charbonneau. He came along too, and so did their baby son, who was not quite two months old when the journey was resumed. Sacajawea carried him strapped to her back.

To the Pacific

The party set off again as soon as the weather allowed, on 7 April 1805, in six canoes and the two pirogues. 'This little fleet,' Lewis wrote in his diary, 'altho' not quite so rispectable as those of Columbus or Capt. Cook, were still viewed by us with as much pleasure as those deservedly famous adventurers ever beheld theirs; and I dare say with quite as much anxiety for their safety and preservation, we were now about to penetrate a country at least two thousand miles in width, on which the foot of civilized man had never trodden; the good or evil it had in store for us was for experiment yet to determine, and these little vessells contained every article by which we were to expect to subsist or defend ourselves.'

Moving west along the river, the party passed the confluence with the Yellowstone and shot and killed their first grizzly bear. One of the pirogues was nearly sunk by a sudden squall. This would have drowned Charbonneau, who could not swim, and all their papers, instruments and medical supplies would have been lost. Lewis wrote that he could not recall the incident without 'the utmost trepidation and horror'.

It was still fiercely cold at night. They began to see mountain ranges, forerunners of the Rockies, and in June they came to the Great Falls of the Missouri. Here a portage was necessary. They made wheels and crude carts and spent three weeks strenuously hauling the boats and baggage across land.

Taking to the river again, they came at last to the Big Belt Mountains, the first rampart of the Rockies, and pushed on southwards to Three Forks, where three streams join to form the Missouri. Here they turned west again, along the north fork, which they named the Jefferson River after the President. It was hard work dragging the canoes over the shoals in suffocating heat, while far above them the mountaintops were white with snow. The men were suffering from strained backs, bruises and boils, and Clark was constipated for days until admitting it to Lewis, who dosed him with pills. They were worried at meeting no Indians, but Sacajawea assured them they were on the right track.

Crossing the heart of the Rockies through the Lemhi Pass, they turned northwards below the 10,000ft (3,000m) peaks of the Bitterroot Mountains. They could take the boats no further, so they unloaded them and sank them in a pool, and went on foot. At last they began to see Indians, the Shoshoni, who were suspicious, kept well away and would not respond to signs. Lewis in desperation was reduced to trying to tie his handkerchief round the neck of one of the Indian dogs with some trinkets in it, but the dog would not let him catch it.

Eventually they managed to corner an elderly Indian woman and a young girl, who took them to the Shoshoni camp. The Indian chief and his warriors were friendly. Sacajawea's brother was among them, there was a touching reunion and the Shoshoni sold the party the horses it badly needed as pack animals, and for food if necessary.

Spending some weeks with the Shoshoni and finding out everything they could about the country ahead, the expedition set out again at the end of August down the Bitterroot Valley. They met a party of Flathead Indians, whose language sounded so strange to them that some of the men thought these must be the Welsh-speaking Indians of legendary fame.

Turning southwest through the Lolo Pass, the party emerged from the Rockies with profound relief into hilly, thickly-wooded country, where they made friends with the Nez Percé Indians. Many of the men were now suffering badly from dysentery, but they made themselves dugout canoes, left their horses with the Indians and took to the water again on the Clearwater River, which led them to the canyons and rapids of the Snake. The Nez Percé kept them company, riding or walking along the bank.

In mid-October the Snake brought the explorers to the mighty Columbia River, here more than 300 miles from the Pacific. They had nothing but kindness from the Indians along the way, though they grew heartily sick of eating salmon and bartered for dogs for a change when they could. Ferocious rapids swept them through the Cascade Mountains and they went on past the site of modern Portland, Oregon, until on 15 November, in pouring rain, after a journey of 4,000 miles (6,435km), they came safely to the mouth of the river and the thundering rollers of the Pacific. 'Great joy in camp,' Clark recorded, 'we are in view of the Ocian, the great Pacific Ocian which we have been so long anxious to see.'

Manifest destiny

The expedition endured a dismal, rain-drenched winter at the stockaded wooden fort they built, Fort Clatsop (a replica stands on the site today). The leaders wrote up their notes and tried to keep the men occupied and out of mischief, boiling

***Above** The way west: covered wagons in the shadow of the towering Rockies, in this Currier & Ives print. Lewis and Clark, and other pioneering expeditions, opened the door for mass emigration to the West along the Oregon Trail, which ran from Independence, Missouri, across the Great Plains to cross the Rockies by South Pass in Wyoming.*

Christmas at Clatsop

Clark's account of Christmas Day, 1805:

"At day light this morning we were awoke by the discharge of the fire arms of all our party & a Selute, Shouts and a Song which the whole party joined in under our windows, after which they retired to their rooms, were chearfull all the morning, after brackfast we divided our Tobacco . . . one half of which we gave to the men of the party who used tobacco, and to those who do not use it we make a present of a handkerchief. The Indians leave us in the evening, all the party snugly fixed in their huts. I recved a present of Capt. L. of a fleece hosrie Shirt Draws and Socks, a pr. Mockersons of Whitehouse a Small Indian basket of Gutherich, two Dozen white weazils tails of the Indian woman [Sacawajea], & some black root of the Indians before their departure . . . The day proved Showery wet and disagreeable.

We would have Spent this day the nativity of Christ in feasting, had we any thing either to raise our Sperits or even gratify our appetites, our Dinner conisted of pore Elk, so much spoiled that we eate it thro' mear necessity, Some Spoiled pounded fish and a few roots."

from *The Journals of Lewis and Clark* (edited by Bernard de Voto)

sea water in kettles to make salt, among other activities. They expected to be picked up and taken home by ship, but no ship appeared and they decided to return by land.

They left on 23 March 1806, with the rain still pouring down, and retraced their steps. They followed much the same route as on the way west, though Clark took the opportunity to explore the Yellowstone River. John Colter, who went off to trap beaver at this stage, was the first white man to see the geysers and boiling mud pools for which the Yellowstone National Park is now famous. When he brought the tale of them back to St Louis, no one would believe him. Meanwhile, Lewis had experienced the only violent brush with Indians of the entire expedition, which left two Blackfoot braves dead and the explorers in flight.

After a comparatively uneventful journey of six months, the party arrived back at St Louis at mid-day on 23 September, joyfully firing off their guns and receiving a hero's welcome from their countrymen, who had given them up for lost.

The two leaders reported to Washington. Lewis was sent back to St Louis as governor, but had only a tragically short time left to live. In 1809 he died in mysterious circumstances near Nashville, Tennessee. Jefferson, who knew he was the victim of severe bouts of depression, believed he had committed suicide. His family believed he was murdered. He was 35 years old.

Clark was also sent to St Louis, in charge of Indian affairs. Sacajawea, Charbonneau and their son lived there for a while as his protegés, but then returned to the West. Sacajawea was reported to have died of a fever in 1812, aged about 25, at Fort Manuel on the Missouri. Clark lived on at St Louis, doing his best to secure decent treatment for the Indians, until his death in 1838.

Lewis and Clark, like Columbus, failed to find a commercial route to the Far East, but in every other respect their expedition was a triumphant success. It brought back a mass of geographical, anthropological and scientific information and it paved the way for the conquest of the West. Fur-trappers and traders, the 'mountain men', moved in to hunt beaver and explore the Rockies. Possession of the West became the 'manifest destiny' of the United States and the expedition's route became the Oregon Trail, a major immigrant route to the West and the Northwest in the 1840s. A powerful trend in American opinion ever afterwards has looked 'inland and toward the Western sea', as Walt Whitman wrote, regarding America as a separate, independent nation rather than as part of an Atlantic community shared with the Old World.

Below *A geyser in the Yellowstone National Park. The first white man known to have seen the natural wonders of this region was John Colter of the Lewis and Clark party.*

Biographical Notes

1770
William Clark born (1 August).

1774
Meriwether Lewis born (18 August).

1801
Lewis became secretary to President Jefferson.

1803
Lewis and Clark appointed to lead the expedition to the Pacific.

1804
The expedition set off from St Louis (14 May).

1805
The expedition reached the Pacific (15 November).

1806
The return to St Louis (23 September).

1809
Death of Lewis (11 October).

1838
Death of Clark (1 September).

SIR JOHN FRANKLIN

An experienced Arctic explorer, Sir John Franklin perished in the race to find the Northwest Passage

The Royal Navy has always been noted for its hydrographers – officers trained for war but invaluable in peace for their skills in seamanship, navigation and chartwork. John Franklin was just such an officer; a seaman who developed a flair for overland travel and became the most celebrated Arctic explorer of his day.

Midshipman Franklin

Born in a quiet Lincolnshire village, Franklin joined the Royal Navy at the age of 14. For the navy it was a time of expansion and action, and the young officer was quickly involved in both. He served as a midshipman through the Napoleonic Wars, seeing action under Lord Nelson at Copenhagen (1801) and Trafalgar (1805). Between bouts of warfare he sailed on a more peaceable mission with his cousin, Matthew Flinders, a navigator who commanded HMS *Investigator*, a survey sloop. Franklin served with Flinders from July 1801 to June 1803, learning navigation, chartwork and seamanship from a master in the craft, and making the first circumnavigation of Australia.

Homeward bound as passengers in a smaller ship, the cousins were shipwrecked on the Great Barrier Reef. While Flinders sailed off in a cutter to secure relief, Franklin remained on the reef with orders to build two boats from the wreckage – an educational experience for a midshipman still in his mid-teens. The castaways were rescued and John Franklin resumed to war. His last naval action was fought at New Orleans (1814); thereafter he concentrated on the navigation and charting that would occupy him for the rest of his naval career.

First Arctic voyage

From 1744 the British Board of Admiralty had offered substantial prize money to the captain and crew of whichever ship should first discover the Northwest Passage, and open up the Arctic sea-route to China. Franklin was one of many officers who responded to the challenge. His first command took him to the Arctic, on orders that were the dream of every young officer of the time. In 1818 the 31-year-old lieutenant was given command of the 246-ton (250 tonne) brig, HMS *Trent*. He was to accompany a slightly larger ship, HMS *Dorothea*, under the overall command of Captain David Buchan, a more senior and experienced officer. Reports from whalers had suggested that this would be a favourable year for penetrating far northward into the ice. Buchan's orders were to explore northern seas between Greenland and Spitsbergen and head as far as the ice would allow towards the North Pole. The ships would then continue across the Arctic basin to Bering Strait, and if possible return via the Northwest Passage.

The Navy took its dream seriously; the two ships were provided with a full research pro-

Left *'He was wrecked on a coral reef off the Australian coast, and with ninety-four persons spent nearly two months on a sandbank only a few feet above the sea-level.' This bracing episode, pictured here in an account of Franklin's adventures, occurred when he was still only in his teens.*

gramme and equipped with all the best modern navigation and scientific instruments. *Dorothea* and *Trent* left the Thames in April 1818 and by early July were sailing bravely into the pack-ice just north of the Spitsbergen archipelago. There the dream ended; though sturdy, the tiny ships were less than a match for the heavy pack-ice, which, stirred by winds and currents, shifted morosely and closed menacingly about them. Within a few days both *Dorothea* and *Trent* had suffered serious damage.

Buchan, an experienced ice-master who had learned his skills in Labrador, knew when to retreat. In late July, after several narrow escapes, he withdrew the two ships with difficulty, emerging into rough seas that tested them to the full. Eventually they returned safely to warmer latitudes. Though unsuccessful in penetrating to the polar ocean, this brief cruise proved invaluable to Franklin, providing a baptism in polar navigation and first-hand experience of managing both ship and crew in polar waters.

First land expedition

With Napoleon safely in exile on St Helena the Royal Navy suffered severe cuts. However, Franklin's navigating skills and polar experience made him readily employable. His next appointment, taken up in 1819, was at first glance a curious one. It involved leading a survey expedition overland in northeastern Canada, though with a maritime purpose. Franklin's instructions informed him that 'the main object of the Expedition was that of determining the latitudes and longitudes of the Northern Coast of North America, and the trending of that Coast from the

Below *The search for the Northwest Passage and the Arctic route to the Far East was the main driving force of Franklin's career and eventually cost him his life.*

Above *Franklin was 61 when he died on 11 June 1847. A search party sent out 10 years later by Lady Franklin found the news of his death written on an official message-pad in a cairn on King William Island. The scene is shown here, below the explorer's portrait.*

Mouth of the Copper-Mine River to the eastern extremity of that Continent'. At the same time a ship commanded by Lt Edward Parry, another Arctic veteran, would attempt to chart the coast from the sea. It was left to Franklin to decide whether to head westward from Hudson Bay or make his way southward across country to the Coppermine River and east along the coast from its mouth. He chose the latter option, and took almost four years to accomplish it.

His journey involved traversing and mapping a network of waterways before the coast was reached. Routes to be followed linked trading posts and small settlements in a wilderness of forest and tundra known only to native trappers and the thinly scattered employees of the fur-trading companies. The Hudson's Bay Company was to provide clothing, ammunition, food and guides.

Franklin's party consisted of John Richardson, a naval surgeon and naturalist, midshipmen Robert Hood and George Hack, seaman John Hepburn, and four experienced boatmen whom Franklin recruited in the Orkney Islands. The officers, not unusually for their time, were a talented group; Richardson was a geographer, geologist, naturalist and anthropologist, and Hood and Back were accomplished artists. Franklin had the enquiring mind of a scientist and an artist's eye, and wrote clear English. Hepburn, the rating of the party, was a good expedition man; at the end Franklin paid tribute to his 'fidelity, exertion, and uniform good conduct in the most trying situations, to which several of the party came to owe their lives'.

An Artist's Eye

On Franklin's first overland expedition to survey northeast Canada, he found the time to record his experiences in a diary.

"Steel River presents much beautiful scenery: it winds through a narrow but well-wooded valley, which at every turn disclosed to us an agreeable variety of prospects, rendered more picturesque by the effect of the season on the foliage, now ready to drop from the trees. The light yellow of the fading poplars formed a fine contrast with the dark evergreen of the spruce, whilst the willows, of an intermediate hue, served to shade the two principal masses of colour into each other. The scene was occasionally enlivened by the bright purple tints of the dogwood, bleached with the browner shades of the dwarf birch, and frequently intermixed with the gay yellow flowers of the shrubby cinquefoil. With all these charms, the scene appeared desolate from the want of the human species. The silence was so great, that even the twittering of the whiskey-johneesh, or cinereous crow, caused us to start. Our voyage to-day was sixteen miles on a S. W. course."

from *Narrative of a Journey to the Shores of the Polar Sea in the Years 1812–22*, John Franklin

They sailed as passengers to Hudson Bay, landing in August at York Factory, an important Company post at the mouth of Hayes River. From there the party set off in heavy 40ft-long (12m) canoes, which they rowed, poled, hauled or occasionally sailed along the shallow rivers. Streams broken by rapids and waterfalls made the going hard; wide lakes provided easier sailing. On good days the party travelled 30 to 40 miles (48–65km), on bad days only one or two.

Hauling the great canoes full of stores and camping gear proved tough work. Autumnal cold bit hard; ice formed on the lakes and streams, casing the oars and making travel impossible. In October the party reached Cumberland House, a log-built trading post on the Saskatchewan River.

There Franklin had been promised guides who would help them on the next leg of their journey north. However, the local Indians were unwilling to travel, and Franklin was told that the nearest guides would probably be found at Fort Chipewyan, at the junction of Lake Athabasca and Slave River some 900 miles further on. He decided not to wait. In the depths of the Arctic winter Franklin, Back and Hepburn, accompanied only by two small dog-drawn sledges with their drivers, journeyed through the snow-bound forest of Fort Chipewyan in just two months.

This was an astonishing achievement. Their clothes, a makeshift combination of European and Indian dress, included leather boots and breeches, a blanket or leather overcoat and fur cap. On their feet they wore clumsy snowshoes of long wooden slats strung together with leather thongs. They cooked over open fires and slept in the snow under brushwood and blanket tents. For food they had pemmican made from fat and dried meat, boiled up in melted snow. Temperatures seldom rose above freezing point; there was little warmth in the sun, which remained low in the sky, often obscured by cloud and mist.

Joined by the rest of his party Franklin forged onward. Living in part off what they could catch, sometimes the men fed well, at other times they came close to starvation. Franklin's journals are filled with detailed accounts of everything he saw; Indians, white folk, plant life, beavers and their dams, buffalo, fishes, birds – all fell before his interested gaze, to be immortalised in his official account of the journey. The expedition pressed on to Fort Providence and Fort Enterprise, where they spent much of the winter of 1820 to 1821.

From there they travelled widely, exploring the hinterland of the fort. Food was scarce and temperatures fell well below 5°F (−40°C), but the men, including Indian and Canadian guides, remained cheerful and busy. When summer came round they moved northward, crossing Point Lake and eventually reaching the turbulent Coppermine River. A hair-raising journey by canoe brought them to the mouth of the Coppermine and the coast, the shore of Coronation Gulf, a wide channel between the mainland and Victoria Island. Franklin explored the Gulf and the complex of bays and islands that lined it.

The land around was bare, inhospitable tundra and game was scarce; often there was hunger in the camp. Franklin had hoped to explore far to the east, possibly to the shore of Hudson Bay, but the men were weak and the brief summer was ending. In late August he headed south-southwest towards Fort Enterprise, where he expected the Company to have provided over-wintering stores. The journey had become a nightmare trek by semi-starved men across bare tundra. The tumbling, northward-flowing rivers that had previously helped them now barred their path; their rations were exhausted and the hunters could find little game. They kept alive on lichens called *tripe de roche*, which they boiled up with scraps of leather from their boots and equipment.

An advance party arrived exhausted at Fort Enterprise to find it empty of men or food.

Left *'And lo! at the door of the fort stood the friendly Indians he had sent with ample succour.' Another illustration from a 19th-century account of Franklin's exploits. It was Indian kindness that saved him and his men from starvation at Fort Enterprise.*

Franklin wrote:

'There was no deposit of provision, no trace of the Indians, no letter from Mr Wentzel [of the Hudson's Bay Company] to point out where the Indians might be found. It would be impossible for me to describe our sensations after entering this miserable abode, and discovering how we had been neglected: the whole party shed tears, not so much for our own fate, as for that of our friends in the rear, whose lives depended entirely on our sending immediate relief from this place.'

Worse was to follow. A search party sent out to seek local Indians returned empty-handed and depleted. Hood was dead, shot by Michel, one of the Indians, who had in turn been executed by Richardson; two others had died or possibly been killed earlier by Michel. There were more deaths from starvation and exhaustion before Back, early in November, succeeded in reaching an Indian camp and securing supplies of meat.

From December their fortunes improved. More Indians approached with food and warm clothing, restoring the strength of the survivors and allowing them to last out the winter. After a long recuperation at Moosedeer Island they made their way back to York Factory and home.

Franklin's account of his expedition, published in 1823, caught the public imagination. He was promoted to captain and appointed Fellow of the Royal Society for the excellence of his scientific reports. In the same year he married Eleanor Porden and, together with Edward Parry, began planning a continuation of his northern survey.

Second overland expedition

Franklin's second Canadian expedition was better financed and planned, and in consequence relatively uneventful. In spring 1825,

18th-Century Arctic Adventure

By the late 18th century, Europeans had explored many thousands of square miles of Arctic territory previously known only to natives. Some sought only adventure; a few were prospecting for minerals, timber or whatever else could be wrung from a forbidding land. The most valued product of the north was fur, of sables, martens, foxes, muskoxen and bears, for example, for which insatiable markets had developed. Many who explored northern lands were hunters, trappers and traders, often representatives of the large fur-trading companies. Some made remarkable journeys, setting up chains of remote trading posts where native hunters could exchange their catches for trade goods. Often they were the first Europeans to meet the natives, and the first colonists of these remote lands.

At sea, the pioneer explorers were sealers hunting for fur seals and whalers in search of baleen (whalebone) and oil. So valuable were these products that governments had to take note; each year the navies of several northern nations sent some of their most experienced navigators to chart Arctic harbours and waterways that sealers and whalers had discovered. Naval exploration centred eventually on four targets – the North Pole, the North Magnetic Pole, and the Northeast and Northwest passages, the Arctic sea routes that everyone hoped would link Europe with the wealth of the orient.

Below *Fur-trapper, by Frederick Remington*

Below *The Passage ran through ice-blocked seas.*

***Right** Franklin's ships, the* Erebus *and* Terror, *had previously been to the Antarctic under the command of James Clark Ross. Stoutly built vessels, they were specially strengthened to cope with ice.*

accompanied again by Back and Richardson, he crossed to the United States and headed north through the Great Lakes into Canada. There he heard, sadly but not unexpectedly, that Eleanor had died of consumption. Continuing northward the party reached Fort Resolution on Great Slave Lake. Franklin had left nothing to chance; provisions were plentiful and the equipment was of the best. In stout canoes the party sailed north along the Mackenzie River to Fort Norman. Back and Richardson headed eastward to Great Bear Lake, where Back supervised the building of winter quarters (called Fort Franklin) and Richardson explored the lake itself. Franklin meanwhile reconnoitred northward along the Mackenzie, in five days reaching the open ocean.

In autumn the party reassembled to pass a cosy winter at Fort Franklin. The following summer they returned to the coast, Richardson heading eastward and circling back to the Coppermine River, while Franklin and Back took their two boats westward in the direction of Alaska. After a lively encounter with acquisitive Eskimos, at a headland that Franklin named Pillage Point, he and Back worked their way laboriously along the coast, reaching a turning point at Cape Beechey (Beechey Point) by mid August. No longer taking chances, they returned uneventfully to the Mackenzie River and Fort Franklin, where they passed a second comfortable winter. No less successfully, Richardson charted much of the coast between the Mackenzie and Coppermine rivers, ascended the Coppermine and wintered at Cumberland House.

Interlude, and the final expedition

Again Franklin returned in triumph to England. Honours, including a knighthood, were heaped upon him. Eleanor had died shortly after his departure for the north, leaving him with an infant daughter. He married Jane Griffin, who warmed the next few years of his life and later played a key role in keeping his memory alive.

Franklin planned further Arctic exploration but the Admiralty, temporarily at least, was no longer prepared to back it. He spent three years commanding a sloop in the Mediterranean, followed by six years as a fair-minded but controversial Governor of Van Diemen's Land (now Tasmania). He returned to Britain at an opportune moment; the Royal Navy was once again promoting a major attempt to discover the Northwest Passage, and their first choice of commander, Sir James Clark Ross, was not available. Though 59 years old, Franklin was an obvious second choice. In May 1845 he sailed with two ships, HMS *Erebus* and HMS *Terror*, with a total of 134 officers and ratings.

Erebus and *Terror* were last seen in Melville Bay (Bugt), off the coast of Greenland, in good shape and heading towards Lancaster Sound. Nothing was seen or heard of the expedition in 1846 or 1847. In June 1848 the first relief expedition was sent out, followed by over a dozen more, some at the behest, and indeed at the personal expense, of Lady Franklin herself.

The story of the two ships was eventually pieced together from many reports, including the stories of Eskimos who remembered seeing strange parties of hungry white men wandering in distress along their shores. *Erebus* and *Terror*, it seemed, had penetrated westward to Beechey Island and wintered there in 1845–6. Released from the ice in the summer, they had circumnavigated Cornwallis Island, and headed south into Franklin Sound (Strait), and in September 1846 they were beset there by ice. There were several deaths, presumably from disease and malnutrition; Sir John Franklin himself died in June 1847. Either before or after this date the survivors, now reduced to 104, left the ships and headed south towards the mainland coast. A trail of abandoned equipment, boats, sledges and skeletons, reaching as far as King William Island, told the tragic tale of their deaths. There were no survivors from Franklin's last expedition.

Biographical Notes

1786
Born in Spilsby, Lincolnshire, England.

1800
Aged 14, entered the Royal Navy.

1801–3
Sailed with Matthew Flinders around Australia.

1818
First command, *HMS Trent*, on an expedition to Spitsbergen and the polar sea.

1819–22
First overland expedition, exploring from Hudson Bay to the Coppermine River.

1825–7
Second overland expedition, from the Mackenzie River to northern Alaska.

1836–43
Governor of Van Diemen's Land (Tasmania).

1845
Given command of expedition to discover the Northwest Passage.

1847
Died near King William Island, Northwest Territory.

LUDWIG LEICHHARDT

A young German scientist and explorer, Ludwig Leichhardt became a national hero in Australia and then mysteriously disappeared

Ludwig Leichhardt owes his place in the annals of exploration not only to his discoveries, but also to the enigma of his disappearance, which kept Australia agog for years. Early in April 1848, the 34-year-old German struck off into the Queensland outback with four other white men, two Australian Aborigines and a substantial caravan of bullocks, mules and horses. They were never seen again.

Over the following years many searches were mounted for the missing expedition, but only uncertain traces were found – trees with 'L' carved on them, bones and scraps of clothing. There were stories of a 'wild white man', who had gone native and was living with Aborigines, but there was no definite proof of his existence. As late as 1938, 90 years after Leichhardt's disappearance, a fresh search was sponsored by the government of South Australia. This time an English Maundy threepenny piece played an intriguing role, but to this day no one knows what happened to Leichhardt and the men who set off with him.

__Below__ Leichhardt's epic journey of 1844–5 took him and his party across much of northern Australia, from the Darling Downs area of what is now Queensland to Arnhem Land and Port Essington in the Northern Territory.

Sailing to Sydney

Friedrich Wilhelm Ludwig Leichhardt was born at Trebatsch in Brandenburg in 1813, the son of a farmer and the sixth of eight children. This was long before the unification of Germany and Leichhardt was by nationality a Prussian. A delicate, nervous child, thin, pale and fair-haired, he did well at school and went on to study at the University of Berlin. He transferred to Göttingen University in Hanover, where he met a young Englishman from Bristol, John Nicholson. To study biology, Leichhardt returned to Berlin, where he struck up a close friendship with John Nicholson's younger brother, William. They shared lodgings together.

To the dismay of his family, who intended him for a secure, respectable career as a teacher or a civil servant, Leichhardt declined to take a degree and announced that he and his friend William Nicholson were going to be a team for the advancement of science, which they would forward by investigating in far-flung and little-known parts of the world. As Leichhardt had no

Nature's Wonders

The unique and extraordinary wildlife of Australia has always fascinated the outside world. Sir Joseph Banks and Daniel Solander were tremendously excited to see their first kangaroo when they reached Australia with Captain Cook, and putting in at Thirsty Bay for water they marvelled at a cloud of millions of blue and black butterflies. Arthur Phillip, the first Governor of New South Wales, sent a live kangaroo back to England for King George III, and when he returned home himself, he took with him a collection of animals and plants which included four live kangaroos and some dingos. Ludwig Leichhardt, too, diligently gathered specimens on his journeys and many white explorers were intrigued or alarmed by fauna ranging from Fubsy koala bears to crocodiles 20ft (6m) long, poisonous snakes and death-dealing spiders.

Dutch voyagers brought back the first reports of kangaroos and wallabies in the 17th century and a Dutchman first described the black swan in 1696, but there were more curiosities to follow. Unique to Australia are the world's only egg-laying mammals – the spiny anteater and the duck-billed platypus. Birds vary from tiny little things half the size of a sparrow to giant flightless, swift-running emus. There is an astonishing creature called the giant earthworm, upto 12ft (3.5m) long and 1ft (30cm) round, which slithers swiftly through its tunnels underground with a greasy gurgling sound. Not for nothing is the continent called 'the land of living fossils'.

Above *A congregation of kangaroos, a species unique to Australia.*

money, this would he achieved at Nicholson's father's expense, which did not particularly please the Nicholson family either.

Leichhardt left Germany for England in 1837 and he and William Nicholson travelled and studied in France, Italy and Switzerland. They decided on Australia as their scene of action, but in the end the Nicholsons prevailed on William not to go. He paid Leichhardt's passage and bought his clothes for the journey, and remained a firm friend and supporter for the rest of Leichhardt's short life.

The young German, approaching his twenty-eighth birthday, sailed from Gravesend in the *Sir Edward Paget* of 600 tons (610 tonnes). The ship called at Cork to pick up Irish emigrants and made the long passage to Sydney, arriving in February 1842.

Into the Outback

Arriving in Sydney, now a city of more than 40,000 people where 60 years before there had been nothing but sea, trees and sky, Leichhardt presented himself to leading citizens, including Sir Thomas Mitchell, Surveyor-General of New South Wales and a veteran Australian explorer himself. He was looked at askance as a foreigner and he made some friends and some long botanical excursions, but no headway.

In 1844, getting no encouragement from Australian officialdom, Leichhardt decided to lead his own private exploring expedition in the northern part of the continent. He was alarmingly inexperienced, but his enthusiasm and self-confidence won him some equally inexperienced followers and a party of 10 started from Jimbour on the Darling Downs west of Brisbane at the beginning of October for a journey that was to last 14½ months and cover almost 3,000 miles (4,830km).

Two of the party soon turned back and Leichhardt went on with four other white men, a boy of 16, two Aborigines, 16 bullocks, 18 horses and four dogs. The expedition started with 1,200lb (545kg) of flour, 200lb (90kg) of sugar and 80lb (36kg) of tea – all of which would be exhausted long before the journey was finished – as well as 30lb (13kg) of powder and eight bags of shot, as the party intended to shoot for food on the way. Each man took two pairs of strong trousers, three shirts and two pairs of stout shoes, and some of them had calico ponchos against rain.

The explorers set off on foot, singing 'God Save the Queen' lustily as they went. As they used up their provisions, they took to riding the horses. The bullocks proved to be a serious problem. None of the party had the remotest idea how to load a bullock properly or how to manage the animals. They had to learn by trial and error. Leichhardt's personal bullock, named Redmond, gave him many a fierce kick, but the explorer became attached to him.

Another difficulty was that no one in the party was a good enough shot. They failed to kill as much game as they needed and so used up their provisions too quickly. At one point on the journey, showing off to a group of Aborigines, they fired at a tree which was full of kites without hitting a single bird – at which the Aborigines burst into shrieks of laughter.

The plan was to keep to the east of the principal mountains, the Great Dividing Range, find a gap through them as far north as they could, keep on northwest to the Gulf of Carpentaria and continue on in the same direction to Port

Essington on the Cobourg Peninsula, where a small military post had recently been established. They had no knowledge of the country ahead and the short-sighted Leichhardt's navigational abilities turned out to he distinctly limited.

Toiling across the continent

Leichhardt reconnoitred ahead for water at each stage and did not move the rest of the party forward until it had been found. He diligently gathered specimens all the way and at first a wary eye was kept for Aborigines, who might or might not be friendly. Leichhardt did not have a high regard for Aborigines and it was his custom to protect himself against native attack at night by hanging from a tree a large pumpkin, hollowed out and carved into a hideous face, with a lighted candle inside.

Tormented by heat, flies and biting ants, the expedition made long detours to bypass areas of dense scrub after an attempt to force the bullocks through it had to be given up as hopeless. They followed the Dawson and Mackenzie rivers north to the Suttor, the Burdekin and the Lynd. They began to kill the bullocks, one by one, and dry the meat to carry with them. By January they had gone only a fraction of the way and the flour ration was down to 3lb (1.3kg) a day for the whole party.

On the way they came across Aborigine camps, many of them just deserted as the natives had cautiously gone to hide. Those they met were almost all friendly and one cheerful party appeared with gifts of boomerangs and emu feathers, to be presented with a Queen Victoria coronation medal in return.

The explorers ate emu, kangaroo, duck, pelican and iguana when they could shoot it or the dogs could catch it, but shortage of food became more and more of a problem and in February Leichhardt had to cut the flour ration in half. The party bickered and wrangled, and grumbled about the slowness of their progress. The two Aborigines gave trouble and Leichhardt was bad-tempered and convinced he had picked the wrong companions for the adventure.

They came to the Mitchell River and made their way westwards across the base of the Cape York Peninsula. One June night, asleep in their tents by the camp fire, and failing to keep a proper watch, they were suddenly attacked by Aborigines hurling spears. They drove the attackers off with gunfire, but not before one of their men, John Gilbert, had been killed and two others wounded. One of them, John Roper, had a wound in the groin and a barbed spear stuck in his arm. The spear had to be pushed all the way through for the head to be cut off.

They buried Gilbert and after two days of rest set off again, afraid of another attack. Within a week, with heartfelt relief, they came to the Gulf of Carpentaria and the whole party broke into cheers. There was still a long way to go, however, as they moved across the fertile plains parallel to the coast, fording many rivers. Leichhardt named one of them the Nicholson, after his English friend (and another, nearby, would one day be christened the Leichhardt). They toiled on over the plains of Arnhem Land, where they were in sufficiently good spirits to hunt emu on horseback. In October they forded the Roper River, which Leichhardt named in honour of John Roper. At last, exhausted and in tatters, they arrived at Port Essington a few days before Christmas, seven men with eight horses left alive and one bullock, the indomitable Redmond.

***Above** Mitchell Falls on the Mitchell Plateau. Leichhardt discovered and named many rivers in northern Australia, including the Mitchell, which he christened in honour of Sir Thomas Mitchell, a redoubtable Scots explorer who was Surveyor-General of New South Wales.*

Conquering hero

Leichhardt and his men rested at Port Essington and were lucky enough to get a passage back to Sydney in a ship called the *Heroine*. It was an appropriate name, as it turned out, for they arrived in March 1846 to be treated as heroes.

Everyone had given them up for dead and expeditions had gone to search for them in vain. They had found an overland route between Brisbane and the north coast, they had discovered numerous rivers and mountain ranges, and, most welcome of all, they brought news of fertile land in the north, which meant more room for the colony to expand. The Sydney *Morning Herald* wrote of 'the joyous, the exultant sensation which this brilliant deed has inspired in the breasts of the colonists'.

For all the public acclaim, private whispers spread about Leichhardt's incompetence as a leader, and Mitchell, the Surveyor-General, was always fiercely jealous of other explorers. The triumphant Leichhardt, however, resolved to lead a second expedition from the Darling Downs. This one would cross northern Australia all the way from east to west and go on down the west coast to Perth. He expected the 5,000-mile (8,045km) journey to take at least two years.

The party of 11 men set off in December, along Leichhardt's previous route, with bullocks, mules, horses and a flock of close to 400 sheep and goats. It was a total failure. Heavy rain, fierce heat and a plague of mosquitoes and sand-flies made things desperately difficult, and attacks of fever and quarrelling among the men made them worse. The animals ran away and the men were too ill and weak to round them up. Only 500 miles (805km) had been covered when the expedition gave up and returned to base, in July 1847.

Leichhardt wrote disconsolately to his brother-in-law in Germany. 'Here I am, back once again from a journey of exploration, but not in the least like a conqueror marching in with banners flying to the jubilation of the multitude. On the contrary, I've been compelled to return worn out by illness and with disgruntled companions whom I've had to lead back to the flesh-pots of Egypt before I had even set foot in unexplored country.'

Although he said publicly that his party had behaved well, Leichhardt privately blamed the failure on his subordinates, who he said were soft and cowardly. When his letter home to this effect was translated and published years later in 1866, the translator used the word 'effeminate'. It created an uproar that seriously damaged Leichhardt's reputation.

Determined to succeed in crossing the continent, Leichhardt set off again from the Darling Downs early in 1848, leading a party of six, including two Aborigines. 'You know well,' he wrote to a friend on 10 March, 'that I consider Exploration of the Continent my great task, which has been allotted to me.' He wrote his last letter on 4 April to the Sydney *Morning Herald* from a sheep station at Mount Abundance. 'I cannot speak in too high terms of my present party,' he said, 'who seem to me well qualified for the long and tedious journey which is before us.' Long and tedious it does not seem to have been. Leichhardt and his men moved off into the outback and into a silence and mystery that has lasted ever since.

Searching for Leichhardt

Leichhardt's transcontinental trek had been expected to take a minimum of two years. As time wore on and no word came of the party, people became worried. In 1852 one of the members of Leichhardt's second expedition led a search in the west of Queensland. He could find no trace of the missing men, but suggested they had probably been killed by Aborigines.

Later in the decade Augustus Gregory led expeditions through northern Australia, partly in search of the lost explorers. These forays made important contributions to Australian exploration, but they found no sign of Leichhardt and his people.

The mystery was much too intriguing to be dropped. In 1864 there was a report that two trees with the letter 'L,' marked on them had been found in the remote northwest of Queensland, but nothing more came of it. Enticing rumours spread of a white man living wild somewhere in the Queensland outback and in 1871 a party led by a police officer, J.M. Gilmour, was sent to investigate. At a waterhole some 500 miles (805km) northwest of Leichhardt's starting point Gilmour found skeletons and pieces of white men's clothing. Gilmour led a second party a few months later, which found a tomahawk and a bit of blanket. There was no sign of any wild white man.

In 1873, however, a horse-thief named Andrew Hume claimed to have encountered deep in the interior a survivor of Leichhardt's party called Adolf Classen, who was living with his Aboriginal wife and three children and did not want to return to the white world. According to Hume, Classen told him that Leichhardt's men had mutinied and murdered their leader and had then been killed by Aborigines. However, Hume had no evidence to support his story.

The popular press kept the mystery alive, with word of fresh searches and tales of a strange iron box that the Aborigines regarded with superstitious awe and were too frightened to open. It was supposed to be Leichhardt's medicine chest.

The 1938 expedition was sparked off by a report that the skeletons of white men had been found at the edge of the Simpson Desert in the middle of the continent. The party found human teeth and bones, pieces of leather and iron, and an English Maundy threepenny coin issued at Easter in 1841. Leichhardt arrived in London from Paris at the end of August 1841, to leave for Australia a month or so later. The coin could have been a memento of England, but in the end the leader of the 1938 search party could only say that the remains discovered seemed as likely to be those of the Leichhardt expedition as of any other vanished party.

Rifts in the Lute

From Leichbardt's letter to his German brother-in-law after arriving safely at Port Essington:

"In my choice of associates I was most unfortunate, for they did everything they could to make the journey unpleasant. A boy of 16, whom I had befriended and taught, because he showed promise, gave me a lot of trouble. A convict (a man transported to Australia on account of wrong-doing) begged me, in Sydney, to take him with me, because he thought that they would grant him a pardon when the journey was over. He behaved well enough, yet he stole dried meat, and had probably been doing so for a long time before I found him out. Mr Gilbert sought in many ways to deceive me, and if he had survived it's likely that I would have enjoyed very few of the fruits of my labour. I discovered his intentions after he was killed. He turned the boy against me, and likewise weakened my hold over one of the blacks. It was unfortunate that I took 2 blacks with me. One led the other astray, so that both resisted me. Roper was an inexperienced and limited young man who seemed to consider it beneath his dignity to obey me; and he thought that he had quite as much right to my things as I had myself . . . None of my associates suffered from illness during the journey except for diarrhoea after eating unwholesome fruit. I myself suffered badly from gall stones. They used to pass out with the urine, but caused me such intense pain that I thought I was going to die. But God was merciful. At the end of the journey my party so harassed me that I doubt that I could have put up with it for as much as another month. I was exhausted, the more spiritually than physically, by the time I arrived at Port Essington. You can well believe how little I enjoy associating with my tormentors now that the journey's over. I'm sick of the very sight of them."

from *The Letters of F. W. Ludwig Leichhardt*, (translated by M. Aurousseau)

Left *After Leichhardt's pioneering trek across the northern area of Australia, further efforts were made to open up the unknown central region of the continent. In 1860 John McDouall Stuart discovered the McDonnell Ranges, stark red mountains broken by steep gaps like this one, Simpson's Gap near Alice Springs. The 1938 expedition to search for traces of Leichhardt was set off by reports of remains found on the edge of the Simpson Desert to the east.*

Biographical Notes

1813
Born at Trebatsch, Germany (23 October).

1841
Sailed to Australia.

1844
Left the Darling Downs on his first major expedition (1 October).

1845
Reached journey's end at Port Essington (17 December).

1846
Started second journey from the Darling Downs; forced to give up after six months.

1848
Left the Darling Downs on his last expedition; wrote his last letter (4 April).

Africa

Most of the Dark Continent remained hidden from European eyes and European conquest until the 19th century

It was in Africa, the evidence suggests, that the human race first emerged from the womb of evolution and from Africa that human beings spread out to explore and settle the rest of the world. A sophisticated civilisation developed in Egypt, whose rulers sent exploring and trading expeditions to the south, along the Nile and down the African coast of the Red Sea. Later the Phoenicians founded colonies along the North African shore, the first settlements in the continent founded by outsiders.

The Phoenicians were skilled and daring sailors. Their seamen sailed through the Pillars of Hercules to discover the Canary Islands and Madeira, and they established settlements on the West African coast. There is even a possibility that a Phoenician fleet in the service of the pharaoh of Egypt sailed the whole way round Africa in about 600 BC.

In the 7th century AD the Arabs conquered Egypt and all of North Africa. Arab merchants established trading links far south into the African interior. In the 14th century the indefatigable Ibn Battutah of Morocco travelled to what is now Somalia, and later to Mali and Timbuktu, reporting that the local cannibals preferred not to eat white flesh because it was not ripe. He returned across the Sahara, living on dates and locusts. The African rulers of Mali had grown immensely rich as middlemen in the trade in West African gold. Mined around the headwaters of the Niger and the Volta, it was exchanged for salt and copper with Arab merchants who ran camel trains from Morocco and Algeria.

Round the Cape

In the 15th century Europeans began to explore Africa, from a mixture of motives – curiosity, an appetite for gold and a missionary urge to spread Christianity. In 1413, or so it was claimed, a Frenchman named Anselme d'Isalguier managed to reach Gao on the Niger in Mali, and came back with a train of black women and eunuchs. In about 1450 Portuguese traders reached Mali from the west coast and in 1470 a Florentine named Benedetto Dei said he had been to Timbuktu.

Meanwhile the Portuguese were thrusting down the West African coast by sea. These voyages were backed by the Portuguese royal family, among them Prince Henry the Navigator, who hoped to find gold and saw himself as a

Above *Rising in cloud-skirted splendour from the plain, the volcanic cone of Mount Kilimanjaro is Africa's highest peak. The first white man to bring back word of it was a missionary named Johannes Rebmann, who journeyed inland from the east coast in 1848. Kilimanjaro was first climbed by Hans Meyer in 1889.*

Left *The piercing gaze of Prince Henry the Navigator, in an idealised portrait. The cross at his breast is a reminder that one of his principal motives in backing voyages down the west coast of Africa was crusading zeal against Islam.*

champion of Christian chivalry against Islam. He was also trying to do what his horoscope predicted. By his death in 1460 the Portuguese had gone as far south as modern Sierra Leone.

Undeterred by adverse winds and difficult currents, sudden fogs and an inhospitable and fever-ridden shore, the Portuguese pressed further and further south. By 1475 they had crossed the Equator. In 1482 Diogo Cão discovered the Congo River (now the Zaire), Africa's second-longest river after the Nile. He sailed up the river as far as Matadi and claimed the whole area for Portugal. Five years later Bartolomeu Dias left Lisbon with three ships under orders from King John II to round the southern tip of Africa. Blown out to sea, he passed the Cape of Good Hope without seeing it in January 1488 and reached land in Mossel Bay, further east. He sailed on up the east coast to Algoa Bay, at which point his crew refused to go any further and he had to return unwillingly home. He had paved the way for Vasco da Gama to round the Cape in 1497, sail on up the east coast to Mombassa and Malindi, and then cross the Indian Ocean to reach India itself.

Gondar and Niger

The discovery of a sea route to India and the riches of the Orient, coupled with the discovery and exploitation of the Americas, took the focus of exploring and imperialist activity away from Africa. However, the Portuguese founded trading posts on the east coast, which was also resentfully investigated by the crews of ships wrecked there. Word of gold, ivory and slaves in the interior attracted interlopers and by the 17th century Portuguese adventurers were ruling as petty chieftains far inland. Further north, the Portuguese hoped to use Ethiopia as a Christian ally against Islam. An embassy was sent there in 1520 and in the following century. Jesuit missionaries made vain efforts to wean the people from their Coptic Christianity to Roman Catholicism.

The Dutch used the route round the Cape of Good Hope to reach their possessions in the East Indies and in 1652 established a naval base on Table Day, at the foot of Table Mountain, where the city of Cape Town stands today. Emigrants came from Holland and Huguenot refugees from France to form a colony – taken over by the British in 1806 – from which settlers, missionaries and hunters explored to the north.

Meanwhile an intrepid Scotsman named James Bruce set out to discover the source of the Nile. Starting from the Red Sea coast of Eritrea in 1769, he made his way up into the mountain fastnesses of Ethiopia to fabled Gondar, ruled by an emperor who claimed descent from Solomon and Sheba. Bruce spent a long time with the court and his white skin caused wonderment among the beauties of the harem. He saw Lake Tana, the source of the Blue Nile, in 1770 and followed the river to its confluence with the White Nile and on down to Aswan and Cairo. He returned with a mass of useful information, but unfortunately made a less favourable impression on London society than on that of Gondar. Nobody believed his account of his experiences and he retired to Scotland, justifiably peeved.

Another Scotsman, Mungo Park, a ship's doctor with an interest in botany, arrived in West Africa in 1795 to solve the mystery of the Niger. No one knew where the great river rose or which way it ran. Some thought it might flow right across Africa to join the Nile. Park travelled with the blessing of Sir Joseph Banks, the presiding genius of British scientific exploration. Equipped with provisions, a compass, a sextant, a big shady

Below *Artist's impression of a Phoenician trading vessel arriving in Egypt. The Phoenicians were the first outsiders to plant settlements on African soil and they built up a thriving commercial empire.*

hat and an umbrella, he set off on horseback up the Gambia River. He was systematically plundered by the local chiefs. One of them kept him in prison for months, but Park escaped and managed to reach Ségou, where he saw 'the majestic Niger, glistening in the morning sun, as broad as the Thames at Westminster and flowing slowly *to the eastward*'.

Park was back in London by the end of 1797 and his book about his travels was a bestseller. In 1805 he led a much stronger expedition inland to the Niger, but his party fell prey to fever and he died at the Bussa rapids, either drowned or killed in a fight with natives. Not until 1830 was it established by two amiable Cornish brothers, Richard and John Lander – they travelled in such enormous straw hats that Africans burst into helpless laughter at the sight of them – that the Niger flows into the Atlantic in the Bight of Benin.

Nile and Congo

It was the 19th century that brought the swift opening up of the African interior to the enquiring European eye and ultimately its wholesale parcelling out among the European powers. Explorers obstinately drove their way across blistering deserts and through fetid malarial jungles, braving local hostility, slave-traders and cannibals, torrid heat, noxious insects, diseases and dangers innumerable.

Among the motives early in the century were commercial, missionary and scientific enthusiasm and the drive to end the slave trade. The Anti-Slavery Society in Britain, for example, had much to do with the expedition that set off from Tripoli in 1850 and crossed the Sahara to Lake Chad. Its principal figure was Heinrich Barth, a young Berliner who travelled 10,000 miles (16,000km) in the next five years, followed the Niger to Timbuktu and resumed to publish a mass of detailed information about the native peoples.

Barth was disappointed by the lack of public interest in his scholarly book, but he inspired another young German, Gerhard Rohlfs, who joined the French Foreign Legion and spent 20 years exploring the Sahara. In the 1860s he went all the way from Tripoli on the Mediterranean to the Gulf of Guinea at Lagos.

Attention had shifted by this time to East Africa, the invitingly unresolved question of the sources of the Nile and reports from missionaries of great lakes and snow-clad peaks in the interior. The missionary Johann Rehmann, for instance, sighted Mount Kilimanjaro, Africa's highest mountain, in 1848. Sent to investigate by the Royal Geographical Society in England, the two formidable egos of Richard Burton and John Hanning Speke left the east coast in harness in 1857 on a famously quarrelsome expedition that discovered Lake Tanganyika and Lake Victoria, which would prove to be the source of the White Nile.

The mystery of the Nile fascinated Samuel White Baker, a romantic who bought his beautiful, golden-haired Hungarian wife, Florence, on impulse at a slave market in Bulgaria. They went off happily together to Egypt. Leaving Cairo in 1861 and crossing the Nubian Desert on camels, they went far south across the Sudan, exploring and hunting big game. Travelling with a villainous gang of slave and ivory dealers, they declined a local chieftain's pressing invitation to exchange wives and eventually reached the lake that Baker named Albert Nyanza, a feeder of the White Nile. They also named the Murchison Falls, now called the Kabalega Falls, in modern Uganda. They ended up as Sir Samuel and Lady Baker.

For the Victorian public in Britain, however, the great hero was David Livingstone, the Scots missionary, geographer and meticulous scientific observer who dedicated himself to rescuing Central Africa from the slave trade, oppression and human misery. His journeys in the 1850s from the centre of Africa to both the west and the east coasts brought the heart of the Dark Continent dramatically to the attention of the outside world. Livingstone also tried to settle the Nile question. Such was his fame that the Anglo-American journalist Henry Morton Stanley became a worldwide celebrity himself for being sent to find the lost explorer and greeting him at Ujiji on Lake Tanganyika with the immortal words: 'Doctor Livingstone, I presume.'

***Below** A slave convoy in the Sudan, in an illustration of about 1880. Arab slave-traders did a flourishing business in black ivory for many centuries in eastern Africa, and the urge to abolish the traffic was one of the motives behind European intervention in the continent.*

***Left** Sir Samuel and Lady Baker pictured in later life, in the* Illustrated London News *in 1873. They made an exciting trip through the Sudan and into modern Uganda in the 1860s to discover the sources of the Nile.*

In 1869-70 the German botanist and plant-hunter Georg Augustus Schweinfurth was the first European to encounter the pygmies of the Congo jungle. Sent by the Royal Geographical Society on another search for Livingstone in 1873, a British naval officer named Verney Lovett Cameron arrived after Livingstone's death, but made a thorough survey of Lake Tanganyika and then followed the Lualuba River to Nyangwe. He believed the river to be the Congo, but this was as far as he could get and he veered off to the southwest to cross what are now Zaire and Angola. He reached the coast at Benguela in 1875 to complete the first European east-west crossing of the continent. Not far behind him came the formidable H.M. Stanley, who returned to Africa in 1874, travelled down the Lualuba, confirmed that it was indeed the Congo and sailed on down the great river to the west coast, which he reached in August 1877.

The Scramble for Africa

Cameron made no secret of the fact that he would like to see the British flag flying over Central Africa. The era of commercial, missionary and scientific exploration in Africa was about to give way to the age of European imperialism. Stanley carved out an empire in Central Africa for King Leopold II of Belgium after the British government had cold-shouldered him. His rival was an Italian-born French naval officer, Count Pierre Savorgnan de Brazza, who in the 1870s and 1880s explored the Ogowé and the Congo, making treaties with native chiefs. He was the founder of the French Congo, which became part of French Equatorial Africa.

The 'Scramble for Africa' began in the 1880s and in 30 years, by the time World War I broke out, the whole continent had been partitioned between seven European nations – France, Britain, Germany, Portugal, Belgium, Spain and Italy. The only independent African states in 1914 were Ethiopia and Liberia.

There was still plenty of scope in Africa for the individual European adventurer – for Mary Kingsley, for example, to explore the interior of what is now Gabon in the 1890s. In the main, however, the new situation required detailed surveying for improved maps, and the construction of railways and roads, as well as scientific investigation into the African environment. This century has seen an immense amount of work by outsiders on the geography, geology, biology, archaeology and anthropology of Africa.

BURTON AND SPEKE

Rival explorers Sir Richard Burton and John Speke contest the true source of the Nile

Towards the end of 1853 Richard Francis Burton arrived in Cairo after a reckless exploit that was to win him lasting fame. A brilliant linguist (he mastered some 25 languages and numerous dialects) who cultivated a reputation for flamboyant behaviour throughout his life, he had disguised himself as a dervish and made the pilgrimage to Mecca – something that was likely to end in death for a non-Muslim. After a few months in Cairo enhancing his reputation for licentious living, he was ready for a new adventure and the reports he heard of Africa persuaded him to go in search of the source of the White Nile. However, this was not the limit of his ambition – three years before Livingstone achieved it, Burton was hoping to become the first European to cross Africa from coast to coast. With this in mind, he obtained leave from his superiors in the East India Company to explore Somaliland and intended then to travel across the continent westward from Zanzibar. His colonel, James Outram, proved obstructive and Burton was forced to begin his enterprise with some reconnaissance missions. On one of these, Burton planned to enter a second forbidden Muslim city, Harar, the centre of the East African slave trade. For another expedition, to Wadi Nogal in northeastern Somaliland, Burton chose as leader an affluent young lieutenant called John Hanning Speke, who was taking extended leave after 10 years of military service and wanted to explore Africa and indulge an

Left *The journey from the coast to Lake Tanganyika was painfully slow, and on the return leg Speke branched off on his own to discover the vast expanse of water that he named Lake Victoria.*

overwhelming passion for killing game. Speke's qualifications for such an expedition were not impressive and Burton seems to have accepted him rather reluctantly, because he was able to provide funds, when the man he would have preferred suddenly died. Whatever the exact circumstances of the decision, it was to have an irrevocable effect on the lives of both these African explorers.

An unpleasant incident in Somaliland

Burton survived his mission to Harar unscathed only because, realising at the last minute that he was in serious danger, he abandoned his disguise and presented himself instead as a British emissary seeking to establish trade links. The ruse succeeded and, despite an ill-advised desert trek, he returned safely. Speke's expedition was far from successful and, in his ignorance of languages, he was easily deceived and humiliated by his chief guide. Despite this, and despite his increasingly low opinion of a man who could not or would not make himself fluent in native tongues, Burton did not dismiss Speke but had the guide punished, and by doing so built up resentment in Somaliland that made itself felt when the expedition proper got under way in April 1855. In a night attack on the explorers' camp early on in the expedition, Speke suffered 11 spear wounds and very nearly died and Burton too was badly injured. His superiors in India were critical of his behaviour and issued a reprimand while Speke was resentful at not being offered any compensation for the financial losses he incurred – something that Burton had promised him at the outset.

Burton returned to England a dejected figure but, by the autumn of 1855, like Speke, he was serving in the Crimea, an experience that he seems to have found deeply shocking. He had not abandoned his African ambitions, however, and back in England during 1856 he persuaded the Royal Geographical Society (RGS) to involve itself in his latest scheme to find a huge lake believed to lie at the centre of Africa and, with it, perhaps also the source of the White Nile. The Foreign Office supported the plan and despite fierce opposition from the East India Company, Burton became leader of a new expedition in which he, surprisingly, invited Speke to participate and Speke, surprisingly, agreed.

In search of Lake Tanganyika and the Nile

The expedition began in December 1856 at Zanzibar, and before departure Burton carried out a detailed survey of this island at the centre of the East African slave trade, through which it has been estimated that 40,000 slaves passed annually. Then, in January, Burton and Speke sailed to Mombasa on the first stage of the long journey, carrying among their equipment a boat, the *Louisa*, which had been cut into portable sections in readiness for reassembly when they reached the lake they were seeking. They began with a preliminary coastal expedition to Tanga and the Pangani River and soon afterwards they were arguing over the choice of route inland. Burton's decision to avoid the territory of the supposedly ferocious Masai people prevailed and finally, after difficulty in obtaining sufficient porters and with animosity between the two of them increasing, they began to move slowly into Africa at the end of June 1857.

Beset by illness and endless trouble with porters, some of whom ran away, the expedition struggled as far as Zungomero, across the Makata Plain, over the Rubeho Pass through the Usagara Mountains and then down to the Ugogo plains. Both men spent long periods desperately ill with fever, sometimes having to be carried in hammocks, and when they penetrated the Kigwa forest and reached the Arab trading station of Tabora, they paused for a month to recover. Even so, illness continued to haunt them and the

Left *Sir Richard Burton was an explorer, adventurer, anthropologist and linguist of prodigious energy and talent. As a young man he built up a knowledge of India by wandering about the bazaars in native dress and in 1853 he made the pilgrimage to Mecca in disguise. He afterwards explored both East and West Africa and also wrote of his travels in the United States and Brazil, as well as translating the* Arabian Nights *and various classic works of oriental pornography into English.*

Left *John Hanning Speke was younger than Burton and of an entirely different temperament. As a young army officer he had done some exploring in the Himalayas before joining Burton in Somaliland and East Africa. The attention he received for his claim to have found the source of the Nile was fiercely resented by Burton.*

journey proceeded painfully slowly, across the Malagarasi River, finally reaching Lake Tanganyika in February 1858. At Ujiji on the lake shore both lay ill again, but Speke recovered sufficiently to explore the lake on his own (achieving nothing, according to Burton) and then, in April, both he and Burton went in search of the River Ruzizi at the northern end of the lake, only to be forced to concede that this was not the source of the Nile.

Disappointed and suffering from a serious shortage of supplies, Burton had to curtail the expedition and begin the return journey by much the same route as before. Back at Kazeh, where he felt particularly at home among the Muslim community, he gave in to Speke's persistent requests to be allowed to travel north alone in search of what was known as Lake Ukerewe. Speke found it 25 days later and named it Lake Victoria. Sure that this was the true source of the Nile, he returned to Kazeh in a state of excitement but Burton reacted to the news with cynicism and refused to go and see for himself. Instead they continued their journey to the coast, reaching Zanzibar after further delays through trouble with porters and illness (Speke succumbed to something not unlike rabies, but against all odds recovered) in March 1859.

As a result of this journey, both Burton and Speke could claim to have explored Lake Tanganyika, but Speke believed that he alone could claim the credit for the discovery of the true source of the Nile. Leaving Burton convalescing at Aden and promising to wait for him before going to the Royal Geographical Society with his information, Speke travelled to England, arriving in May 1859. Within a day or so of his arrival he had a meeting with Sir Roderick Murchison, President of the RGS, and, in his *Journal of the Discovery of the Source of the Nile*, published in 1863, he quotes Sir Frederick as responding to his theory about the source of the river with the words, 'Speke, we must send you there again'. This, of course, was exactly what Speke wanted – the leadership of a new expedition which, in his own words, would be 'avowedly for the purpose of establishing the truth of my assertion that the Victoria N'yanza, which I discovered on 30th July 1858, would eventually prove to be the source of the Nile'.

Speke had apparently gone back on his word and yet, when Burton arrived in England shortly afterwards and received the Royal Geographical Society's Gold Medal in acknowledgement of his discovery of Lake Tanganyika, he included in his acceptance speech a handsome tribute to his colleague. 'To Captain Speke,' he said, 'are due those geographical results to which you have alluded in such flattering terms. Whilst I undertook the history and the ethnography, the languages and the peculiarity of the people, to Captain Speke fell the arduous task of delineating an exact topography, and of laying down our positions by astronomical observations – a labour to which, at times, even the undaunted Livingstone found himself unequal.' At this stage the RGS gave every appearance of considering Burton's own proposals for a further expedition to Africa, but it was Speke's scheme that won Sir Roderick Murchison's support. In theory Burton was to be given command of another venture, but he was offered no money to finance it and the whole idea may have been nothing more than a feeble attempt to keep him quiet.

Speke returns to the Nile

The man chosen to accompany Speke on his return to Lake Victoria was Captain James Grant, a friend from Indian army days who was a talented artist and botanist. The two set out from Portsmouth bound for Zanzibar in the spring of 1860, and before leaving Speke wrote to Burton in an attempt to make peace. His approach was rejected and soon after his departure Burton published his account of *The Lake Regions of Central Africa* in which he gave a less than complimentary assessment of Speke's work, pointing out various errors in his calculations and attacking him personally.

With 115 porters Speke and Grant sailed from Zanzibar to Bagamoyo at the end of September. Again, the route across Masai territory had been rejected in favour of the longer but well-established caravan trail to Kazeh. Before, Speke had urged Burton to take the Masai route; now, in charge of his own expedition, he was not prepared to risk the unknown.

Speke had instructions from the RGS to go round Lake Victoria, find the source of the White Nile and trace the course of the river as far as the mission station at Gondokoro. A former mining engineer called John Petherick, who had explored part of the Upper Nile himself, was to leave boats and supplies there for them, after travelling up river from Khartoum. Speke reached Kazeh at the end of January 1861 after a journey of over 100 days, which, as before, was marred by frequent illness. On the journey all but two of the porters deserted and supplies were frequently stolen, but Speke managed to supplement a meagre diet through his skill in hunting and shooting game.

After a long wait at Kazeh for improved weather and replacement porters the expedition moved slowly on again, only to be delayed further by a local chief demanding tribute payments. Things improved when they reached the kingdom of Karagwe, where they enjoyed the hospitality of King Rumanika for several months and where Grant was left, suffering from a leg wound that refused to heal, while Speke made his way, early in 1862, to the territory of Mutesa, the Kabaka (ruler) of Buganda.

'The Nile is settled'

Speke was the first European ever to visit Mutesa, who was sometimes called the father of the Nile and known to be violent and erratic in his

Above *Lake Victoria with the source of the Nile. The controversy over the great river's origin aroused passionate excitement in Victorian England, but Speke's claim to have located it in Lake Victoria has proved to be correct.*

behaviour. The visitor was treated like royalty and stayed four and a half months in all, but there were times when Mutesa's behaviour began to look threatening. He would not be contradicted and he insisted on Grant being brought to see him, despite his illness and lack of mobility. Mutesa was reluctant to allow his guests to leave, but when news was brought to them in April that another expedition of white men had been seen in the region to the north, Speke assumed that this was Petherick and he became eager to set off.

They did not finally get away until early July 1862, and accompanied by an escort supplied by Mutesa they travelled to Baja. Speke sent the still-weak Grant by a direct route to the intended rendezvous with Petherick while he himself went in search of the source of the Nile. After reaching the river at Urondogani on 21 July, Speke followed its course on foot for a week before he came to the point known locally as 'the stones', which he named the Ripon Falls (now the Owen Falls) after Lord Ripon, Murchison's successor

Left *Illustration of an incident when Speke intervened with Mutesa, the ruler of Buganda, to save a woman's life. Speke was the first European to visit the formidable Kabaka of Buganda.*

as President of the RGS. There was now no doubt in his mind. Lake Victoria, he said, 'is the great source of the holy river which cradled the first expounder of our religious belief'.

After this triumph there was frustration. Permission to proceed to the rendezvous with Petherick had to he obtained from King Kamrasi, but he had so far refused to see Grant and when Speke returned to join his companion they were delayed a further two months before eventually being allowed to leave by canoe and travel as far as the Karuma falls. From here they continued overland via Jaifa and Apuddo to Gondokoro, but instead of finding Petherick they were greeted by Samuel White Baker, a good friend of Speke's who was also seeking the source of the Nile. It was in boats provided by Baker that Speke and Grant and 19 porters who had stayed loyal to the expedition sailed to Khartoum.

On arrival Speke sent a telegram to the RGS announcing: 'The Nile is settled' and this, the first communication to arrive in London from the expedition since the end of September 1861, told a public much concerned for their safety that the explorers were alive and well. From Khartoum the travellers went to Cairo, where Speke had the porters photographed for inclusion in his book of the journey, and announced that 'they all volunteered to go with me again, should I attempt to cross Africa from east to west through the fertile zone'.

Controversy rages

He was to make no such journey. He and Grant returned to England where they were welcomed as national heroes. Speke received the RGS Gold Medal, and before the end of 1863 he had published his *Journal of the Discovery of the Source of the Nile*, with maps and illustrations provided by Grant. The book provoked a good deal of critical comment and disbelief. It was suggested that the expedition had not done a sufficiently thorough job, and it was true that the evidence offered for the source of the Nile was incomplete and unconvincing – the north and south of Lake Victoria had been investigated, but no one had demonstrated for sure that it actually was one lake. At the same time, Speke's carping references to the behaviour of Petherick were considered ungentlemanly and he went on to offend the officers of the RGS by delivering an inadequate report of his expedition for publication in the Society's learned journal. Arguments about the true nature of the Nile raged for months. Speke quickly wrote another book, *What led to the Discovery of the Source of the Nile*, in which Burton was vigorously attacked, and Burton, who had been employed in Foreign Office work in West Africa for a number of years, returned to England more than ready to participate in the controversy.

Everything was set to come to a head during the annual conference of the British Association for the Advancement of Science at Bath in September 1864, at which it was intended that both Burton and Speke should take part in a debate before an audience of distinguished explorers and geographers. On the day before the debate was due to take place, the two met again for the first time in years at the conference venue and, according to an account of the event by Richard Burton's wife, Isabel, Speke seemed to turn to stone and left the room saying something that suggested he did not plan to come back. That afternoon he died in what was officially described as a shooting accident, but

__Below__ 'Natives of Equatorial Africa, part of the retinue of Captain Speke' in a Victorian illustration. As in other parts of the world, white explorers in Africa relied heavily on local guides, guards and porters.

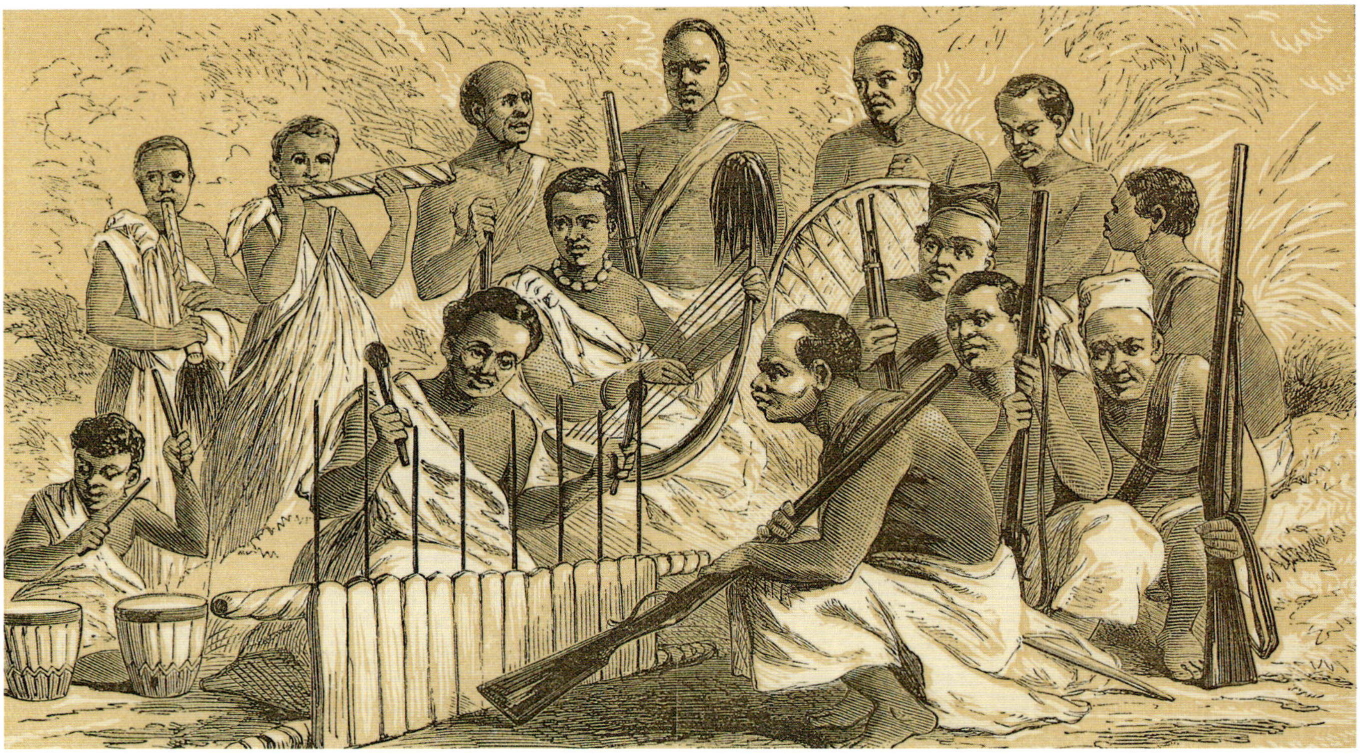

there were immediate suspicions that he had committed suicide and there can never be complete certainty as to what actually happened. Burton wrote, 'Nothing will be known of Speke's death; I saw him at 1.30 p.m. and at 4 p.m. he was dead. The charitable say that he shot himself, the uncharitable that I shot him.'

Over 10 years later, Henry Morton Stanley carried out detailed surveys of Lake Tanganyika and Lake Victoria, and demonstrated that the former had no connection with the Nile. Speke's theory had been vindicated and, shortly before his death in 1890, Richard Burton, who spent his later years writing, translating and working on a number of Foreign Office assignments (he wrote in all over 40 books), finally conceded this.

Above *Two feluccas, or traditional sailing barges, glide sweetly in unison over the Nile near Luxor. The world's largest river, the Nile was the lifeblood of Egypt and of Ancient Egyptian civilisation. Its source was an enticing mystery for centuries.*

The Nile

The length of the Nile from the Ripon Falls to the sea is just under 3,500 miles (5,600km), and the question of where this huge river rises exerted a strange fascination for centuries. In the ancient world the expression 'to seek the head of the Nile' was used to suggest an impossible task, rather like looking for a needle in a haystack. Speke was right, but he lacked the evidence to convince others. The Nile emerges from the north of Lake Victoria at the Ripon Falls; after about 240 miles (385km) it enters Lake Albert, flows out again to Gondokoro and then through the swamp territory known as the sudd, for nearly 500 miles (805km). It next receives two major tributaries before it is joined by the Sobat River. The name 'White Nile' was applied to the river from this point as far as Khartoum, where the less clear 'Blue Nile' joins it and the river continues for almost 2,000 miles (3,220km) more before reaching the Mediterranean. James Bruce, a Scottish explorer, found the source of the Blue Nile in 1770 and believed he had solved the whole problem of the river's origin. He was, of course, wrong and neither was he the first European to reach the Blue Nile – he had been preceded by Portuguese Jesuit missionaries who were at work in Ethiopia in the 17th century.

Biographical Notes

Richard Francis Burton

1821
Born on 19 March at Torquay, Devon.

1853
Travel led to Mecca and Medina disguised as a Muslim.

1856
Embarked on expedition with Speke to Lake Tanganyika.

1859
Received RGS Gold Medal.

1890
Died in Trieste.

John Hanning Speke

1827
Born on 4 May at Bideford, Devon.

1855
Accompanied Burton on expedition into Somaliland.

1856
Travelled with Burton to Lake Tanganyika.

1858
Found Lake Victoria and believed it was the source of the Nile.

1860–3
Led expedition to the source of the Nile.

1864
Died from gunshot wound in England.

DAVID LIVINGSTONE

A missionary turned explorer in the name of God

Exploration and evangelism have often gone hand in hand. The Christian duty to spread the gospel sent medieval monks trekking across Asia and gave later explorers a spiritual motive and papal authority to justify their sometimes violent activities. In the 19th century, when missionary zeal was at its height in Britain, David Livingstone travelled to Africa expecting to make huge numbers of converts. Arriving at a well-known mission station, he was shocked and disappointed to discover how few Africans had actually accepted Christianity. He considered sending a message back to the London Missionary Society to tell them that one of their officers was failing in his duty, but soon he realised for himself that conversion was not so easily achieved. These frustrating early experiences resulted in his transformation into an explorer.

Below *Explorer, Christian missionary and dedicated opponent of the slave trade, David Livingstone was one of the heroes of Victorian Britain and was eventually given a hero's tomb among the great in Westminster Abbey.*

David Livingstone was born on 19 March 1813 at Blantyre, near Glasgow, where he lived with his devoutly religious parents and four brothers and sisters in a tiny, one-room tenement flat. At the age of 10 he started at the local cotton-mill, working from six in the morning until eight at night and going on after that to evening classes, where he did so well that he was eventually accepted to study medicine at a local college. The concept of the medical missionary – a person who would provide both practical and spiritual help – was a new one, which Livingstone had recently read about. This, he decided, was to be his vocation. At the training centre of the nonconformist London Missionary Society (LMS) in Essex he was regarded as an oddity, a loner whose brusque manner seemed likely to repel rather than attract converts, and at the end of a probationary period he was nearly asked to leave. One teacher stood up for him and he survived to benefit from further medical training in London sponsored by the Society. In 1840 he qualified as a doctor and was ordained as a member of the LMS. China was his first choice of destination, but this proved impossible as tension was building up there prior to the Opium War. He appealed against the Society's plan to send him to the West Indies and at last it was agreed that he should set out for Africa.

First impressions

After a journey to the Cape, during which he studied navigation and the Setswana language, Livingstone arrived at the end of July 1841 at the mission station of Kuruman just south of the Kalahari desert and beyond the border of the British Cape Colony. Disillusionment was rapid. The mission was a modest place – not at all the impressive settlement Livingstone had been promised, and very soon he was writing letters that revealed his desire for independence and his ambition to conquer new ground beyond the areas in which other missionaries were already at work. Livingstone's Christian faith appeared unshakable throughout his life but he seems to have combined it with ambition and a desire for personal acclaim. He was quick to assert his independence. After only a month at Kuruman he was travelling north into Bechuanaland (Botswana) with another missionary (and without official permission) looking for a suitable site for a new settlement. Over the next few months he tried to establish himself at two sites without success, and nearly died in the attempt when he was badly mauled by a lion at Mabotsa. Undaunted, after a long enforced convalescence,

he made his headquarters at Kolobeng in the territory of Sechele, chief of the Bakwena people. Sechele was Livingstone's only Christian convert and his attachment to the practice of polygamy is said to have proved stronger than his supposed religious fervour.

Kolobeng, too, was an inhospitable place, and before long Livingstone was travelling again. In June 1849, in company with William Oswell, a hunter who financed the expedition, he made a journey across the Kalahari to Lake Ngami. They were the first Europeans to reach the lake, the Royal Geographical Society (RGS) awarded Livingstone a prize for his efforts and even the

Left *Livingstone was mauled by a lion soon after his arrival in Africa, and the injured left arm troubled him for the rest of his life. This is an artist's impression of the scene.*

Below *Livingstone was an efficient and meticulous geographer and his journeys mapped much of southern and central Africa.*

LMS expressed its approval for the publicity which the expedition had given to the Society's presence in Africa. At this point Livingstone's ambition becomes clear. He declared that 'the Lake belongs to missionary enterprise,' but he was convinced that there was a vast river system to the north of it and he wanted to be the man to investigate it, and to study the native Makololo people, without giving Oswell a chance to claim any of the credit. With recognition from the RGS he could now consider himself a genuine explorer and he promptly arranged his own independent expedition, which involved his young children and pregnant wife in a dangerous desert trek. A third journey, again with Oswell, was more successful and culminated in the explorers' arrival, in August 1851, at the banks of the Zambezi at a point near Sesheke. The sight of the huge, fast-flowing river left Livingstone in no doubt as to what he should do next. The route into the interior of Africa from the Cape was a difficult one and increasingly threatened by warring factions. If the Zambezi could be shown to be navigable it might offer British missionaries and traders a better route in from the east, and, equally, there might be a suitable approach from the western coast. With this in mind, Livingstone sent his wife and children home from the Cape to an uncertain and poverty-stricken fate, spent some time studying the use of sextant and chronometer watch and planned his most ambitious journey yet.

Above *Suffering from Malaria on his way up the Zambezi in the 1850s, Livingstone is taken to pay his respects to Shinte, a local African chief, who treated him as an honoured guest.*

Across Africa from coast to coast

Between September 1854 and May 1856, David Livingstone undertook the first known crossing of the African continent by a European. He travelled 4,000 miles (6,435km) from central Africa to the west coast and then to the east, taking bearings and keeping a detailed journal all the way. His journey was described by the President of the RGS as 'the greatest triumph in geographical research which has been effected in our times'. It was an expedition conducted with minimal resources and no British sponsorship – Livingstone's only companions were 27 native porters provided by Chief Sekeletu of the Makololo.

From Sekeletu's capital at Linyanti, Livingstone went first to Sesheke and then on by canoe up the Zambezi, preaching as he went and always halting on the sabbath. At Libonta (Libonda) they moved from Makololo territory to the country of the Balonda where Livingstone was forced to detour overland to pay his respects to the local Chief, Shinte, who received him formally, sitting in state, dressed in a kilt and attended by over 1,000 subjects. After 10 days as a guest of Shinte, who provided seven more men to accompany the expedition, Livingstone continued overland through Balobale territory to Lake Dilolo and across the central African watershed. Then, for over a month they resisted the threats and violence of the Bachokwe who demanded tribute payments in exchange for free passage through their land. Conditions grew worse, the porters became anxious to turn back and Livingstone fell ill with malaria, but he held the expedition together, convinced that God was with him. At last they entered Portuguese Angola at Kimeya and suffered no more intimidation on

Left *David Livingstone photographed in England. He returned from Africa in 1856, to receive a medal from the Royal Geographical Society for his discoveries and to rouse opinion in Britain against the slave trade.*

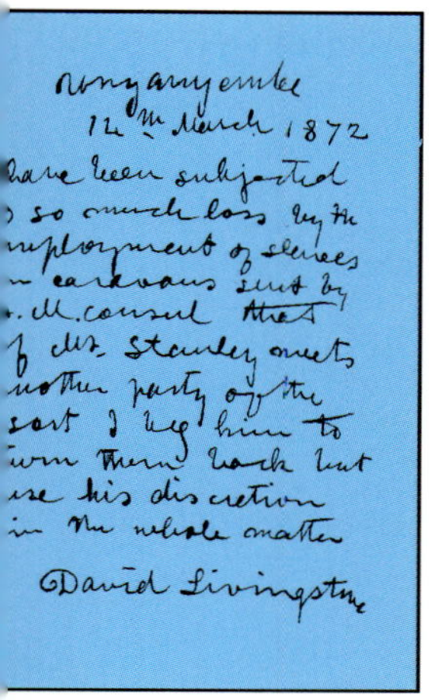
Unyanyembe
12th March 1872
have been subjected
to so much loss by the
employment of slaves
in caravans sent by
H.M. consul that
if Mr Stanley meets
another party of the
sort I beg him to
turn them back but
use his discretion
in the whole matter
David Livingstone

Above *A note to H.M. Stanley in Livingstone's hand, dated March 1872, refers to the difficulties caused him by slave caravans.*

their way to the coast at Luanda, although Livingstone grew weaker and weaker with fever.

In one sense this alone was a triumph of achievement, but Livingstone was not satisfied – he knew that the route from the west coast was not a viable one, particularly because of the prevalence of the tsetse fly, and so he now planned to cross Africa and investigate the eastern route. After four months in Luanda and another year's journey back to Linyanti, during which time he heard that he had been awarded the RGS Gold Medal, he set off again almost at once, again with Sekeletu's practical support. He started his 1,000-mile (1,610km) journey at the beginning of November 1855, this time with over 100 Makololo porters, travelling along the left bank of the Zambezi. Only a fortnight into the journey Livingstone deviated from his planned route and travelled by canoe to the place on the Zambezi known as Mosi-oa-Tunya, 'the smoke that thunders'. In his journal written at the time, Livingstone does not sound particularly impressed with these waterfalls and he hopelessly underestimated their size, but later he was to produce florid descriptions of what he named the Victoria Falls, talking about scenes which 'must have been gazed upon by angels in their flight.'

Next Livingstone went on to the Batoka plateau, keeping some way north of the Zambezi and convincing himself that this would be a hospitable area for substantial European settlement. If this dream was to be realised, the Zambezi must be proved navigable – Livingstone returned to the left bank and continued through a region that the Portuguese had been forced to abandon some years before. Armed tribesmen appeared ready to obstruct his crossing of the Luangwa River, outside Zumho, but again, fortified by prayer, Livingstone was able to continue unscathed. Convinced that he was doing God's will and that, therefore, his plans would succeed, he became careless and failed to inspect the whole line of the Zambezi between Mpende and Tete.

After a month's enforced rest at Tete to recuperate from illness, Livingstone continued to the mouth of the Zambezi and Quelimane, arriving in May 1856. Here he received a discouraging letter from the LMS expressing irritation at enterprises 'only remotely connected with the spread of the gospel' and offering little hope of future financial support. When he boarded ship for England he was on the point of resigning from the Society.

The Great Zambezi Expedition

Despite the disgruntled reaction of the LMS, Livingstone was immediately acclaimed a hero in England, receiving honorary degrees, lecturing to huge audiences and, before long, earning a huge sum in royalties from sales of his book *Travels and Researches in South Africa*. When he proposed another expedition, to sail up the Zambezi and establish a research station on the Batoka plateau, influential people listened, not realising the extent to which he had been carried away by his own enthusiasm. Livingstone had decided that the Zambezi was 'God's Highway' – the means by which Africa was to be opened up to Christian civilisation and trade, and the British government and the RGS willingly sponsored the expedition that was intended to make this dream come true. This time Livingstone was the leader of a large team including a geologist, an artist and an engineer. He had resigned from the LMS and now had a government salary and the official title of HM Consul to Quelimane.

Things went wrong from the start. The *Ma Robert*, the ship built specially for the journey from the mouth of the Zambezi to Kafue, proved

Left *The Victoria Falls on the Zambezi, as illustrated in Livingstone's book,* Missionary Travels and Researches in South Africa, *which was published in 1857. The Africans, more poetically, called the falls 'the Smoke that Thunders'.*

inadequate and Livingstone quarrelled with three of his companions. One left early of his own accord and Livingstone later dismissed the other two. Starting from the Zambezi delta in April 1858, the expedition did not reach Tete until September. Two months later Livingstone's folly in failing to inspect the entire river became clear. Ahead of them lay an impossible obstacle – the Kebra Bassa (Quebra basa) Gorge. Livingstone the national hero had made an enormous blunder but his belief in divine guidance kept him going; how the government, the RGS and the other members of the party maintained their faith in Livingstone is a more difficult question.

Livingstone's response was to change the route, sail up the Shire River, and investigate Malawi. Desperate to find a new site for the research base (which was, after all, the whole point of the expedition), he selected an area in the southern uplands, but the place was to prove unhealthy, the first missionaries sent there soon died and the station itself was short-lived. The list of disasters continued with the sinking of the *Ma Robert*, the death of Livingstone's wife,

Left *Too weak to walk, Livingstone was carried on a litter on what proved to be his last journey, to Lake Bangweulu, where he died of dysentery. His faithful Africans bore the body and the explorer's papers and instruments across country to Zanzibar, and from there it was shipped to England.*

Henry Morton Stanley

Stanley is chiefly remembered for his encounter with Livingstone at Ujiji, but there was far more to him than that. He deserves credit as a great explorer in his own right and one who was capable of astonishing feats of endurance. Originally named John Rowlands, he was born in Wales in 1841, went into a workhouse when still a young child and then escaped to America, where he adopted the name of a man who acted as his benefactor, Henry Hope Stanley. After periods of service on both sides in the Civil War, he began a career in journalism, and the meeting with Livingstone, which was a journalistic assignment and no mean achievement, persuaded him to continue the investigation of the central African river systems that Livingstone had begun. In 1874 he returned to Africa at the head of an expedition sponsored by two newspapers, his own *New York Herald* and the *Daily Telegraph*. The plan was to carry out further studies of the river systems and Stanley, travelling with three Europeans and over 300 porters was, like Livingstone before him, equipped with a boat, the *Lady Alice*, which was transported in sections and launched on Lake Victoria and Lake Tanganyika. Stanley's research confirmed that there was no connection between the Nile and Lake Tanganyika, vindicating Speke's theory about the source of the Nile, and, after a perilous journey during which nearly half of his men died, he also established that a river that Livingstone knew as the Lualaba was actually part of the Congo (later Zaire). When the British government showed no interest in the region Stanley had explored, he accepted a commission from King Leopold of Belgium, under which he returned to the Congo in 1879 to supervise the construction of a railway and, in effect, he secured the territory of the Congo Free State for the king, although his relationship with this capricious and cruel monarch was inevitably fraught with difficulties. After another extraordinary venture known as the Emin Pasha Relief Mission to rescue a German botanist trapped in southern Sudan, Stanley's reputation suffered severely. He wrote a number of books, gave lectures and even succeeded in winning election (by a small majority at the second attempt) to the British parliament as Liberal-Unionist MP for North Lambeth, but he had little patience with the parliamentary system and achieved no great distinction. When he died in 1904 there was talk of his being buried next to Livingstone in Westminster Abbey, but the suggestion was rejected, apparently because he was held to have led too violent a life.

Above *H.M. Stanley, photographed in the costume he wore when he met Livingstone at Ujiji.*

further fragmentation of the expedition and orders to bring the whole expensive enterprise to a close even before two new ships that had been brought to the area could be launched on Lake Malawi. The Great Zambezi Expedition lasted six years and resulted in the gathering of accurate geographical and geological information which contributed directly to the colonisation movement known as the 'Scramble for Africa'.

Livingstone reached England again in July 1864 and this time his reception was cool and polite. He spent six months writing his *Narrative* of the expedition, playing down the problems and the quarrels, and then began to think about another expedition.

***Above** 'Dr Livingstone I presume.' The famous meeting at Ujiji, when H.M. Stanley found the great explorer in 1871.*

The Last Journey 1866–1873

In spite of everything, Livingstone won the support of the RGS for another venture and, although this time the Government was not helpful, he found private sponsors and also provided some funds of his own. He had ambitions to settle two of the great contemporary puzzles – the source of the Nile and the Congo. He also wanted to investigate Lake Nyasa and the central African watershed. And he believed that the establishment of an inland settlement would help to end the slave trade that was carried on so vigorously in that region. His starting point was Zanzibar and this time he had no European companions and travelled with 60 native porters and a number of Indian soldiers whom he soon dismissed. They sailed first to the mouth of the Rovuma River and then went to Lake Malawi (Nyasa), but they were in dangerous territory and often under threat. Their route took them round the lake from the south to the northwest and at this point some of the hired men deserted and returned to Zanzibar, where they claimed that Livingstone was dead. He did indeed fall ill in April 1867 while exploring Lake Tanganyika, and his situation was not helped by the theft of his medicine chest, but he recovered well enough to pursue his search for the source of the Nile, investigating Lakes Mweru and Bangweulu. He began to suffer badly from tropical ulcers, and theft of supplies was a constant problem. However, he did not give up until he was shocked into doing so by a massacre that took place when Zanzibari slave-traders fired into the crowded market-place at Nyangwe. At this, Livingstone retreated to Ujiji on the shore of Lake Tanganyika where, in October or November 1871, for the first time in five years, he set eyes on another European.

***Below** The coffin arriving at Southampton.*

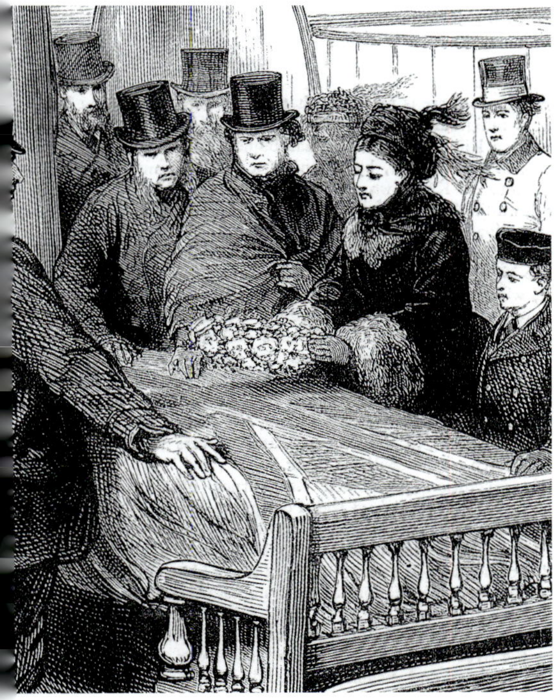

Meeting at Ujiji

The story of Stanley's mission and his greeting, 'Dr Livingstone, I presume,' has entered popular folklore. Stanley was a journalist on the *New York Herald*, travelling with instructions to 'find Livingstone' at a time when there was considerable alarm about the fate of the missionary explorer. Stanley arrived at a time when lack of supplies was becoming a serious problem for Livingstone and he restored his morale to the extent that, before long, the two men were exploring the north of Lake Tanganyika and discovering that this, at least, was not the source of the Nile. In March 1872 Stanley finally left. Livingstone refused to join him but requested more porters and supplies. When these arrived he set out once again, this time to explore Lake Bangweulu, near which he died on 1 May 1873, without knowing that, as a result of Stanley's reports, he was once more regarded as a hero in Britain – so much so that his embalmed body was transported back for a state funeral and burial at Westminster Abbey.

Biographical Notes

1813
Born at Blantyre, Scotland.

1840
Ordained and qualified as a doctor.

1854–6
Crossed Africa from coast to coast.

1858–64
Led Great Zambezi Expedition.

1866
Began exploration of central African river system.

1871
Meeting with H.M. Stanley at Ujiji.

1873
Died near Lake Bangweulu.

BURKE AND WILLS

The most famous exploring expedition in Australian history ended in tragedy

On 21 January 1863 a solemn funeral procession moved slowly through the city of Melbourne, watched by a huge and respectful crowd. A military band led the way with doleful music, houses along the route were draped in black and soldiers lined the streets. Two coffins under an open canopy rested on a funeral car of gigantic proportions, drawn by six black-plumed horses. At the cemetery the coffins were lowered into a grave, above which was subsequently set a 34-ton (35-tonne) stone inscribed to Robert O'Hara Burke and William John Wills, 'comrades in a great achievement, companions in death, and associates in renown.'

The two men whose remains were interred in solemn state that day had set out with high hopes and confidence from the same city almost 2½ years earlier, in 1860. Melbourne was a thriving town of 140,000 people, which had made its fortune in the Gold Rush of the previous decade. It was well placed to mount an expedition that would attempt to make the first crossing of the continent of Australia by white men, all the way from the south coast to the north.

The unknown interior

Australia's entire coastline had been surveyed long before, and settlements and sheep ranches had spread round the perimeter of the continent. What no one knew and everyone wanted to know was what lay in the middle, in the huge blank space on the map? Was there a great inland sea, as many thought? Was there good sheep pasture to be exploited? Did the heart of Australia have a future?

Attempts to answer these questions had been going on for 20 years. In 1840 Edward Eyre headed north from Adelaide for about 400 miles to Lake Toreens before turning back. Four years later, Charles Sturt led a strong party north from

Below The expedition set out from Melbourne in 1860. There was much public excitement about the camels, though they proved to be difficult to handle and alarmed the horses.

Left *Robert O'Hara Burke, the expedition's leader, was an Irishman of courage and charm, but without experience of the bush.*

Right *William John Wills, the English doctor's son, who became second-in-command.*

Below *The expedition was the first to cross the continent all the way from tidal water to tidal water, south to north.*

Adelaide up the Murray and Darling rivers and then further north into one of the most ferocious summers on Australian record, with temperatures up to 132°F (55°C) in the shade. Though penned up at a water hole for six months by the terrible heat, Sturt discovered Cooper Creek (or Cooper's Creek originally), which he named after Charles Cooper, a distinguished South Australian lawyer. He made probes further north, but was finally forced to give up when about 150 miles (240km) from the geographical centre of Australia.

In 1845–6 Sir Thomas Mitchell, heading towards the central region from the east, crossed the Great Dividing Range and penetrated into what is now western Queensland to discover the Barcoo River. The imperious Sir Thomas believed, mistakenly, that the Barcoo would be found to flow into the Gulf of Carpentaria and offer a badly needed route to the north coast. In 1858, however, Augustus Gregory travelled southwest along the Barcoo to Cooper Creek, confirming that the two rivers were the same.

The explorers

By this time a committee had been formed in Melbourne to organise an expedition to strike right across the continent. Interest mounted, well-to-do citizens gave money, and the government of Victoria contributed twice what had been raised from private sources. The obvious person to lead the expedition was Gregory, but he did not want to go. The job was advertised in the press and of the 14 applicants the choice fell on Robert O'Hara Burke.

Burke was a bachelor superintendent of police in his late thirties. He evidently charmed the committee, but with hindsight it is generally agreed that he was a bad choice. An Irishman of panache, dashing and impetuous, he had no experience of exploration or of living in the bush. Born at St Clerans, near Loughrea in County Galway, he had been an officer in the Austrian cavalry and served in the Irish police before emigrating to Australia in 1853 and serving bravely and effectively as a police officer in the gold camps. He was a man who relished action and had been disappointed by his failure to get into the Crimean War.

The second-in-command was to be an Englishman named George James Landells, who was appointed because he was believed to understand camels. The novel decision to take camels on the expedition set the public agog and Landells was packed off to India to acquire some.

The next man in the pecking order would turn out be a more important figure than Landells, who did not last long. William John Wills was an English doctor's son from South Devon, who had arrived in Australia a year before Burke. He was 26 when the expedition left Melbourne. A trained surveyor, he was a steady, dependable, loyal subordinate and it is his diary and letters that supply most of the information about the expedition. Burke kept a diary, too, but it is comparatively brief and uninformative.

The 15 other members of the party included a German named William Brahe and an Irishman named John King, who had served in the British Army in India and was enlisted by Landells along with the camels.

To Cooper Creek

Crowds of spectators turned out to cheer the expedition on its way as it started from Melbourne on 20 August, with its camels roaring, horses cavorting and a train of wagons laden with enormous quantities of equipment, from provisions to guns and fishing tackle, camel shoes, tents and camp-beds, books to read and gimcrack mirrors and beads to present to Aborigines.

It soon became clear that the expedition was weighed down by its own baggage. The party made slow progress through farming country in pouring rain. The wagons stuck in the mud. The camels frightened the horses and the male camels fought over the females. After three weeks the lumbering caravan reached the Murray River.

Burke was worried. He knew he had a rival in the field, in John McDouall Stuart, who had served with Sturt. Stuart had left Adelaide in March in a bid to reach the north coast. Burke did not want to be merely the second man to cross the continent, but Stuart had a long start.

Perhaps this was what made Burke short-tempered and high-handed. He quarrelled fiercely with Landells, who eventually resigned in fury and went back to Melbourne. Wills was moved up to second-in-command and John King was put in charge of the camels. The expedition ground slowly on.

It was October by the time they reached Menindee, an unprepossessing hamlet of tumbledown shacks on the Darling River. The summer heat was coming and it was now the wrong time of year to attempt the interior, but Burke could not bear to hang about for months at Menindee. He decided to push swiftly ahead with a select group travelling light for Cooper Creek, more than 400 miles to the north. The rest of the expedition would follow on more slowly with the bulk of the supplies.

Below *Cooper Creek, seen from the air. Known as the Barcoo River in its upper reaches, the stream flows from Queensland southwest towards Lake Eyre. It splits into numerous channels and dries up altogether for long periods of time.*

State of Nature

The Aboriginal inhabitants of Australia were still in the Stone Age when the first white explorers and settlers encountered them. They had never invented the wheel or writing, they did not grow crops or herd cattle, they wore practically no clothes and had only the simplest tools and weapons. They had no concept of private property, which often embroiled them with whites.

The Aborigines, or 'blackfellows' as the settlers called them, lived in small nomadic groups by hunting and gathering. The men stalked and speared kangaroos, wallabies and emus, dug or smoked out wombats from their burrows, trapped turkeys and ducks, killed koala bears with throwing sticks and caught fish in nets and traps. To the women, who were very much the subordinate sex, fell the task of gathering food – fruits and berries, nuts, seeds and roots, shellfish and such insects as witchety grubs, beetles, ants and grasshoppers.

To Captain Cook, in their simplicity the Aborigines were 'far happier than we Europeans'. For all their apparent primitiveness, their religious beliefs turned out to be hauntingly rich and strange, and they certainly understood their environment and how to survive in it far better than the white explorers who came to grief in the outback. They had extraordinary skill in tracking, their memory for country was astonishing, and some whites who got to know them believed they had telepathic powers. What they could not survive unscathed was the impact of European civilisation. As early as 1789 an epidemic of smallpox killed them in droves. Drink and guns ruined the lives of many more and their numbers have steadily dwindled.

Left *Aboriginal culture could not stand up to the impact of European ways.*

Among those with Burke were Wills, King, Brahe and an easy-going former sailor named Charlie Gray. There was also a man named William Wright, who knew the bush and would act as guide. They set out on 19 October with 16 camels and 15 horses over a vast plain which, unknown to them, would one day reveal millions of pounds worth of silver in the Broken Hill area. The party came to the strange region of spiky hills and deep pools that the Aborigines called Mootwingee and regarded as a peculiarly sacred place, where they made drawings and carvings on the rocks, of men, kangaroos and emus, snakes and boomerangs and the outlines of human hands and feet. Today it is a national park.

The white men shunned the place and hurried on. On 29 October Wright was sent back to Menindee to bring on the rest of the party. Burke and the others pressed ahead through blazing heat. On 11 November they reached Cooper Creek, where the river ran sweetly through eucalyptus and mulga trees. Birds and fish were plentiful, but so were mosquitoes, flies and rats of such insatiable appetite that all the supplies had to be hung from tree branches on strings. The heat was 109°F (43°C) in the shade. They made camp and rested, and waited for Wright to come up from Menindee with the main supplies.

The strike to the gulf

Days went by, weeks went by, and there was no sign of Wright. By the middle of December Burke could restrain himself no longer. He divided his forces again. Brahe and three others were left at the Cooper Creek camp, while Burke took Wills, King and Gray with him in a dash for the Gulf of Carpentaria. They would walk the whole way, 750 miles there and 750 miles back, carrying dried horsemeat, water and other supplies on Burke's horse and six camels. They each had a gun and a bedroll, but little extra clothing and no tents. Burke expected to be back at Cooper Creek in three months at the outside. They left on 16 December.

In his book *Cooper's Creek* Alan Moorehead gave a vivid account of the four men tramping monotonously on, leading the groaning camels, for 11 hours or more each day, covering 12 to 15 miles a day, changing direction to avoid swamps or to cross ridges. They laboured through the heat, besieged by swarms of flies, halted now and again by blistering sand-storms. They found a plant called portulaca, which they could boil and eat, but little else they could live on.

They crossed the Tropic of Capricorn and in January the Selwyn Range rose ahead of them, rugged hills that they struggled through into a country of thin scrub and spinifex grass, eucalyptus and paperbark trees, and towering anthills. Now the tropical rain poured down, day after endless day, turning the ground to a morass of mud. It was so hot they moved by night. At last they came to the Cloncurry River and followed it to the Flinders River.

On 10 February, only some 30 miles from the sea, it became impossible to get the camels any further through the mud. King and Gray stayed with them, while Burke and Wills went on with the horse. That night they tasted the water in the river and it was too salty to drink. They had reached tidal waters close to the Gulf shore, but the next day they decided that they could not get through the mangrove swamps to the sea itself. 'It would have been well to say that we reached the sea,' Burke wrote sadly, 'but we could not obtain a view of the open ocean, although we made every effort to do so.' Two disappointed men trudged wearily back to King and Gray. They had, however, crossed the continent successfully from tidal water to tidal water, and had done it first, as Stuart had been forced to turn back.

A shattering blow

On 12 February the party started back to Cooper Creek. The journey was a nightmare of exhaustion and starvation. They had less than one-third of their rations left. The rain was relentless, the ground a bog, the heat thick and enervating. They had no tents, so they slept in the wet, and their clothes fell to bits. They caught a snake and cooked it. They killed the horse and four of the camels and ate them. Gray was caught stealing the precious flour. He kept complaining of feeling ill. They thought he was malingering, but on 17 April they found him dead in his bedroll. They were so weak that it took them all day to dig him a shallow grave.

Four days later, in the evening, three men and two camels tottered into the camp at Cooper Creek to suffer a shattering blow. There was no one there. Following instructions blazed on a tree, they dug in the ground and found a box with a month's rations and a pencilled message from Brahe in a bottle. He and his men had left the camp that very morning, only a few hours before. If Burke and his party had not stopped to bury Gray, they would have arrived in time.

Brahe had waited four months, rather than three. Wright and the main stores had never appeared. His men were coming down with scurvy and the temperature was 112°F (45°C) in the shade. He did not know what had happened to Burke, so he pulled out to return to Menindee. On the way he encountered Wright, at last moving slowly forward. The reasons for Wright's delay were never satisfactorily explained and he lived the rest of his life under a cloud of public disapproval.

The last act

The three men at Cooper Creek were faced with an appalling dilemma. They were too exhausted to hurry on through the night after Brahe (he was actually only 14 miles [23km] away). Wills wanted to follow him to Menindee, but Burke decided they would head southwest down Cooper Creek for the police post at the ominously named Mount Hopeless, only 150 miles (241.5km) off. It must have seemed the sensible course, but it proved a death sentence.

Brahe and Wright rode to Cooper Creek and arrived on 8 May, 15 days after Burke, Wills and King had left. They failed to realise anyone had been there and rode back south.

Burke, Wills and King were some 30 miles away, struggling exhaustedly along the creek. Friendly Aborigines gave them fish. The country was drying out and the creek's various channels began to peter out. At a waterhole one of their two camels was hopelessly stuck in a morass of mud. They were not strong enough to pull it out and had to shoot it, which meant they had to carry its load themselves.

They were growing weaker and weaker, though kindly Aborigines, who had little enough to eat themselves, occasionally cooked them fish or delicious fat rats, done in their skins. The branch of the creek they were following turned north, the wrong way. Leaving it, they made a defiant forced march of six days towards Mount

***Above** Burke, Wills and King struggling to reach Mount Hopeless as their exhausted camel dies: an artist's impression of the scene by G.W. Lambert.*

The Last Letter

Wills wrote his last letter on 27 June 1861, to his father.

My dear Father,

These are probably the last lines you will ever get from me. We are on the point of starvation, not so much from absolute want of food, but from want of nutriment in what we can get . . . We have had very good luck and made a most successful trip to Carpentaria and back to where we had every right to consider ourselves safe, having left a depot here, consisting of four men, twelve horses and six camels. They had sufficient provisions to have lasted them for twelve months with proper economy. We have also every right to expect that we should have been immediately followed up by another party with additional provisions and everything necessary for forming a permanent depot at Cooper's Creek. The party we had here had special instructions not to leave until our return, unless from absolute necessity. We left the creek with nominally three months' supply, but they were reckoned at little over the rate of half rations, and we calculated on having to eat some of the camels. By the greatest good luck we crossed to the Gulf through a good deal of fine country, almost in a straight line from here. On the other side the camels suffered considerably from wet, and we had to kill and jerk one soon after starting back. We had now been out a little more than two months, and found it necessary to reduce the rations considerably, and this began to tell on all hands, but I felt it by far less than either of the others. The great dryness and scarcity of game and our forced marching prevented us from supplying the deficiency from external sources to any great extent, and we never could have held out but for the crows and hawks and the portulac. The latter is an excellent vegetable and I believe secured our return to this place. We got back here in four months and four days and found that the others had left the creek the same day. We were not in a fit state to follow them . . . I leave you in sole charge of what is coming to me, the whole of my money I desire to leave to my sisters; other matters I will leave for the present.

Adieu, my dear Father. Love to Tom [his brother].

W.J. Wills

[P.S.] I think to live about four or five days. My religious views are not the least changed and I have not the least fear of their being so. My spirits are excellent.

quoted in *Cooper's Creek*, Alan Moorehead

Biographical Notes

1821
Burke born at St Clerans, Ireland.

1834
Wills born at Totnes, England (5 January).

1853
Burke migrated to Australia; Wills arrived in Victoria.

1860
The expedition left Melbourne for Menindee (20 August); advance party left Menindee (19 October); reached Cooper Creek (11 November); reached tidal water at the Gulf of Carpentaria and turned back (11 February 1861); returned to Cooper Creek (21 April); deaths of Burke and Wills (late June 1861).

Hopeless. They covered 45 miles (72km), but they could find not a drop of water and they had to turn wearily back to the creek.

Wills by superhuman effort trudged back to the main Cooper Creek camp, but there was no one there and he returned to Burke and King. All they could do now was to wait and hope to be rescued. They lived on a plant called nardoo, whose seeds can be laboriously pounded into a floury paste and baked in a camp fire. They found it not very nutritious.

Wills was failing fast. On 29 June the other two went to look for Aborigines who might help them. Wills had written a final letter to his father, and read it to Burke and King before they left so that they could be sure he had said nothing unfair to them. They left him, but did not get far. After a few miles Burke collapsed and told King to leave him with his pistol in his hand and not to try to bury him. He died of starvation and exposure early in the morning, perhaps on 30 June, near the bank of a waterhole under a coolibah tree. There is a cairn there to his memory today. King went back to Wills and found him lying dead where they had left him.

On 13 September a rescue party from Melbourne arrived at the main camp on Cooper Creek, to find it deserted. Casting about, they met some Aborigines who were evidently excited to see them. Among them was a blackened, starved figure in rags and the remains of a hat, desperately weak and half out of its mind. It was John King.

The tragedy had a profound impact on Australia and has never been forgotten. Ironically, as Alan Moorehead pointed out, if Burke and Wills had returned to Cooper Creek a day earlier and survived their successful expedition, they would be less remembered today.

__Below__ The plant that the Aborigines called nardoo, otherwise sometimes known as 'clover fern'. Its pods can be ground between stones to make a starchy paste. Burke, Wills and King were reduced to living on this at the end.

Pioneer Women Travellers

'Ladies should never undertake expeditions to the more solitary districts without escort.'

KARL BAEDEKER

Above *Amelia Earhart, the pioneer American flyer, seen here with her plane in 1930. Two years later, she was the first woman to fly the Atlantic solo and in 1935 she flew from California to Hawaii. In 1937 she disappeared in the Pacific during a bid to fly round the world.*

It is possible to find books on exploration written relatively recently which declare that this is almost exclusively a male activity. Throughout the centuries, the argument goes, a typically masculine combination of strength, competitiveness and ambition has driven men to discover unknown continents, plant flags on top of inaccessible mountains and generally defy death and disease in the interests of extending their empires.

It cannot be denied that men have been the pioneers of exploration, often motivated by a strangely childish desire for fame which few women share, but also helped in their ambitions by a social structure that supported their adventurous quests while making it unthinkable for a female to, say, learn about navigation or join a party of reckless buccaneers and sail around the world. It is the pioneers with which this book is chiefly concerned, but if women have been denied the major prizes of world discovery, they have still made great contributions to the art of exploration and embarked on their own highly demanding personal quests.

Domestic discoveries

At the end of the 17th century Celia Fiennes travelled through every county in England on horseback and produced a valuable record of life and manners at that time. The subject matter may be on a domestic rather than an international scale, but this does not diminish the achievement and Celia Fiennes earned her place among contributors to the literature of exploration. She pointed out the folly of rushing abroad before one knows one's own country and wished that 'all persons, both Ladies, much more Gentlemen, would spend some of their tyme in journeys to visit their native land, and be curious to inform themselves and make observations of the pleasant prospects, good buildings, different produces and manufactures of each place'.

It is fair to say that, although there are quite enough dull, privately printed ladies' journals to reveal that, for some, travel does nothing to broaden the mind, serious women travellers have often recorded their discoveries and written up their observations with an academic rigour superior to that displayed in the accounts

Right *Dame Freya Stark at home in her study at Asolo, northern Italy. She was inspired to travel by reading* The Arabian Nights *as a child and made her first trip to the Middle East in 1927 ostensibly to restore her health.*

of many of their better educated male counterparts. Nor is there any shortage of distinguished female explorers. In her guide to women travellers, *Wayward Women*, published by Oxford University Press in 1989, Jane Robinson lists some 400 female adventurers and their publications, leaving no doubt as to women's appetite and aptitude for travel and the diversity of their experience.

Marital teamwork

Women accustomed to a life of sheltered gentility, or condemned for years to think of themselves as virtual invalids, have often surprised themselves and everyone else by their ability to cope with, and even thrive in, the most difficult conditions, from desperate cold and hunger in Tibet to deadly fever and threats of cannibalism in equatorial Africa. Many made their own decision to travel in spite of conventions that would have them behave differently, and relished their release from domestic tedium. However, some were rudely uprooted from the society they knew and were expected to trail after husbands who tended to regard a wife as just another part of the necessary baggage when their employment or their desire for adventure took them away from home. Although it can inspire exceptional teamwork, exploration is more often an activity for individualists and true co-operation between men and women is rare. The successful and happy partnership of Samuel and Florence Baker in Africa is as strange as the story of how it all began when Samuel purchased his future wife, a Hungarian refugee, at a slave market in present-day Bulgaria. Together they discovered Lake Albert Nyanza and the Murchison Falls. According to her husband, she was not a 'screamer' and several times ensured the success of their expeditions by calming rebellious porters, persuading traders to help them and wisely conserving the food rations.

Below *Lady Mary Wortley Montagu, who had a brilliant reputation in literary and intellectual circles in England, explored Turkey when she accompanied her husband on a posting there and described life in Constantinople in delightful letters home.*

In 1716 Lady Mary Wortley Montagu was unusual in being delighted at the chance to travel east with her husband when he became British ambassador in Turkey, and her *Letters*, describing a year-long journey to Constantinople and unfamiliar eastern scenes, were a huge success. Mary Livingstone, wife of David, had a less happy time. She was the daughter of a missionary, accustomed to Africa and aware of her religious duties, so to some extent she knew what to expect, but her uncomplaining ability to tolerate difficult desert journeys while pregnant and with several small children in tow, says much for female powers of endurance. Eventually her husband, who complained about her frequent pregnancies as if they were nothing to do with him, sent her home, where she struggled to survive with little money and later, on her return to Africa, she soon developed a fever and died.

The story of Harriet Tytler's experiences in India during the Mutiny also calls for admiration. Born in India, and the wife of an Indian army officer, she was the only 'lady' to witness and survive the three-month siege of Delhi by the British in 1857. She chose to stay, rather than be evacuated from the city, because the birth of her son was imminent. He was safely delivered, on a cart, in the most horrific conditions. Although Harriet Tytler's account of the events was written as a reminiscence 50 years later, it gives a good sense of all the horror and of the stoical resistance and religious faith that enabled her to cope with it. At one point, seeing a dead sepoy, she caught herself saying 'Serve you right for killing our poor women and children who had never injured you'. She realised that 'At any other time my heart would have been full of pity and sorrow at such awful sights, but after all we had suffered . . . pity had vanished and thirst for revenge alone remained. Such are the effects of warfare upon the hearts of gentle, tender-hearted women.'

Alone against the elements

The willing woman traveller is not necessarily a typical feminist; she may simply feel no concern with such petty distinctions as gender, seeing no reason to be restrained in her activities and feeling irritated when her achievements attract attention not for themselves but because the protagonist is a woman. Some, including Dame Naomi James the first woman to sail solo round the world, in 1977, have found widespread media attention more trying than any journey. Amy Johnson, a Yorkshirewoman working in London in the 1920s, took a first flying lesson out of curiosity and then crammed enough lessons into her spare time to qualify as a pilot. She also became a skilled aircraft engineer, working on equal terms with men in a thoroughly male-dominated business and, in 1930, flew solo in an open-cockpit plane from England to Australia, taking nearly three weeks to complete the journey. This and later flights offer an example of determination and achievement which few people have equalled, but Amy Johnson reckoned that her celebrity status caused the break-up of her marriage. It is possible also that her achievements made her feel invulnerable. Working in air transport during World War II she insisted on delivering a plane in appalling conditions. The plane crashed and she died in 1941.

Right *Mary Kingsley, who travelled deep into Africa and enjoyed her freedom immensely, maintained at all times the strict decorum of a well-bred Victorian lady.*

Freedom – with a long skirt

In the past, many women chose to maintain the conventions of femininity in an unusual setting. Gertrude Bell who, in 1888, was the first woman to take a first class degree in History at Oxford, began a life of exploration in the Middle East in an attempt to forget an unhappy love affair (another reason for travel often considered to be exclusively male). She consulted her parents in everything and always remained an opponent of the movement to give women the vote. Mary Kingsley, who once said that she went out to West Africa to die, found instead that Africa gave her a new *joie de vivre*, but at no point was she willing to surrender the decorous standards of clothing and behaviour which she had been brought up to consider appropriate for a Victorian lady. May French Sheldon, an American was another traveller in Africa at the end of the 19th century who chose to wear long skirts and even a blonde wig. She exercised ruthless discipline and was known as 'Lady Boss'. Her frilly dresses did not prevent her from carrying out serious studies of tribal customs and contributing to the understanding of East Africa, to the extent that the Royal Geographical Society rewarded her with a Fellowship in 1892.

Isabella Bird did not start travelling alone until she was 40 in 1872, after years of suffering from back trouble. A clergyman's daughter, she had lived the life of an invalid reluctantly and felt that Victorian propriety sapped her energy. 'I wish I cared for people,' she wrote, 'and did not feel used up by them.' She came to the conclusion that a servant's life would suit her and that 'manual labour, a rough life and freedom from conventionalities added to novelty would be a good thing'. Her life was dramatically transformed after a dangerous sea voyage and a prolonged stay on Honolulu. After that she visited Japan, travelled in the Rocky Mountains with some distinctly dubious companions, and also ventured as far as China, Korea and Tibet. She wrote books about her experiences (including the well-known *A Lady's Life in the Rocky Mountains*) and was one of the first women to be made a Fellow of the RGS.

Below *Dame Naomi James was the first woman to sail single-handed round the world, in two days less than it had taken Sir Francis Chichester. She is seen here before a transatlantic yacht race in 1980.*

Spiritual journeys

A Frenchwoman, Alexandra David-Neel, born in 1868, was the first western woman to enter the forbidden Tibetan city of Lhasa, but this was just one remarkable achievement in a life that also involved performing with a Parisian opera company, interviewing the Dalai Lama in exile at Darjeeling, journeying through war-torn China, receiving an invitation to lecture in comparative religion in Belgium, and spending 10 months living as a hermit in a cave in the Himalayas. Her devotion to the serious study of Buddhism was enough to earn her the status of an honorary lama, which no other western woman has achieved, and her visit to Lhasa was provoked by the fact that the British Resident in Sikkim actually ordered her out of Tibet.

Alexandra David-Neel is one of those whose expeditions to distant places combined with a desire for an inner, spiritual journey – something which would be immediately understood by the 20th-century Swiss traveller Ella Maillart. An accomplished skier and yachtswoman, she wrote of her *Forbidden Journey* in the 1930s from Peking to Kashmir, and also about other treks in India and Afghanistan, and then spent five years in southern India studying with a guru and practising prayer and meditation.

Alexandra David-Neel and Ella Maillart, like many other travellers from the west, found that travel opened their eyes to the truths of eastern philosophies, but if religious feelings gave meaning to their journeys, these were feelings of a very different sort from those that motivated most Christian missionaries, whose task it was to replace native beliefs with the Christian gospel. Many women left the comfort of their homes to take the good news to the heathen in inhospitable parts of the world, and the image of the Victorian missionary lady is a familiar one, but there were also some remarkable attempts at evangelism in earlier years. In 1658, very soon after the establishment of the Religious Society of Friends (or Quakers), Katharine Evans and Sarah Cheevers became convinced that it was God's will for them to take the message of Quakerism all the way to Alexandria. They got no further than Malta, where Jesuits suspected them of being witches and detained them for more than two years, during which they clung tenaciously to their beliefs. Eventually they were sent back to England, where they published an account of their 'Cruel Sufferings (for the Truth's sake)'. For such women there was no distinction between male and female when it came to doing God's work. A voice within told them what to do and if that meant attempting a perilous journey, they were ready to go.

Few women have believed in such precise instructions from the Almighty, but many have responded to an instinctive desire to explore. Amelia Earhart, the pioneer American aviator who, in 1932, became the first woman to fly solo across the Atlantic, perhaps spoke for many of them, before and since, when she said that women 'must try to do things as men have tried. When they fail, their failure must be but a challenge to others'.

Above right *Amy Johnson, the Hull-born English flyer, is seen here with her Gypsy Moth plane* Jason, *in which she flew solo from England to Australia in 1930. On the way she flew blind through sandstorms, and had to make a forced landing in Java to patch the wings with sticking plaster.*

Right *Alexandra David-Neel explored oriental beliefs as well as forbidden territory when she went to the Himalayas and Tibet. She is the only western woman to have been accepted as an honorary Buddhist lama.*

MARY KINGSLEY

An exceptional Victorian woman who exchanged a life of stifling drudgery in England for one of high adventure in West Africa

One of the few surviving photographs of Mary Kingsley shows a lean, upright figure dressed with all the dignity and decorum to be expected of a Victorian matron. It is a picture redolent of lavender water and starched primness but the determined face peering out above a high collar and a firmly knotted bow has an enigmatic expression. This woman might he about to utter a severe rebuke to a wayward child or tradesman, but the appealing and sometimes riotous humour of her book *Travels in West Africa* leaves one in no doubt that she could equally well be about to give way to peals of laughter.

Right *The indomitable Mary Kingsley was a self-educated anthropologist and naturalist of distinction and described her African journeys with sympathy and humour.*

Early years in England

Her first thirty years were spent at home, in London and Cambridge. Much of this time Mary was tied to the home, caring for her unhappy, invalid mother and a younger brother who was provided with the education which Mary would have valued dearly and which, as a woman, she was denied. Her father, George Kingsley, brother of the novelist and author of *The Water Babies*, Charles Kingsley, travelled the world as a private physician to one aristocrat or another. George was an amateur naturalist and ethnologist and his accounts of his wanderings in his letters and on his periodic returns home excited and inspired Mary. Apart from some lessons in German, provided specifically so that she could be of assistance to her father, she educated herself, devouring volumes on exploration from her father's library as well as delving passionately into chemistry, zoology, physics and medicine, and making it her personal mission to sort through her father's papers and support him in his work.

During 1892 her parents died within a few weeks of one another, but her sense of duty was such that she still did not consider her time her own until her brother's decision to leave England relieved her of the obligation to keep house for him. Suddenly the woman who spoke of herself as always having lived 'in the joys, sorrows and worries of other people' was free, and if one major sense of purpose, that of caring for others, had been removed, she lost no time in finding another. 'In 1893' she wrote, 'for the first time in my life, I found myself in possession of five or six months which were not heavily forestalled, and feeling like a boy with a new half-crown, I lay about in my mind as to what to do with them.' Her decision was to go to Africa and to carry out the sort of research into native tribal customs which had taken her father to other distant parts of the world. Already something of an amateur anthropologist and naturalist, she was more than ready to leave her books and theories behind and to investigate the realities of life in a world very different from her own.

First foray into Africa

After a recuperative journey to the Canary Islands, which served as a preview to Africa, Mary Kingsley left England on her first African expedition in August 1893, equipped with a long waterproof sack stuffed with blankets, boots, books and anything else which would not fit into her portmanteau or black bag. As she travelled from London to join her ship at Liverpool she considered the significance of the fact that no return tickets were available on the West African cargo steamers and she wondered why the very first expression in her phrasebook was 'Help, I am drowning'.

During this first journey on the steamer *Lagos*, once it had been established that she was neither a missionary nor a representative of the World's Women's Temperance Association sent to spy, she received much practical advice from the ship's captain and from the traders who worked the African coast. Later, it was generally as a trader that she carried out her researches on African soil, using tobacco as her principal currency. It gave a credible purpose to her journey to those who might otherwise be baffled at the sight of a white woman travelling in such wild country (she also used the excuse that she was looking for her lost husband), and helped to finance her expeditions.

The 1893 journey took her by sea to Freetown in Sierra Leone and down the coast to what is now Luanda in Angola, stopping at various ports along the way.

After initially getting cold feet and taking a Portuguese boat back up the coast to Cabinda in the hope of catching a boat back to England, which she missed by a day, Mary decided to stick it out. In Cabinda she met R.E. Dennett, an English ex-trader and student of African languages, folklore and traditions, who found her accommodation in a rather run-down dwelling briefly occupied by Stanley and served as a sort of tutor to Mary on things African.

One evening in a Cabinda village Mary came upon a family bolting out of their hut, which had been invaded by swarming driver ants, and so obviously distressed at having left something behind that she thought it must be their baby.

'I joined the frenzied group, crying, "Where him live?" "In him far corner for floor!" shrieked the distracted parents, and into that hut I charged. Too true! There in the corner lay the poor little thing, a mere inert black mass, with hundreds of cruel Drivers already swarming upon it. To seize and give it to the distracted mother was, as the reporter would say, "the work of an instant." She gave a cry of joy, and dropped it instantly into a water barrel, where her husband held it down with a hoe, chuckling contentedly. Shiver not, my friend, at [such] callousness . . . that there thing wasn't an infant – it was a ham!'

Next she sailed down the Congo River to Matadi where she travelled on the Congo Free State Railway – 'one of the most risky things you can do in all Africa' she wrote. (A year previously an engine had careered into a pile of dynamite

Above *Mary Kingsley's expeditions in the 1890s took her into the Congo and Gabon regions of West Africa and deep into the equatorial jungles.*

Left *The port of Liverpool in the 1880s, with the Cunard liner Campania. Mary Kingsley started both her West African journeys from Liverpool, then England's major west-coast port.*

left on the line.) In the French Congo, Mary continued on foot with just a small group of African bearers, trading with villagers and collecting fish and insect specimens until finally reaching the port of Libreville, where she caught a ship home to England.

Second voyage out

In December 1894 Mary Kingsley left Liverpool aboard the steamer *Batanga* on her second West African journey. After 12 months of frustration in London – keeping house for her feckless brother and writing an account of Africa which she later withdrew from publication because she disliked its amateur tone – she was free once more. This expedition had the blessing of Dr Günther of the British Museum, who had commissioned Mary to collect fish from the area between the Niger and Congo rivers and had given her the equipment to enable her to do so scientifically.

Disembarking at Calabar, she spent some time exploring the Cross River area and conducting a valuable study of the little-known Bubi tribe on

Below *Mary Kingsley's canoe on the Ogowé, close to the equator in Gabon. On this second African journey she had a commission to collect specimens for the British Museum.*

the Spanish island of Fernando Pōo (Bioko). She then travelled to Lagos, where another ship took her to the French Congo port of Glass. She planned to make a detailed investigation of the Gabon region and this involved an ambitious, not to say reckless, journey along the Ogowé (Ogoové) River running almost along the line of the equator.

As far as Lambaréné the journey was an exceptionally beautiful and reasonably straightforward one by paddle-steamer, but the name of one of the settlements beyond gave a suggestion of what lay ahead; Talagouga, Mary Kingsley tells her readers, means Gateway of Misery. Here, the French Mission Evangelique was her base for expeditions into almost impenetrable equatorial jungle and here she taught herself to manage a native canoe so well that, with a crew of eight local Galoa people, she survived a journey further upriver to the magnificent Alembe rapids. The voyage was punctuated with regular capsizes and calls to abandon ship. Apparently unhampered by her long, thick, black skirt, Mary Kingsley appears to have leapt easily in and out of

Crocodiles

"A crocodile drifting down in deep water, or lying asleep with its jaws open on a sand-bank in the sun, is a picturesque adornment to the landscape when you are on the deck of a steamer, and you can write home about it and frighten your relations on your behalf; but when you are away among the swamps in a small dug-out canoe, and that crocodile and his relations are awake, he is highly interesting and you may not be able to write home about him – and you get frightened on your own behalf. For crocodiles can, and often do, in such places, grab at people in small canoes.

On one occasion, one chose to get his front paws over the stern of my canoe, and endeavoured to improve our acquaintance. I had to retire to the bows, to keep the balance right, and fetch him a clip on the snout with a paddle, when he withdrew, and I paddled into the very middle of the lagoon, hoping the water there was too deep for him or any of his friends to repeat the performance. Presumably it was, for no one did it again. I should think that crocodile was eight feet long; but don't go and say I measured him, or that this is my outside measurement for crocodiles. I have measured them when they have been killed by other people, fifteen, eighteen and twenty-one feet odd. This was only a pushing young creature who had not learnt manners."

from *Travels in West Africa*, Mary Kingsley

Above *Mary Kingsley died tragically young in 1900, carried off by enteric fever while nursing Boer prisoners-of-war in South Africa. This photograph, taken that same year, shows Boer fighters.*

the water. As ever, she emphasises the comic side of her adventures and plays down the dangers.

On her safe return to Lambaréné, with countless warnings ringing in her ears, she soon set off on a week-long journey through the jungle between the Ogowé and the Rembwé (Rembové) rivers. She had encountered some of the notorious Fang tribespeople before, but this expedition took her to Fang villages untouched by any outside influences – places where the rumoured Fang cannibalism was most likely to be seen. In the village of Efoua Mary Kingsley discovered some fairly persuasive evidence:

> 'I went in for another doze, and the town at last grew quiet. Waking up again I noticed the smell in the hut was violent, from being shut up, I suppose, and it had an unmistakably organic origin. Knocking the ash end off the smouldering bush-light that lay burning on the floor, I investigated, and tracked it to those bags, so I took down the biggest one, and carefully noted exactly how the tie had been put round its mouth; for these things are important and often mean a lot. I then shook its contents out in my hat, for fear of losing anything of value. There were a human hand, three big toes, four eyes, two ears, and other portions of the human frame. The hand was fresh, the others only so so, and shrivelled. I subsequently learned that although the Fangs will eat their fellow friendly tribesfolk, yet they like to keep a little something belonging to them as a memento.'

Mary reacted to this experience with complete composure and went on to several more settlements, finally reaching Agonjo (Akondjo) and then canoeing down the Rembwé. It was the sort of journey everyone said could not be done and, as so often, Mary Kingsley proved them all wrong. Her second West African expedition ended with a flourish when she climbed Mungo Mah Lobeh (Mount Cameroun), perhaps the first woman to have done so. When she finally boarded ship again for England it was with every intention of returning to her beloved West Africa as soon as possible. In fact she was never to see this part of the world again.

Travels in West Africa and beyond

After *Travels in West Africa* had reached a wide audience she also published *West African Studies*, and a *Story of West Africa*, and edited some of her father's work, which appeared as *Notes on Sport and Travel*. Her collection of specimens resulted in three new varieties of fish being identified and named after her, but her liberation was sadly short-lived. Despite all the attention and the belief that she was doing worthwhile work in her own right, she never lost her sense of duty to others and it was this that took her to South Africa in March 1900 to nurse Boer prisoners of war at Simonstown. In West Africa she had survived exposure to danger and disease, but here enteric fever killed her at the age of 37.

Mary Kingsley is seldom named among the first rank of explorers and adventurers, and it is

Missionaries

Firmly agnostic in her upbringing, Mary Kingsley had a low opinion of missionaries and their impact on those they attempted to convert. Before she left England on her first expedition she was advised to read some missionary literature for an insight into the places and the native people she would encounter. She found little of use to her because 'these good people wrote their reports not to tell you how the country they resided in was, but how it was getting on towards being what it ought to be.' The missionaries also tended to paint a damning picture of the West African traders – the very people whom Mary valued for their help and support. She is scathing in her condemnation of the Hubbard, a sort of woman's smock imposed on Africans by missionaries:

'I think these things are one of the factors producing the well-known torpidity of the mission-trained girl: and they should be suppressed in her interest, apart from their appearance, which is enough to constitute a hanging matter. . . . What idea the pious ladies in England, Germany, Scotland and France can have of the African figure I cannot think, but evidently part of their opinion is that it is very like a tub.'

Exempt from her criticism were the members of the French Mission Evangelique – people she considered to be engaged in a perfect, purely spiritual activity. Another missionary who won her respect was Mary Slessor, a Scotswoman known to all as 'Ma'. Mary Slessor lived for years in the Calabar region, where she was noted for her work rescuing twin babies – regarded in local folklore as offspring of the devil. Mary Slessor lacked the arrogance of some missionaries and took the trouble to understand the people among whom she lived.

Despite such exceptions, Mary Kingsley wryly observed that 'if the aim of life were happiness and pleasure, Africa should send us missionaries instead of our sending them to her'.

***Left** Mary Kingsley was one of the first Europeans to view Africans and their arts, crafts and way of life with a non-judgemental eye and in an effort to understand rather than change them. She brought these Benin brass armlets back to England with her.*

Biographical Notes

1862
Born in London.

1892
Death of both her parents.

1893
Travelled to West Africa to explore Angola and parts of the Congo River.

1894
Returned to England with specimens of beetles and fishes.

1894–5
Second voyage to Africa: travelled up the Ogooué River.

1897
Published *Travels in West Africa* and was much in demand to give lectures.

1900
Died while nursing sick prisoners-of-war in South Africa.

sad that whole histories of African exploration have been written without any reference to her at all. As a writer, she knew what made a good story and presented herself as a rather blundering, accident-prone individual, always missing her footing, tumbling through the roof of a native hut or landing up to her neck in murky water. The comedy is appealing but does not conceal any lack of scientific rigour. She made a point of reporting only those things that she knew from personal experience and never accepted an explanation of any native custom from one person alone. Her efforts to understand the outlook of the tribal people she met were sincere and, unlike many of the missionaries whose work she distrusted, she did not set out to judge them. While not rejecting colonialism, she wrote books and gave lectures drawing on her experience in an attempt to increase British understanding of West African people and their way of life, and suggesting how imperial rule might be altered for the better.

The path that led directly into the West African jungle from a life of stifling drudgery in Victorian England was a previously untrodden one, and one which Mary Kingsley made her own.

FRIDTJOF NANSEN

Nansen, the 'gentle giant' of Arctic exploration, reached a new furthest point north while exploring the Arctic basin

From Viking times to the present, Scandinavia has spawned a succession of seamen and maritime explorers, nurtured in the sheltered harbours of its endless coastline, and prompted by poor natural resources to find a living elsewhere. First came the Vikings, coastal farmers who spread across northern seas and colonised from Kiev to Labrador.

Then came the whalers, sealers and fishermen, who explored Arctic waters to Svalbard, the ice edge and beyond. Their counterparts today are Scandinavia's maritime scientists – explorers who see new truths about the world's oceans. Of these Fridtjof Nansen was among the first and greatest.

Below *Dr Fridtjof Nansen, seen in his skiing gear in Franz Josef Land in about 1896.*

The early years

Born in Store Froen, close to the Norwegian capital Christiania (now Oslo), Nansen was raised in a prosperous and lively family, with parents who stimulated his interests and encouraged his mental and physical development. Tall, broad, athletic and enquiring, with a dominant but gentle personality, he studied zoology at his local university and might well have become a teacher or university research worker. But a wise zoology professor suggested he spend some time on a summer voyage to the Arctic, taking passage on a sealing vessel and studying the anatomy of seals killed on the ice.

From March to the end of summer, 1882,

Nansen lived the hard life of a sealer, tracing the ice edge along the east Greenland coast. Greenland's formidable mountains and glaciers were often visible, sparkling in summer sunshine with the interior ice-cap rising behind.

On return to Norway, Nansen was appointed curator of the Bergen zoological museum, continuing his studies of animal anatomy during working hours and skiing, climbing and walking the fells when time and weather allowed. His vision of Greenland persisted; its massive icecap, unique in the northern hemisphere, had barely been visited and never explored. An accomplished cross-country skier, with one Arctic season behind him already, Nansen convinced himself that the Greenland ice-cap could and should be crossed, and that he was the one to attempt it.

Crossing Greenland

At the end of the 20th century, crossing the Greenland ice-cap is relatively simple for any group of fit, sensible young people with money to buy equipment from sporting goods stores. Nansen in 1887 began by having to raise money for the expedition, but had also to design his own equipment, for skiing and tobogganing were not yet established sports and gear suitable for long cross-country journeys did not exist.

Raising money was not easy, even for a small, economical expedition, for Norway was a poor country and exploration in Greenland, a distant land under Danish control, had no immediate appeal to government or taxpayer. A wealthy Dane, Augustine Gamel, eventually became his sponsor. In designing equipment Nansen showed remarkable ingenuity, based on his hard-won experience of winter travel in Norway. He fashioned lightweight skis, ski bindings, a light flexible sledge, a boat, inner and outer clothing suitable for the long trek, and a system of aluminium cooking posts based around the recently-introduced kerosene pressure stove, designed for maximum economy of fuel. The Nansen sledge, based on his design, is still widely used in many forms by polar explorers. The

Below *The slow, drifting three-year journey of* Fram *across the Arctic ocean brought back a vast quantity of scientific information, subsequently published in six substantial volumes.*

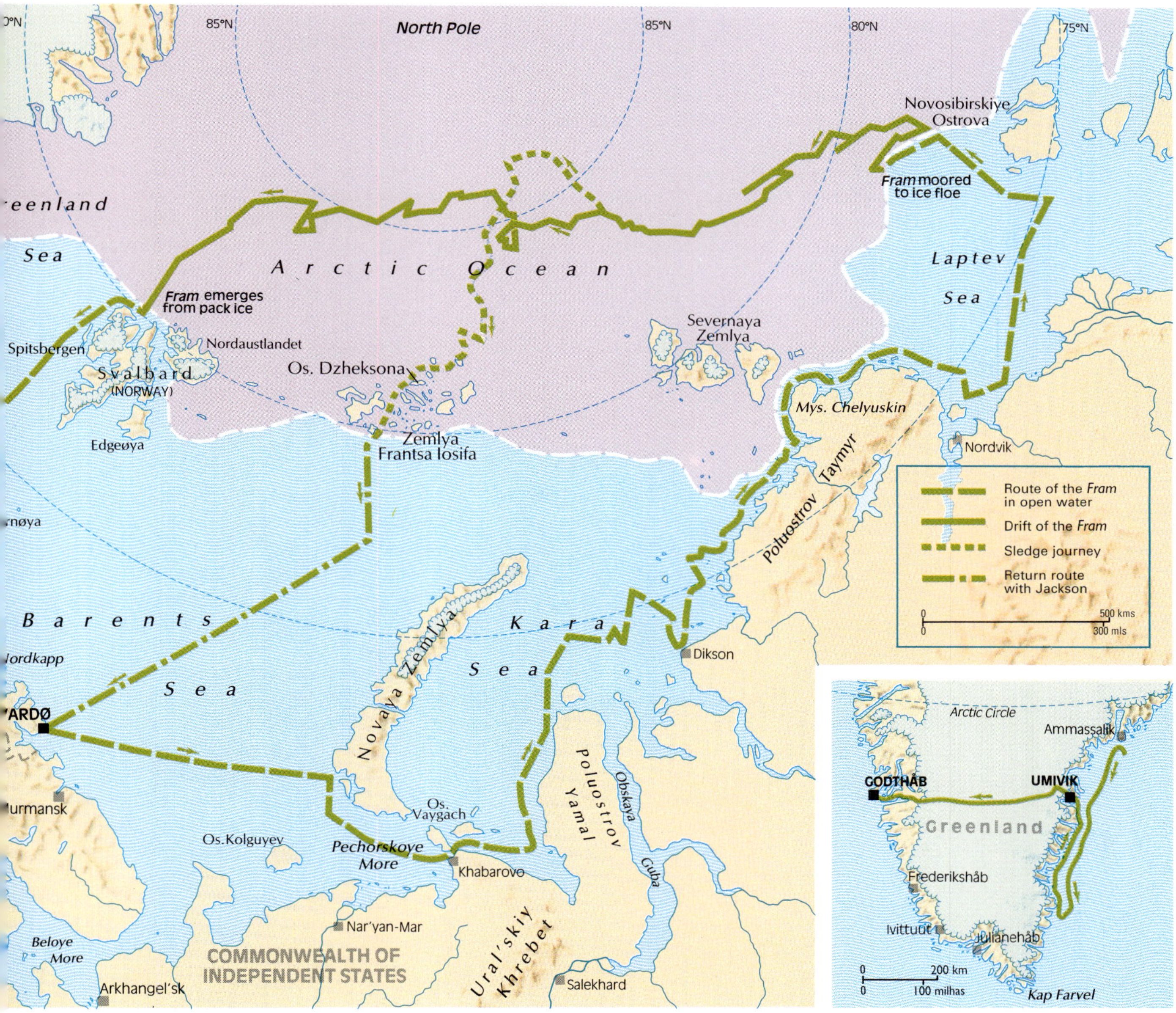

Above *The Nansen sledge is based on the one specially designed by the explorer for his expedition across Greenland in the 1880s, and has been used by many polar expeditions. This one was photographed in the Antarctic.*

Nansen cooker was for many years standard equipment for polar travellers.

For his travelling companions Nansen recruited three Norwegians, Otto Sverdrup, Oluf Dietrichson and Kristian Trana, and two Finmark Lapps, Balto and Ravna. All were young; Nansen was 26, and the oldest member, Sverdrup, was 33. The five-man party left Christiania in early May 1888, sailing via Leith and Iceland to join up with the sealing fleet that was already working in Arctic waters.

From Iceland the sealer *Jason*, a small steamboat, took them northward along the east Greenland coast, where a stream of heavy pack-ice flowed steadily down from the north. On 7 July, close to Angmagssalik (Ammassalik), *Jason* nosed into the ice and Nansen and his party were put down onto the floes. They had with them ½ ton (½ tonne) of camping gear, food and scientific equipment, and two small boats; the boats were seaworthy enough to row across the sometimes turbulent open water between the ice floes, but light enough to haul out when the ice pressed closely around them.

Some 10 miles (16 km) of shifting ice and open water separated them from the shore where they hoped to start their crossing of Greenland; the party expected to be on land within a few hours. However, it soon became clear that they had underestimated both the difficulties of floe-hopping and the strength of the southward-flowing current.

However fast they moved westward, from time to time the jostling movements of the floes brought them uncomfortably close to the open sea, where they were lashed by heavy surf. This was uncomfortable and dangerous enough, but more seriously, they found themselves drifting rapidly southward at a speed much greater than their westward progress. For 10 days they watched the panorama of the east Greenland coast sliding past, as they drifted some 300 miles (480km) south of their landing point.

Eventually they reached the inshore coastal water and began the long haul back north. After a further two weeks' travel, involving 200 miles (320km) of sailing and pulling, they landed at Umivik, which Nansen had noted as one of several likely places to start their inland journey. It was further south than he had intended and, because Greenland tapers southward, the crossing would be shorter than he had planned. However, time was pressing; it was already long past midsummer, and it was not his intention to spend winter in tents on the Greenland ice-cap.

The crossing began on 10 August. Nansen and Sverdrup found a route up a heavily crevassed glacier, returning to lead up the rest of the party with five heavily-laden sledges. For the first four weeks they were climbing, steeply at first and then almost imperceptibly. For the first few days they were hot, but temperatures fell as they climbed, and biting winds reminded them that summer was almost over. Snow surfaces varied, sometimes deep and soft, at other times wind-crusted and gritty, making the sledge-runners drag as though through soft clay. It was hard, gruelling work, faced cheerfully by the Norwegians but less so by the Lapps, who began to find the whole operation both boring and dangerous. By 12 September hard slogging had brought them to the summit; one week later they were running downhill with the wind behind them, sledge sails set, and the men skiing hard to keep up.

Throughout the journey Nansen and his colleagues maintained records of weather and snow conditions, took astronomical fixes, monitored their height above sea level, and plotted a course that would bring them down into Godthåb, a small Danish and Eskimo settlement on the west coast. On 19 September they caught their first glimpse of mountains and ran into the first crevasses of the western slopes. Soon they were descending through a range of spectacular mountains, following the glacier that runs into Godthåbfjord. A week later they crossed from ice-cap to moraine and dropped to the coastal plain. Leaving most of their equipment to be recovered later, they marched over tundra towards the sea. Finally, Nansen and Sverdrup sailed to the settlement of Godthåb in a ramshackle boat, hastily constructed from bamboo marker-poles, theodolite legs, willow twigs and a canvas tent-floor.

It was now early October and the last boat of the season had sailed from Godthåb. However, the party spent a happy winter in the settlement, enlivening the tiny community with their presence. Nansen took the opportunity to study the Eskimos, later writing a valuable work on their ethnology. He and his party returned in triumph to Copenhagen in May 1889.

Crossing the Arctic Ocean

Nansen wrote up his expedition reports, married Eva Sars, the daughter of a distinguished zoologist, and moved back to Oslo, where he became curator of the university zoology museum. Now his thoughts turned to the Arctic Ocean, and the possibility of a scientific expedition both to study the polar basin and to reach the North Pole. No polar expedition had so far managed to penetrate the compact ice of the Arctic basin; many had tried, and several had been lost in trying.

His attention focused on the remarkable story of *Jeanette*, an American expedition ship that in 1879 had foundered among pack-ice off the Siberian coast. Three years later wreckage from *Jeanette* had appeared in the pack-ice of Julianehäb, a settlement near the southeastern corner of Greenland. Driftwood and human artefacts from Siberia had also turned up along the Greenland coast. Clearly the pack-ice that Nansen had ridden through the summer of 1888 originated in the Arctic basin, so the ice that packed the basin was constantly mobile.

Nansen envisioned a small but sturdy ship, built to withstand ice pressure, that could enter the pack-ice off the Siberian coast and ride the drift in safety. This could offer the best opportunity for reaching the Pole. Not surprisingly few shared his vision; Arctic seamen and scientists condemned it as dangerous and bound to fail. However, his powerful presence and gentle, intelligent persuasion raised funding from the Norwegian government, public and scientific community. Slowly, Nansen's vision became reality.

With Colin Archer, a Norwegian shipbuilder and designer, he developed a steel-hulled ship of 787 tons (800 tonnes) displacement some 115ft (35m) long, 40ft (12m) broad with a draught of less than 5½ft (5m). *Fram* ('Forward') was a round-bottomed schooner with both sails and a steam engine, capable of making 7 knots in good conditions. Her accommodation met new standards in comfort and practicability and her holds were capacious, for Nansen was planning in terms of a five-year expedition, in which the ship would become a floating scientific base. *Fram* was launched in 1892, and in 1893 set off on her long journey across the polar basin.

The crew of 12 included Captain Otto Sverdrup of the Greenland party, a medical officer, and a young but widely experienced crew. During the planning stages Nansen had made it clear that reaching the North Pole was not the main objective:

"... for to reach this point is intrinsically of small moment. Our object is to investigate the great

Below *A glacier near Etah in northern Greenland. Nansen and his party made the first crossing of the Greenland ice-cap, skiing and hauling or sailing their sledges. They made careful observations all the way.*

unknown region that surrounds the Pole and these investigations will be equally important from a scientific point of view whether the expedition passes over the polar point itself or at some distance from it."

There were few trained scientists willing to embark on so hazardous and uncertain a venture, but Nansen inspired all his men with the need to take systematic observations at every opportunity.

Fram sailed from Vardø to Novaya Zemlya and headed eastward along the Siberian coast. At Khabarovo, in the Kara Sea, they picked up stores and sledge dogs, then continued eastward. It was a leisurely journey through relatively open water; here and there they stopped to hunt reindeer and polar bears. On 6 September they negotiated Proliv Vil'kitskogo and four days later rounded Cape Chelyuskin (Mys Chelyuskin). On 25 September Nansen judged that they had steamed and sailed far enough. *Fram* was made fast to an ice floe in 78° 50′N, and by the end of the month was frozen into the Arctic pack. The drift of *Fram* was erratic and slow, but she wandered, as Nansen had predicted, well west of north across the Arctic basin. Soundings through the ice indicated when the ship had left the Siberian shelf and crossed into deeper water. During October pressure began to build up in the ice, heralded by creaking and groaning, and manifest when the jumbled floes began to pile up around the ship. In Nansen's words:

". . . you hear a sound like the thundering rumble of an earthquake far away on the great waste: then you hear it in several places, always coming nearer and nearer. The silent ice world re-echoes to traverse deep water: the Arctic basin."

As the ship drifted erratically onward it became apparent that they would miss the North Pole by many miles. Nansen therefore determined that two of them should leave *Fram* and head towards the Pole on foot. He and Lieutenant Johanssen sledged off on 14 March 1895 in 84° 04′N, a position some 400 miles (645km) from the Pole. It was a hard journey over rough ice; they had little food with them, and no chance to replenish stocks in the desert in which they found themselves.

After 25 days they had travelled across the drifting ice to 86° 14′N, and decided that that was enough. With no clear knowledge of where *Fram* might be, they turned southeastward and headed toward Franz Josef Land (Zemlya

Below *Nansen and Johanssen wave farewell to* Fram *as they set off with their dog-teams for the North Pole. They were forced to turn back when about 230 miles (370km) from their goal.*

Frantsa Iosifa), where they hoped to find a habitable expedition hut and a stock of food. Making landfall eventually on Frederick Jackson Island (Os. Dzheksona) in late August, they were prevented by open water from going further. There was no ready-made shelter but, inventive as always, Nansen dug a hole in the raised beach of the island, laid across it a driftwood framework and roofed it over with walrus hide. The two men lived there, cold and often hungry, but in reasonable safety, until 19 May 1896.

Continuing their travels over the Franz Josef archipelago, on 17 June, by an extraordinary chance, they met Frederick Jackson, a wealthy British yachtsman well known for his explorations in this sector of the Arctic. With him they returned to Norway, reaching Vardø on 13 August. *Fram*, meanwhile, had broken out of the ice close to Svalbard, and under Sverdrup's command made her way back to Norway, to arrive about the same time. The expedition members were all reunited in Christiania on 9 September 1896.

Aftermath

Nansen's book *Fram over polhavet*, translated into English as *Farthest north*, appeared in 1897. It caught the public imagination as few other polar books had. Nansen continued his career as a research scientist, and became the expert that all others consulted in polar matters. When Norway achieved independence in 1905, figures of world status were needed to represent her in diplomatic circles, and Nansen found himself more and more in demand. After World War I, in which Norway remained neutral, he represented his country in the newly-formed League of Nations. He achieved fame once again, this time with the 'Nansen Passport', a document that was issued to displaced persons in the aftermath of the war. He died, a much revered figure, in 1930.

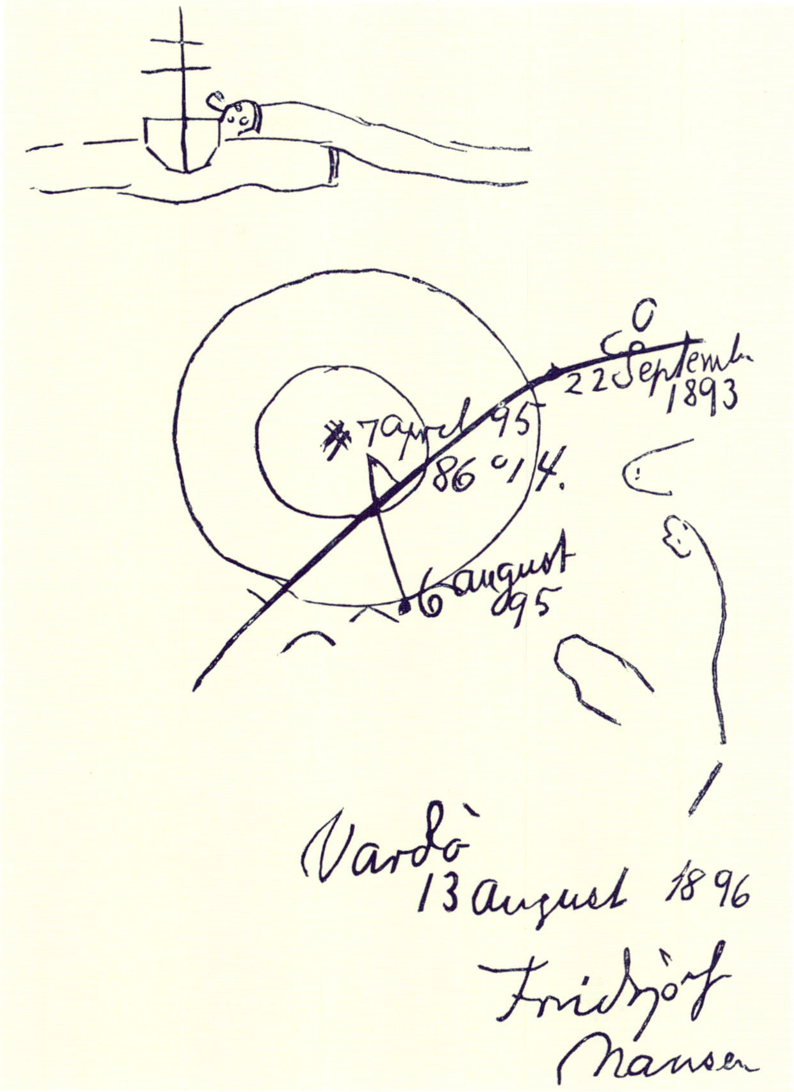

***Above** Nansen's scribbled sketch plan of his attempt on the North Pole in 1895, done when he reached Vardø in the following year. His polar exploits and his subsequent work for refugees after World War I won him international renown and he was awarded the Nobel Peace Prize in 1922.*

Arctic Exploration in Nansen's Time

In the 18th century, Arctic exploration had four main objectives: reaching the North Pole, finding the North Magnetic Pole, and exploring the Northeast and Northwest Passages. By the late 19th century, Nansen's time, the last three of these had been discovered; all that remained was the North Pole itself. Whether it would be found on land or in mid-ocean was still anyone's guess, though Nansen and other oceanographers were convinced, from accumulating evidence of currents and ice movements, that the Arctic basin was largely empty of land. It was, however, likely to be full of pack-ice – impenetrable barriers of ice 3ft (1m) or more thick that formed each winter on the Arctic fringes, and dispersed southward each spring and summer.

Behind the outer ring of annual pack lay immense fields of heavier ice several years old, forming an even more formidable barrier to small ships. This perennial ice was known to circulate slowly in ways that were not fully understood, occasionally leaving gaps of open water that lured ships to their destruction. So many losses, so many narrow escapes, had made all mariners intensely wary of Arctic pack-ice. Hence the radical nature of Nansen's approach to allow a ship to be frozen in and drift with the pack – and the fear and derision with which the idea was met.

Biographical Notes

1861
Born 10 October in Store Froen, Norway.

1880
Entered university to study zoology

1882
First visit to the Arctic in sealing ship *Viking*; first sight of Greenland.

1888–9
Led a party of five in the first crossing of the Greenland ice-cap.

1893–6
The *Fram* expedition across the Arctic basin.

1930
Died.

SVEN HEDIN

A tireless and dedicated explorer of the world's most inhospitable regions

In April 1880 the Finnish explorer, A.E. Nordenskiöld, arrived in Stockholm aboard a ship called the *Vega*. His expedition had been away for almost two years and had been feared lost, but, after 10 months trapped in ice at the extreme eastern end of the Arctic coast of Siberia, the steam-powered *Vega* had become the first vessel to find a way through the Arctic Northeast Passage. In Stockholm she received an ecstatic welcome. Among the crowds was Sven Hedin, who was 15 at the time, and that day decided his career. He heard the cheers roaring like thunder from the quays, streets, windows and roofs and he thought, 'I, too, would like to return home that way'.

His first ambition was to be an Arctic explorer and to find the North Pole, something for which he prepared himself, not only by reading and drawing maps, but also by rolling about in snow and sleeping by open windows during the long Swedish winters. Later, all his powers of endurance were to be severely tested, but not in the Arctic. While still at school, he was offered a job as a tutor at Baku on the Caspian Sea, and the journey out was a captivating experience, involving a dramatic trek up and down a zigzag army road cut through the Caucasus mountains. Asia soon became the focus of Hedin's ambitions as an explorer, and his name came to he particularly associated with the history of the exploration of Tibet.

First journeys

In April 1886, when his teaching contract was over and he had learned to speak Persian and Tatar, Hedin set off on his first expedition,

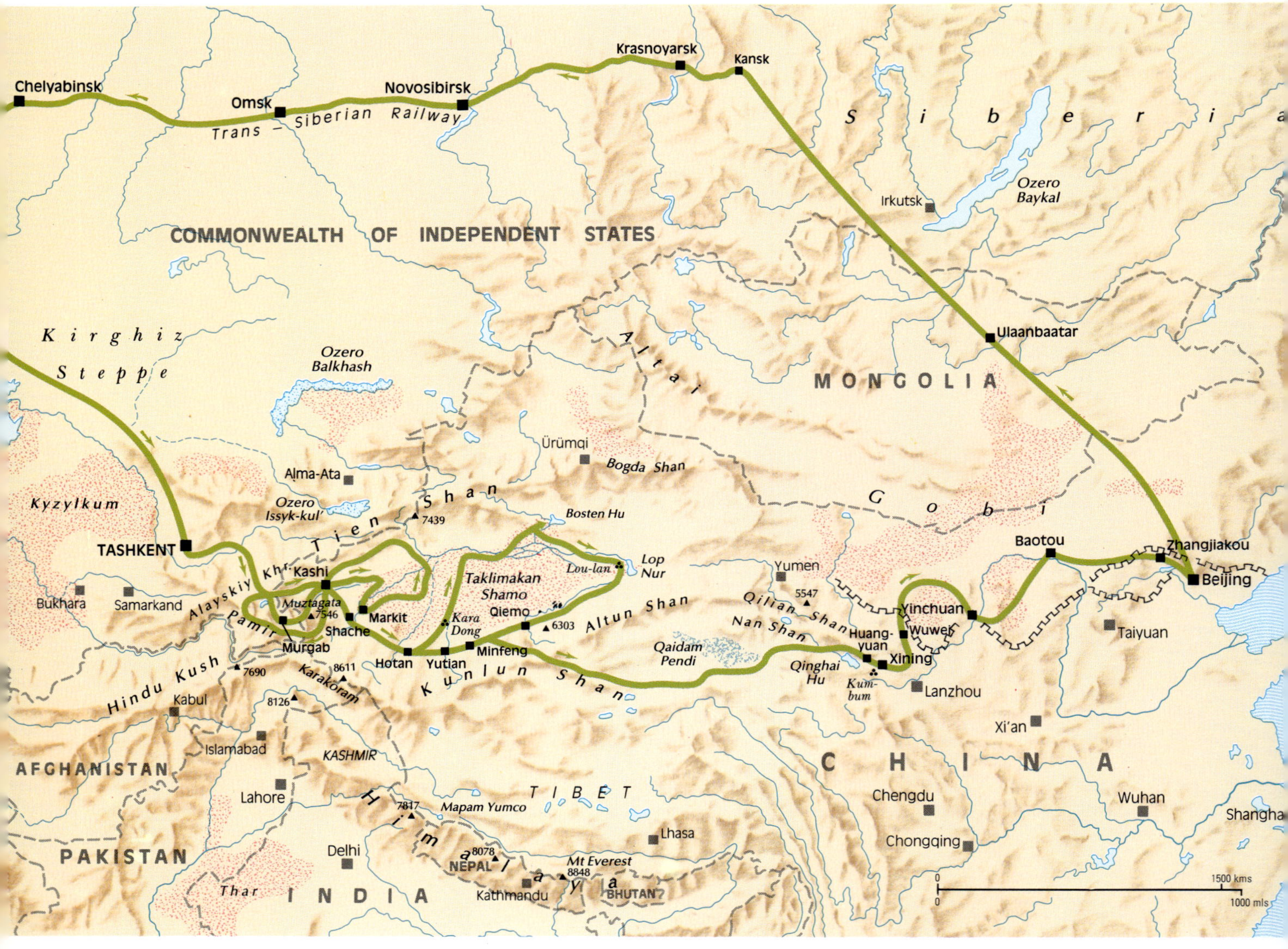

***Below** Hedin's journeys in the 1890s took him across 'the roof of the world' in the Pamirs and into regions of Central Asia still almost unknown to outsiders.*

travelling on horseback, originally with one companion and then alone, south through Persia to the sea at Bushire. Here he took a ship to Basra, and then continued to Baghdād. From there, with no servant and very little money, he rode to Kermanshah, travelling with merchant and pilgrim caravans for part of the way. He continued on to Tehran, Baku and Constantinople before returning home, where he published an account of his journey.

He soon left again, accompanying a royal embassy to the court of the Shah of Persia. When the official business in Persia was over, in June 1890, Hedin continued his exploration of the East, visiting Bukhara and Samarkand and entering Chinese Turkestan before returning to Sweden. At this point he felt that his apprenticeship as a traveller was over. 'Now,' he said, 'I was content with nothing less than to tread paths where no European had ever set foot.'

Exploration on a grand scale

His next journey was to last three years and seven months, during which time he mapped a total distance of 6,200 miles (10,500 km), nearly one third of which was over land previously uncharted. Hedin left Sweden in October 1893, going first by carriage, pulled by a succession of horses, across the icy Kirghiz Steppe for 1230 miles (2080 km) to Tashkent. The next stage of the journey took him across the Pamir mountain region, otherwise known as the roof of the world. Encouraged, like many a traveller before him, by warnings that the route he proposed was impossible, and that he would die in the attempt, Hedin made his way with three servants along the valley of the Isfairan River, and along a treacherous path through the Alai mountains (Alayskiy Khr). There was a constant danger of slipping on the ice, and one of the seven pack- horses did just this and fell to its death. The temperature was at times as low as −37°C and a human skeleton in the snow and signs of a bloody struggle warned the travellers of the presence of ravening wolves, but Hedin and his small party eventually made it to their next stopping place, the Russian fort of Pamirsky Post (Murgab).

They went on, through the Chugatai Pass and crossed from Russian into Chinese territory, where they were regarded with suspicion but allowed to continue. Hedin had to travel blindfold for a while to protect his seriously inflamed eyes from the cold. He began to recover as the temperature grew warmer on the approach to Kashgar (Kashi), which they reached at the beginning of May 1894. However, he could not resist the temptation to return the way he had come and climb Mustagh-ata (Muztagata), at 24,757ft (7,546m) known as the 'Father of the Ice Mountains'.

Next, from his base at Kashgar, Hedin planned an expedition to the Takla Makan desert (Taklimakan Shamo), where there were rumoured to be ancient towns buried in the sand. Travelling with two horse-drawn carts, they first followed the Kashgar-daria (Kaxgar He) and Yarkanddaria (Yarkant He) rivers. After a pause at Merket (Markit), Hedin set off again, this time with eight camels and their drivers, while the locals shook their heads and remarked that 'They will never come back'. Before long, this prediction was proving alarmingly close to the truth. Their water supplies were inadequate and, already weak, they ran into a fierce sandstorm. With three of their camels already dead and their water exhausted. Hedin collapsed and the rest of the camel train left him. Later he staggered after them and caught them up, but now all of them, including the animals, were overcome by exhaustion. Desperation drove some of the servants to drink sheep's blood and camel urine, but this could not save them and soon almost all were dead. Hedin himself finally found water and he and a servant were rescued by travellers.

Left *A photograph of Sven Hedin shows the explorer looking suitably determined as his eagle gaze seems to scan the far horizons. As a teenager he imagined himself discovering the North Pole, but he grew up to spend much of his life among the mountains and desert wastes of the East.*

Nowhere in his account of these events does Hedin say that he was tempted to abandon exploration after such a near brush with death. Instead, after recovering his strength in a shepherd's desert camp, he was eager to move on again. Most of his baggage and scientific instruments had been lost, and he made another expedition into the Pamirs while waiting for replacements. Then, at the end of 1895, he left Kashgar for Khotan (Hotan), and from there ventured back into the desert, where his guides took him to the buried town of Takla-makan. He saw posts and wooden walls sticking out of the dunes, collected some plaster figures of the Buddha, and reflected that 'No explorer had an inkling, hitherto, of the existence of this city'.

Eager to continue on routes untrodden by any other explorer, he next decided to follow the course of the frozen Keriya-daria, a plan that brought him to Kara-dung (Kara Dong) (the Black Hill), another buried town where Buddhist teaching had once prevailed, and to an area inhabited by rare wild camels. Hedin's next goal, on the way back to Khotan, was the Lop Desert mentioned in Marco Polo's *Travels*, the inland delta of the Tarim River (Tarim He), and the Lop Nor lake (Lop Nur), which had been seen by one of Hedin's heroes, the Russian general Nikolai Przhevalsky, in 1877, and whose exact position was an enigma that Hedin hoped one day to solve. On this occasion he explored the river system to the east and made an extraordinary journey by canoe along narrow waterways lined by thick reeds that were often over 20ft (6m)) tall.

Into Tibet

Back in Khotan, Hedin prepared himself for another challenge – his first journey into Tibet. With a caravan of 21 horses, 29 donkeys and six camels, eight servants and 17 Taghlik guides, he travelled to Keriya (Yutian) and Niya (Minfeng) before following a river valley up to the Dalai-Kurgan district a height of 11,000ft (3,350m). From here they travelled east for two months without meeting another human being. At altitudes over 15,000ft (4,570m) many of the party fell ill and progress was slow. Hedin reported that 'it was with a group of invalids that I made my entrance into northern Tibet'. They were travelling through unknown and unnamed regions and gradually the conditions became too much even for the animals; soon they were reduced to five camels, nine horses and three donkeys.

At last they met some Mongolian peasants, and Hedin paused long enough to learn something of the language and buy replacement horses before pressing on. Conditions improved as they travelled between the plains of Tsaidam (Qaidam) and the Tibetan mountains and spent the nights at Mongol tent-villages, but there were threats from Tangut robbers to deal with, and another barren region to negotiate as they approached the Yak River (Bukhain-gol/Buh He) and the Koko-nor (Qinghai Hu) (Blue Lake) at an altitude of about 10,000ft (3,050m).

Below *A yak caravan high among the mountains of Tibet. Hedin covered so many miles in Tibet that the British apologised to him for taking the virginity of the bride he had coveted – meaning Lhasa. Later, his pro-Nazi sympathies did harm to his reputation.*

Lhasa

Remote and mysterious, the Buddhist holy city of Lhasa sits 12,000ft (3660m) up in the Tibetan Himalayas near a tributary of the Brahmaputra River. Noted for its numerous monasteries, Lhasa is dominated by the holiest temple in Tibet, the four-storey Gtsug-lag-khan, built during the 7th century AD, and by the Potala Palace. This was formerly the winter home of the Dalai Lama, the leader of the Buddhist Dge-lugs-pa (or Yellow Hat) sect and the spiritual and temporal leader of the country.

Lhasa was the ancient capital of Tibet, but lost this authority in 842 AD, when the ruling king was assassinated. In subsequent years the city developed into a religious centre of unique importance and became home to thousands of Buddhist monks.

As was the case with Christian monasticism, new, more austere sects or orders tended to develop whenever there were signs that an established order was giving way to decadence.

The Yellow Hat sect, founded in the 14th century by Tsong-kha-pa, advocated a return to celibacy and abstinence from alcohol and meat, and placed great emphasis on intellectual activity. In 1642 Lhasa again became the capital of Tibet. Its reputation as an almost inaccessible city in a land where Europeans were not welcome inevitably attracted explorers (Sven Hedin among them) who were looking for a new challenge in a world where there were few unknown regions left.

Each Dalai Lama is believed to be a reincarnation of the last. The present one was born in 1935, enthroned in 1940 and driven into exile in India in 1959 following an unsuccessful Tibetan revolt against the Communist Chinese forces that invaded and occupied Tibet in 1951.

Once over the Khara-kottel Pass they were in a more populated area and finally reached a city, Tenkar (Huangyan), where members of a Christian mission looked after them. Hedin now visited the temple-city of Kum-bum and stayed with members of the China Inland Mission at Sining (Xining), where he dismissed all but one of his party before setting off on the last stage of his journey to Peking (Beijing). There was still a huge distance to cover, via Liang-chow-fu (Wuwei), Ning-sha (Yinchuan), and across the Yellow River (Huang He) to Bao-to (Baotou) and Kalgan (Zhangjiakou), but the journey was a reasonably good one, with hospitable mission stations along the way.

After 12 days in Peking he began the journey home, via Mongolia and Siberia, using the Trans-Siberian Railway (then complete as far as Kansk) and covering, 1,800 miles (2,897km) by carriage and sledge. Pausing at St Petersburg for an audience with Tsar Nicholas II, he mentioned his plans for another expedition and received a promise of support. Then, on 10 May 1897, a steamer finally brought him back to Stockholm. His parents and friends gave him a joyful greeting, but, he notes sadly, 'there was no trace of the triumphal procession that I had dreamt of as a schoolboy, that time when Nordenskiöld returned to Stockholm. The whole city was thinking only of the great exhibition which was then about to open'. However, Hedin's achievements were soon acknowledged publicly by the King and virtually every geographical society in Europe held a reception in his honour.

A lost city in the desert

Two years later, Hedin was on his way to Asia again on another extraordinary journey, during which he made his way across the Gobi Desert. He discovered the remains of the city of Lou-lan, which had been abandoned some 1,500 years earlier when the waters of the Lop Nor lake had retreated. Hedin excavated a Buddhist temple and a number of houses and found coins dating from the year 7 and 14 AD as well as some of the oldest known paper documents. The discovery of Lou-lan had diverted him from his original purpose – to enter the forbidden Tibetan city of Lhasa disguised as a pilgrim. He now tried to go ahead with this plan, but despite his disguise and his lama companion, the Tibetans became suspicious and intercepted him. He continued through Tibet, with an official escort watching over him, into India and then home.

One more attempt on Lhasa

He was still obsessed with Tibet, and in particular with the region marked 'unexplored' on a map published by the Royal Geographical Society in 1906. 'It was my ambition,' he said, 'to obliterate that word, to supplant it by the correct names of mountain ranges, lakes and rivers, and to cross and recross the white spot in as many directions as possible.' He tried again to get to Lhasa and failed. However, by 1906 this was no longer a major disappointment because, since his last journey, there had been a brief British military invasion, and much of the mystery of the forbidden Tibetan city had been dispelled. Instead, Hedin could be content with exploration of the Transhimalaya mountain region, investigation of Lake Manasarowar (Mapam Yumco) and speculation about the source of the Brahmaputra River (Maquan He).

Throughout his long life, Hedin continued to travel extensively and produced detailed accounts of all his journeys, including nine volumes of text and three of maps on *Southern Tibet*, which contributed much to current understanding of the region. If it was the overwhelming enthusiasm of the crowds greeting Nordenskiöld in 1880 that encouraged him as a boy to become an explorer, he soon demonstrated that he was not really motivated by mere hopes of fame. Rather, he was totally dedicated to the business of travel, discovery and scientific reporting.

Biographical Notes

1865
Born Stockholm.

1886
First journey in Persia.

1890
To Bokhara and Chinese Turkestan.

1893–7
Major Asia expedition.

1900–1
Attempted to reach Lhasa.

1906–8
Further travels in Tibet.

1952
Travelled widely until death in 1952.

The Polar Regions

'And now there came both mist and snow
And it grew wondrous cold:
And ice, mast-high, came floating by,
As green as emerald.'

S.T. COLDRIDGE
The Rime of the Ancient Mariner

Above *'Ice, mast-high . . .' Icebergs and sea ice at Melville Bay, high on the west coast of Greenland. John Ross passed this way in 1818 in command of a British naval Arctic expedition. With him was his nephew, the young James Clark Ross, who was to become a distinguished polar explorer.*

If any proof were needed of the determination of human beings to master their environment in the teeth of the most daunting dangers and obstacles, the history of the polar regions would supply it. The Antarctic is so inhospitable that it has never been settled and the Arctic, if not quite so desolate, is hardly a welcoming place. It consists largely of floating ice and even in high summer the temperature hovers around freezing point. Even so, explorers have risked and not infrequently lost their lives investigating both regions.

The Antarctic is a continent of solid ground surrounded by icy water, while the Arctic is an ocean of floating ice surrounded by permanently frozen ground. Taking its name from the constellation of the Great Bear ('bear' is *arktos* in Greek), it is the region between the North Pole and the northern tree line, above which no trees grow. Most of the area is occupied by the Arctic Ocean, which covers about 5½ million sq miles (approximately 14 million sq km).

Golf in the Arctic

The earliest human beings to explore and settle in what is now the Canadian Arctic came originally from Asia across the Bering Strait. They were the ancestors or the present-day Inuit ('the people'), better known to the outside world as Eskimos. The Norse colonised southern Greenland, but the modern history of white exploration of the Arctic begins in the 15th and 16th centuries with attempts by English and Dutch seamen to find a northern route to the Far East. John Cabot was trying to reach China across the North Atlantic when he collided with Newfoundland in 1497. He was to have many successors.

Right *John Cabot, the 15th-century sea captain who found Newfoundland in his way when trying to reach China across the North Atlantic.*

***Left** The Dutch navigator Willem Barents, who led three expeditions along the Arctic coast of Russia. A winter in the ice killed him in 1597. He left his name to the Barents Sea.*

In the 16th century English and Dutch venturers tried to get through to the East the opposite way, along the northern coast of Russia. A Dutchman, Willem Barents, piloted three expeditions in the 1590s, discovered Bear Island and Svalbard (Spitsbergen) and rounded the northern tip of Novaya Zemlya. He and his men, who encountered icebergs, pack-ice, polar bears, walruses and the local Samoyed aborigines, were the first men to play golf in the Arctic. Barents did not survive the third voyage.

The Russians began systematic exploration of their Arctic coast in the 18th century, but it was not until the 19th that the Northeast Passage was at last successfully negotiated, by Adolf Nordenskiöld, a Swede born in Finland, who left Tromsö, Norway in the *Vega* in July 1878 and reached the Pacific a year later.

As near to heaven

It was the Northwest Passage, however, that fascinated British explorers, from Gilbert, Frobisher and Drake in Elizabethan days to Captain Cook, Sir John Franklin and many more. Sir Humphrey Gilbert in the 1570s forcefully pointed out the huge advantages the Northwest Passage held for England (the distance from London to Japan is less than 8,000 miles (12,870km) by that route). He was drowned in a storm in the Atlantic in 1583, saying cheerfully not long before his ship went down, 'We are as near to heaven by sea as by land'.

The map is sprinkled with the names of explorers who braved freezing temperatures, ferocious gales and monstrous seas, icebergs and crushing pack-ice, frostbite, scurvy and starvation: Frobisher, Davis, Hudson, Baffin, Foxe, James, Ross, McClure . . . Relationships with the Eskimos spanned the scale from murderous to amicable. John Davis's men in the 1580s danced hornpipes to entertain the natives and played a football match against them. A Danish expedition under Jens Munk spent an appalling winter at Port Churchill on Hudson Bay in 1619–20, which only three of them survived. Thomas James's vivid journal of his adventures in the ice helped to inspire *The Ancient Mariner*.

Though the attempts failed, each explorer added to the store of knowledge and experience. A strong tradition of British Arctic exploration grew up that has endured ever since, and the quest for the Northwest Passage unlocked the doors, not to the riches of Cathay but to those of the fur trade, which was a major factor in the European exploration and settlement of North America. The Hudson's Bay Company, the principal British fur-trading concern, was given its charter in 1670.

In the 19th century, with Britannia ruling the waves after the defeat of Napoleon, fresh attacks on the Northwest Passage were launched by the British Admiralty, which found the Arctic a useful training ground for officers. In 1818 the government confirmed an earlier offer of a prize of £20,000 for the discovery of the Passage, and over the next 30 years naval expeditions led by John Franklin, George Back, William Parry, John Ross and his nephew James Clark Ross explored Arctic waters. At the same time prospectors from the Hudson's Bay Company, travelling overland in sledges pulled by huskies and copying Eskimo methods of living off the land, explored northern Canada.

Tragedy struck when Franklin left England with the *Erebus* and the *Terror* in 1845 and did not return. His ships were caught in the ice and he and his men died. The numerous search parties sent to find him added considerably to the stock of Arctic knowledge. In 1850 a naval expedition under Robert McClure in the *Investigator* approached from the west, from the Bering Strait, and was stuck in the ice for two winters.

***Above** The Arctic was home to the Inuit.*

***Below** Speeding over the Arctic snow.*

They sledged overland and were rescued by another ship, coming from the east, which took them home through Baffin Bay in 1854. McClure and his crew were the first Europeans to traverse the Northwest Passage, though in the 'wrong' direction and without their ship.

The North Pole

Using boats mounted on sledge runners, William Parry attempted to reach the North Pole in 1827, but had to turn back at 82° 45′N, some 500 miles (800km) short of the goal. Reaching the Pole was not a practical possibility until steamships had replaced sailing vessels. American expeditions between 1853 and 1873 probed north from Baffin Bay and in 1875–6 the British Arctic Expedition reached 83° 20′N by sledge. In 1879 an American naval officer, George Washington de Long, set off from the Bering Strait in the *Jeanette* to cross the Arctic Ocean, but the ship was caught and crushed in the ice and de Long and his crew starved to death.

De Long's attempt inspired the formidable Norwegian zoologist Fridtjof Nansen to try the same exploit in a specially strengthened boat, the *Fram*, which between 1893 and 1896 drifted across the Arctic from Siberia to Svalbard, gathering a treasure of scientific information on the way. In May 1895 Nansen left *Fram* to strike across the pack-ice for the North Pole itself and reached 86° 14′N.

The North Pole became a goal to be attained for its own sake – like Mount Everest – and competition to be the first to reach it became intense. In 1900 an Italian party, led by a naval officer and distinguished mountaineer, Umberto Cagni, got as far as 86° 34′N by sledge from Franz Josef Land. Between 1903 and 1906 the Northwest Passage was at last successfully navigated by the great Norwegian explorer, Roald Amundsen in *Gjöa*. Admundsen hoped to be the first man to the North Pole, but in 1909 an American naval officer, Robert Peary, claimed to have reached the Pole by sledge with a party of Eskimos. How close he actually came to it is in dispute, but the frustrated Amundsen turned to the South Pole instead.

With 20th century technology applied to the frozen North, in 1926 the American airman, Richard Byrd, flew over the North Pole and a few days later Amundsen and the Italian aviator, Umberto Nobile, flew over it in an airship and dropped flags on it. Thirty years later, regular commercial flights over the polar region were pioneered by Scandinavian Airlines.

Right Captain Scott on skis during the Antarctic expedition from which he did not return.

Below Pressure ice piled up in Greenland. Treasures of courage, endurance and determination have been expended on conquering the frozen worlds of the two Poles.

Left Roald Amundsen, the great Norwegian explorer who won the race against Scott to be the first to the South Pole.

The American submarine *Nautilus* made the first voyage under the North Pole in 1958. In 1969 the British Trans-Arctic Expedition led by Wally Herbert reached the North Pole by dog-sledge in the course of the first surface crossing of the Arctic, from Point Barrow in Alaska to just short of Svalbard. In 1978 a Japanese mountaineer, Naomi Uemura, reached the Pole from Ellesmere Island, north of Greenland, alone with his dog-team. Between 1979 and 1982 Sir Ranulph Fiennes and Charles Burton made the first circumnavigation of the globe by way of both poles. By earlier standards, the North Pole was becoming almost crowded.

The White South

The last continent to be explored is the coldest, most arid and most inhospitable of all. The ice sheet covering Antartica is 3 miles (4 km) thick in places and contains 90 per cent of the world's fresh water in some 7 million cubic miles (about 30 million cubic km) of ice. The cold is phenomenal and temperatures have been recorded down to −87.2°C (−128.6°F). The only human inhabitants are the temporary personnel of research stations.

Captain Cook sailed the whole way round Antarctica in the 1770s, but did not actually set eyes on it. The honour of being the first to do that is usually accorded to two Russian navy ships under Captain Fabian Bellingshausen, which sighted an ice-covered area of what is now the Princess Martha Coast in January 1820, in the course of circumnavigating the continent. A few days later Lieutenant Edward Bransfield of the Royal Navy discovered what he named Trinity Land (now Graham Land) and later in the year an American sealer, Nathaniel Palmer, also sighted land.

The initial sightings were followed up by various expeditions in the 1830s and 1840s. Captain Dumont d'Urville of the French navy named Adélie Land and, less flatteringly, the Adélie penguin, after his wife. An American expedition was led by Lieutenant Charles Wilkes of the US navy and a British one by James Clark Ross. Though battered by fierce storms, Ross's expedition discovered the Ross Ice Shelf and Victoria Land, and its members were reduced almost to incoherence by the astonishing beauty of the icy landscape under clear blue skies. Ross wrote that 'we gazed with feelings of indescribable delight upon a scene of grandeur and magnificence far beyond anything we had before seen or could have conceived'.

The 'heroic age' of Antarctic exploration had to wait until the 1890s and 1900s. A Belgian expedition of 1897–99 led by Adrien de Gerlache with Roald Amundsen among the party was the first to winter in the Antarctic. The first expedition to winter there on land, in Victoria Land in 1899–1900, was led by a Norwegian, Karsten Borchgrevink. German, French and Scottish expeditions soon followed and in 1901 Captain Scott arrived in *Discovery*, to make the deepest penetrations yet into the Antarctic, reaching 82° 17′S. The South Pole became the glittering prize and in 1909 Ernest Shakleton was only 97 nautical miles from it when forced to turn back.

In 1910 Scott made a second expedition, which turned into a race against Amundsen for the South Pole. The Norwegian, who was the more professional and better organised, won the race and reached the pole with his dog-sledges on 14 December, 1911. Scott and his party, hauling their sledges themselves, arrived on 17 January 1912. Disappointed and exhausted, they died on the return journey.

With the Pole conquered, the emphasis turned to surveying and scientific exploration, with significant American, British and Norwegian expeditions between World War I and World War II. Richard Byrd flew over the South Pole in 1929, and in 1935 another American, Lincoln Ellsworth, demonstrated the practicability of the airplane as a means of transport in the Antarctic by flying across the entire continent. In 1940 a US Navy expedition photographed much of the Antarctic from the air.

In 1957 a British party led by Vivian Fuchs started from the Weddell Sea and a New Zealand party led by Sir Edmund Hillary, the conqueror of Everest, from the Ross Sea on the opposite coast. They met at the South Pole in January 1958 and each party went on to cross the continent overland for the first time. They used tractors and sno-cats, and Fuch's team covered 2,185 miles (3,515 km) in 99 days. In 1990 an international expedition crossed Antarctica at its widest point with dog-sledges on a journey of 4,000 miles (6,435 km).

Scientific research work has continued in Antarctica in a spirit of international cooperation. Nowadays, tourists visit the continent by ship and take flights to view the blinding beauty of the White South, where not so long ago only the bravest pioneers ventured at the risk of their lives.

***Above** A congregation of King penguins assembled amicably in the Antarctic.*

***Below** An improbable place to meet, as Sir Edmund Hillary (left) and Dr Vivian Fuchs kept a rendezvous at the South Pole in 1958.*

ROBERT PEARY

Looking for fame through Arctic exploration, Robert Peary struggled for years to be the first at the North Pole

Robert Peary was born on 6 May 1856. His father, Charles Peary, died when Robert was less than three years old. Mary, his mother, brought up the boy, her only child, on her own. Robert passed with credit through high school and Bowdoin College, graduating in 1877 in civil engineering. After an apprenticeship in the US Coast and Geodetic Survey he was commissioned as a civil engineer in the United States Navy, assigned to construction tasks in the US and overseas.

From an early age Arctic exploration had fired Peary's imagination. Especially exciting to him were the journeys of US and other explorers of the previous generation, especially Elisha Kent Kane, Isaac Israel Hayes and Charles Francis Hall, all of whom had explored northern Canada and Greenland beyond Baffin Bay. All had worked alongside Eskimos and used Eskimo techniques of travel and survival. No one had yet reached the North Pole; of Peary's particular heroes, Hayes had claimed to have sledged northward to 81° 35′N; Hall had reached 82° 11′N by sea. Captain George Nares, of the British Royal Navy, had recently led an expedition that, from Cape Sheridan, northern Ellesmere Island, had sledged to 83° 20′N. An even more recent expedition under Adolphus Greely had reached a similar latitude from Lady Franklin Bay. Many of Greely's party had died of starvation when their relief ship failed to reach them.

Recipe for success

Peary was ambitious, and saw Arctic exploration as a way of achieving fame. Long before his first visit to the Arctic he planned a polar expedition that would penetrate as far north as possible by sea with a small party – ideally of three experienced white men, accompanied by Eskimos and their wives. The party might have to wait several years for the right opportunity to make a dash over the Arctic sea ice to the Pole. Many of his subsequent expeditions followed this pattern.

These plans were laid mostly in the steaming rain-forests of Nicaragua where Peary, as a naval engineer, was surveying the route for a possible trans-American canal, an alternative to that proposed through Panama. The scheme reached an advanced stage of planning before finally being abandoned.

As a prelude to polar adventure, Peary in 1886 presented a paper to the National Academy of Sciences on a scheme for surveying the ice-bound east Greenland coast by crossing the ice-cap from the more accessible west. The ice-cap had not yet been crossed, and exploration of the north Greenland coast might provide a useful starting point for a polar journey.

Nansen's subsequent crossing of Greenland took much of the glamour from the project. However, on leave from the navy in June 1886, in the company of Christian Maigaard, a more experienced traveller, Peary made a brief visit to

Below left *Lieutenant Robert Peary of the US Navy, in his early forties: from a photograph taken in Newfoundland in 1898.*

northern Greenland. The two men trudged inland some 100 miles (160 km) across the ice-cap, climbing to about 7,500ft (2,285m). The excursion gave Peary practical experience.

Shortly before returning to Nicaragua, Peary met and employed as his valet a black, Matthew Henson, who became his faithful servant and later his companion on all major expeditions. On leave one year later he married Josephine Diebitsch.

Expeditions to northwest Greenland

Peary's experience on the Greenland ice-cap encouraged him to seek leave – the first of many – from the navy to mount a more serious Arctic expedition. Nansen had crossed Greenland in a relatively low latitude; he would begin by crossing it further north and exploring the unknown northern coast. In June 1891 he sailed from Brooklyn with his bride Jo, Matthew Henson, and a party consisting of Evind Astrup, a

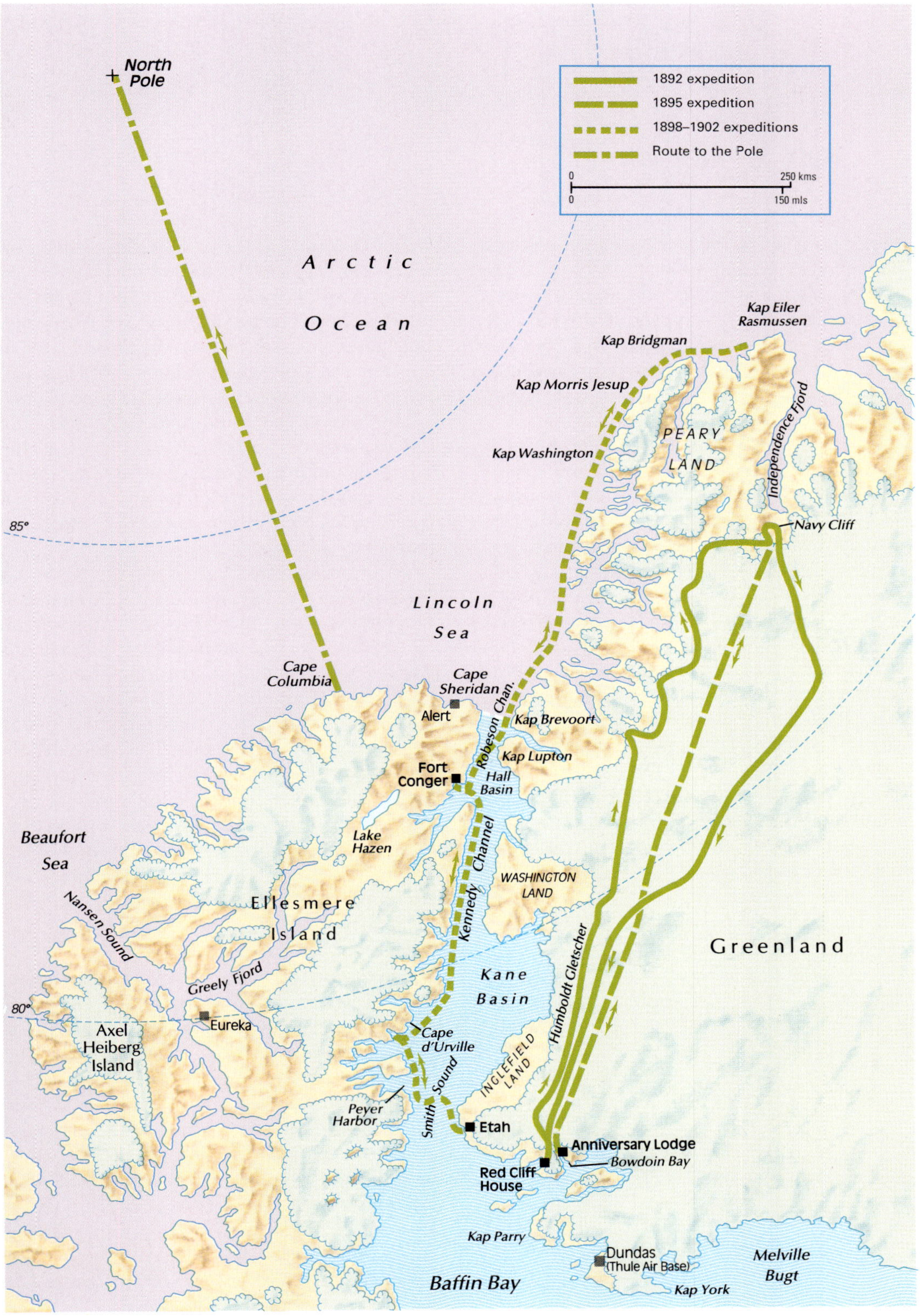

Below *Peary pressed ever further north into Greenland and Ellesmere Island to realise his dream of being the first to the North Pole. Whether he actually succeeded in reaching it is in serious doubt.*

Below *A winter blizzard swirls round a remote settlement in Greenland. Peary's sledging expeditions through northern Greenland in the 1890s earned him popular acclaim.*

Left *Peary's camp in the Arctic wilderness, an illustration from a French magazine. The goal of reaching the North Pole and the hardships of Arctic exploration caught the imagination of the popular press in Europe and America.*

Norwegian skier, John Verhoeff, meteorologist and geologist, Langdon Gibson, a hunter, and medical officer Frederick Cook, later to become his bitter rival in the conquest of the Pole. His small steamer, *Kite*, was shared with paying passengers whose fares helped to defray expedition expenses.

At McCormick Bay, northwest Greenland, some 80 miles (130km) north of present-day Dundas near the settlement of Thule, Peary supervised the building of Red Cliff House, a small living hut. Astrup, Cook, Gibson and Verhoeff travelled by boat along the coast, encouraging local Eskimos to call at the hut, where they could be interviewed and photographed. The purpose was partly ethnological; Peary and Cook wanted to acquire good records of the physical characteristics of these little known people. However, Peary was interested too in discovering which were the best drivers and who had the best dog-teams to help him with fieldwork.

After a cramped winter in Red Cliff House and several short runs to try out the teams, Peary and Astrup set off in May 1892 on the major journey of the expedition. Six weeks of difficult travel over the ice-cap brought them to what appeared to be the northeast corner of Greenland, from where, beyond a towering cliff, they could see the ice of the Arctic Ocean. Taking longer than expected over their 1,200 mile (1,930km) journey, they returned in early August to find themselves almost given up for lost, and the relief ship about to leave without them. Peary learned of the recent disappearance of Verhoeff from a boating party in nearby Bowdoin Bay. Cook, who was in charge of the party, wrote this off at the time as an unfortunate accident; later he was to refer to it darkly as suicide by a young man driven to ending his life by the injustices of Peary and the persecution of his wife.

On returning to civilisation, Peary's stories of travel and adventure caught the public imagination, for a moment giving him the fame that he felt was his due. The ethnological and meteorological records of the expedition were well received in scientific circles, and the long sledging journey across northern Greenland was highly acclaimed. Peary himself recognised that, although he had almost certainly crossed the 82nd parallel north on his long journey across Greenland, much of the mapping was inadequate and uncertain; it was still not clear whether the north Greenland coast provided better opportunities than Ellesmere Island for a march to the Pole. He enjoyed the adulation, but soon began planning a return visit.

A strenuous campaign of fund-raising lectures, personal appearances and buttonholing influential people raised the money he needed for a longer expedition, this time involving a bid for the North Pole. Opportunity came in 1893; again the navy granted him leave, and Peary sailed for Greenland on 23 June. Henson and Astrup sailed with him as before, but not Frederick Cook, with whom Peary had quarrelled over publication of results from the last expedition. The party arrived on 20 August and set up house in Bowdoin Bay, just a few miles east of their old base. On 12 September Jo, who was again with her husband, gave birth to their first child, Marie.

The Ideal Arctic Team

"One intelligent white man would represent the head, two other white men selected solely for their courage, determination, physical strength, and devotion to the leader would represent the arms, and the driver and natives the body and legs. The presence of women an absolute necessity to render the men contented; farther than this they are in many respects as useful as men, and are nearly if not quite their equals in strength and endurance."

from Peary's diary, quoted in *The Noose of Laurels*, W. Herbert

Below *Matthew Henson, Peary's black valet and companion, is seen here in 1907 in* Harper's Monthly. *Henson was with Peary in 1909 in what successful assault on the North Pole. Years afterwards, in 1959, Henson claimed that he himself had actually reached the pole first.*

Below right *A French cartoon of 1909 shows Cook and Peary coming to blows over which of them deserved the glory of being the first to the Pole.*

Frederick Cook: Hero or Rogue?

Born on 10 June 1865 in Hortonville, New York, Frederick Albert Cook was one of five children of immigrant parents. His father, a general practitioner, died when Frederick was five; reared in poverty by his mother, Cook worked hard to qualify in medicine. He had a small New York practice when Robert Peary, nine years his senior, invited him to join his first expedition to Greenland.

Cook proved a good doctor and efficient expedition man. Peary thought highly enough of his surgeon to appoint him second-in-command. On returning to New York, Cook completed his ethnological and medical reports. Their joint ethnological work was presented by Peary in his own name, though with an acknowledgement of Cook's involvement. When Cook sought to publish some of his medical findings in his own name, Peary refused him permission, and the two parted company. Thereafter Cook and Peary circled each other warily, each appreciative of the others' good qualities but forced gradually from amity into rivalry, and ultimately into open hostility.

Like Peary, Cook wanted to find fame in polar exploration. He tried but failed to mount an Antarctic expedition of his own, and in 1897 sailed south with the Belgian research expedition of Adrien de Gerlache. In the ship *Belgica*, this was the first ever to overwinter in Antarctica. Both the expedition leader and Roald Amundsen, mate of *Belgica*, later paid tribute to Cook's qualities as a doctor and shipmate.

In 1901 Cook sailed north at the request of the Peary Arctic Club to locate Peary, then on his third expedition to Greenland. In 1903 he reconnoitred a route up Mt McKinley, Alaska's highest mountain, and in 1906 claimed to have made the first ascent to the peak. Though accepted at the time, some of the evidence he presented was later shown to be false, and his claim was discredited. In 1907 he led an Arctic expedition, privately funded by John R. Bradley, which rather improbably combined hunting in the Smith Sound region with a dash to the North Pole. Cook returned to civilisation in 1909, claiming to have reached the Pole with two Eskimo companions on 21 April 1908. This was almost a year before Peary's claimed achievement. Again his evidence was closely examined by experts and found wanting. Thereafter he was no longer regarded as credible by the exploring fraternity.

Frederick Cook.

In 1923, by then an oil consultant, Cook was convicted of making statements calculated to defraud potential shareholders; he received a 14-year prison sentence of which he served half. In 1940 he received a presidential pardon, and in the same year suffered a serious stroke from which he died. Many remain convinced that Cook was a maligned man and that he, not Peary, was the first to reach the North Pole.

Peary's second expedition, spanning two winters, was an almost unmitigated disaster, to which bad weather and indifferent planning alike contributed. A major ice-cap journey, planned to involved three separate survey parties, failed at the outset. Sledges were blown away by hurricanes, boats damaged by a freak tidal wave, food and equipment were lost in the snow. Only an unscheduled coastal journey by Astrup to Case York (Kap York) could be called a success, but Peary quarrelled with Astrup over it, and indeed over equally trivial matters with most of his men. When the ship returned at the end of winter, all but Henson and one other, Lee, elected to leave.

The second season was less traumatic but achieved little. Peary, Henson and Lee completed a journey to the northeast that did little more than repeat the long journey of the previous season. Peary recouped some of his financial loses by bringing back to the USA two large meteorites, together weighing over 1 ton (1 tonne), and selling them to the American Museum of Natural History. With monumental insensitivity he also sold the bones of several Eskimos, and brought back six Eskimos live for the museum scientists to study. These trophies did not hide the thinness of the expedition results.

Back to Smith Sound

The expeditions across Greenland convinced Peary that the route to the Pole lay where he had earlier assumed it to lie – northward from Smith Sound. To follow this through, he sought and was granted leave for five years. In July 1898 he once again headed north towards Ellesmere Island, intending to reoccupy Fort Conger, Adolphus Greely's old base close to the Arctic Ocean. However, heavy pack-ice forced him to winter his ship *Windward* off Cape D'Urville in Kane Basin.

By chance Otto Sverdrup, in Nansen's old ship *Fram*, was wintering a few miles further south, on a Norwegian-backed expedition to explore both Ellesmere Island and the north Greenland coast. From a conversation between the two leaders Peary gained the impression that the Norwegians were trying for the Pole. He decided to forestall them by making a winter journey along the coast to Fort Conger, some 250 miles (400 km) to the north.

These suspicions and the decision to travel cost him dearly. With Henson, Dedrick (his doctor) and four Eskimos and dog-teams he set off in late December. Two weeks later, after a bitterly cold and difficult journey, the three Americans and two of the Eskimos struggled into Fort Conger. Greely's old huts were intact but grim and forbidding. The men started fires in the stoves and prepared warm food. When Peary came to remove his boots, he found that both feet were badly frozen; when he removed the fur liners, parts of his toes came away with them.

Dr Dedrick trimmed and cleaned up the stumps of the damaged toes; in a later operation he removed all but the little toes from both feet. Peary was confined to bed, while Henson and the Eskimos went hunting for musk oxen to keep the party alive. A 10-day journey in mid-February got them back to the ship, with Peary riding on one of the sledges. By late May 1899 he had returned to Fort Conger, where the huts were taken apart and rebuilt on a smaller scale. He also collected together the abandoned papers of the Greely expedition and packed them for return by his ship.

The expedition wintered at Etah, an Eskimo settlement on the Greenland shore of Smith Sound. Returning in late March 1900 to Fort Conger, Peary used it as a point of departure for one of his best considered journeys – a 400-mile (645km) long exploration of the north Greenland coast. At the nothernmost point, which he named Cape Jesup (K. Morris Jesup) after a New York supporter, he made a short foray on to the sea ice of the Arctic Ocean, but turned back after a few miles to continue the coastal survey. Returning to Fort Conger in early June, he and his Eskimo hunters laid in supplies of game to see them through a further winter.

Early in the following April Peary, Henson and an Eskimo made a further brief foray to the north, but turned back after only a few days. On

Above *An illustration from* Scribner's Monthly, *in 1893, showed Peary and the relief expedition that had almost given him up for lost in Greenland the previous year.*

Below *'The return from the furthest North.' An illustration from the* Graphic, *in 1907, shows Peary's ship* Roosevelt *entering New York Harbour on the explorer's return from the Arctic. His claim to have reached a new furthest north in the previous year is now doubted.*

***Left** A wintry landscape with broken sea ice near Etah in northern Greenland. This is the country through which Peary and his parties struggled.*

17 April, abandoning all hope of further progress that year, he turned south and sledged towards Kane Basin, where he hoped to receive news of his relief ship, *Windward*. En route he met a party coming north from the ship, and learnt that *Windward* was beset in Peyer Harbour, where she had been since late in the previous summer. Furthermore, Jo and his daughter Marie were onboard. The family was reunited on 6 May 1901.

Frederick Cook, sent north by Peary's supporters to discover what had happened to the great man, visited him in early August 1901. He found Peary 'wrecked in ambition, wrecked in physique, wrecked in hope', and 'worried, anxious, discouraged as I have never seen him before'. He could hardly walk, and showed symptoms of pernicious anaemia. For the latter, Cook prescribed raw meat and liver, which Peary refused to consider.

Cook had no prescription for the general malaise that seemed to possess Peary, other than to advise him that his travelling days were over. Peary made no immediate reply, but the following summer found him once again stumbling across the Arctic Ocean pack-ice, to claim a furthest-north latitude of 84° 7′.

Towards the North Pole

Now Peary's work was substantially supported by the Peary Arctic Club, a fraternity of wealthy New Yorkers led by Morris K. Jesup of the American Museum of Natural History. Formed in 1899, the Club became active to meet Peary's latest needs. Its members were motivated by a patriotic wish to see an American – their American – first at the Pole, and perhaps by an understanding that their names would be immortalised on Peary's polar maps. That, together with interest from newspapers, encouraged a weary old man in his final bid for immortality.

Peary made two subsequent attempts on the North Pole, accompanied each time by the ever-faithful Henson and teams of Eskimos. Returning to the Arctic in 1905, in a new ship, *Roosevelt*, provided by the Club, Peary seemed once again his old, vigorous self. Fighting ice on the fringes of the Arctic Ocean he wrote of '. . . the thrill, the shock of hurling the *Roosevelt*, a fifteen-hundred ton battering ram, at the ice to smash a way through . . .', and of '. . . the upward heave, the grating snarl of the ice as the steel-shod stem split it . . .'. Picking up Eskimos, dog-teams and meat on the way, he punched his way through to Cape Sheridan, on the northeast corner of Ellesmere Island, and secured the ship for the winter.

March and April 1906 he spent out on the pack-ice, on a hazardous trek toward the North Pole supported elaborately by Eskimo teams. Though a long and difficult journey was undoubtedly made, Peary's claim to have reached 87° 06′ on 21 April is seriously open to question by those who have studied his records.

For his final polar bid, Peary sailed from the US, again in *Roosevelt*, in July 1908. Wintering as before at Cape Sheridan, he chose as his point of departure Cape Columbia, some 90 miles (145 km) to the west. From there he set out on 1 March 1909, again with support from Eskimo teams and as always accompanied by Matthew Henson. Again he made a long northward journey over the shifting pack-ice of the Arctic Ocean, subjecting himself, his men and his dogs to the hazards and discomforts of primitive sea-ice travel. Again his record of the journey is open to doubt; although he travelled a long way towards the Pole and returned safely, whether or not he got there is seriously doubted by analysts.

Peary's fans in New York were in no doubt of the outcome; he had reached the Pole, and now he returned to a hero's welcome. Despite doubts expressed at the time and later, he was fêted at home and abroad, promoted by the navy to Rear-Admiral, and awarded medals and decorations for his achievements. He died of pernicious anaemia on 20 February 1920.

Biographical Notes

1856
Born in Cresson, PA, USA.

1877
Graduate in civil engineering, Bowdoin College, Maine.

1879
Employed as draughtsman by US Coast and Geodetic Survey.

1881
Commissioned in Civil Engineering Corps of the US Navy, working on Nicaraguan Canal project.

1886
Brief expedition to the Greenland ice-cap.

1891–2
First major expedition to north of Greenland.

1989–95
Second expedition to north of Greenland.

1898–1902
Third expedition to north Greenland.

1905–06
First polar expedition: claimed farthest north, 87° N.

1908–09
Last expedition: claimed conquest of the North Pole (6 April 1909).

1920
Died.

SIR ERNEST SHACKLETON

Ernest Henry Shackleton was born on 15 February 1874, the second child and first son of Henry Shackleton, an Anglo-Irish landowner, and his wife Henrietta. Though proud of his Irish birth and background, Ernest was brought up an Englishman. In 1880 the family moved to Dublin, where Henry became a medical student. He qualified as a general practitioner in 1884, and moved to south London, settling eventually into a practice in Sydenham. Ernest was schooled at Dulwich College, where he gained a reputation for charm, intelligence and hard work in subjects that caught his interest, together with a taste for adventure. The college served him well, cultivating in him a love of literature and a respect for learning that lasted throughout his life.

Shackleton pioneered the route to the South Pole and made a breathtaking open-boat journey across the world's wildest ocean

However, routine studies held no appeal; action and travel were what he sought, and at 16 he was apprenticed to train as an officer in the merchant marine. His first ship, the square-rigged *Hoghton Tower*, took him several times round Cape Horn to the Pacific Ocean, and around the Cape of Good Hope into the Indian Ocean. It was a hard but sound training. Young Ernest was fully extended by the seamanship, and taxed by the navigation and other studies that he had to master for professional examinations. Qualifying as a Second Mate, he sailed the world for five years in a tramp steamer.

From 1896 when he took his First Mate's ticket, to 1899 when he transferred to the prestigious Union Castle Line, there was little about Shackleton to distinguish him from a thousand other merchant service officers, save a streak of culture; shipmates noted the library of good literature in his cabin and his unusual ability to quote poetry on watch. Inwardly he was restless: the routine became tedious and again he sought adventure beyond anything that the service could provide.

Discovery expedition

Shackleton's chance came in 1900, when he heard that Lt Robert Falcon Scott RN, recently appointed to lead the British National Antarctic Expedition, was seeking recruits with maritime training to man his ship HMS *Discovery*. Shackleton applied and was appointed Third Officer, a position for which his many years in sail equipped him well. He helped to order stores for *Discovery*, load her up and prepare her for the long voyage to Antarctica.

They sailed in August 1901, crossing the world to New Zealand, then heading south into the sector of Antarctica which Sir James Clark Ross had explored many years before. *Discovery*, a slow, ill-designed barque with an auxiliary engine, lumbered her way south, breaking through the pack-ice to arrive at her destination, McMurdo Sound, early in February 1902. Shackleton became a popular figure: his energy, efficiency and cheerful disposition soon permeated every corner of the ship and expedition.

He and Scott got on well together. When they reached Antarctica the ship was secured and the sea froze around it; the snow built up, and the men prepared for the long, cold winter ahead. Shackleton's interests spread to the sledging programme. In the shortening days of autumn and early winter he learned to ski, drive the dog-teams and camp in the snow. He also put his literary talents to editing the ship's newspaper.

Left *The Discovery in the ice during Scott's Antaractic expedition, which left Britain in 1901. Shackleton, who was experienced in the handling of sailing ships, served as Third Officer.*

Opposite page *Ernest Shackleton. Described by one of his contemporaries as 'a human dreadnought', and given to quoting Robert Browning at length, he had a cheerful, outgoing personality that made him one of the best-liked of all polar explorers.*

Below *Advertising one of Shackleton's lectures, illustrated by magic lantern slides, in December 1909. Shackleton was a popular hero, but had little or no money and depended on lecture earnings and book royalties.*

As the winter wore on Scott planned a long spring sledging journey into the interior of the continent, perhaps even to the South Pole. They would start as soon as the days lengthened and the bitter cold of winter was over. Among the other officers of the party there was much speculation over whom Scott would choose to accompany him. Eventually he chose Edward Wilson, the ship's junior doctor and naturalist, and Ernest Shackleton.

It was a long, cruel journey over an almost featureless desert of snow. The dogs, poorly trained and underfed, soon gave up: many died or were killed to feed the others. The men had to haul the sledges themselves – a backbreaking task on poor rations. Scott had learned little from the pioneering work of the Scandinavian explorers: their clothing, sleeping bags, sledges and tents were poorly designed and barely adequate for the job.

The three men struggled on to 82° 15′S, a record for Antarctica but still over 500 miles (805km) from the Pole. On the return journey all three showed signs of scurvy, due to malnutrition. Shackleton was worst hit, but more than scurvy was involved: he suffered breathlessness and other symptoms suggesting heart trouble that left him almost helpless. At times he had to walk beside the sledge or ride on it.

Safely back on the ship Scott and Wilson soon recovered, but Shackleton remained an invalid for over a month. Much against Shackleton's own wishes, Scott decided, to send him home on the relief ship, which had just arrived in the Sound. So Shackleton returned from the expedition a year earlier than expected, with a feeling of failure and frustration that changed the course of his life. Back in Britain, where he gave lectures on the expedition, he determined that his life as a seaman was over; he would become an explorer in his own right.

Nimrod expedition

With no money of his own, Shackleton had first to earn a living. Using contacts made in the geographical world he became the secretary of the Royal Scottish Geographical Society, a small but influential society based in Edinburgh. He married and for a time seemed settled, but social life in Edinburgh soon palled. After a year he again became restless and put up for election to Parliament. When this failed he became involved in small businesses and other money-making enterprises, none of which brought him the riches he sought. Fortunately his wife Emily had a small income that kept the home together.

Finally in 1906 Shackleton's plans matured, and he announced his intention of mounting a private expedition to Antarctica, with the objective of reaching the South Pole. Public activities had brought him a wide range of friends and acquaintances in Scotland, several of whom he called on for the money to make a start.

Shackleton himself inspired confidence, but he had no official support and fund-raising was never easy. Scott, who had returned from Antarctica a national hero, was planning a polar expedition of his own, and made no secret of his irritation that a former subordinate was competing against him. Shackleton invited Edward Wilson and others of his old shipmates to join him, but all declined.

Money promised to him did not materialise, and to the very last moment before sailing the expedition was heavily in debt.

In August 1907 King Edward VI inspected *Nimrod*, the tiny expedition ship, and gave the operation his approval. However, when *Nimrod* sailed for Australia, Shackleton remained behind in England, still trying to raise money for the supplies that he would need to take aboard before the last leg of the journey. He caught up with his ship in Lyttelton, New Zealand, and finally left for Antarctica in early January 1908.

Shackleton had intended to approach the Pole from the Ross Ice Shelf, but landing proved difficult and the interior was unknown. He returned instead to McMurdo Sound, setting up a small hut on Cape Royds, some 17 miles (27km) north of the old *Discovery* hut and 750 miles (1,250km) from the Pole. Here in late January and early February he disembarked eight Manchurian ponies, thirteen men, an Arrold-Johnson motor-car, stores for over a year, and a motley collection of sledge dogs from New Zealand. *Nimrod* returned to civilisation, leaving the shore party to secure for the winter.

From the Cape Royds hut a party of six men climbed Mount Erebus, over 12,000ft (3,794m) high, and for the first time looked down into its steaming crater. After midwinter Shackleton began moving stores southward, providing

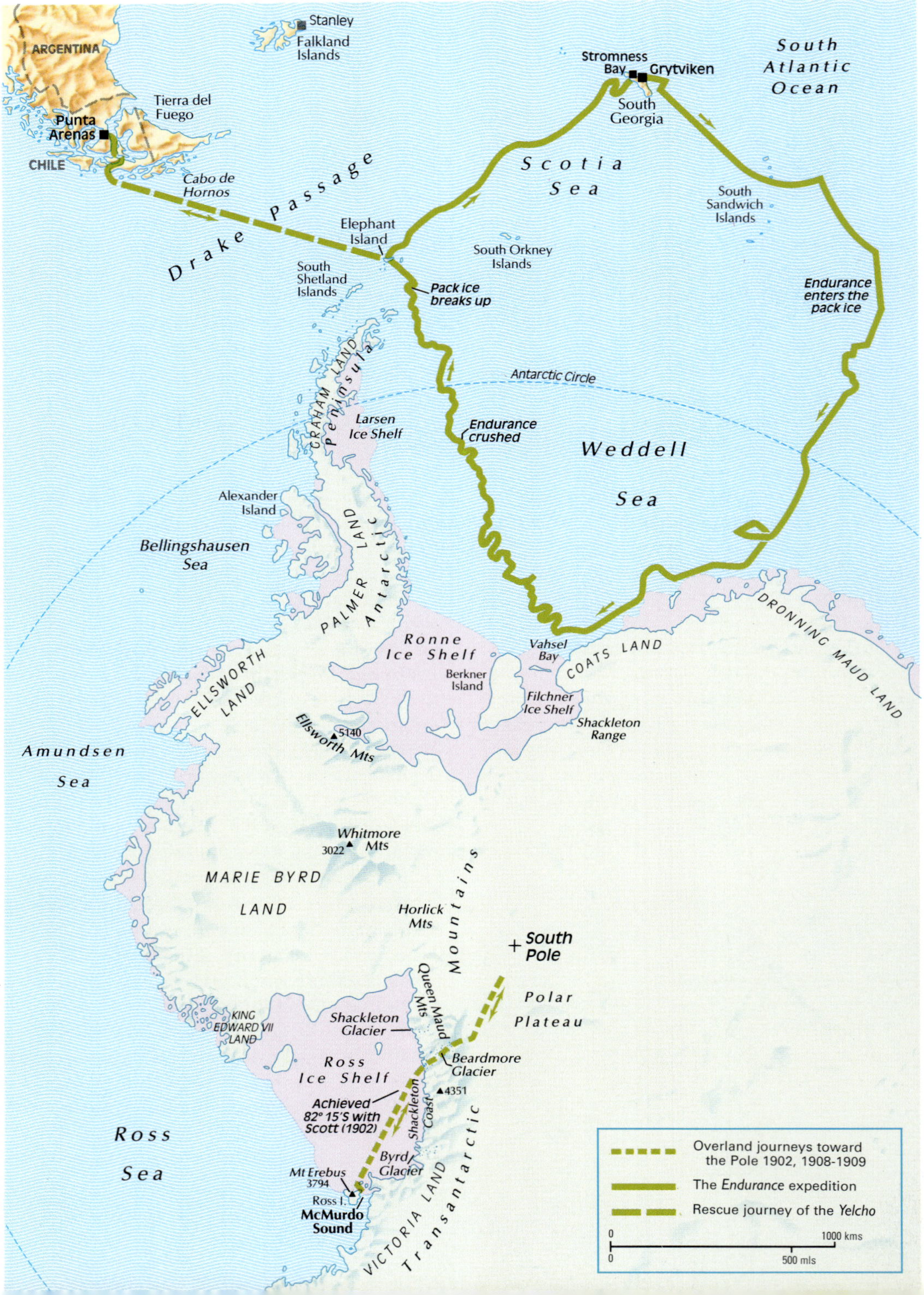

Below *Scott, Wilson and Shackleton probed a record distance into Antarctica in 1903. In 1909 Shackleton and his party penetrated to within 97 miles (156 km) of the south Pole, the exploit for which Shackleton was knighted.*

Below *Shackleton's hut at Cape Royds. Prefabricated and insulated with cork, it measured 30ft by 19ft (9m × 5.75m) and was home to 15 men. This photograph was taken in 1965.*

Above *Adélie penguins at Cape Royds in 1965. In the background is Mount Erebus, which some of Shackleton's party climbed in 1908.*

depots across the Ross Ice Shelf for the long polar journey he was planning. The motor vehicle proved ineffective; ponies (now reduced to four) and dogs were involved, but much of the work was done by man-hauling, the slowest, hardest and most dispiriting method of polar travel.

Shackleton's main journey began on 29 October. With Eric Marshall, the expedition doctor, Frank Wild and Jameson Boyd Adams, he set off across the Ross Ice Shelf on a track close to that which he, Wilson and Scott had travelled some six years before. They made good time, achieving 82°S (the earlier record) in less than a month and pressing on south, converging slowly on a magnificent chain of mountain peaks. Assisted by the floundering ponies (which were shot one by one as they wore out) the four men climbed through the range up a glacier over 100 miles (160km) and 30 miles (48km) wide.

By Christmas Day they had climbed to over 9,000ft (2,745m): a few days later they had reached the polar plateau, and on New Year's Day 1909 they stood less than 200 miles (320km) from the Pole. Already on reduced rations to eke out their food supplies, they realized that the Pole lay beyond their grasp. On 9 January, with 97 miles (156km) still to go, a sick and hungry party abandoned the Pole and started the 730 mile (1,175km) trek back to base.

Returning to pick up the expedition in January 1909, *Nimrod* first gathered in two other sledging parties that had worked in the mountains west of McMurdo Sound. Through February the ship waited with increasing anxiety for signs of the polar party. Their instructions were to leave not later than 1 March, and time was running out. The polar party too was racing against time: weakened by hunger and dysentery, and hampered by bad weather, theirs was a desperate struggle to reach the coast before the ship sailed.

Here Shackleton's leadership and resourcefulness took over. In a series of forced marches they reached the coast, and he and Wild forged ahead, crossing steep, icy slopes to reach Hut Point by 1 March. The ship's party found them, and Shackleton, though almost exhausted, led a rescue team back to recover Marshall and Adams. On 4 March, with everyone safely aboard, *Nimrod* headed northward through thickening ice.

Though the expedition had failed to reach the Pole, Shackleton returned a hero. He was fêted in many countries and lionized in Britain: the government paid off most of the expedition's debts, and Shackleton received a well-acclaimed knighthood. A lecture tour and a popular book, *Heart of the Antarctic*, maintained and extended his public image, and brought him a little income to sustain his new position in society. However, by the standards of the time he remained a poor man, still depending on Emily's income to maintain his growing family.

Trans-Antarctic expedition

In the southern summer of 1911–12 Roald Amundsen reached the South Pole and returned safely to his base on the Ross Ice Shelf. Robert Scott too reached the Pole, finding a tent and messages left by Amundsen a few weeks earlier.

Reaching the Pole was no longer an objective for Antarctic exploration: what could take its place? Shackleton and the German explorer Wilhelm Filcher reached a similar conclusion – Antarctica must be crossed from one side to the other, preferably by the shortest land route between the Ross Sea and the Weddell Sea.

Filchener sailed first in his ship *Deutschland*, which was caught in the pack-ice of the Weddell Sea and narrowly escaped destruction. Undeterred, Shackleton planned a double expedition: one ship would enter the Weddell Sea and an overwintering party would approach the Pole from that side. A second ship would enter the Ross Sea, and parties from McMurdo Sound would lay depots that would enable the polar party to continue their crossing. With help from the British government and from private backers, the Imperial Trans-Antarctic Expedition became reality.

Shackleton's ships, *Endurance* and *Aurora*, were ready by August 1914, on the eve of World War I. When war was declared, Shackleton placed *Endurance* at the disposal of the British Admiralty, but was told unequivocally to proceed. He sailed south from Plymouth on 8 August, reached Buenos Aires in mid-October, and in December entered the pack-ice of the Weddell Sea. Pressing south towards Vahsel Bay, in the southeastern corner of the ice-filled sea, *Endurance* became surrounded by pack-ice, and began to drift helplessly.

Aurora too had problems. Sailing from Hobart in December she reached McMurdo Sound in early January. While offloading at Cape Evans, Scott's old base, she was blown from her moorings and beset by pack-ice. Unable to return, she too drifted helplessly, leaving an ill-equipped party of 10 with the awesome responsibility of laying the depots for the polar party.

Endurance drifted for nine months in a clockwise circle that took her south, west and finally northward. In late October pressures built up in the ice around her, crushing the wooden hull and finally sinking her. At the first signs of danger Shackleton got the men, the dogs, the lifeboats and many of the stores on to the ice, setting up a camp. In mid-November the ship sank, but the camp continued to drift northward for a further five months. Early in April they reached the northern edge of the pack-ice, which began to disintegrate under them. The party of 28 men took to the three lifeboats, rowing and sailing their way to Elephant Island, in the South Shetland group.

Half-frozen, wet and exhausted, they landed on a narrow beach under steep cliffs. After a few hours' rest they moved to a second point called Cape Wild after the expedition's second-in-command, which gave them better shelter from sea and wind. Those who were still capable of action built a hut with walls of beach cobbles and scree, roofed by two of the lifeboats, which were upturned and draped with canvas sails.

Shackleton realized that nobody knew or would guess where they were; he would have to seek help. He wasted no time. The third boat, *James Caird*, was fitted with a half-deck heavily made from packing-cases and canvas, and reinforced with the mast from one of the other boats. Within three days of landing he left, with a crew of five others, to sail to South Georgia for help.

South Georgia stood to the east, some 700 miles (1,125km) away across the world's roughest ocean. Other land lay nearer to the west, but South Georgia was down-wind and easier for a sailing boat to approach. Shackleton knew that whalers were operating with shore stations and sea-going ships. It provided by far the best chance of help.

James Caird, 22ft (6.7m) long and less than 7ft (2.1m) across, left Elephant Island on 24 April. Heading north to avoid the last of the pack-ice, she turned northeastward and sailed before the wind. Frank Worsley, the captain of *Endurance*, navigated as best he could with sextant, pocket compass and chronometer. All took turns at steering and look-out. Under cover of the half-deck the men cooked their food over a primus stove and between watches slept in cold, wet sleeping-bags.

To the South Pole

The South Geographical Pole is a point in the cold heartland of Antarctica, about 10,000ft (3,048m) above sea level on a featureless, ice-covered plateau. Long before its exact geography was known, explorers realised that it must lie a long way from the sea. They still had to approach by sea, but reaching the Pole would require a march – and probably a climb – over inland ice. That in turn would require an overwintering station on land, so that full advantage could be taken of an early start in spring.

It paid sea-borne expeditions to travel as far south as possible by sea: hence Scott and Shackleton's approach along a sea-route pioneered by Ross in the previous century, and Amundsen's subsequent agreement that a polar journey should start from the Ross Sea. Though it is possible to reach almost as far south in the Weddell Sea, the pack-ice there was known to be more difficult and dangerous.

Explorers realized that the combination of high altitude and high latitude would make a south polar journey difficult, even in summer: living and travelling conditions would be much harsher than in an Arctic summer. The long distances overland would require careful logistic planning of sledge-loads, depot laying and other techniques. Though thousands of people inhabiting the Arctic were familiar with life in cold climates, few who were involved in southern polar exploration, other than the Scandinavians, began with the necessary skills and experience.

Scott, Shackleton and the British explorers had little experience of snowcraft, sledging or cold-weather survival, and seemed to mistrust their ability to learn. By contrast, Amundsen and his Norwegian team were skilled skiers and cross-country sledgers, who quickly made themselves expert drivers of dog-teams. Scott and Shackleton's curious and sometimes irrational trail methods contrasted sharply with the meticulous planning carried out by Amundsen, whose attention to detail, learnt from Eskimos during his long Arctic apprenticeship, made possible his spectacular dash to the South Pole.

Below *Shackleton's ship* Endurance *gets under way after leaving the London docks for the Antarctic in 1914.*

Most of the time they were wet; sometimes the temperature dropped and they froze. Once, ice built up on the boat and had to be chopped away with axes. Normally they ran before the wind; occasionally they had to ride out gales, tossing and heaving in impossibly choppy seas. On 8 May, their fifteenth day afloat, they peered through mist and hail and sighted the dark, forbidding cliffs of South Georgia. It took two further days to beat into King Haakon Bay and make a landing.

Their landfall and landing were miracles achieved, but they still had some way to go. King Haakon Bay was on the deserted southern side of the island, while the whaling stations lay on the more sheltered north side. After feeding, drinking and resting on dry land, Shackleton again took to the boat and moved the party to a more sheltered beach. After a further week of waiting for clear weather, he, Worsley and Second Officer Tom Crean set off to cross the island.

One hundred miles (160km) long and up to 20 miles (32km) wide, South Georgia is made up of ice-capped mountains alternating with steep, crevassed glaciers. Winds of hurricane strength are not uncommon. The island had never before been crossed, and the party had no equipment other than a primus stove, pan, rope and axe. Their map was little more than a sketch. They started out by moonlight at 2.00am in the morning of 19 May. Good weather held; climbing to over 2,500ft (762m) crossing ice fields and rocky plateaux they saw South Georgia's fiords and headlands laid out before them. Finally they made their descent on the north side, reaching the whaling station at Stromness Bay by tea-time on 20 May.

The whalers were cooperative; Shackleton was able to charter a whale-catcher and, with a volunteer crew, return immediately to Elephant Island. However, pack-ice surrounded the island and he was unable to approach. He went on to the Falkland Islands, from whence an Argentine whaler made a second attempt to reach Elephant Island. Shackleton journeyed to Punta Arenas, where a small pilot ship *Yelcho*, was placed at his disposal. On 30 August, with Shackleton aboard, *Yelcho* finally reached Elephant Island and took off the marooned men.

Below The hut and Mount Erebus.

Above *South Georgia, the last resting place.*

Aftermath

Shackleton returned to a Europe deeply involved in war. He undertook propaganda work for Britain in South America, and served briefly with the army in Russia. After demobilization his debts, still unpaid from the last expedition, and the old problem of earning a living, returned. Picking up the threads of his former life, he lectured and wrote the book of the Trans-Antarctic Expedition. Recovering from war, the world had lost interest in polar exploration.

In 1920 Shackleton planned an expedition to Arctic Canada, which came to nothing. In 1921 he was more successful, planning and developing an expedition to the Southern Ocean that would circumnavigate the Antarctic continent and visit isolated islands in the south Atlantic and Pacific oceans. Funded largely by John Rowett, an industrialist and old school friend, he pulled the expedition together and on 21 September 1921 sailed from London in *Quest*, a tiny whale-catcher. Many of his old shipmates from *Endurance* sailed with him; 'the boss', as he was known, still commanded the respect of those who had served with him.

This was his last expedition. Ill health dogged Shackleton across the South Atlantic Ocean. In South America he suffered acute chest pains and, arriving in South Georgia in early January, he was overcome by a series of heart attacks. Sir Ernest Shackleton died aboard *Quest* in Grytviken Harbour, and was buried in the whalers' graveyard overlooking the bay.

Biographical Notes

1874
Born in Kilkea, County Kildare, Ireland.

1890
Joined the Merchant Navy: rounded Cape Horn in a square-rigged sailing ship.

1896
Earned First Mate's qualification.

1901–3
Joined Scott's National Antarctic Expedition. Sledged with Scott and Wilson to 82° 15'S; invalided home.

1904–6
Secretary, Royal Scottish Geographical Society; unsuccessful parliamentary candidate and businessman.

1907–9
Led British Antarctic Expedition, sledging to within 97 miles (156km) of the South Pole.

1914–17
Led Imperial Trans-Antarctic Expedition: lost ship in pack-ice of Weddell Sea.

1922
Died at Grytviken, South Georgia.

ROALD AMUDSEN

When Admundsen heard that Peary had beaten him to the North Pole, he went to the South Pole instead

Roald Amundsen was born on 16 July 1872 at Hvidsten, an estate close to the Norwegian capital Christiania (Oslo). His father and grandfather were mariners, ship-builders and ship-owners, and he, like his three elder brothers, was destined to join the prosperous family business. Roald passed a happy childhood in Christiania. Educated in a good local school, he spent his spare time in the nearby forests, along the shore and in the family boatyard. Skiing and skating were his winter pastimes, sailing and fishing in summer.

When he was 14 his father died at sea. His brothers left home, and young Roald found himself alone with a much loved but over-protective mother. She planned for him a career in medicine and a comfortable, respectable life ashore. Roald preferred travel, adventure and discovery. At 15 he was an avid reader of travel books. The hero who first stirred his imagination was Sir John Franklin, the British Arctic explorer who had died while searching for the Northwest Passage. In 1889, witnessing Fridtjof Nansen's triumphant return from Greenland, Roald made up his mind: he would become a polar explorer himself.

While his friends played football, Roald hardened his muscles with cross-country skiing. He camped out in the snow; to his mother's horror he slept with his bedroom window wide open in the bitter winter cold. At 18, a dutiful son, he entered university to read medicine. At 21, when his mother died, he abandoned his course and joined the army, continuing his regime of hard outdoor exercise whenever possible.

Training for adventure

Polar explorers throughout the 19th century had tended to drift into exploration, learning as they went. Roald Amundsen thought out his future more carefully. To qualify for expedition leadership, he reasoned, he would first need to become a master mariner. Then he would have to gain polar experience, preferably with others who had something to teach him. He would need to study every possible source of written information – every published and unpublished expedition account. Finally, to achieve scientific credibility like his hero Nansen, he would need a scientific training. The next few years he devoted to achieving these qualifications: by his late 20s Amundsen was equipped to lead polar expeditions as few had been before him.

Firstly, in 1894 he signed on to the sealing barque *Magdalena* as a seaman, and sailed to the Arctic. Within two years he had learnt how to handle a ship in ice, and qualified as an officer. Good fortune quickly brought him further experience. In July 1896, returning from an Arctic voyage in the sealer *Jason*, he entered Sandifjord harbour to find a Belgian ship in the process of fitting out for an Antarctic expedition. Unhesitatingly he volunteered to join as an unpaid mate. The expedition leader, Adrien de Gerlache, was impressed with his keenness and qualifications – a ship's officer who could also ski

***Below** Roald Amundsen was the first man to navigate a ship through the long-sought Northwest Passage between the Atlantic and the Pacific. This was in* Gjöa *in 1903–6.*

and travel over snow. Appointed Second Mate, Amundsen sailed with *Belgica* in 1897.

It was neither a happy expedition nor a particularly successful one. Sailing south to Cape Horn and the Antarctic Peninsula, Amundsen soon realised that he was among amateurs. The leader intended to take *Belgica* across the Pacific sector of the Southern Ocean and winter near Cape Adare. however, beyond Alexander Land in March 1898, the ship became caught up in storms, and the inexperienced captain and first mate drove her into the pack-ice. Amundsen was appalled:

"Skirting the Antarctic ice field on our westward way, we encountered another terrific gale blowing from the north. We were in imminent danger of being blown against the wall of ice that lay to the south of us. The instinct of any navigator accustomed to the Polar seas would have been to use every effort to get away to the north and into the open sea. This we could have done. But at this juncture my two superior officers saw an opening in the ice field to the south of us and decided to ride before the storm into this opening. . . . By the time we had ridden out the storm, we were probably more than a hundred miles within the ice field."

The ice closed behind them, and *Belgica* spent an enforced winter drifting westward in the Bellingshausen Sea – the first-ever ship to winter in Antarctica.

Unprepared for the ordeal, her crew responded badly. Fear and scurvy took over, affecting several of the officers and men, including the captain. Despite his youth, Amundsen took charge: having experienced many sub-Arctic winters in southern Norway, he remained healthy and unperturbed. So did Frederick Cook, the ship's doctor, who had travelled with Robert Peary in the Arctic and was not afraid of wintering in a stout though ill-provided ship. He and Amundsen ensured that fresh seal meat was served to deal with the scurvy. While the other officers languished, they used their wits to keep themselves and the crew occupied, mentally and physically. Between them the two young veterans maintained morale until the sun returned and the ship was released. Amundsen left *Belgica* in disgust, returning to Norway more than ever convinced that exploration was a job for professionals.

Northwest Passage

Still determined to equip himself for exploration, Amundsen returned to sea and in 1900 qualified as skipper, able to command his own ship in Norwegian home waters. The Arctic beckoned, especially the Northeast Passage that had so narrowly defeated Sir John Franklin, and the North Magnetic Pole, unvisited since the expedition of Sir James Clark Ross in 1831. The geographical North Pole too was as yet unconquered. Recognising that a scientific expedition would attract more attention and support than

Right *The hawk-faced Amundsen was perhaps the most professional and formidable of all modern explorers. He was also an excellent leader and his expeditions had a more relaxed and humorous atmosphere than his severe portraits might suggest.*

Below *The forbidding harshness of the Antarctic is matched only by its extraordinary, almost unearthly beauty, which has touched the hearts of even the most reserved and phlegmatic explorers. This scene is in the Antarctic Peninsula.*

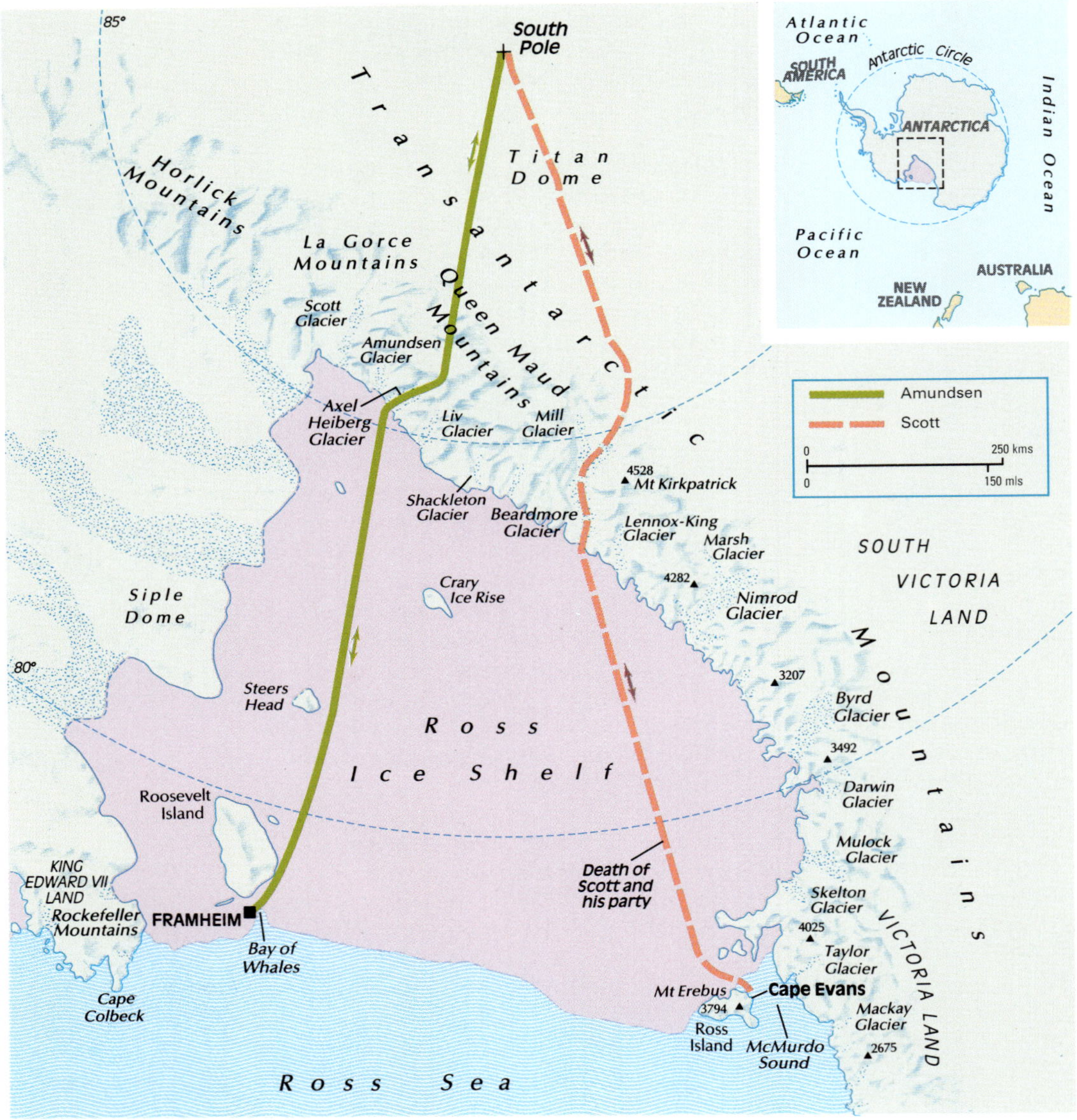

***Left** The routes taken by Amundsen and Scott in the race to the South Pole. Amundsen's party was better trained, better equipped and better led.*

one mounted purely for exploration, Amundsen combined two objectives in one: his first expedition would navigate the Northwest Passage and re-locate the North Magnetic Pole.

On the *Belgica* expedition he had occupied himself with a study of geomagnetism. Now he travelled to Hamburg to receive a training in geomagnetic observation from the highly respected physicist George von Neumayer. Later in the same year he bought a 46-ton (47tonne) wooden fishing smack, *Gjöa*, 72ft (22m) long. For the next two years he sailed northern waters, testing and modifying his little ship, sealing to defray expenses, trying out crew, taking magnetic observations for his mentor, von Neumayer, and gaining the seatime necessary for his ocean-going master's certificate.

Most of Amundsen's personal fortune was tied up in Gjöa; for floating the expedition, which required five years' stores and much expensive equipment, he had to beg and borrow money. In this he was ably supported by Nansen, whose respect he had earned and whose patronage brought him some official recognition and support. Yet on 16 June 1903, when Gjöa set sail for the Northwest Passage, Amundsen had far outrun his resources and was deeply in debt. He and his six companions slipped out of harbour at night to avoid creditors.

In Greenland they loaded more stores and equipment, including 17 sledge dogs. Overburdened, the tiny ship crossed Baffin Bay and entered the maze of relatively uncharted waters that they hoped would give them passage.

Amundsen chose to follow Franklin's track into Lancaster Sound. In late August he arrived off Beechey Island, where three of Franklin's crewmen were buried, then headed south down James Ross Strait to seek a harbour for wintering. Rounding King William Island he found a small, sheltered bay, which he called Gjöahavn (Gjoa Haven). There they secured the ship for the winter, built an observatory ashore for geomagnetic observations, and laid in a stock of caribou meat. Before long a group of some 200 Netsilik Eskimos came to join them, settling close to *Gjöa* for the winter.

Amundsen befriended the Eskimos, learning their language and taking the opportunity to discover all he could of their culture, especially their clothing and skills of travel, hunting and survival. Though untrained in ethnology, he was a patient and careful observer. His research became a unique study of lasting value. The expedition passed a busy winter. In March and April Amundsen and Peder Ristvedt, his engineer, sledged northward along Boothia Peninsula to the position where Ross had discovered the Magnetic Pole, only to find that the pole had shifted northward. They spent a further two weeks searching for it before returning to the ship.

Valuing enormously his experiences with the Eskimos, Amundsen decided to spend a second winter of learning and sledging from Gjöahavn. In August 1905 they resumed their voyage westward, passing through the relatively unknown waters of Simpson and Dease straits, and finally emerging into the broader waters south of Victoria Island. There they sighted a whaling ship, *Charles Hanson*, which to their delight had come from San Francisco via the Bering Strait: they had reached the western end of the Passage.

However, the journey was far from over. Heavy ice lay between them and Bering Strait, and *Gjöa*, though sturdy, had little power to force her way between the floes. In early September Amundsen decided that another winter was inevitable: he stopped at King Point, close to Herschel Island, and secured *Gjöa* in a bay behind a grounded ice floe in the company of several whalers. From there he sledged with Eskimo companions and one of the whaling captains to the nearest telegraph office at Fort Egbert (Eagle), Alaska, a journey of some 500 miles (805km) over the mountains. Having telegraphed the news that he had traversed the Northwest Passage, he returned to Herschel Island. In June *Gjöa* began the last leg of the journey, arriving in San Francisco in October 1906.

Polar expedition

A gift from the newly-fledged state of Norway, writing and a spell of international lecturing paid off the debts of the *Gjöa* expedition and gave Amundsen enough money to live on. For him the Northwest Passage had been a proving ground, an opportunity to learn more of his chosen profession of polar explorer. Now he was determined on a second, more ambitious northern journey – to drift, like Nansen, across the north polar basin, and if possible to reach the Pole itself. Nansen too had long had this journey in mind, but affairs of state occupied his time. Generously he yielded the use of the research ship *Fram* to Amundsen, and promised his full support.

In seeking financial backing for his new expedition Amundsen presented the journey as a scientific exploration of the north polar basin: achieving the Pole would be incidental. Characteristically, he spent weeks in Bergen learning the skills of oceanography. However, he recognised the value of the Pole as a money-raising attraction. Even with *Fram* provided by the state, together with a substantial grant, he still had to raise funds from private sources.

In September 1909 the newspapers announced the claim of his old shipmate, Frederick Cook, to have reached the North Pole. For Amundsen this immediately removed much of the attraction of his proposed expedition. When later in the same month Robert Peary announced that he too had reached the North Pole, Amundsen gave up all ambitions to make an Arctic

Below *The* Fram *played a remarkable part in polar exploration. Built in Norway, she was christened by Eva Nansen in 1892 and drifted across the Arctic Ocean under her husband's command. Subsequently used as a storage hulk, the ship then carried Amundsen's expedition to the Antarctic.*

journey. Overtly he continued with his plans: secretly he determined instead to try for the South Pole.

Secrecy was essential; he had no wish to antagonise Captain Scott, the British explorer who was known to be embarking on a south polar expedition, and known to guard jealously his assumed rights to the Pole. Amundsen could be sure that, in the circumstances, his own government would not wish to antagonise Britain by supporting a rival south polar venture. When *Fram* sailed from Norway on 7 June 1910, only Amundsen's brother and a handful of his closest colleagues shared his secret. Not until 9 September, from Madeira, did Amundsen announce to the world that the South Pole was his true objective.

His crew took the news philosophically. The South Pole would be an achievement, probably more interesting and certainly yielding quicker results than the long trans-Arctic drift that all had anticipated. With their full support, and knowing that Scott was already heading south, Amundsen pressed forward. From Madeira *Fram* made a non-stop swoop towards Australia and into the Ross Sea. By mid-January 1911 they had reached the eastern end of the Ross Ice Shelf; by the end of the month the shore party had set up Framheim, the prefabricated hut and tents where the polar party, with their teams of over 100 dogs, would overwinter.

On 4 February the Norwegians received a visit from *Terra Nova*, Scott's expedition ship. Scott himself and his wintering party were already ashore at Cape Evans, McMurdo Sound. The ship carried Lt Victor Campbell and a northern party who planned to winter in King Edward VII Land. The explorers and ships' companies exchanged cordial greetings and information, and parted on good terms, Campbell withdrawing in view of the Norwegians' presence, to work in South Victoria Land. Shortly afterwards *Fram* departed for Buenos Aires and a long oceanographic cruise in the Southern Ocean. Throughout late February, March and early April Amundsen and the wintering party worked hard to lay depots in a line southward across the ice shelf, in preparation for their journey the following spring.

The winter passed quietly, with everyone preparing physically and mentally for the coming ordeal – the race to the Pole. Desperate to be there before Scott, Amundsen and his polar party of four started out in late August, but a spell of intense cold drove them back to the protection of Framheim. Finally they set out on 15 October.

Had they known more of the British operation, they would have had less to worry about. Scott's party set off from Cape Evans over a week later. Though travelling over a known route, Scott's party was comparatively ill-equipped and poorly trained, depending largely on man-hauling for motive power. Earlier or later, Scott stood no chance against the hard-won professionalism of Amundsen. Neither his tractors, nor his sad, mishandled ponies and dog-teams, nor least of all his strategic planning, at any stage posed a challenge to the Norwegian bid.

Despite his preparations and superlative efficiency, Amundsen's polar journey was far from easy. His route, unknown at the outset, took him a total of 1,400 miles (2,250km) across heavily crevassed shelf ice, almost 10,000ft (3,048m) up a steep, winding glacier, and across the featureless polar plateau. The five-man party, with four superbly-trained dog

Captain Scott

Born on 6 June 1868, Robert Falcon Scott became an officer cadet in the Royal Navy at the age of 13. His early career was prosaic and uneventful: he travelled the world, qualified as a torpedo officer, and by his early 30s seemed set to climb slowly the ladder of command. Though unqualified in any way for polar work, in 1900 he was appointed to command the National Antarctic Expedition, Britain's contribution to a turn-of-the-century wave of international polar exploration. In HMS *Discovery*, a newly-built wooden research ship, he sailed south with a team of scientists to McMurdo Sound (see 'Shackleton'). In the course of the expedition, accompanied by Ernest Shackleton and Edward Wilson, he sledged across the Ross Ice Shelf in the direction of the South Pole, reaching latitude 82° S.

The expedition, which completed two winters, was judged successful and Scott was promoted to Captain. After further service with the fleet he was granted permission to organise a second Antarctic expedition, this time with the avowed intention of reaching the South Pole. In their ship *Terra Nova* his party left Britain on 15 June 1910, reaching McMurdo Sound, Antarctica, a few days before Amundsen's arrival off the Ross Ice Shelf. Equipped with ponies and motor tractors, and following a route that Shackleton had already pioneered, Scott seemed fully capable of reaching the Pole before Amundsen. However, the tractors failed, the ponies proved disappointing, and the five-man polar party reverted to man-hauling. They reached the South Pole on 17 January 1912, almost five weeks after the Norwegians. All died of malnutrition and exhaustion on the return journey.

***Above** Captain Scott and party, photographed in January 1911 with Scott placed sixth from the right.*

***Left** The Norwegian flag flies in triumph at the South Pole in December 1911 as Amundsen takes a sextant reading to make sure he has found the right spot. A packing-case is used as the base for an artificial horizon.*

teams, climbed the glacier in four days: at the top all but 18 of the dogs were shot, their work done. The rest of the journey was accomplished in style. The party reached the South Pole on 14 December 1911.

After circling the Pole to make sure they had got there and cooking a celebratory meal, they returned the way they had come. They kept up a good pace, following a line of cairns and flags put up on the way out, skiing expertly down the glaciers, riding the sledges whenever possible.

Again it was not an easy journey: crevasses yawned on every side, and all the dangers inherent in intense cold and remoteness accompanied them every day. However, they were fit, well-fed, superbly skilled in their snowcraft and, above all, successful. They returned to Framheim on 26 January 1912, to find *Fram* waiting at the ice edge, and sailed for home.

Aftermath

The heroic death of Scott and his companions took some of the gilt from Amundsen's achievement. However, he became a legend in his own time – the archetypal explorer of both polar regions who had lived to tell his tale. World War I, in which Norway remained neutral, gave him an opportunity to mend his fortune: from profits in shipping he built and equipped a new expedition ship, *Maud*, in which to drift across the Arctic Ocean. From 1918 to 1922 he returned to the Arctic, sailing and drifting along the Siberian coast from east to west, but failing to enter the main circulation towards the Pole.

He experimented with aircraft, exploring the Arctic basin in seaplanes financed by Lincoln Ellsworth, a wealthy US amateur explorer. In May 1926, with Ellsworth and Umberto Nobile, a flamboyant Italian pilot, he crossed the Arctic from Spitsbergen to Alaska in *Norge*, an Italian dirigible. Though he had quarrelled violently with Nobile on every aspect of the flight, Amundsen joined the search for him when Nobile's airship *Italia* was lost in the Arctic two years later. This act of humanity was his last exploration: Roald Amundsen disappeared on a flight between northern Norway and Svalbard on 17 June 1928.

A Historic Event

At the South Pole, the Norwegian team planted their country's flag with simple ceremony. Amundsen wrote:

"I had determined that the act of planting it – this historic event – should be equally divided among us all . . . this was the only way I could show my gratitude to my comrades in this desolate spot. They understood and accepted it in the spirit in which it was offered. Five weather-beaten, frost-bitten fists they were that grasped the pole, raised it high in the air, and planted it as the first at the geographical South Pole."

from *My Life as an Explorer*, Roald Amundsen

Biographical Notes

1872
Born in southern Norway.

1890
Entered medical school.

1894
First Arctic voyage on sealing ship.

1897–9
In Antarctica with Belgian expedition.

1900
Qualified as skipper: bought own boat.

1903–6
Re-located the North Magnetic Pole: sailed the Northwest Passage.

1910–12
Expedition to the South Pole.

1918–20
Maud expedition to Northeast Passage.

1926
Flight across the Arctic.

1928
Lost with aircraft between Norway and Svalbard.

RICHARD BYRD

Richard Evelyn Byrd began his career of travel and adventure at the age of 12, when he journeyed unaccompanied from his home in Virginia to stay with family friends in the Philippine Islands. He was destined for a career in law, but schooling at military academies and a year at the University of Virginia gave him a taste for something more adventurous. He entered the US Naval Academy, Annapolis, graduating as ensign in 1912.

Undistinguished during his training, he seemed set for a life of routine and slow progress up the ladder of promotion. However, an accidental fall into the hold of a ship left him with a permanently damaged leg: unfit for further sea duties, in 1916 Lt Byrd was placed on the retired list and consigned to deskwork involving naval reserve units and training.

Byrd was among the first to see how aircraft could revolutionise exploration, and his Antarctic expeditions filled in the map of Antarctica

The development of naval aviation opened a new door: in 1917 he trained as a pilot and in 1918 became involved in a plan to fly some of the US Navy's largest seaplanes across the Atlantic Ocean to the European theatre of war. One aircraft made the crossing, the first-ever trans-

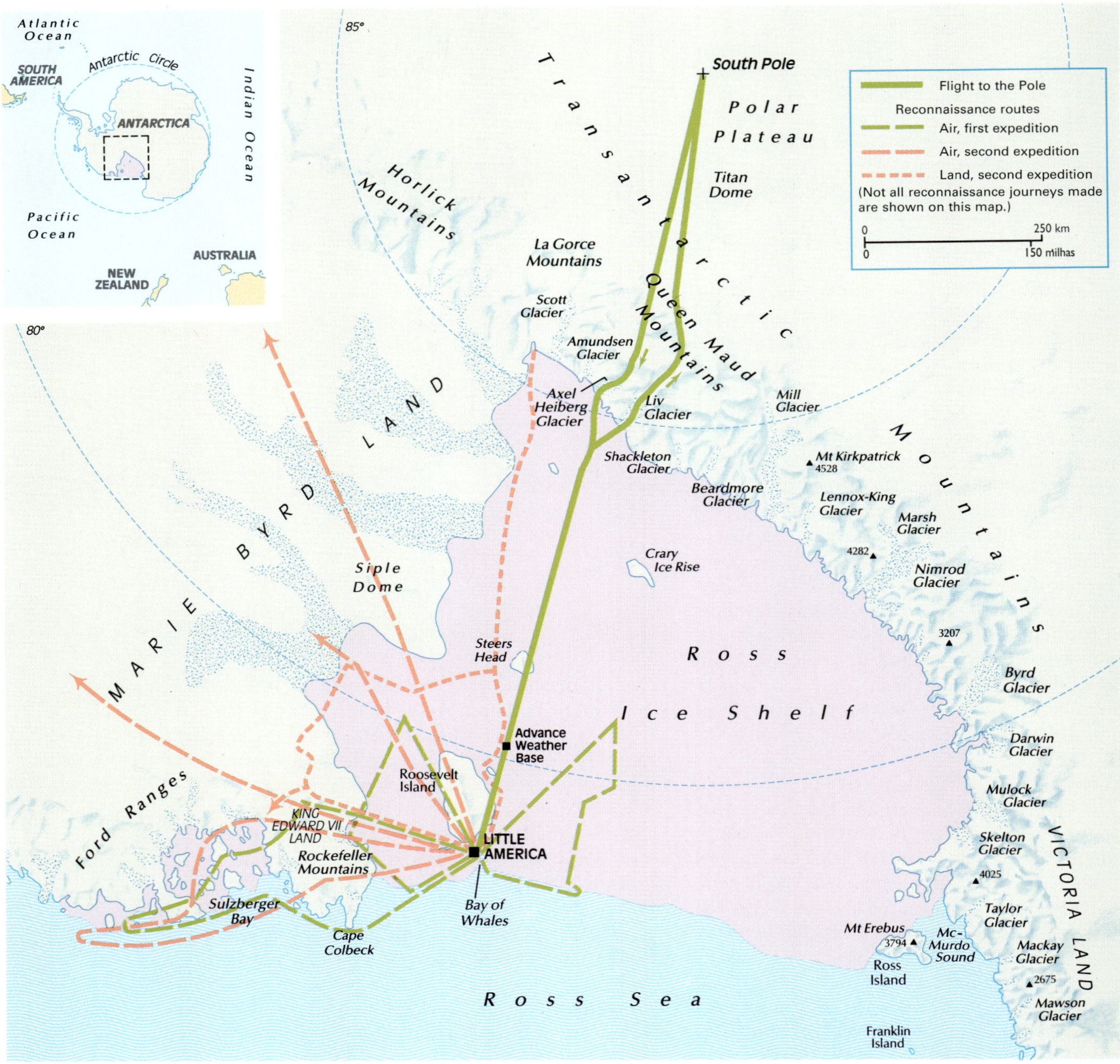

Atlantic flight. Though Byrd himself was not on board, the experience he gained in logistic planning, calculating distances, weather conditions and safety factors made him an expert, then almost unique, in the long-range routing of aircraft. The end of the war brought an end to the exercise, and Byrd was again transferred from active service to the reserve.

Arctic flights

In 1925 the US Navy considered sending *Shenandoah*, one of its airships, on a flight across the Arctic basin from Alaska to Svalbard, taking in the North Pole. Byrd was among the team drawn together to work out the logistics. The airship was damaged in a storm during trial runs and the flight was cancelled. However, Byrd became fired with the idea of using aircraft, preferably seaplanes (which were then among the largest aircraft, with the longest range) to explore some of the unknown areas of the Arctic basin. His special status as a reserve officer gave him the freedom to plan an expedition of his own. He sought private funding from prominent industrialists and bankers – Edsel Ford and John D. Rockefeller Jr were among his sponsors. However, he sought also the cooperation of the Navy, arguing that it should continue its traditional involvement in Arctic exploration, but using the new methods at its disposal.

It was a timely argument, for the naval air arm was struggling through a difficult infancy, and its supporters welcomed the chance to show what the new service could do. When Byrd petitioned for the use of some of its seaplanes to fly the Arctic, possibly to the North Pole, his request was taken seriously.

It happened that an experienced Arctic explorer, Donald Macmillan, was at that time planning an expedition to Greenland. He too had the idea that an aircraft would help exploration, though he lacked Byrd's expertise and vision. Simultaneously with Byrd he asked the navy for the loan of a seaplane for reconnaissance and transport, in support of his ground-based dog-teams. The Navy wanted to help both, but only a limited number of seaplanes could be spared. The suggestion was made that Byrd might postpone his own plans and form a small semi-independent unit to accompany and support Macmillan.

So in summer 1925 Byrd found himself based

Above *Richard Byrd is second from the left in this photograph. On the extreme right is Bernt Balchen, who piloted the plane in which Byrd flew over the South Pole in 1929.*

Below *An iceberg in the Weddell Sea, from which Sir Vivian Fuchs and his party crossed the Antarctic to the South Pole and the Ross Sea in the 1950s.*

Above *Admiral Byrd in action. The great pioneer of exploration from the air, he flew over the North Pole in 1926 and the South Pole three years later. His subsequent expeditions in the 1930s and 1940s mapped the huge areas of the Antarctic.*

at Etah, in west Greenland, and flying over Ellesmere Island and the coast and western ice-cap of Greenland. His flights covered in minutes the areas where Peary and other famous explorers had struggled for months. He was all too well aware that, out there to the north over the Arctic Ocean, stretched an unencumbered route to the Pole itself.

It was not an entirely happy expedition, for Macmillan and Byrd, representing the old and the new in Arctic exploration, disagreed on many points. Macmillan's ad hoc planning did not appeal to the meticulous Byrd, and did not allow the aircraft to make an effective contribution to the work of the expedition. However, Byrd gained first-hand experience of cold-weather operations and the problems of navigating close to the earth's magnetic pole, where ordinary magnetic compasses became almost useless. He saw that, even with the small and relatively clumsy aircraft available to him, flying to the North Pole would be relatively easy; indeed it would not be difficult to explore a considerable area of the Arctic basin in a single, well-planned season.

His plans went further: if the Arctic could be explored by air, then what about Antarctica? Virtually the whole southern continent awaited discovery; on so vast a scale, long-distance reconnaissance flights would be by far the most expeditious method of discovering what was there.

In the following year Byrd took a private expedition to Svalbard (Spitsbergen) and from there flew to the North Pole. It was to have been a US Navy expedition, but the Navy found that it could not support him, and turned him down. Unperturbed, he sought help from some of the wealthy sponsors who had supported his earlier expedition, and from institutions, businessmen and the public. Such was his reputation for straight dealing and reliability that he quickly raised enough to buy the equipment and services he needed. These included two aircraft, a ship, and a crew of 50, many of them volunteers.

In early April he sailed from Brooklyn; by late April he had reached Svalbard, his chosen point of departure, and early on 9 May, piloted by Floyd Bennett, Byrd took off in his ski-equipped, tri-motored Fokker aircraft. It was a seven-hour flight to the Pole across almost featureless sea ice, and a slightly longer flight back. There were no new discoveries of land. The main dangers lay in engine failure or navigational miscalculation, either of which might have forced a landing on the rough, inhospitable sea ice. Byrd and Bennett had to work hard to stop themselves falling asleep at the controls.

It was a daring but well-conceived flight, and Byrd's careful planning made it a relatively uneventful one. The event preceded by a few days a much longer and technically more difficult airship flight by Roald Amundsen and Lincoln Ellsworth over the north polar basin, but it was Byrd who scooped the headlines. On return to base he released the news of his flight by radio; on returning to the US in June 1927 the two fliers found themselves fêted as national and international heroes. Byrd had a full mandate to continue exploring in whatever direction he chose.

Byrd in Antarctica

From the Arctic Byrd learned many useful lessons, not only about polar flight but also about managing cheap, inadequate ships with volunteer crews, and operating on budgets that, however substantial, were never quite enough for the job in hand. He had learned, too, the value of good publicity, and reached the conviction that any future exploration, on a scale that appealed to him, would be accomplished not through the Navy, but only with funding from wealthy patrons and the public at large.

Now Byrd turned his attention to the Antarctic, determining to conquer it by air. As a diversion, in late June 1927 he took part in a race to cross the Atlantic by air, completing a course from Newfoundland to the coast of France. However, Antarctica was his main preoccupation. He planned a two-year expedition that would include a flight to the South Pole, plus extensive exploration in the region that Amundsen, Shackleton and Scott had made famous half a generation before.

Byrd's first Antarctic expedition, funded almost entirely by private and public sponsors (including the prestigious National Geographic Society) was the largest and most expensive geographical expedition of its time. Two ships were involved, *City of New York* and *Eleanor Bolling* (named after Byrd's mother), and Byrd also made use of whale factory ships to carry himself and some of his cargo south. The expedition sailed from New Zealand early in December 1928, reached the edge of the Ross Sea pack-ice by the middle of the month, and early in January set up a base, Little America, in the Bay of Whales, a semi-permanent indentation in the Ross Ice Shelf, which Amundsen also had used.

By the end of January, Little America was almost complete, an overwintering camp for 42 men with 80 sledge dogs and three aircraft. Before the end of summer Byrd made several reconnaissance flights, discovering and photographing with aerial cameras many square miles of continental territory that no man had ever seen before. A flight to the Rockefeller Mountains, piloted by Bernt Balchen and led by geologist Laurence Gould, ended in a minor disaster: the aircraft was blown from its mooring and damaged beyond repair. The men were rescued, but the aircraft remained behind in the snow.

At the end of winter Byrd began making preparations for the expedition's major flight to the South Pole. This involved a distance of over 800 miles (1,285km), some 150 miles (240km) further than the north polar flight, and a climb to over 12,000ft (3,655m). Both factors would make for heavy fuel consumption, and Byrd felt it necessary to lay an emergency depot of fuel and food along the route.

At 3.29 on the morning of 28 November, Byrd, photographer Ashley McKinley and radio operator Harold June, piloted by Bernt Balchen, took off for the South Pole. Their route from Little America followed closely that taken by Amundsen some 18 years earlier. Along it they overflew Gould's geological party, whose role was the useful but more mundane one of detailed ground survey by dog-sledge.

Flying to the Pole

Byrd described the scene in the aircraft as they approached the polar plateau:

"McKinley was 'fighting' with his camera all over the plane. I was navigating. June was sending radios, dumping gas from cans to tanks, estimating gas from six tanks, and between times taking pictures. Later he took his turn at the controls . . . Our activity was in violent contrast to the stillness of the lifeless white spaces below."

Byrd had to decide which glacier to ascend – the Axel Heiberg, which Amundsen had used and surveyed, or a neighbouring glacier that might offer an easier run:

"Should we tackle Axel Heiberg, altitude known, but width and air currents unknown? The bordering peaks might be so high that the currents they created would dash us to the ground, hovering as we were near the absolute ceiling of our plane. Or should we take the unknown glacier, which looked feasible? Beyond the wider pass there might be mountains to block us. We had to choose now – and the choice would be irrevocable because we did not have enough gasoline to enable us to fly up a glacier and back again and try another. And we had to choose quickly – we were heading into the mountains at a speed exceeding a mile a minute."

from *The National Geographic magazine*, Volume 58(2)

Below One of the expedition's aircraft was damaged beyond repair in a flight to the Rockefeller Mountains in 1929 and had to be abandoned to the engulfing snow. John D. Rockefeller Jr was one of Byrd's wealthy backers.

Shortly after 9.15 they had to jettison emergency food bags to rise to the height of the polar plateau, which they cleared by a few hundred feet. Thereafter it was a steady run to the Pole, which they reached at 1.15. By 4.45 in the afternoon they had returned to the foot of the glaciers, and located and landed at the depot, where they refuelled. Six hours later, after a flight of 15 hours and 51 minutes, they were safely back in Little America.

Again Byrd released the information by radio and hit world headlines. However, through December and January he and his aviation group made a far more valuable contribution to exploration, by overflying many square miles of King Edward VII Land and other localities and bringing back an excellent photographic record of mountains, lakes and ice coasts. Meanwhile, Laurence Gould and his sledging party were quietly establishing a record of their own: their detailed, painstaking work in the mountains involved one of the longest scientific journeys by dog-sledge on record. They brought back both valuable scientific data and astronomical fixes that helped to consolidate the aerial survey.

The expedition landed in Dunedin, New Zealand, in March 1930, releasing a flood of information to press and radio. On return to the US some weeks later, Byrd found his own country ready to honour him, and widespread interest throughout the world. The public had supported his expedition: now the public heard about it through radio, cine-films and the printed word. Byrd reached a far wider audience than any explorer before him, and the public responded with a wave of adulation for himself and his team.

The second Antarctic expedition

Now appointed Rear Admiral on the retired list, Byrd rode the wave effectively. He had scratched the surface of Antarctica: now he planned a second, more elaborate expedition that would explore more thoroughly some of the new lands he had discovered, and if possible discover more.

The economic depression that blanketed both the US and Europe made planning and fund-raising a nightmare. Byrd succeeded with a call to American patriotism. This time there was no spectacular flight to the Pole; it was to be a scientific and geographical expedition in the 'American' sector of Antarctica; it would declare US interest in the new continent, and provide what might be needed for some future claim for US sovereignty. For almost two years Byrd and an energetic staff of volunteers begged, borrowed and traded to raise the two ships, four aircraft (including one of the newly developed autogyros) and the tons of stores and equipment needed for a large overwintering party.

The ships of the second Byrd expedition, *Bear of Oakland* and *Jacob Ruppert*, left the US in October and November 1933. On the approaches to Antarctica, Byrd made several reconnaissance flights in the big Curtiss-Wright Condor seaplane, but failed to see any convincing coastline. Reaching the Bay of Whales in mid-January 1934, the party reoccupied and refurbished Little America, digging out cases of food and equipment (including two near-serviceable aircraft) and augmented the camp with eight new buildings. When the last ship left in early March there remained 56 men, 150 sledge dogs and – uniquely – three Guernsey cows and a calf.

While daylight remained the sledging parties with tractors and dogs set off to lay depots as far as possible into the interior, and a prefabricated hut for a small advanced weather base, nominally for three men, was tractored to its site just south of the 80th parallel of latitude. In mid-March Byrd made the controversial and inherently dangerous decision to spend the winter there alone.

***Below** Majestic icebergs lie like anchored ships in the Antarctic. The fierce cold posed special problems for aviators in polar regions and navigation was exceptionally difficult.*

On 22 March he handed over command of the expedition to Thomas Poulter, a physicist, and was flown out to where the shack was being erected. One week later the construction team returned to Little America. Byrd maintained weather observations, read, and for a time seemed able to cope with his solitude. However, on several occasions he was almost gassed by fumes from the stove and generator engine; the quality of his radio transmissions deteriorated, and Poulter judged it necessary to pay him a visit. The team that in August made a risky journey to rescue him found the admiral sick, unkempt and living in squalor, from which it took him two months to recover.

With the return of the sun in early August the sledging teams limbered up for action, and from October several took to the field. A biological party under Paul Siple explored Marie Byrd Land, and geological and survey parties explored the shelf-ice and mountains to south and east of Little America.

In November and December the aviation group made several memorable flights, particularly to discover if there was any indication of a channel connecting the two deep indentations in Antarctica, the Ross Sea and the Weddell Sea. They established that high ice surfaces lay in every direction beyond the Ross Ice Shelf: whatever lay below the ice, following their work Antarctica could safely be represented on maps as a single ice-covered continent.

Again Byrd returned to the US in triumph. Though geographers niggled over some of his interpretations and the superficiality of much of his aerial exploration, the public took the more sensible view that Byrd and his team had made history – a great and positive achievement in exploration. The government too gave its highest accolades. Though it was not official US policy to claim the newly discovered territories, the government was well aware that Byrd's well publicised achievements would strengthen possible future claims, to match those that Britain, Norway, France and other countries were currently lodging.

The US in Antarctica

Byrd's success persuaded the government that Antarctic exploration was no longer a matter for private enterprise. In 1939 he was appointed head of the US Antarctic Service, and placed in command of a hybrid expedition, largely but not entirely government funded. The USAS expedition had two bases, one at Little America under Paul Siple, the other at Stonington Island, far down the west side of the Antarctic Peninsula, under Richard Black. Both base leaders and many others involved had served their apprenticeships with Byrd, and now carried his methods forward. The expedition, planned to last for several years with changing personnel, ended under threat of war in 1941.

During World War II Byrd advised on cold-weather clothing and equipment, and helped in planning bases and long-range air routes in the Pacific Ocean. In the post-war years he played nominal roles in a number of US Navy forays into Antarctica.

In 1946–7 he took part in Operation Highjump, revisiting the continent and again flying to the South Pole. In 1955 he was called from retirement to start a new initiative, US Antarctic Programs. Though he again revisited Antarctica in 1955–6 he played little part in the planning or design of USAP; he was far-sighted enough, however, to take an interest in the planning that led to the international Geophysical Year 1957–8, when the US established permanent stations in McMurdo Sound and at the South Pole. Byrd did not live to see this: he died aged 68 on 11 March 1957.

Biographical Notes

1888
Born 25 October.

1908–12
United States Naval Academy.

1916
Retired from active duty due to damaged leg.

1917
Trained as naval pilot.

1925
First Arctic flights over Greenland and Ellesmere Island.

1926
Flight to the North Pole.

1928–30
First Antarctic expedition: flight to the South Pole.

1933–35
Second Antarctic expedition.

1939–41
United States Antarctic Service Expedition.

1946–7
Leader, US naval operation Highjump.

1955
In charge of United States Antarctic Programs.

1957
Died 11 March.

FREYA STARK

A name synonymous with the art of travel writing

In the first volume of her autobiography, *Traveller's Prelude*, Dame Freya Stark reveals that her parents were 'singularly mobile, even for that age of easy frontiers. Before I was a year old we spent ten days in the country near Paris, travelled to England (at four months), visited in Basingstoke and Torquay, and settled close to Dartmoor for the summer. At nine months I again travelled, visited in Paris, spent a first Christmas with the Genoa grandmother and settled down for a year and a half of only minor movements in the little town of Asolo near Venice'. If these experiences bred in the infant an eagerness to devote her life to travelling, it was to be a long time before any such ambitions were fulfilled.

Her early years were marred by a near-fatal accident in an Italian factory when her hair was caught in some machinery, and by a succession of illnesses. She worked for a while as a nurse during World War I, after which long years of poor health left her desperate to escape from confinement and get on with the business of living. Many people with such a background might have chosen to spend their lives at home close to competent medical help, but Freya Stark's reaction was the opposite. A woman with an instinctive love of the outdoors and of climbing in the Italian Alps, she felt that it would be better to die rather than go on living as an invalid, and so the prospect of foreign travel held few fears for her.

'The whole of my future must be rearranged'

As a convalescent with time on her hands, she had applied herself to learning Arabic and then went on to improve her skills at the School of Oriental Studies in London – the Middle East was to be her first destination. On 18 November 1927, satisfied that her mother could manage without her, but aware that her own physical strength was still poor, she boarded a ship bound for Beirut. This first seven-month period of travel included an extended stay at Brummana, above Beirut (where her health slowly improved and warnings about never being able to walk more

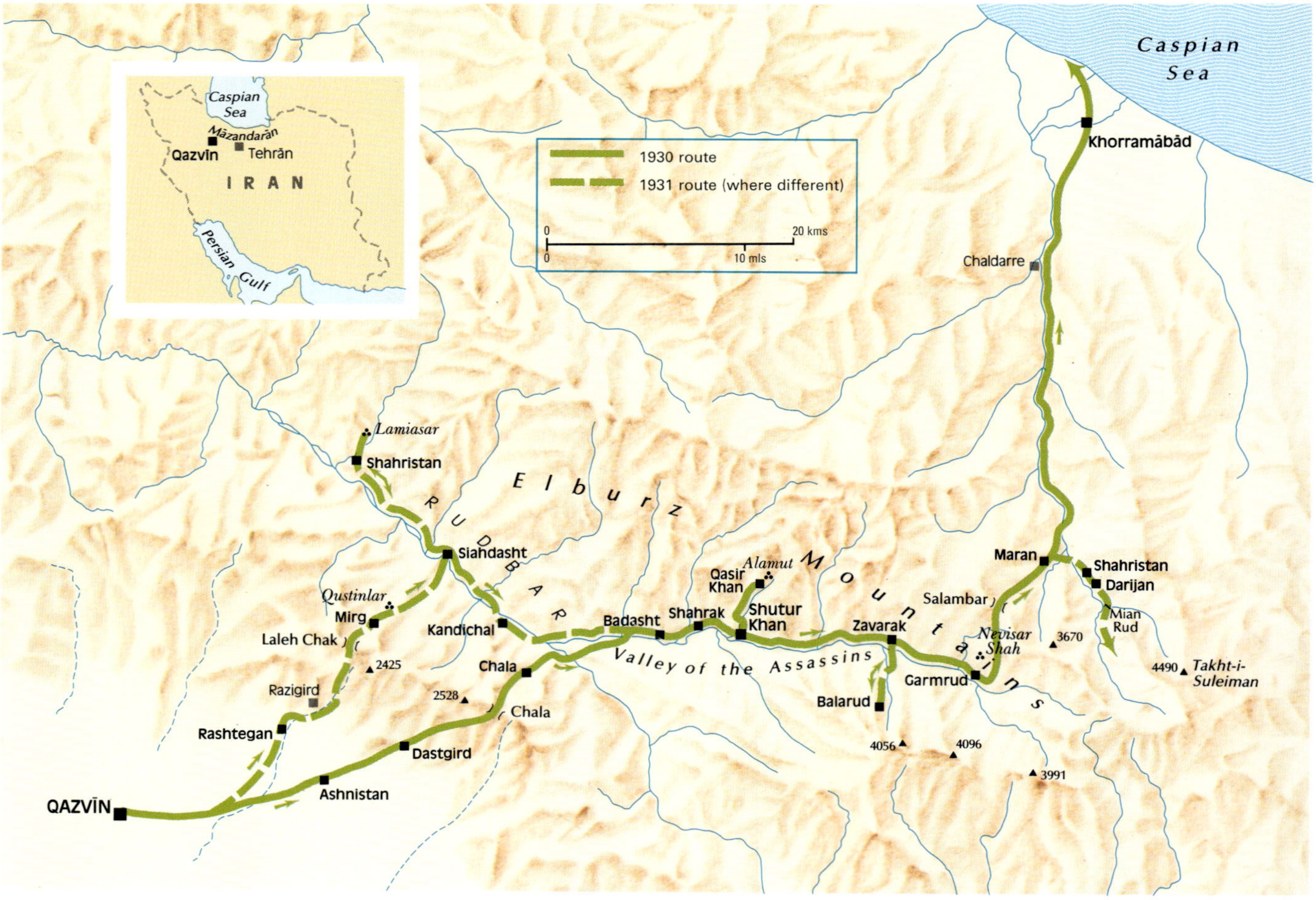

***Below** Freya Stark's journeys in 1930 and 1931 took her into the Valley of the Assassins in the mountain depths of Iran, where few Europeans had ever ventured.*

than ½ mile [1km] were gladly dismissed), and visits to Damascus, Jerusalem and Cairo. She returned to Italy 'with a feeling, dim but insistent, that the whole of my future must be rearranged'.

She went next to Canada to visit her father, published her first article, about the Druze in Syria, and then, in September 1929, followed up a longstanding invitation to go to Baghdād, where her first impressions of members of the British Civil Service were that these people displayed attitudes far more foreign to her than any of the opinions held by the native residents of the Middle East. She for her part was seen as something of a rebel because she refused to live at the British Club, preferring instead to lodge with a shoemaker's family and so improve her Arabic. Within a few months she was also learning Persian in preparation for another journey.

To the Valley of the Assassins

In April 1930 Freya Stark left Baghdād and travelled over the Paitak Pass to Hamadan in Persia on the first stage of an expedition in search of the fortress of Alamut, which had belonged to the Persian sect known as the Assassins.

Marco Polo had referred to these places in his *Travels*, but the modern map indicated only vaguely an Alamut district. Enquiries revealed that the remains of a castle were still standing at a place called Qasir Khan and that it could be reached from the town of Qazvīn. Arriving at the Grand Hotel there armed with several letters of introduction, she found that her intended journey roused considerable interest and many offers of help, although the local police were inclined to treat her with suspicion. She was fortunate in meeting Dr As'ad el Hukuma, one of the owners of the Rock of Alamut. He supplied her with an escort, a muleteer called 'Aziz, who arrived to begin the journey with two deputies, his mother and his son.

A Rationale for Travel

In her many books Freya Stark speaks of herself as a traveller, and says that in the beginning she travelled 'single-mindedly for fun,' but she found that:

"Some more ascetic reason than mere enjoyment should be found if one wishes to travel in peace: to do things for fun smacks of brevity, immorality, almost, in our utilitarian world. And though personally I think the world is wrong, and I know in my heart of hearts that it is a most excellent reason to do things merely because one likes the doing of them, I would advise all those who wish to see unwrinkled brows in passport offices to start out ready labelled as entomologists, anthropologists, or whatever other -ology they think suitable and propitious."

from the preface to *The Valley of the Assassins*, Freya Stark

Above *Freya Stark, photographed in Italy. Defying poor health and a weak heart, she spent years indomitably climbing mountains, exploring remote regions of the East and writing vividly of places and people.*

They rode first to Ashnistan and then prepared for the trek across the mountains at the village of Dastgird, where the arrival of a Christian woman was regarded with distaste. As they approached the Chala Pass they met a succession of Alamut traders leading mules carrying heavy loads of Caspian rice. At last they reached the top of the mountain ridge and looked down into the Valley of the Assassins spread out beneath them, with a mountain known as King Solomon's Throne prominent in the distance. Their map was sketchy to say the least and Stark made it one of her tasks to discover the local names for the various features along the route in an attempt to compile a more accurate plan of the region. Gradually, 'by sifting and collating, by telling Ismail that he was a liar and getting 'Aziz to ask every likely man we met, I gradually got the landmarks of my line of march; and also acquired such a reputation for geographical curiosity that strangers would come up and bring me names unasked'.

After a pause at Chala, they continued to the point where the Alamut and Talaghan rivers meet and, after an hour climbing up all old cliff-face path, found their way into the Valley of the

***Above** Ruins of the Assassins' castle at Alamut.*

The Assassins and Their Valley

In 1071 a young Persian known as Hassan al-Sabbah became a member of the Ismaili sect. Freya Stark records how this movement broke away from the dominant Shi'ites in Persia and established a dynasty of Fatimite caliphs in Egypt who were known for their love of learning and their religious tolerance. Hassan himself formed a separate movement within the Ismaili known as the Assassins. He is said to have obtained recruits by drugging them with hashish and taking them to the castle of Alamut, where they would wake up in a beautiful complex of gardens and believe themselves to be in paradise. The name Assassins is derived from hashish, and Hassan's followers did indeed assassinate their political opponents. They had a network of castles in northern Persia, many in the so-called Valley of the Assassins in Luristan. Their influence also spread to Syria where they came into contact with the Crusaders, and they may have influenced the way the Knights Templar organised themselves.

Assassins. They waded across the Alamut River and continued on through Badasht and Shahrak to Shutur Khan, where the area policeman asked questions and searched their luggage but made no objection to their plans. Next day they crossed the Qasir Rud and approached their goal, the castle of Alamut at Qasir Khan. Here, in addition to examining the castle, they found plentiful fragments of ancient pottery. What Stark saw there so impressed her that she was eager to return one day.

For now, however, they continued to the villages of Zavarak and Garmrud, where small, flat-roofed houses crowded together on a mountain slope with the castle of Nevisar Shah looming high above them. The villagers told Stark that she was their first European visitor for years and added that no European had ever climbed up to Nevisar Shah. Nor was it a place that many of the villagers had visited. This was a challenge that could not be resisted and, escorted by a hunter armed with a huge and primitive gun, Stark climbed up to the scant remains of the castle and was intrigued to find discarded 13th-century pottery of a type that matched the kind she had seen previously at the castle at Qasir Khan.

More castles and a serious illness

On her way from Garmrud, over the Salambar Pass en route for the Caspian Sea in the summer of 1930, Freya Stark saw once again the mountain known as Takht-i-Suleiman, or King Solomon's Throne, and just over a year later, in August 1931, she returned with plans to climb it. While she was waiting to start from Qazvīn she heard about another castle of the Assassins, whose name was Lamiasar, but whose exact position was far from clear.

She knew only that it lay in the district of Rudbar and that it would be dangerous to go there because of the prevalence of malaria, but she decided to risk it. Travelling with one servant and two mules she went northeast from Qazvīn to Rashtegan and on up into the mountains to a pass that was known locally as Laleh Chak, but was not named on the map she was using. Here she met three Kurdish farmers who took her to stay in their tiny village of Mirg and told her that years before some other English people had stayed there – surveyors who had been compiling maps of the region. After a night sleeping on the roof of one of the houses, a villager took the travellers to see the ruins of another castle, Qustinlar, before sending them on their way to Lamiasar. They reached Lamiasar with the help of a local guide via a winding mountain track, often so narrow that it was impossible to ride. Finally, they had to leave the mules behind as they came close to the castle, and had to scramble up the rock-face to the western gate. Here, as at Alamut, there were thousands of pottery fragments, signs of an elaborate water system and the remains of numerous buildings within an area about 1500ft long by 600ft wide (457 × 183m). Freya Stark left the

Above *Freya Stark took this photograph of the northern slopes of the Salambar Pass in 1930. She received much help and kindness from the local people, who were astounded to find a white Christian woman exploring their remote country.*

castle knowing that there were many other ancient sites scattered around this region waiting to be explored, but her muleteer apparently begged the local guide to mention no more castles and she soon began to feel too ill to argue.

Too weak to continue, she lay at a small shrine near the village of Kandichal, attended by local women but fully expecting to die. After three days, when heart trouble developed, she sent to Qazvīn for medical help and her muleteer returned with a bottle of digitalis and a letter in which some unknown well-wisher 'hoped that I now realised the gravity of my situation and would abandon this foolish idea of wandering unprotected over Persia'. She recalls that she was on the point of abandoning, not only her travels, but also life on earth and certainly intended to go straight to hospital in Tehran at the first opportunity. However, on the sixth day, feeling stronger, she changed her mind and, with a mixture of tenacity and recklessness, decided to try to reach King Solomon's Throne after all.

Progress was understandably slow: 'Even on the level ground it took us three hours to reach the far side of the defile from Kandichal, and when we had done so, I lay on my quilt, injected camphor to steady my troublesome heart, and fed myself on white of egg and brandy, the only food I dared risk.' After six and a half hours travelling, they reached the village of Shutur Khan where they were remembered from their visit of the previous year and warmly welcomed. Just as things looked as if they might improve, however, Stark realised that she was now also suffering from malaria.

A Persian doctor, staying in a village five hours ride away, was brought to her bedside, where he diagnosed dysentery and malaria, dispensed quinine in huge quantities, and cheerfully proposed that the invalid should make the five-hour journey back to his village. He promised that she would be well within a week. After another arduous ride along the Alamut valley and up into the Elburz range of mountains, they reached the village of Balarud, where she was invited to choose a house in which to stay. When she did so, the inhabitants cleared out their belongings and left. From the window of her room there was an excellent view of King Solomon's Throne.

With competent attention from the doctor she grew stronger and began to enjoy her convalescence: 'It was pleasant to think that we were not marked on any map; that so far as the great world went, we were non-existent; and yet here we were, harvesting our corn, living and dying and marrying as busily as elsewhere.' Soon, she was well enough to move on, and she was still intent on reaching her original destination.

Right *Snowy Mount Damavend, 'smooth and serene above all earthly things', as Freya Stark wrote, rises to 18,600 ft (5,670m) in the Elburz Mountains.*

An attempt on King Solomon's Throne

From Balarud they travelled down again to the Alamut valley and followed the route of the previous year from Garmrud up to the Salambar Pass, where Stark spent three hours taking bearings and collecting data for a better map of a region where the names of villages and landmarks were unknown beyond the immediate locality. At Shahristan in the Darijan valley, she found that 'the people rushed to me as if I were a circus. Twenty times or more I was asked to show myself full length to new audiences'. Here they met a man who offered to guide them to King Solomon's Throne. They rode on to the village of Darijan, up the valley to a point above Mian Rud, 'the place between rivers', where they camped for the night.

The next day their local guide had vanished and they were faced with a path that 'appeared to continue straight over a wall of rock some thousands of feet high'. Stark estimated that the climb would take 10 hours and doubted that she was sufficiently recovered from her illness to tackle it. At nightfall their guide resumed, and the next morning he led them on for four and a half hours to the top of a ridge. From here they could only contemplate the mountain peak, which appeared to be completely inaccessible. Freya Stark learnt later that this was a deliberate attempt to prevent her from climbing to the top. There was an easy mule track that would have led them to a place far closer to the summit, but a Hungarian engineer who had been working on a survey of his own in the area had threatened their guide with appalling retribution if he took the Englishwoman to the peak of King Solomon's Throne.

The disappointment was considerable, but Freya Stark continued her study of this region, known as Māzandarān, and her work did much to improve knowledge of this inadequately mapped area. After that, she never ceased to travel. She became an expert on the Middle East, advised the British Ministry of Information on Arabian affairs during World War II, explored China, became a regular visitor to Turkey, and retraced the path of Alexander the Great from Caria to Cilicia.

An individual approach to travel

Much of the history of exploration concerns individuals who left home to claim new territory for nationalistic and commercial reasons. Others were inspired by religious ideals, scientific curiosity or a desire for personal fame. In the late 1920s, Freya Stark was not embarking on a life

***Above** The Elburz Mountains, cloaked in snow, make a barrier to the south of the Caspian Sea. Among their secluded valleys the murderous sect of the Assassins had its strongholds. Its leader was called the Old Man of the Mountains.*

***Right** The village of Shutur Khan, photographed by Freya Stark in 1930. It lies close to the Assassin fortress at Alamut on the great rock from which the sentries kept watch.*

of exploration in any of these senses, but rather on one of quiet observation and reporting.

Freya Stark did not start out ready labelled and subsequently became a most distinguished, prolific and adventurous travel writer. She succeeded in this through an ability to be an unobtrusive witness of events – something that was her clear intention from the start. In a letter written in January 1929 she said that she would like to keep a little shop in an eastern town such as Aleppo or Hama, because this would give great possibilities for observation.

Writing at a time when popular tourism was gaining ground and the most remote regions were beginning to be within the grasp of anyone with some cash and two or three weeks to spare, she speculated on the difference between 'wild' and 'domestic' attitudes to travel. The domestic creature, she reckoned, liked 'to have the views of outside brought in to vary the sheltered panorama; and, though it may travel from the Crystal Palace to Timbuctoo, the park precincts will never be abandoned. The genuinely wild is not interested in 'seeing the world', it is exclusively interested in *being*; it digests the world as a cow chews its cud not for what the grass looks like but for what it does inside . . . these creatures travel, even if they are sitting motionless and chained'. With such an outlook, as Freya Stark has shown, it is still perfectly possible to be an explorer, both of the world and of human nature. She lives, in her one hundredth year, in Italy and her books of travel writing and autobiography bear witness to her ability to absorb a landscape and distill the essence of its character and its people in a way which countless readers can enjoy.

***Above** Māzandarān in 1920.*

Biographical Notes

1893
Born in Paris.

1927
First journey to the Middle East.

1929
Went to live in Baghdād.

1910
Journey to Valley of the Assassins, Luristan, Persia.

1931
Further travel in Luristan and Māzandarān followed by 60 years travelling, writing and lecturing all over the world.

THOR HEYERDAHL

Thor Heyerdahl's journeys, reconstructing the voyages of ancient civilisations, sought to separate fact from myth

By the middle of the 20th century there were few places on earth that remained to be explored. Regions that had eluded earlier travellers because of brutality of climate or sheer impossibility of access had gradually become attainable as a result of technological advances and better global communications. After centuries during which explorers had been putting new names on maps and demonstrating that the world was a larger place than people thought, air travel was now bringing continents closer together.

At the same time, or so it seemed to the young Thor Heyerdahl in Norway in the 1930s, the modern western way of life was cutting people off from nature and denying them an appreciation of true humanity. Perhaps most of the world's surface had been efficiently mapped, but this did not mean that all the mysteries had been solved or that the majority of people had any better understanding of themselves. Heyerdahl was to pioneer a new type of exploration – one that tried to reproduce ancient seafaring conditions and to demonstrate that, long before the great European voyages of discovery, people were capable of travelling vast distances across the oceans.

Primitive man, according to Heyerdahl, was not so primitive after all, and his way of life was often more dignified than that of a modern city-dweller. It was to test the truth of this theory and to see what he could learn by turning his back on modern civilisation, that, in 1937, at the age of 22, he went with his 20-year-old wife to live on the Polynesian island of Fatu Hiva in the Marquesas group (Îles Marquises).

An experiment in living

They had chosen an island that was rich in fruit and vegetables and where they could reasonably expect to be self-sufficient. The islanders

Below *In voyages across the South Pacific, the Atlantic and the Indian Ocean, Thor Heyerdahl demonstrated the sea-going capacities of early civilisations.*

***Left** The youthful explorer. A stay in the Marquesas Islands in the 1930s alerted him to early South American settlement of the Pacific.*

accepted them and built them a weatherproof hut when it became clear that their own efforts at building would not withstand the first storm. Heyerdahl's feelings about the modern world were confirmed and, thinking in a way that recalled von Humboldt's cosmos theory of 100 years earlier, and anticipated today's emphasis on 'green' issues, he became acutely aware of how everything is interconnected: 'Civilised man had declared war against his own environment and the battle was raging on all continents, gradually spreading to these distant islands. In fighting nature man can win every battle except the last. If he should win that too he will perish, like an embryo cutting its own umbilical cord.'

Heyerdahl was taken to see a unique rock carving on the island depicting numerous figures of gods and men, a huge fish and, most intriguing of all, 'a crescent-shaped ship with a curved bottom, a very high bow and stern, a double mast and rows of oars'. This ship was nothing like the native canoes and rafts, but looked more like an ancient Egyptian reed boat, and he began to wonder if there could possibly be some connec-

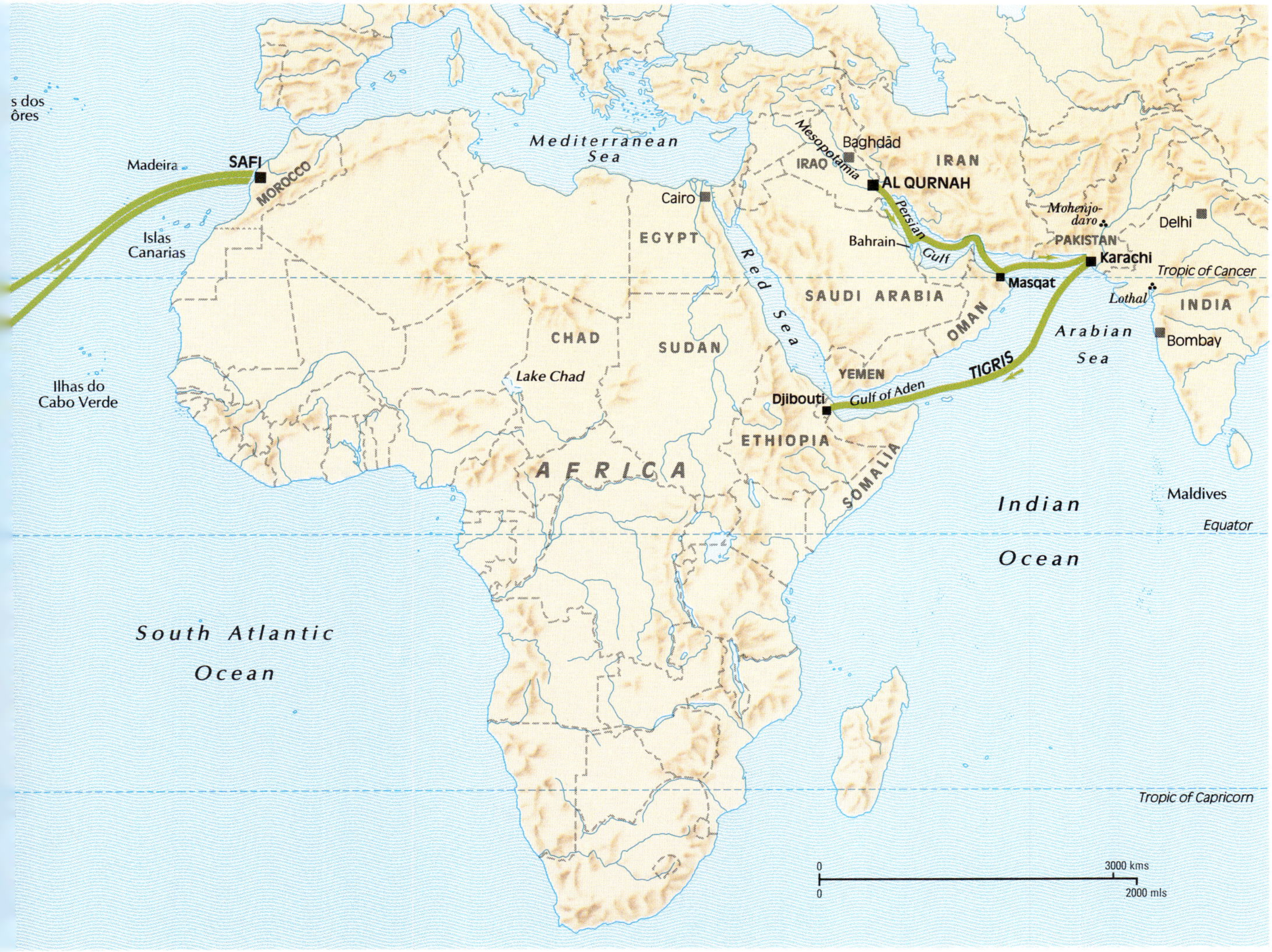

tion. Later, when visiting a neighbouring island, Hiva Oa, another mysterious connection seemed to suggest itself when he was shown some giant red stone statues and photographs of apparently similar statues from Tiahuanaco near Lake Titicaca in Bolivia.

The Polynesian islanders themselves spoke of ancestors who came from the east and they had plants, such as the sweet potato, that were native to Latin America – was there a chance that the established view that the Polynesian Islands had been populated by people from Asia was wrong? Were the islands originally inhabited by people from South America whose traditional rafts had travelled westwards from the Peruvian coast carried by the constant east winds? Nearly 10 years later, long after the Fatu Hiva experiment had been abandoned in the face of increasing concern about illness, and after a period of active service during World War II, Heyerdahl still wanted to find the answer to that question.

The *Kon-Tiki* expedition

After the war, Heyerdahl set his theory about migration from Peru to the Polynesian Islands down on paper and went to the USA in search of an audience. He could not even get anyone to read his manuscript, and in a New York museum he was told that it would have been quite impossible for ancient South American peoples to cross the Pacific, because they had no boats. When he protested that they did have balsa-wood rafts, he received a sarcastic reply: 'Well, you can try a trip from Peru to the Pacific Islands on a balsa-wood raft.' Some months later, with a team of five other men and a green parrot, he did exactly that.

The *Kon-Tiki* raft was built in the naval dockyard at Callao in Peru and launched on 27 April 1947. The Peruvian authorities had inspected the vessel and their faith in its seaworthiness was such that they immediately insisted on Heyerdahl signing documents absolving the navy and the government of all blame, should disaster strike. According to the most optimistic estimates it would be at least 97 days before there was any hope of landfall in the Polynesian Islands, and the members of the expedition set sail with predictions of doom and disaster ringing in their ears. The team, Herman Watzinger, Torstein Raaby, Knut Haugland,

Bengt Danielsson and Erik Hesselberg, had not been selected for their skills in seamanship, but even the most accomplished mariner would have been a beginner where manoeuvring a balsa-wood raft was concerned. Steering and managing the sail was a struggle at first, but the raft itself proved remarkably seaworthy, riding with the waves rather than acting as an object of resistance to them.

Twentieth-century expertise had condemned the primitive craft as hopelessly inadequate, but over the next three months Heyerdahl and his team proved that traditional methods of raft building worked, and that a vessel which fell laughably short of any modern standards of seaworthiness was actually perfectly designed for a 4,000-mile (6,435km) journey from the Peruvian coast to the islands of the Pacific. The raft could also carry a great deal – not only six men (one of whom took 73 books on sociology with him to read on the voyage), but ample provisions, scientific instruments, radio equipment, a rubber dinghy, and plenty of water. And when the water began to taste brackish, after about two months, they were already well into regions where rainfall provided constant fresh supplies. Neither was there any shortage of fresh food – the man taking his turn as cook would often find enough fish for breakfast lying on the deck in the morning.

The voyage involved occasional struggles with rough weather, and encounters with rare and even unknown fish, and also with sharks that sometimes came too close for comfort, and yet the greatest difficulty was not sailing but stopping. When they eventually came in sight of the island of Angatau after exactly 97 days at sea, they spent a whole day trying to find a safe approach through a coral reef, and eventually had to give up. Three days later *Kon-Tiki*'s voyage ended on another reef, and the crew made their way from the wreck to an uninhabited island nearby. Here they were visited by people from Raroia Island, where they stayed for some time until a French schooner was sent to collect them. They were taken to Tahiti, where a Norwegian steamer bound for America took them and *Kon-Tiki* on board.

Throughout the journey Heyerdahl had kept a diary, and his account of the *Kon-Tiki Expedition*, first published in 1950, became an international bestseller, while the crew's efforts to film their activities won them an Oscar for 'camera achievement'. Ironically, after all the difficulty he had experienced in finding support for the venture, the success of this 20th-century voyage of exploration had caught the imagination of a huge international audience and soon turned him into a celebrity. Since then, Heyerdahl himself and many others have attempted to re-enact a variety of historic journeys, seeking to understand the ancient conditions by going back to traditional methods of construction and engineering. Heyerdahl had virtually invented a new type of exploration but, in future, the chances were that film cameras and crowds would always be in attendance, and that there could never be another experience like that of the *Kon-Tiki*.

Opposite page *Kon-Tiki breasts the Pacific swells, invisibly assisted by the powerful force of the Humbolt Current. The balsa-wood raft was built on Inca principles. Other balsa rafts made successful Pacific voyages after Heyerdahl's success in 1947.*

Above *Heyerdahl at* Kon-Tiki *steering oar.*

To Easter Island

Heyerdahl's work, however, had only just begun. He did not claim that the *Kon-Tiki* expedition had done any more than show that it was *possible* for people to have travelled from Peru to the Polynesian Islands on board a balsa-wood raft. However, despite, or perhaps because of, the huge public interest in the voyage, the academics and the experts were still inclined to ignore his theories. Some saw the whole enterprise as no more than a sort of schoolboy adventure with no scientific validity.

In response, Heyerdahl wrote an 800-page book on *American Indians in the Pacific*, and began to make plans for another expedition. Further experiments with balsa-wood rafts had taught him that, with skilful use of the centreboards, these craft could actually be made to tack. The ancient seafarers from Peru were not necessarily condemned to a one-way voyage across the Pacific. They could manoeuvre their vessels and sail close to the wind if they chose, and communications with the South Sea Islands could well have been regular and deliberate, and not just the result of chance.

In 1955 Heyerdahl decided to go in search of more evidence on Easter Island where, in the 18th century, the first European visitors had reported seeing three distinct races of people, some dark, some with reddish skin and some white skinned with red hair and strange, extended earlobes. It was this third group that seemed to show particular reverence for the

island's huge and mysterious stone statues, known as *moai*. These take the form of great heads standing on average 15ft (4.5m) tall, with elongated ears, and sometimes wearing hats or top-knots made of a different red stone. Ear extension is a practice known to have existed in pre-Inca Latin America, and, according to Easter Island tradition, the Long Ears had come from the east. Clearly, this place had to be investigated. In a quarry on the island, Heyerdahl's team of archaeologists discovered one statue unlike the *moai* but very similar to the kneeling figures known at Tiahuanaco. They also found that some of the people of Easter Island knew how to build boats from reeds – a skill that might well have been transmitted by the reed boat builders of Lake Titicaca.

Heyerdahl's extensive research persuaded

Above *The giant stone statues on Easter Island are one of the world's most intriguing mysteries.*

Below *The reed boat* Ra II *in which Heyerdahl crossed the Atlantic in 1970.*

Ancient Boat-building

Rafts made of balsa logs had been in use along the Peruvian coast since before the time of Columbus, and Heyerdahl drew on descriptions of these, including one by Pizarro's pilot, Ruiz, to build the *Kon-Tiki*. Numerous experts insisted that such a raft would sink long before it was anywhere near its destination because the logs would quickly absorb water, and that would be the end of it. To guard against this, Heyerdahl insisted on using newly felled trees full of water-resistant sap.

Nine balsa tree-trunks were bound together with hemp rope, with the longest log, measuring 45ft (13.5m) placed in the middle and shorter ones on either side. The raft thus had a slightly projecting bow with the forward ends of the nine logs shaped to glide through the water. Its sides measured about 30ft (9m).

Other experts protested that rope would soon work – loose they must use wire. Heyerdahl ignored this advice and was vindicated later when he realised in rough seas how quickly wire would have sawn through the soft logs and caused the whole thing to disintegrate. Thinner balsa logs were lashed across the raft at intervals of 3ft (1m), and a deck of split bamboos was constructed over these in such a way that water could circulate below it and pass through the gaps between the nine logs as if through a sieve.

Slightly towards the stern, a small open cabin was built of bamboo canes with walls of plaited bamboo reeds and a roof covered with thick banana leaves. In front of this were placed two masts of hard mangrove wood, which were lashed together at the top.

A square sail was hung from a yard made of bamboo stems. A long steering-oar was pivoted from the stern and five fir planks, slotted through gaps between the logs, acted as centreboards and also turned out to assist with steering.

him that Long Ears from Latin America were the first people to settle on Easter Island, although, again, he could not produce enough incontrovertible evidence to satisfy all of his critics. He now asked another question. He believed in a pattern of migration between Latin America and the islands of the South Pacific, but who were the people who originally populated Latin America. Were they indigenous or did they arrive from another continent, and if so, how did they travel? Heyerdahl remembered the stone carving of what looked like a reed boat on the Polynesian island of Hiva Oa. He had also noticed that papyrus boats shown in ancient wall paintings in the Valley of the Kings, in Egypt, resembled some painted on pottery in Peru, and he decided to conduct some more nautical research.

The *Ra* expeditions

In 1970 Heyerdahl crossed from the ancient port of Safi in Morocco to the West Indies in a reed boat called *Ra II*. This successful voyage came after a false start: the original *Ra*, constructed according to the traditional reed boat-building methods practised on Lake Chad, had sailed the previous year. The steering mechanism and a number of structural elements had been copied from Egyptian wall paintings, but without any real understanding of how they functioned. There had been no time for detailed tests, and it was only when the ship was at sea that its shortcomings became clear.

After two months and 3000 miles *Ra* was badly damaged in a storm and, although (contrary to expert opinion) the papyrus rolls of which the hull was made were still proving remarkably buoyant, the expedition was curtailed. With an international crew of eight, *Ra II*, built according to the slightly different traditions of Lake Titicaca, and incorporating improvements that the first voyage had shown to be necessary, reached her destination in the West Indies in 57 days. Another of Heyerdahl's theories about primitive oceanic transport was shown to be perfectly feasible.

The *Tigris* Expedition

From the days of his first experiment in living on the Pacific island of Fatu Hiva, Heyerdahl had kept a clear vision of the unity of the world and the interconnectedness of all forms of life on earth. The tracing of possible patterns of migration between continents was a means of improving understanding of these links, and he now began to consider if there was some way in which he could apply his methods to the theory that three great ancient civilisations (Sumeria, Mohenjo-daro and the mysterious place known to the Egyptians as the Land of Punt) had originated somewhere in Mesopotamia. He fixed on the idea of creating another reed boat to discover how it would survive a journey on the Indian Ocean. The *Tigris*, intended to be a replica of an ancient Sumerian vessel known as a *ma-gur*, was built with local berdi reeds by Marsh Arabs in southern Iraq, but with assistance from the Lake Titicaca Indians who had constructed *Ra II*. Launched from Qurna (Al Qurnah) in Iraq in 1977, she proved an excellent sailing ship and somehow the reed hull withstood the appalling pollution at the head of the Persian Gulf.

The voyage demonstrated the possibility of an ancient sea route between Dilmun (on Bahrain Island), which the Sumerians referred to as their ancestral home – and the Mohenjo-daro civilisations of the Indus Valley. *Tigris* actually sailed to Karachi, but an ancient port, capable of accommodating larger ships, has been excavated at Lothal in what is now the Indian state of Gujarat. To complete the picture, Heyerdahl wanted to sail to Somalia, which is believed to be the site of Punt, but war in Ethiopia and the Yemen made this impossible. In March 1978, *Tigris* reached the republic of Djibouti, adjacent to the Somali border, but, for what were described as security reasons, she was forbidden to travel further.

Heyerdahl burnt the ship, in perfect condition, and sent a message to the United Nations declaring that this was a protest against the inhuman elements of the modern world. 'Our planet,' he said, 'is larger than the bundles of reeds that bore us across the sea, but still small enough to risk the same threats, unless those of us living acknowledge that there is a desperate need for intelligent co-operation if we are to save ourselves and our common civilisation from what we are turning into a sinking ship.'

In recent years Heyerdahl has led archaeological expeditions to the Maldives, and returned to Easter Island as leader and organiser of a joint Norwegian and Chilean archaeological project. At the age of 77 he still travels and writes.

Left *Heyerdahl sailed the Sumerian-style reed boat* Tigris *down the Persian Gulf, to India and across the Indian Ocean to East Africa. In 1978 he burned her as 'a torch that will call men to reason' and to 'the cause of peace.'*

Biographical Notes

1914
Born 6 October, Larvik. Norway.

1937
Spent a year on the Pacific Island of Fatu H va.

1947
Kon-Tiki expedition.

1955–56
Expedition to Easter Island.

1970
Ra II expedition, from Morocco to West Indies.

1977–78
Tigris Expedition

1982–84
Expeditions to the Maldives.

1986–88
Further research on Easter Island.

HILLARY AND TENZING

After 30 years of repeated and gallant attempts, the conquest of Everest thrilled the world

The Himalayas, whose name means 'abode of snows', stretch for some 1,550 miles (2,500km) of jagged, steep and snow-covered peaks. The Great Himalaya range itself, the backbone of the system, contains 9 of the 14 highest mountains in the world. It was not until 1852 that Mount Everest, on the border of Tibet and Nepal, was authoritatively declared to be the highest of them all. A hundred years later its height was calculated at 29,028ft (8,848m) give or take a little. The mountain is getting higher by about ½in (13mm) a year, pushed up by the pressing together of the landmasses, and in 1990 was said to be 1½ft (46cm) higher than it was when Hillary and Tenzing climbed it in 1953.

***Below** The conquerors of Everest enjoy a friendly snack together, many thousands of feet below the scene of their triumph.*

'Because it is there'

The mountain was known to British India as Peak xv until it was christened in 1865 in honour of Sir George Everest, a former surveyor general of India. For untold centuries before that, however, it was known in Tibetan as *Chomolungma*, 'Goddess Mother of the World', and to the local Sherpa tribespeople as 'the mountain so high that no bird can fly over it'. Mountaineers gazed at it with longing, but until 1920 the authorities in Tibet and Nepal would not allow foreigners to approach it.

In that year the Alpine Club and the Royal Geographical Society jointly established an Everest Committee and, with support from the British government, they won the Dalai Lama's approval for an expedition. Nepal would not relent, so it was only from the northern, Tibetan side that an assault on the great mountain could be launched. In 1921 a reconnaissance party carefully examined the northerly approaches. One of its members was George Mallory, who until the expedition of 1953 was to be the most famous of Everest mountaineers. A schoolmaster, who had originally intended to be a clergyman, Mallory had begun climbing in the Alps as a Winchester schoolboy. It was he who gave the famous answer, when asked why he wanted to climb Everest: 'Because it is there.' He would die on the mountain before his 38th birthday.

The reconnaissance expedition duly reported, and in 1922 the first of many sieges of Everest was mounted by British climbers with local Sherpa porters. The advance was up the North Col, the main ridge on the northern side, and Mallory and two others eventually reached 26,985ft (8,217m), the highest point ever known to have been attained by human beings up to that time, but they were exhausted and suffering from frostbite and had to retreat. Later an attempt was made with oxygen, which reached a new high of 27,300ft (8,321m) before falling back. A third attempt was frustrated by an avalanche.

A second expedition followed in 1924, but exceptionally low temperatures and the worst storms in living memory made climbing peculiarly difficult. Even so, two of the party got to 28,126ft (8,573m). A final strike was made, with such little oxygen as the expedition had left, by Mallory and Andrew Irvine. They were last seen moving up and going well, only some 800ft (about 245m) below the summit, when mists swirled across and hid them from view. They

Summits Under Siege

The conquest of the high places of the earth has been the province of a special breed of explorer. It is also a modern achievement, as a liking for spectacular scenery and a taste for mountain climbing did not develop until the 18th century. Mont Blanc, the highest peak in Western Europe, was climbed in 1786 by a doctor from Chamonix with a local guide, and two Swiss brothers reached the top of the Jungfrau in 1811.

The modern sport of mountaineering, however, like so many other international sports, was essentially a British creation. In its early days, it was also fundamentally an amateur pursuit, the preserve of well-to-do sportsmen who could afford the time and the expense. They climbed with the assistance of local guides, who were paid professionals and left the glory to the amateurs. Swiss guides, especially, gained a high reputation.

The Alps were subjected to sustained assaults by British climbers after Sir Alfred Wills scaled the Wetterhorn in 1854 and the Alpine Club was founded in London in 1857. Interest soon spread beyond Britain and similar clubs were established in France, Switzerland, the United States, New Zealand and other countries.

A spectacular early achievement came in 1865, when Edward Whymper led a successful assault on the supposedly unscaleable Matterhorn after six previous attempts. The dangers of the sport were brought home on the descent, when four of the party slipped and were killed and only the fact that the rope broke saved Whymper and two guides from the same fate. Whymper, undaunted, went on to explore Greenland and the Andes Mountains of South America, where he was the first to climb the towering peak of Chimborazo in Ecuador, at 20,702ft (6,310m), in 1880.

Above *Edward Whymper and his party take a well-earned rest and plant a flag on the snow-clad summit of the Matterhorn.*

The principal peaks of the Alps and the Pyrenees having been stormed by the early pioneers, interest shifted to the Caucasus, North and South America, Africa and New Zealand. Kilimanjaro, the highest peak in Africa, was climbed by two Germans, Hans Meyer and Ludwig Purtscheller, in 1889. Dizzying Aconcagua (22,839ft/6,959m), the topmost peak of the Andes, was conquered by Mattias Zurbriggen in 1897. In 1913 Mt McKinley, the highest mountain in North America, succumbed to a party led by Hudson Stuck, an English-born Protestant clergyman in Alaska who held the majestic appointment of Archdeacon of the Yukon.

Long before this, the eyes of the world's mountaineers had naturally turned to the sky-challenging, snowcapped summits of the Himalayas. These great peaks are not only extremely high, but often extremely difficult to approach. As the 20th century wore on, however, they attracted climbers not only from Europe – British, Austrians, French, Germans, Italians, Russians – but from India, China and Japan. At the same time, the casual, gentlemanly and individualistic air of mountaineering's early days changed. Assaults on high peaks became much more like military operations, and in particular like sieges. Parties of climbers with small armies of porters and massive quantities of supplies and equipment made disciplined, carefully planned, methodical approaches to the summit. The besiegers advanced on the citadel by stages, establishing a succession of camps higher and higher up the mountain, to which supplies were laboriously brought up and where climbers could rest before moving up again until close enough to the summit to strike for it. It was this type of operation which finally took Everest.

never returned. Whether they reached the top, and what happened to them, no one knows.

Further assaults

The tragedy put a damper on Everest attempts for a while, but in time other Himalayan peaks were tackled. In 1930 an unsuccessful attempt was made on the daunting Kanchenjunga on the border of Nepal and Sikkim, the world's third highest mountain at 28,169ft (8,586m). In 1931 the peak of Kamet was conquered by Frank Smythe, a frail climber who had been invalided out of the Royal Air Force with the advice never to try to go upstairs quickly for the rest of his life. It did not stop him scaling Kamet, which was the first mountain over 25,000ft (7,620m) ever to be climbed.

Smythe was on the next Everest expedition, in 1933, which was defeated by ferocious weather, as was the assault of 1936. In that year Bill Tilman and an American-British party climbed Nanda Devi, another monster over 25,000ft (7,620m), and Tilman led the 1938 attack on Everest, which included Smythe and another notable British mountaineer, Eric Shipton. They were greeted by piercing blizzards, snowdrifts and temperatures down to −34°C (−30°F). That same year an American expedition attempted K2, the second highest mountain in the world.

No expeditions were possible during World War II, but once it was over climbers could take advantage of improved oxygen equipment. The invention of nylon also had a dramatic effect on

both climbing ropes and climbing clothes. In 1950 the colossus of Annapurna, the first mountain over 26,247ft (8,000m) ever scaled, yielded grudgingly to a French Alpine Club party led by Maurice Herzog. The Chinese took control of Tibet that year and closed Everest's northern approaches to outsiders, but Nepal and the southern flanks were now open.

Such earlier scanning of the southern side as had been possible had not been encouraging, but in 1951 a reconnaissance party was organised under the leadership of Eric Shipton. One of its members was a beekeeper from New Zealand named Edmund Hillary, a tough and amiable character in his early thirties. His father was a local newspaper editor turned apiarist and the son had recently taken over the family business. He had not taken up mountaineering until the comparatively late age of 26.

Shipton's reconnaissance party identified a possible route up the mountain from the south and was frustrated to discover that the next climbing season, of 1952, had already been booked by the Swiss. 'It is surprising how much we resented this news,' Hillary wrote, 'as though we were the only ones who had any right to the mountain.'

The Swiss expedition hired as its sirdar, or foreman, of the Sherpa porters a certain Tenzing Norgay. Other Sherpas were content to be porters and had no desire to climb to the top of their homeland's shimmering peaks, but Tenzing was different. He was an ambitious and determined mountaineer who had cut his teeth on British expeditions in the 1930s and he was a full climbing member of the Swiss party. The Swiss launched their attack from the south by the route Shipton's party had identified and Tenzing and Raymond Lambert climbed to a height of above 28,200ft (8,595m). To sighs of British relief, intense cold and fierce winds made it impossible for them to go any higher.

The top of the world

The British expedition that was at last to succeed arrived at the Thyangbuche Monastery, some miles to the southwest of Everest, late in March 1953. Shipton had been expected to lead it, but the command had gone instead to a little-known army officer, Colonel John Hunt. This had caused sharp acrimony, but Hunt proved to be an excellent leader. There were 12 climbers, most of them Britons with Oxford, Cambridge or army backgrounds, and a high-altitude force of 36 Sherpas, with Tenzing Norgay as both sirdar of Sherpas and a full climbing member of the party. He was teamed with Hillary. The party acclimatised for a while, or as Hillary put it,

'rushed around the hills climbing 19,000 and 20,000 feet peaks' to adjust to the altitude.

The route chosen lay up the Khumbu Glacier and then up the long, rising valley of the Western Cwm to the face of Lhotse, a formable peak itself, and up that to the South Col, at roughly 26,000ft (7,925m). From there a steep climb would lead up the South-East Ridge to the South Summit of the mountain, from which they hoped to gain the final summit.

A base camp was established and a way was found over the gaping crevasses and tottering ice towers of the dangerous Khumba Icefall to the Western Cwm. When they were safely past it, Hillary commented: 'It was a pleasant change to have a place to sleep without any sense of impending doom.' A succession of camps was now planted up the Western Cwm, but the lead climbers had serious difficulty getting up the Lhotse Face. Progress slowed and in mid-May the advance guard was halted for several days by icy winds. Hunt sent Wilfrid Noyce forward and with one of the Sherpas he managed to reach the spur leading to the South Col, a smallish plateau of boulders and ice, which Noyce said looked 'absurdly solid and comfortable at first glance' after the climb. Strewn about on it were the remains from the Swiss expedition of the year before.

Hunt had meanwhile sent Hillary and Tenzing on. They were both strong and determined climbers, with a cheerful disposition and a certain ruthlessness. Hunt joined them on the South Col with Charles Evans and Tom Bourdillon, who were to try for the South Summit. Forging doughtily on through thick snow, Evans and Bourdillon reached it, the highest place on which human feet had ever trodden, at 28,575ft (8,765m). They were sorely tempted to try for the main summit, but would they be able to get back? Their oxygen would not hold out. They had a fierce argument, muffled by their masks, but Evans, in charge, decided it was too risky and they turned reluctantly back.

A Good Team

"On re-reading my diary after twenty years I get the impression that I must have been rather an uncomfortable person at times on the expedition – restless, competitive and a little argumentative. Yet my memories of the expedition have revolved about the good times . . . about the people I liked and laughed with; the tough jobs we did together and the feeling that everyone was giving of their best according to their strength and temperament at the time. We were a good team – of that I am convinced and it was this team spirit more than anything that ultimately got Tenzing and me to the summit. If you accept the modern philosophy that there must be a ruthless and selfish motivation to succeed in sport then it could justly be claimed that Tenzing and I were the closest approximations we had on our expedition to the climbing Prima Donnas of today. We wanted the expedition to succeed – and nobody worked any harder to ensure that it did – but in both our minds success was always equated with us being somewhere around the summit when it happened."

from *Nothing Venture, Nothing Win*, Edmund Hillary

Left *Mount Everest, showing the successful line of assault in 1953. The southern approach was not initially considered promising.*

Below *Seen from some 20 miles (32km) away to the south, the 'Goddess Mother of the World' towers up in majestic beauty on the borders of Nepal and Tibet.*

Left *Tensing Norgay on the summit of Everest on 29 May 1953. An exceptionally determined and powerful climber, he was not content with the accustomed Sherpa role of porter, and he had come close to vanquishing the great mountain with the Swiss expedition of the previous year.*

Lower down, meanwhile, were an anxious Hillary and Tenzing, who according to Hunt's plan were to make the final strike for the summit. Hillary was ashamed to feel envy and fear that Evans and Bourdillon might get there first, and Tenzing could not conceal his dismay. To their intense relief, Evans and Bourdillon returned, exhausted.

On 28 May Hillary and Tenzing moved up the South-East Ridge and made themselves an uncomfortable ledge in the frozen snow for their tent. They had an evening meal of sardines and apricots, and Hillary had to sleep sitting up to hold the tent against occasional fierce gusts of wind. The thermometer in the tent showed −27°C (−17°F). In the morning the wind had dropped and the sky was a blazing blue. They thawed their frozen boots over the primus stove and started at 6.30am. They reached the South Summit at 9am and examined the ridge leading up higher still. They changed their oxygen bottles and set off roped together, with Hillary in the lead cutting steps in the snow above an alarming precipice. Presently they came to a vertical rock wall, 40ft (12m) high. Hillary managed to clamber up a crack in it using his crampons and ice-axe, and then helped Tenzing up by pulling on the rope. 'As I heaved hard on the rope Tenzing wriggled his way up the crack and finally collapsed at the top like a great fish when it has just been hauled from the sea after a terrible struggle.'

The rock wall was the last obstacle. They went on up the ridge and suddenly at 11.30am found themselves standing on the highest spot on earth, with a panoramic view over the Himalayas that no one had ever seen before. They shook hands delightedly, took photographs, ate some strengthening mint cake and flew the Union Jack, the flag of Nepal and the United Nations flag. Hillary left a crucifix on the summit on Hunt's behalf and Tenzing, who was a Buddhist, an offering of sweets and biscuits. They stayed about 15 minutes and started back down the mountain.

The aftermath

Everest had fallen! The sensation was worldwide and the acclaim intense. Hillary and Hunt were both knighted (and Hunt was later made a life-peer) and Tenzing received the George Medal. Tenzing, who did not much care for Hillary's description of him being hauled up the rock wall like a stranded fish, was hailed as the supreme hero of the exploit in India and Nepal. He devoted himself mainly to training the next generation of mountaineers in India. Hillary also did much useful work in India and in 1958 was the first man

Left *The successful Everest expedition flew into London Airport on 3 July 1953. Tenzing, who is cheerfully waving a Union Jack, is flanked by Colonel Hunt (left), the party's leader, and Edmund Hillary (right).*

to reach the South Pole overland since Captain Scott.

After 1953, however, mountaineers began to abandon the siege-style methods which had brought success on Everest and resumed to the ways of earlier days, with smaller parties travelling light and moving fast, often without oxygen. Since 1953 Everest has been climbed over and over again. The second ascent was by a Swiss expedition in 1956, the Chinese claimed to have reached the summit by the North Col in 1960, and there have been successful climbs by parties from America and Canada, Japan, Britain, Yugoslavia, Poland, Australia and France. The first women to scale the mountain were a Japanese and a Tibetan, both in 1975, and in 1978 Everest was climbed without oxygen by two Austrians, Reinhold Messner and Peter Habeler. Tenzing foresaw a day when tourists would be carried to the summit by helicopter. 'And a cable-car to the top? I hope not. That would be horrible, but not impossible.'

Skill and Courage

"Since that moment when Edmund Hillary and I shook hands on a high patch of snow, looked down on the huge panorama of peaks and glaciers and valleys and clouds, and remembered for a moment or two – we were only on the summit for about fifteen minutes – those who had tried before us and failed, then thanked God for our own success and prayed for a safe descent, and scratched in the snow to bury little things like a pencil and a bag of sweets and a cat made of black cloth – since that moment a new generation of men and women have been born both in Solo Khumbu and in the world outside that now wonders what all the fuss was about . . .

It is like this: for the final ascent of Everest there was a long build-up for the climbers themselves and for those who followed the adventure. For me too. For everyone therefore the ascent in 1953 was a great climax. For many, many years, ever since Everest was recognised as the earth's highest mountain, men had tried to conquer it. It was almost a permanent challenge. Mostly they tried by the northern route through Tibet, and all had failed, though there were some tremendous achievements, especially when you take into account the real lack of knowledge of very great heights and what was needed to survive them, also the primitiveness of much of the equipment and clothing and supplies, and finally the mental attitudes which held people in check . . . You have only to look at the photographs to see the difference, especially the clothing, the boots – and even hats! Yet the will to succeed was the same and the very great skill and courage. How else could Mallory and Irvine have got as high as they did with all those disadvantages – some say that they actually got to the top and fell on the descent? Others, too, like Smythe, Norton, Somerville, Odell, who got very close to succeeding.

So our excitement in the end is very understandable, I think, the sense of accomplishment at having done so much at last, climbing on the backs, one might say, of all those who had gone before, Sherpas as well as Europeans: for quite a few of my own people had died on those expeditions and among those who did not die were some who got very high on the mountain."

from *After Everest*, Tenzing Norgay Sherpa

Biographical Notes

1914
Tenzing Norgay born at Tami, Nepal.

1919
Edmund Hillary born in Auckland, New Zealand (20 July).

1951
Hillary joined the British Everest Reconnaissance Expedition, led by Eric Shipton.

1952
Tenzing was a member of a Swiss expedition to Everest, and with Raymond Lambert climbed to above 28,200ft (8,595m).

1953
British Everest Expedition, led by Colonel John Hunt; Evans and Bourdillon reached the South Summit (26 May); Hillary and Tenzing climbed to the topmost summit (29 May).

1958
As leader of the New Zealand contingent on the British Commonwealth Trans Antarctic Expedition, Hillary reached the South Pole overland (4 January).

1977
Hillary led the first jet boat expedition up the River Ganges.

1986
Death of Tenzing Norgay (9 May).

Space

'Come, my friends,
Tis not too late to seek a newer world . . .
for my purpose holds
To sail beyond the sunset, and the baths
of all the western stars, until I die.'

ALFRED LORD TENNYSON
Ulysses

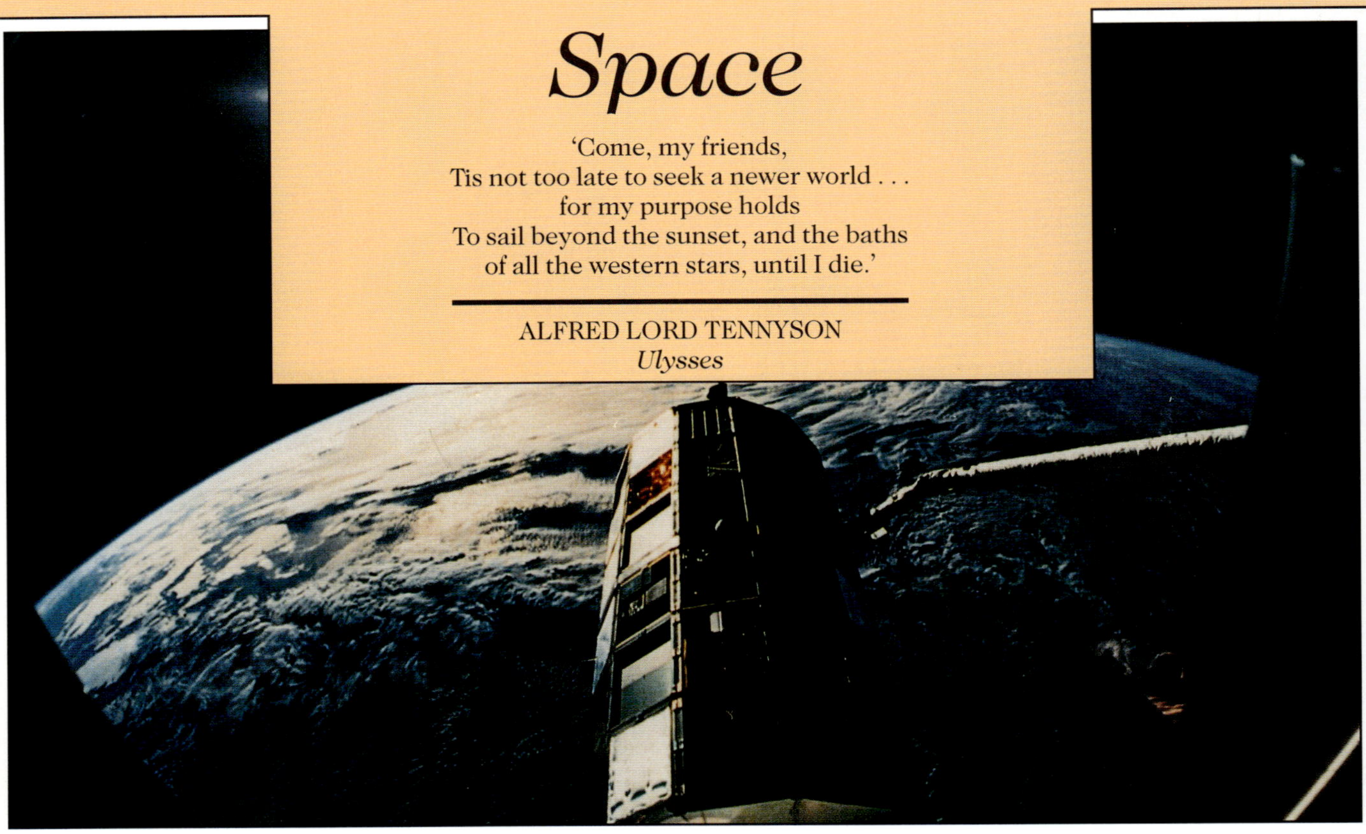

'The *Eagle* has landed.' The voice of the American astronaut Neil Armstrong, who had just settled his spider-like vehicle gently on the surface of the moon, was heard by an estimated 500 million people all around the world who watched on television. They saw Armstrong clamber down the ladder in his clumsy spacesuit to stand on the dusty surface. 'That's one small step for a man, one giant leap for mankind.'

The moon landing must surely rank as the most remarkable single achievement in the entire history of exploration. It came less than 200 years after the first balloonists rose uncertainly into the sky. In 1783 at Versailles, King Louis XVI of France, Queen Marie Antoinette, their patched and powdered court and a huge crowd watched as an ornately decorated balloon designed by the Montgolfier brothers was inflated with hydrogen, rose in stately fashion and flew for eight minutes or so before descending into a wood. In a cage slung below it were a sheep, a duck and a cockerel. They survived the journey undamaged except that the cockerel was kicked by the sheep. The world's first air passengers, they were the humble forerunners of today's space-exploring astronauts and cosmonauts.

Rising higher

Balloons were almost immediately employed for scientific purposes, which included both the examination of the atmosphere and the observation of the earth. As balloonists rose higher and higher, lack of oxygen and severe cold caused fainting and even death, but the obstacles were overcome and by the 1930s the Swiss physicist, Auguste Piccard, was making balloon asents into the stratosphere, to above 50,000ft (15,240m) in a pressurised cabin. By this time, of course, the development of the airplane was well under way and planes, like balloons and airships, were used to survey inaccessible regions of the earth. Antarctica, for instance, has been examined far more thoroughly from the sky than has been possible on the ground.

In the early development of space technology, observation of the earth was a key objective. Satellites were put into orbit in increasing numbers after 1957 for purposes ranging from military surveillance and intelligence gathering to geological research, oceanography, weather forecasting and communications, including satellite television. There are more than 3,000 of

Above *Science fiction came to life in the space age as American and Soviet technology grappled with the challenge of a voyage to land human beings on the moon.*

Below *Forerunners of the astronauts were the balloonists. Here Auguste Piccard rests after a record ascent at Zurich in 1932, which took him up into the stratosphere to 55,563ft (16,940m).*

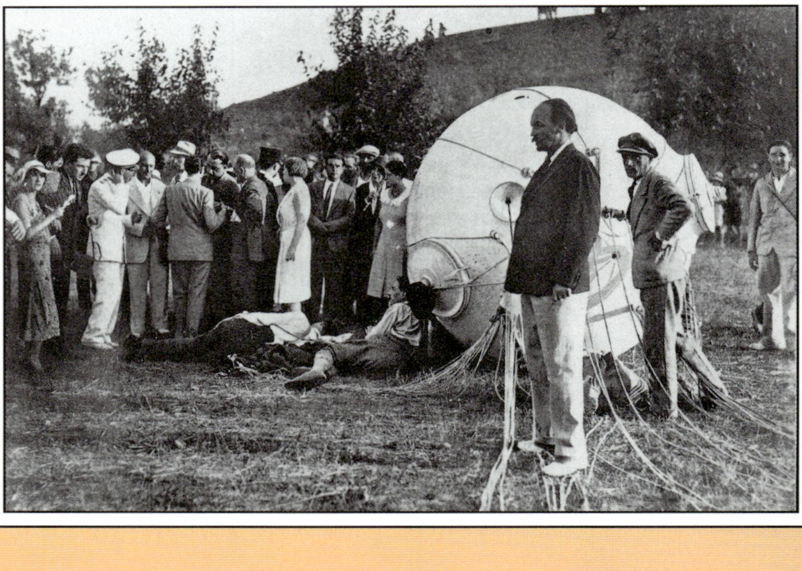

them, stationed in remote orbit round the planet, sent up from Russia, the United States, Japan and European countries.

The first weather satellite, *Tiros I*, was launched by the United States on 1 April in 1960. The first live television transmission between the USA and Europe was relayed by *Telstar* in 1962. These earth-directed activities, however, have aroused far less public excitement than the exploration of space itself, especially in craft carrying human beings.

The space age

Human beings had long dreamed of voyaging to the stars, but as late as 1956 the Astronomer Royal in Britain was reported as dismissing the whole idea of space travel as 'bilge'. On 4 October 1957, however, the space age began when the USSR launched the first satellite to orbit the earth. According to the reports, *Sputnik 1* was a small sphere, only 22in (56cm) in diameter and weighing 184lb (83.4kg), circling the earth more than 500 miles (800km) into the sky about once every 95 minutes at a speed of 18,000mph (28,962 km/h).

This was startling enough, but only a month later the Soviet Union announced that a dog named Laika was in orbit, circling the earth in a much larger satellite, *Sputnik 2*. What was more, the last stage of the rocket that had propelled *Sputnik 2* into space was still attached to it, which meant that the Russians had contrived, astonishingly, to put a weight of about 6 tons (6 tonnes) into orbit.

The dog died after about a week in the Sputnik. The first American attempt to launch a satellite failed, in December, when the Vanguard rocket blew up on take-off, but *Explorer 1* went up safely from Cape Canaveral in Florida early in 1958. Weighing 31 lb (14 kg), it was only the size of a grapefruit, but it paid an immediate exploration dividend by confirming the existence of the Van Allen radiation belts. In July, the National Aeronautics and Space Administration (NASA) was set up to take charge of America's space programme.

The Soviets were forging on, and the rivalry with the Americans began to heat up. In 1959 a Soviet Luna spacecraft flew past the moon, while NASA placed a contract for a capsule in which an astronaut could orbit the earth. The Americans recovered two monkeys named Able and Baker alive after a space flight, and the Soviets recovered two dogs and a rabbit. In September the USSR's *Luna 2* hit the moon, the first man-made object ever to do so. A month later *Luna 3* went into orbit around the moon, and the pictures it sent back to the earth were the first to reveal the dark side of the moon.

In 1961 came a tremendous sensation when the USSR sent the first human being into space and recovered him. On 12 April an R-7 rocket lifted off from the Baikonur Space Centre in Kazakhstan and thrust into orbit the spaceship *Vostok 1*. Inside it was a 27-year-old air force officer, Yuri Gagarin, who orbited the earth in a flight of 108 minutes and landed again safely. The first human being to view the earth from space, Gagarin was killed in an air accident in 1968.

The achievement was a red flag to the American bull. President Kennedy announced that the United States would put a man on the moon before the decade was out. The space race was on in earnest and on 20 February 1962 John Glenn became the first American to orbit the earth, in a capsule called *Friendship*, which lifted off from Cape Canaveral and splashed down in the sea off Puerto Rico five hours later.

Below *Colonel John Glenn, photographed in London in 1966. He was the first American astronaut to orbit the earth, in 1962.*

Left *Two Soviet cosmonauts, Yuri Gagarin and Valentin Tereshkova, were the first man and the first woman in space, in 1961 and 1963 respectively. The Soviet Union led the way in the space race initially, but was overtaken by the United States.*

Left The American astronaut Neil Armstrong commanded the successful flight to the moon in 1969 and was the first human being ever to step on to the moon's surface.

The giant leap

The full force of American drive, engineering skill, organisational ability and money was now propelling NASA's Apollo programme to put the first man on the moon. Even so, it took the rest of the decade to do it. Meantime, the first pictures of the planet Venus came back to earth from an American space probe in 1962. In the following year Valentina Tereshkova of the Soviet Union at 26 years old became the first woman in space, and both the Americans and the Soviets sent spacecraft to examine Mars.

The next excitement occurred in March 1965, when for the first time a human being left a spaceship to dangle in space. Attached by a thin cord to his *Voshkod 2* spacecraft, Alexei Leonov of the Soviet Union floated about for 10 minutes or so and turned a somersault. In the time he was out in space he travelled about 3,000 miles (4,827km). The first American to undertake EVA, or 'extra-vehicle activity', was Ed White, who spent 14 minutes outside his *Gemini 4* spacecraft the following June. He propelled himself about with a compressed oxygen gun and enjoyed the romp so much that he had to be persuaded back into the spaceship.

The growing number and length of flights gave more Russian and American personnel experience of space, of weightlessness and of moving in the black void outside the spacecraft. The American astronaut Buzz Aldrin described the feeling. 'I have no particular fear of heights, but I was nevertheless surprised to see that a hundred and fifty miles above the surface of the earth there was no awareness of height at all. I was secure and comfortable, though encumbered, in the space suit . . . the view was spectacular, the colours of the earth – a benign combination of blue, brown and green, with white and grey clouds formed above – the colours of life.'

Tragedy struck in January 1967 when Ed White and two other American astronauts were burned to death. During a run-through for the countdown their spacecraft burst into flames as the result of an electrical fault in its miles of wiring. With 2 million working components, an Apollo spacecraft was the most complicated vehicle ever built, and this was the first fatal accident that had occurred in the American space programme.

The programme continued, and in October 1968 astronauts on an Apollo flight spent 11 days in space, which was longer than would be needed for the voyage to the moon and back. The next flight, *Apollo 8*, took human beings for the first time beyond the orbit of the earth. The first two stages of the rocket put the craft into earth orbit and the third stage fired it out beyond earth's gravity at exactly the required speed and direction to reach the moon, be caught by the moon's gravity and go into orbit round it. The astronauts orbited the moon 10 times and returned safely home to earth.

The stage was now all set for the decisive step. On 16 July 1969, 169 days before the deadline of the end of the decade, enormous crowds gathered on the Florida beaches to watch the take-off for the moon, while millions more watched fascinated on television. At 9.32am Eastern Standard Time, the monstrous Saturn rocket, standing 350ft (107m) high at its gantry and developing 7½ million lb (approximately 3½ million kg) of thrust, stirred as fire billowed out round its base, and to a huge crescendo of sound rose majestically into the sky at the beginning of a journey of 240,000 miles (386,160 km).

The first and second stages of the Saturn rocket fell away, and at close to 120 miles (195

Below The earth seen from space, with the African and Arabian deserts showing up clearly. One of the powerful motives behind the exploration of space was to discover more about the earth.

km) from base the third stage boosted the speed up above 24,000mph (38,616km/h) to thrust the command module, Columbia, out of the earth's gravitational pull on course for the moon. There were three astronauts on board, Neil Armstrong, Edwin (Buzz) Aldrin and Michael Collins, and it took three days to cover the distance. The moon came looming up, huge and awesome, filling their window. About 60 miles (97 km) above the surface they went into orbit around the moon.

When the moment came, on 20 July, Armstrong and Aldrin crawled into the weird-looking lunar module, *Eagle*. Released from Columbia, which stayed in orbit, it descended gently towards the surface. At the tense command centre at Mission Control in Houston, crammed with hopeful but anxious technicians, an alarm was heard, but it was checked out and ignored. Eugene Kranz, the flight director, said calmly, 'We're go', and Armstrong and Aldrin 240,000 miles (386,160km) away were told, 'We're go.' Armstrong had to steer away from an awkward crater strewn with boulders, and the module touched down. Armstrong said, 'Houston, Tranquillity base here. The *Eagle* has landed.' Mission Control replied, 'Roger, Tranquillity, we copy you on the ground. You've got a bunch of guys about to turn blue. We're breathing again. Thanks a lot.' After a few moments in Houston, Eugene Kranz said irritably, 'Okay, keep the chatter down in this room.'

Far away on the pale and dusty moon, Armstrong was joined on the surface by Aldrin. In their white spacesuits, heavy gloves and boots, and helmets with gleaming visors like TV screens, they lumbered about collecting samples of dust and rock, taking photographs and planting the Stars and Stripes flag. The moon, so long apostrophised by lovers, priests and prophets, had felt at long last the tread of human feet.

Among the stars

On earth, with the space race won, media attention turned away in other directions and there was a certain feeling of anticlimax. The immense cost of space operations also came in for criticism. After the initial moon landing, however, useful scientific exploration continued.

The Americans made a second moon landing in November 1969. Two astronauts spent 32 hours on the surface, walked as far as 1,000ft (305m) away from their lunar module and collected 50lb (22kg) of samples to take back to the earth. In July 1971 two more American astronauts went for a drive on the moon in a strange-looking wheeled buggy and gathered samples from the edge of Elbow Crater.

Several more moon landings followed, while unmanned spacecraft were sent far out into the distant reaches of the solar system. In 1973 an American space probe, *Pioneer 10*, reached Jupiter and in 1983, Neptune. American probes launched in 1975 landed instruments on Mars, which disappointingly found no signs of life there. The Soviets and Americans had meanwhile put space stations into orbit and 1977 saw the maiden flight of the American space-shuttle, a re-usable launch vehicle. The shuttle *Challenger*'s crew of seven were tragically killed in 1986 when the craft exploded on lift-off. However, the development programme went ahead, while unmanned probes discovered new moons attendant on Saturn and Neptune. The challenge to 21st-century exploration clearly lies in space.

Below left *The second man on the moon. Buzz Aldrin descends the ladder from the module* Eagle *onto the powdery surface.*

Below *A Soviet re-usable space-shuttle is ready for take-off, perched on its gigantic Energia booster rocket.*

INDEX

ACKNOWLEDGEMENTS

Thanks are due to the following for permission to reproduce copyright material

Penguin Books Ltd for extracts from *The Vinland Sagas* translated by Magnus Magnusson and Herman Pálsson, *Marco Polo: The Travels* translated by Ronald Latham, and *The Conquest of New Spain* by Bernal Diaz translated by J.M. Cohen;

Croom Helm for an extract from *Adventures of Ibn Battuta* by R. Dunn:

The Estate of Alan Moorehead for an extract from *Cooper's Creek* by Alan Moorehead;

Allen & Unwin, now Unwin Hyman, an imprint of HarperCollins Publishers Limited for an extract from *After Everest* by Tenzing Norgay Sherpa.

The extract from *Nothing Venture, Nothing Win* by Edmund Hillary, © Edmund Hillary 1975, is reproduced by permission of Hodder & Stoughton Ltd/New English Library Ltd.

The Automobile Association would like to thank the following photographers, libraries and associations for their assistance in the preparation of this book:

B & C ALEXANDER PHOTOGRAPY 122 Arctic icebergs, 164 Nansen's sledge, 165 Glacier nr Etah, 172 Icebergs and sea ice, Melville Bay, 173 Dog sled, 174 Ice – Greenland, 176/7 Greenland Village, 181 Broken ice – Greenland.

J ALLAN CASH PHOTOLIBRARY 130 Mt Kilimanjaro, 137 R. Nile, 139 Felucca on R. Nile, 148 Cooper Creek.

E T ARCHIVE 25 Cathay and Empire of the Great Khan, 35 Mecca in Ottoman times, 54 Portuguese ocean greyhounds, 63 Moctezuma, King of the Aztecs, 66/7 Cortés – conquest of Mexico.

MICHAEL HOLFORD 1 Viking picture stone, 14 Detail – Odysseus and sirens, 22/3 Viking sword, 38 Pilgrim caravan, 545 Arrival of St Francis Xavier at Goa, 60 Manuscript of Magellan, 65 Aztec goddess, 74 Gold ceremonial knife, 76 Gold puma, 78 Indian, 81 Indian village.

HULTON PICTURE COMPANY 152 Amelia Earhart, 153 Freya Stark, 154 Naomi James, 155 Amy Johnson, 175 Hillary and Fuchs, 182 Sir Ernest Shackleton, 183 *Discovery*, advert for Shackleton's lecture, 186 *Endurance*, 195 Commander Byrd, 201 Freya Stark, 212 Hillary and Tenzing, 217 Everest team, 219 Col. John Glenn, 220 Neil Armstrong, 221 Apollo II & Aldrin.

JOHN CLEARE-MOUNTAIN CAMERA 170 Yak caravan, Tibetan plateau (Colin Monteath), 214 Mt. Everest.

KON-TIKI MUSEET Front cover *Ra II*, 207 Thor Heyerdahl, 208 *Kon-tiki* raft, 209 Heyerdahl on *Kon-tiki*, 210 *Ra II*, 211 Burning *Tigris*.

A J LAMBERT 70 Amazon River.

MARY EVANS PICTURE LIBRARY 4 Compasses and navigational instruments, 26 Cossacks conquer Siberia, 35 Ibn Battuta, 42 Landing of Jacques Cartier, 43 Prospector in American West, Emigrants, 53 Vasco da Gama, 61 Death of Magellan, 64 Spanish armour, 69 Vespucci, 82 Sieur de la Salle claiming L. Mississippi, 84/5 Canoe with outrigger – New Guinea, 85 Sir Francis Drake, 86/7 Dutch trading ships, 91 Pirate, 92 Dampier's ship under attack, 95 Robinson Crusoe, 98 Cook at Botany Bay, 100 Cook takes possession of New South Wales, 108 Botany Bay, 109 Sir Joseph Banks, Dodo, 110 Charles Darwin, 111 HMS Beagle, Gorillas, 115 Meriwether Lewis at Missouri Falls, 122 Canadian fur trapper, 123 *Erebus* and *Terror*, 131 Henry the Navigator, Phoenician trading vessel, 132/3 Slave convoy in Sudan, 133 Samuel White Baker, 135 Sir Richard Burton, 142 Livingstone sick with fever, 144 Livingstone's last journey, 145 Livingstone's body brought home, 146 Burke and Wills leave Melbourne, 151 Burke and Wills exploration, 153 Mary Wortley Montagu, 155 Alexandra David-Neel, 156 Mary Kingsley, 159 1890s Liverpool liner, 160/1 Boer War, 167 Route to N. Pole, 172 John Cabot, 173 Willem Barents, 173 Eskimo, 175 Capt. Scott, 176 Robert Peary, 178 Peary's camp, 178 Matthew Henson, 179 F A Cook, Cook and Peary fight (cartoon), 180 Peary and relief expedition, *Roosevelt* 192/3 Amundsen at S Pole, 213 Whymper's team on Matterhorn, 218 Picard and balloon.

NATIONAL MARITIME MUSEUM S Cook landing at Mallicolo, 96 *Endeavour*, 97 Capt. Cook, 101 *Resolution* and *Discovery* in Nootka Sound.

NATURE PHOTOGRAPHERS LTD 108 Breadfruit (S C Bisserott), 110 Giant tortoise (P R Sterry).

NOVOSTI 219 Gagarin and Tereshkova, 221 Energia booster rocket.

T OLIVER 21 Brattahlid, 22/3 E. Greenland.

PITT RIVERS MUSEUM 161 Benin brass armlets.

POPPERFOTO 174 Roald Amundsen, 187 Hut and Mt. Erebus, 192 Capt. Scott and party, 196 Byrd.

ROYAL BOTANIC GARDENS KEW 110/1 Stapelias – Masson's illustration.

ROYAL GEOGRAPHICAL SOCIETY 102 Von Humboldt, 203 Salambar Pass, 205 Village – Mazandaran, Iran, Shutur Khan, 216 Tenzing on summit of Everest.

SOUTH AMERICAN PICTURES 69 Stilted houses, Venezuela, 71 Col. P H Fawcett, 73 Inca drinking vessel, 77 Cuzco Sacsahuaman Fort, Inca sun god mask, 104 Cave in N. Venezuela, 105 Canaima Falls, 106/7 Mt. Chimborazo, Ecuador.

SPECTRUM COLOUR LIBRARY 6/7 Schweickart's space walk, 16 Palace, Persepolis, 31 Mt. Ararat, 36 Cairo and Al Rifai, 39 The Citadel, Cairo, 51 Cape of Good Hope, 70/1 Machu Picchu, 84 Alice Springs, 87 Easter Island, 93 Papua, N. Guinea, 94 L. Toba, Sumatra, 125 Kangaroo, 126/7 Mitchell Falls, 129 Simpson's Gap, 149 Aborigine, 210 Easter Island, 218 View from spacecraft *Columbia*, 220 Earth from space.

B STONEHOUSE 175 Penguins, 184/5 Shackleton's hut, 185 Antarctic, 187 S. Georgia, 189 Antarctic, 195 Ice packs, 198/9 Icebergs.

THE BRIDGEMAN ART LIBRARY 28 Marco Polo, frontispiece from The Book of Ser Private Collection, 29 Le Livre de Merveilles: Marco Polo on his Travels Bibliotheque Nationale, Paris, 30 Les Livres du Graunt Caam, 14th-century MS: University of Oxford for the Bodleian Library, 32 Banknote of the Ming dynasty: from the Kublai Private Collection, 46 Illustration of Ferdinand and Isabella, Library of Congress, Washington D.C., 48 Illustration of Columbus at the Royal Court, Library of Congress, Washington D.C., 66 One of a pair of panels, Museo de America, Madrid, 75 Pizarro seizing the Inca of Peru by Millais, (1826–96) Christie's London, 107 Gymnotus Aequilabiatus and Gymnotus Electricus by Von Humboldt, Royal Geographical Society, London

THE HUTCHINSON LIBRARY 202 Castle of the Assassins, 203 Mt Damavend, 204 Elburz Mountains.

THE MANSELL COLLECTION Back cover First view of the Rockies, Endpapers Start of Burke and Wills expedition 2/3 Cortés and army, 17 Alexander the Great, 18 Battle of Issus, 21 Discovery of Greenland by Erik the Red, 25 Hsuan Tsang, 26 Devil dancers, Tibet, 33 Marco Polo Catalan map, 38 Pilgrimage to Mecca, 41 Ste Croix, Canada, 42 Henry Hudson *The Half Moon*, 45 Christopher Columbus, 47 Columbus – sword and cross, 50 Vasco da Gama, 51 Vasco da Gama's ship, 57 Magellan, 58/9 Magellan sailing the straits, 63 Cortés, 67 Mexico before conquest, 72 Pizarro, 81 Sieur de La Salle, 83 Murder of La Salle, 88 John MacDouall Stuart, 91 Dampier, 97 Detail of Cook's voyages, 101 Cook landing in Tasmania, 103 Von Humboldt, 113 Thomas Jefferson, 114 William Clark, 116/7 Pioneers, 118 Sir John Franklin – shipwrecked, 120 Sir John Franklin, 121 Franklin and Indians, 135 Capt. Speke, 137 Source of the Nile, 138 Natives of Equatorial Africa, 140 & 142 David Livingstone, 143 Writing by Livingstone, Victoria Falls, 144 Henry Morton Stanley, 145 Livingstone and Stanley, 147 Robert O'Hara Burke, William John Wills, 151 Nardoo plant, 154 Mary Kingsley, 158/9 Mary Kingsley's canoe, 162 Dr. Nansen, 166 Dr. Nansen and Lt. Johnson, 169 Sven Hedin, 171 Laughing Buddha, 189 Amundsen, 191 The *Fram*.

TOPHAM PICTURE SOURCE 97 Wreck of plane.

WORLD PICTURES 24 Mt. Annapurna.

YALE UNIVERSITY PRESS 22 Vinland map.

ZEFA PICTURE LIBRARY (UK) LTD 9 Fort Kait Bey, Alexandria, 27 Potala Palace, 40 & 41 Dominican Republic, 68 Orinoco River, 80 Niagara Falls, 88/9 Aborigines, 114 Kansas City, 117 Geysers, Yellowstone Park.